International and Comparative Law in the Asia Pacific

International and Comparative Law in Asia is an ambitious and timely series dedicated to exploring the dynamic and multifaceted landscape of legal systems across Asia. The series aims to provide a comprehensive and scholarly examination of the legal traditions, contemporary practices and challenges, and law reforms in jurisdictions across the Asia Pacific, offering valuable insights into their convergence and divergence within the broader context of international law and comparative law. Each volume will delve into specific areas of law, offering in-depth analyses and comparative perspectives that highlight the unique legal landscapes of individual countries while also identifying common trends and regional patterns.

The primary objectives of this series are multifaceted and aim to achieve the following:

1. Bridge the Gap Between International and Domestic Law: Enhance understanding and foster dialogue among legal scholars, practitioners, and policymakers by exploring the interaction between international law and the diverse legal systems of Asia.
2. Advance Comparative Legal Research: Develop the field of comparative law in Asia by conducting in-depth analyses that highlight the similarities and differences among legal systems, such as Singapore, China, Australia, Japan, Korea, Malaysia and Hong Kong. This will provide a foundation for understanding how various countries address similar legal issues.
3. Promote Harmonisation of Laws: Facilitate the harmonisation of laws across Asia by identifying common legal principles and encouraging the adoption of best practices. This objective aims to support regional integration and cooperation.
4. Integrate International Law: Examine the influence of international legal norms, treaties, and institutions on domestic legal reforms, assessing how Asian countries contribute to and are shaped by international law.
5. Support Human Rights and Social Justice: Focus on the implementation of international human rights standards in Asian jurisdictions, addressing challenges such as gender equality, minority rights, and the rule of law. This objective aims to promote social justice and legal empowerment.
6. Analyse Economic and Commercial Law: Given Asia's central role in the global economy, the series will cover aspects of trade, investment, and commercial law. It will analyse regional trade agreements, foreign investment laws, intellectual property rights, and the impact of globalization on domestic legal frameworks.
7. Address Environmental and Sustainable Development Law: Explore legal responses to environmental challenges, climate change, and sustainable development initiatives. This will provide insights into regional and international efforts to promote environmental sustainability with a clearer legal framework.
8. Examine Dispute Resolution and Law Reforms: Assess various dispute resolution mechanisms, including arbitration, mediation, and judicial reforms. The objective is to evaluate the effectiveness of these mechanisms in providing justice and resolving conflicts in diverse legal contexts, such as the International Commercial Courts in Singapore and China.
9. Foster Legal Scholarship and Education: Promote the development of legal scholarship and education in Asia by providing a platform for high-quality research and discussion. This will support the academic and professional growth of legal experts in the region.
10. Explore Law and Technology: Investigate the intersection of law and technology, focusing on how emerging technologies such as artificial intelligence, blockchain, and cybersecurity are shaping legal frameworks and practices in Asia. This objective aims to address the legal challenges and opportunities posed by technological advancements.

Alex Wan · Peng Guo

Good Faith Obligation

A Comparative Perspective

Springer

Alex Wan
Swinburne Law School
Hawthorn, VIC, Australia

Peng Guo
Swinburne Law School
Melbourne, VIC, Australia

ISSN 3059-2178 ISSN 3059-2186 (electronic)
International and Comparative Law in the Asia Pacific
ISBN 978-981-97-7034-2 ISBN 978-981-97-7035-9 (eBook)
https://doi.org/10.1007/978-981-97-7035-9

This Springer imprint is published by the registered company Springer Nature Singapore Pte Ltd.
The registered company address is: 152 Beach Road, #21-01/04 Gateway East, Singapore 189721, Singapore

Editorial Advisory Board

Preface and Acknowledgements

This book embarks on a journey to explore the relevance of the obligation of good faith in Australian contract law. The obligation of good faith, despite its introduction over three decades ago in the landmark decision of *Renard Constructions (ME) Pty Ltd v Minister for Public Works*, remains one of the most pivotal yet unresolved issues of Australian contractual law. Over the years, there have been numerous judicial attempts to establish a foundation for a consistent approach in applying good faith obligation. However, finding common ground in the judicial attempts have been elusive and at times frustrating. The discourse has often devolved into a comparative debate between common law and civil law approaches which has to an extent polarised the scholarly discussion.

This book aims to scrutinise whether the continued relevance of good faith obligation can be upheld in arm's length contractual relationships based on the reasonable expectations of the contracting parties. To achieve this, the discussion in this book revisits the current legal approaches and utilises economic analysis to discern whether there is a continuing role for an obligation in good faith in commercial contracts.

The research in this book is divided into three main parts. Part I delves into the historical and contemporary context of good faith obligation from other jurisdictions to ascertain whether it would be fitting for Australia to adopt the obligation and its relevance to commercial contracts. Part II considers the approaches taken by the Australian courts thus far with the obligation of good faith and explores its application using contractual construction as an alternative pathway. The final part considers good faith through a law and economics analysis, allowing for an evaluation of whether the obligation of good faith is viable, practical, and efficient.

In addition to the economic analysis, an empirical methodology using a case study approach was introduced to analyse and capture good faith provisions in a specific commercial contracting setting. The empirical approach is intended to be illustrative and is used as a platform to observe the relevance of good faith. This aligns with Eisenberg's view that legal theories are significantly influenced by the way doctrinal propositions relate to social propositions, which include both empirical and economic propositions that are relevant, meritorious, and can be utilised by lawmakers. Notwithstanding, the book's main approach maintains a conventional doctrinal legal research that utilises case law analysis and legal theory. The combined use of economic principles and empirical methodology in this book adds another dimension into the research, offering insights into the viability of the obligation of good faith in Australian contract law.

Lastly, but certainly not least, we would like to acknowledge and thank our two research assistants, Mr. Jiaqi Wang and Ms. Sian Donazzon for their tireless editorial work rendered in this project. And finally, we would like to add a note of thanks and appreciation to a number of unnamed past and present colleagues at Swinburne University of Technology who have supported and encouraged this project as well as provided insightful comments on the work along the way. Dr. Wan also thank his wife for her continuous understanding and support and Dr. Guo thank his family for their unconditional love, endless support and unwavering patience.

Melbourne, Australia
June 2024

Dr. Alex Wan
Dr. Peng Guo

Introduction to the Series

International and Comparative Law in Asia is an ambitious and timely series dedicated to exploring the dynamic and multifaceted landscape of legal systems across Asia. The series aims to provide a comprehensive and scholarly examination of the legal traditions, contemporary practices and challenges, and law reforms in jurisdictions across the Asia Pacific, offering valuable insights into their convergence and divergence within the broader context of international law and comparative law. This series will also delve into specific areas of law, offering in-depth analyses and comparative perspectives that highlight the unique legal landscapes of individual countries while also identifying common trends and regional patterns.

The primary objectives of this series are multifaceted and aim to:

1. Bridge the Gap Between International and Domestic Law: Enhance understanding and foster dialogue among legal scholars, practitioners, and policymakers by exploring the interaction between international law and the diverse legal systems of Asia.
2. Advance Comparative Legal Research: Develop the field of comparative law in Asia by conducting in-depth analyses that highlight the similarities and differences among legal systems, such as Australia, China, Japan, Korea, Malaysia, and Singapore. This will provide a foundation for understanding how various countries address similar legal issues.
3. Promote Harmonisation of Laws: Facilitate the harmonisation of laws across Asia by identifying common legal principles and encouraging the adoption of best practices. This objective aims to support regional integration and cooperation.
4. Examine Dispute Resolution and Propose Law Reforms: Assess various dispute resolution mechanisms, including arbitration, mediation, and judicial reforms. The objective is to evaluate the effectiveness of these mechanisms in providing justice and resolving conflicts in diverse legal contexts, such as the International Commercial Courts in Singapore and China.
5. Foster Legal Scholarship and Education: Promote the development of legal scholarship and education in Asia by providing a platform for high-quality research

and discussion. This will support the academic and professional growth of legal experts in the region.

I hope this series will contribute to the development of international and comparative law in the Asia Pacific area. In addition, I would like to extend my deep gratitude to the editor from Springer and esteemed members of the editorial advisory board, whose invaluable support has been instrumental in bringing this series to fruition. Their expert guidance and unwavering assistance have played a pivotal role throughout this endeavour.

Melbourne, Australia
June 2024

Dr. Peng Guo
(Editor-in-Chief)

Contents

Part I

Part I

Chapter 1
Overview

1.1 Introduction

Good faith as a contract law obligation is controversial and frustrating. This is largely because it is ill-defined. The concept of good faith, in terms of function and interpretation, elicits diverse and conflicting perspectives from the judiciary and legal scholars. Despite this, the principle of good faith is increasingly acknowledged and continues to exert a growing impact on a range of contracts contextually. It is for this reason that good faith obligation as a contractual concept has been hailed as one of the most important unresolved contractual issues in contract law.[1] Good faith obligation inherently fits the objective of any established contract law system in that it has the ability to promote fair and equitable dealings in contractual performance.[2]

The aim of this book is to consider the reasons why and, more importantly, to appraise whether the obligation of good faith continues to have relevance and utility as a contractual term in arm's length commercial business dealings. In this respect, Australia is chosen as a focus jurisdiction for this discussion with a comparative outlook towards the experience in the United States (US) and China as a contrasting civil law jurisdiction (with a limited mention of selected European jurisdictions). To accomplish this, the book will primarily focus on the relevance of good faith obligation in the context of Australian contract law, investigate current legal approaches, and consider whether good faith obligation commands a place in Australian law as a viable and practical contracting principle. The third aspect uses a law and economics analysis to consider whether good faith is economically relevant and beneficial in practice. From the foregoing, a conclusion will be drawn as to the

[1] John W Carter and Andrew Stewart, 'Interpretation, Good Faith and the "True Meaning" of contracts: The Royal Botanic Decision' (2002) 18 *Journal of Contract Law* 182, 190; Sir Thomas Bingham in the foreword to Reziya Harrison, *Good Faith in Sales* (Sweet & Maxwell, 1997) vi.

[2] Johan Steyn, 'The Role of Good Faith and Fair Dealing in Contract Law: A Hair-Shirt Philosophy?' in Johan Steyn (ed), *Democracy Through the Law: Selected Speeches and Judgments* (Routledge, 2004) 213.

A. Wan and P. Guo, *Good Faith Obligation*, International and Comparative Law in the Asia Pacific, https://doi.org/10.1007/978-981-97-7035-9_1

continued desirability of having an obligation of good faith in Australian contract law.

The approach of the book confines the application of good faith obligation in the performance and enforcement of contractual terms in commercial contracts based on the reasonable expectations of the contracting parties. However, it will not explore the operation of good faith across the full spectrum of commercial contractual circumstances. This limitation is in recognition of the well-developed meaning of good faith obligation in particular contractual settings, such as in insurance contracts, employment contract,[3] or under a tortious[4] and equitable duty.[5]

This introductory chapter is intended to provide an overview and justification for the book. It also sets the framework for this research contribution.

1.2 Research Background

In general, the underlying public policy of commercial contract in Australia is freedom and certainty of contract, a policy that has been commonly relied upon by those seeking to counteract the development of contractual good faith obligations.[6] This view is not without merit when judged against the reality of commercial agreements that have been negotiated at arm's length.[7] The justification being that the preservation of the sanctity of contract should not be impinged by the impact of the implied obligations of good faith where the parties have not contemplated their inclusion.[8]

---

[3] E.g. *Hunter Business Finance v Australian Commercial and Equipment Finance* [2003] NSWSC 122, [71]; *Victoria University of Technology v Wilson* [2004] VSC 33, [145]; interestingly, the High Court held that there is no general implied obligation to act in good faith in contracts of employment unless it forms part of the contract by express or implied provisions: *Commonwealth Bank of Australia v Barker* [2014] HCA 32, [42], [107].

[4] E.g. in *Gibson v Parkes District Hospital* (1991) 26 NSWLR 9.

[5] Such as company directors, partners, and trustees.

[6] Lord Justice Staughton, 'Good Faith and Fairness in Commercial Contract Law' (1994) 7 *Journal of Contract Law* 193, 194: 'businessmen prefer certainty to justice, and like to know where they stand'; Maree Chetwin, 'Relational Contract Theory and the Good Faith Debate' (2003) 9 *New Zealand Business Law Quarterly* 211; Rick A Bigwood, 'Symposium Introduction: Confessions of a "Good Faith" Agnostic' (2005) 11 *New Zealand Business Law Quarterly* 371.

[7] *Walford v Miles* [1992] 2 WLR 174.

[8] Justice Rogers in *GSA Group Ltd v Siebe plc* (1993) 30 NSWLR 573, 579: 'courts should not be too eager to interfere in the commercial conduct of parties … where … the parties are wealthy, experienced, commercial entities able to attend to their own interests.'; Michael Bridge, 'Does Anglo Canadian Law Need a Doctrine of Good Faith?' (1984) 9 *Canadian Business Law Journal* 385, 412; Gunther Teubner, 'Legal Irritants: Good Faith in British Law or How Unifying Law Ends Up in New Divergences' (1998) 61 *Modern Law Review* 11; James Davies, 'Why a Common Law Duty of Contractual Good Faith is Not Required' (2002) 8 *Canterbury Law Review* 529.

In contrast, the relevance of good faith has already been recognised by the Australian judiciary. Sir Anthony Mason used the remarks of Kelly J in the Canadian case of *Gateway Realty Ltd v Arton Holdings Ltd (No.3)*,[9] and queried:

> why are good faith and fair dealing superior objects to obsessive insistence on total clarity and certainty in contract? And why is emphasis on the need for good faith and fair dealing not likely to lead to the resolution of business disputes?[10]

In the same vein, Sir Anthony Mason also wrote that 'the quality of Australian commercial life could only profit from an infusion of good faith.'[11] Gleeson CJ also commented that

> The demand of justice, as seen through modern eyes, are much less likely to be met by formal and inflexible rules which treat hard cases with the dismissiveness sometimes manifested in earlier times. The citizens ... have an attitude towards all forms of authority which is questioning, demanding and self-assertive. They seem to place less value upon predictability than former generations.[12]

Such comments from prominent members of the judiciary reveal a changing judicial attitude and a retreat from the classical model of adversarial contracting.[13] These views represent a shift towards a more welcoming approach towards an obligation of good faith in commercial contracting.[14] The seminal good faith decision in *Renard Constructions (ME) Pty Ltd v Minister for Public Works*[15] ('*Renard Constructions*') provides the judicial gateway to consider good faith obligation in commercial contracts in Australia. Priestley JA in *Renard Constructions* observes that the implication of good faith and fair dealing is a reflection of 'community expectations of contractual behaviour.'[16] This is an acknowledgement that the courts should treat contract cases individually with a focus on contracting fairness and provides the strongest indication that the scope of good faith application can accommodate the contracting parties' commercial intent.

One of the common elements in case law that sees good faith obligations arise in commercial contracts have been contracts that may be described as relational where

---

[9] (1991) 106 NSR (2d) 180.

[10] Anthony Mason, 'Contract, Good Faith and Equitable Standards in Fair Dealing' (2000) 116 *Law Quarterly Review* 66, 89.

[11] Sir Anthony Mason, 'Foreword' (1989) 12 *University of New South Wales Law Journal* 1, 3.

[12] Anthony Murray Gleeson, 'Individualised Justice—The Holy Grail' (1995) 69 *Australian Law Journal* 421, 430.

[13] Mason, 'Contract, Good Faith and Equitable Standards', above n 10, 70; Michael Bridge, 'Good Faith in Commercial Contracts' in Roger Brownsword, Norma J Hird and Geraint Howells (eds), *Good Faith in Contract: Concept and Context* (Dartmouth Publishing Co,1999) 150.

[14] The High Court decision of *Royal Botanic Gardens and Domain Trust v South Sydney City Council* (2002) 186 ALR 289, [40], recognised the importance of good faith obligation in contractual performance. The court, however, did not rule on the issue of good faith, as the occasion for its consideration was deemed inappropriate. This decision will be revisited in Chap. 4.

[15] (1992) 26 NSWLR 234.

[16] Ibid 268.

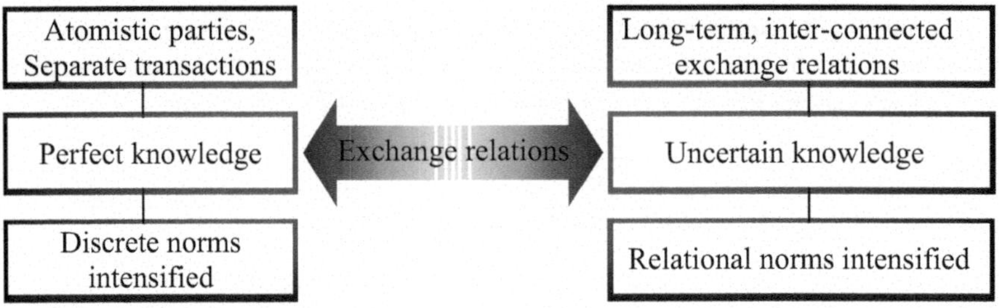

Fig. 1.1 Diagram adapted from Macneil's theory illustrating the contractual norms[20]

certain expectations of cooperative contractual behaviour implicitly operate.[17] This does not necessarily mean that the parties are operating outside the ambit of arm's length transaction but only that there is a degree of shared mutuality in achieving contractual objectives, which arguably is common in all contracts.[18]

Macneil states that legally binding contracts span a spectrum, with highly discreet contracts at one extreme and highly relational at the other.[19] A diagrammatic illustration is depicted below (Fig. 1.1).

In highly relational exchange situations, contracting parties mutually seek to maintain cooperative relationships and establish contractual norms that avoid 'behaviour promoting individual parties' goal orientation.'[21] In this sense, the term 'relational commercial contract' or 'commercial contracts that are relational in nature' refers to the type of contracts that Macneil characterises as 'intertwined'—these contracts regulate relationships that are not only ongoing but also evolve over time, and they

[17] See Nicholas C Seddon, 'Australian Contract Law: Maelstrom or Measured Mutation?' (1994) 7 *Journal of Contract Law* 93, 96; Paul Finn, 'Good Faith and Fair Dealing and "Boats against the current"' (Paper presented at the 2nd Biennial Conference on the Law of Obligations, Melbourne, 16 July 2004) 6–7; Charles J Goetz and Robert E Scott, 'Principles of Relational Contracts' (1981) 67 *Virginia Law Review* 1089, 1091; *Bobux Marketing Ltd v Raynor Marketing Ltd* [2002] 1 NZLR 506; *Hospital Products Ltd v United States Surgical Corporation* (1984) 156 CLR 41; Jeannie M Paterson, 'Good Faith in Commercial Contracts: A Franchising Case Study?' (2001) 29 *Australian Business Law Review* 270; Elisabeth Peden, *Good Faith in the Performance of Contracts* (LexisNexis Butterworths, 2003) 170; Chetwin, 'Relational Contract Theory', above n 6, 211; *Archibald Barr Motor Co Ltd v ATECO Automotive New Zealand Ltd* (High Court, Auckland, CIV 2007–404-5797, 26 October 2007), [79]; *Gibbons Holdings Ltd v Wholesale Distributors Ltd* [2008] 1 NZLR 277.

[18] *Computer Services Pty Ltd v Digital Equipment Corporation (Australia) Pty Ltd* (1988) 5 BPR 11,110; Randy E Barnett, 'Conflicting Visions: A Critique of Ian Macneil's Relational Theory of Contract' (1992) 78 *Virginia Law Review* 1175, 1206.

[19] Ian R Macneil, 'Relational Contract Theory as Sociology: A Reply to Prof Lindenberg and de Vos' (1987) 143 *Journal of Institutional & Theoretical Economics* 272.

[20] Ian R Macneil, *The New Social Contract: An Inquiry into Modern Contractual Relations* (Yale University Press, 1980).

[21] Aksel I Rokkan, Jan B Heide and Kenneth H Wathne, 'Specific Investments in Marketing Relationships: Expropriation and Bonding Effects' (2003) 40 *Journal of Marketing Research* 210–224, 212.

often incorporate good faith provisions.[22] Examples of such contracts include franchise agreements,[23] and various forms of alliancing and partnering arrangements where contracting parties may even agree not to engage in litigation in the event of a dispute but resolve them through agreed norm channels.[24] The operation of good faith obligation in contracts where such forms of relational circumstance are established tend to be less controversial. The consensus in such contractual settings is that good faith obligation and a duty of cooperation and loyalty are implied.[25]

On the other hand, discreet exchanges focus on maximising self-interests and contracting parties are guided strictly by agreed-upon exchanges.[26] Discreteness refers to the separation of the contractual exchange transaction from all other interactions among the participants, both concurrent and thereafter.[27] The presence of a market, which is a fundamental assumption of the discrete transaction system, negates the need for any ongoing relationship between the contracting parties in the event of a contractual disagreement.[28] This is the characterisation of an arm's length

---

[22] Macneil, 'Relational Contract Theory as Sociology', above n 19, 274–275; Barnett, 'Conflicting Visions', above n 18.

[23] Franchise agreements are not one-off deals. They incorporate arrangements that are classified as long-term relationships where the basis for economic gains will be ongoing harmony and commitment to a common cause. The long-term mutual obligations of the parties are dependent upon coordinated action and cooperation, and the parties have an interest in the franchise relationship succeeding even though their relationship remains inherently vertical. The franchisee effectively puts his or her economic fate in the hands of the franchisor: See *Dymocks Franchise Systems (NSW) Pty Ltd v Bilgola Enterprises Ltd* (1999) 8 TCLR 612, [63], [236]; Veronica L Taylor, 'Contracts with the Lot: Franchisees, Good Faith and Contract Regulations (1997) *New Zealand Law Review* 459, 459; Stephen Corones, 'Implied Good Faith and Unconscionability in Franchises: Moving towards Relational Contract Theory' (2000) 28 *Australian Business Law Review* 462, 467.

[24] These type of contracts include contracting strategy that promotes Early Contractor Involvement (ECI), which incorporate a risk sharing philosophy where compensation mechanisms are adopted toward ensuring everyone wins or everyone loses: See, e.g. Roger Quick, 'Queensland ECI Contract' (2007) 24(1) *International Construction Law Review* 3, 15; Matton Van den Berg and Peter Kamminga, 'Optimising Contracting for Alliances in Infrastructure Projects' (2006) 23(1) *International Construction Law Review* 4; Chris Skeggs, 'Project Partnering in the International Construction Industry' (2004) 20(4) *International Construction Law Review* 456; Jim Ross, 'Introduction to Project Alliancing' (Paper presented at *Alliance Contracting Conference*, Sydney, October 2003) 21.

[25] For example, *Yam Seng Pte Ltd v International Trade Corporation Ltd* [2013] EWHC 111; *D & G Cars Ltd v Essex Police Authority* [2015] EWHC 226; *GEC Marconi Systems Pty Ltd v BHP Information Technology Pty Ltd* (2003) 128 FCR 1 [230]; *AMC Commercial Cleaning (NSW) Pty Ltd v Coade* [2011] NSWSC 932; See also George M Cohen, 'The Fault that Lies Within our Contract Law' (2009) 107 *Michigan Law Review* 1446; Andrew Terry and Cary Di Lernia, 'Franchising and the Quest for the Holy Grain: Good Faith or Good Intentions?' (2009) 33 *Melbourne University Law Review* 542; Anthony Gray, 'Good Faith in Australian Contract Law After Barker' (2015) 43 *Australian Business Law Review* 358.

[26] Barnett, 'Conflicting Visions', above n 18, 1177–1178.

[27] Ian R Macneil, 'Contracts: Adjustments of Long-Term Economic Relations under Classical, Neo-Classical and Relational Contract Law' (1978) 72 *Northwestern University Law Review* 854, 856.

[28] Ibid 861.

contract in this book and the task is to understand the relevance and utility of good faith obligation in this type of contractual setting.

The judicial approach to good faith application in arm's length commercial contracts has been described as tortured both in its applications of precedents and the relevant legal tests prescribed.[29] This has largely been the result of members of the judiciary favouring the traditional approach in contract law and those who do not see the need for good faith infusion into Australian commercial life.[30] Underpinning the traditional approach is the classical model of contract, which is an adversarial premise modelled on the economic theory of laissez-faire, where contracting parties seek to maximise their own respective interests.[31] Classical contract law exclusively focuses contractual relations at the static point of contract formation that formally dictates the fundamental ground rules for 'self-maximising private ordering.'[32] This approach stems from an ideology of liberal individualism (or market individualism)[33] with the primary aim of securing an autonomous subject in the respective, individualistic contract participant.[34] Thus, the execution of contractual obligations and the exercise of contractual rights and discretions would be governed solely by the parties' adherence to mutual freedom and equal opportunity, disregarding all other valid considerations of reasonable expectations, in the pursuit of self-interest.

Australian contract law has generally followed the classical paradigm and rejected the obligation of good faith as an overriding principle regardless of contractual setting.[35] This is consistent with the approach of English common law where notions of good faith are thought to manifest in contract law via piecemeal doctrines such as estoppel, relief against forfeiture, mitigation, unconscionability, reasonableness and implied terms.[36] Good faith has also been regarded as incompatible with an

---

[29] Tyrone Carlin, 'The Rise (and Fall?) of Implied Duties of Good Faith in Contractual Performance in Australia' (2002) 25(1) *University of New South Wales Law Journal* 99, 122.

[30] Mason, 'Foreword', above n 11, 1–3.

[31] Mason, 'Contract, Good Faith and Equitable Standards', above n 10, 70; cf Roger Brownsword, 'Positive, Negative, Neutral: The Reception of Good Faith in English Contract Law' in Roger Brownsword, Norma J Hird and Geraint Howells (eds), *Good Faith in Contract: Concept and Context* (Dartmouth Publishing Co, 1999) 13, 32.

[32] Jay M Feinman, 'Relational Contract Theory in Context' (2000) 94 *Northwestern University Law Review* 737, 738; Melvin A Eisenberg, 'Why There is No Law of Relational Contracts' (2000) 94 *Northwestern University Law Review* 805, 807.

[33] Ian R Macneil, 'The Many Futures of Contract' (1974) 47 *Southern California Law Review* 691; cf Rick A Bigwood, 'Conscience and Liberal Conception of Contract: Observing Basic Distinctions Part II' (2000) 16 *Journal of Contract Law* 191, 203.

[34] Bigwood, 'Conscience and Liberal Conception', above n 33, 1, 19.

[35] Apart from legislative references.

[36] John W Carter and Elisabeth Peden, 'Good Faith in Australian Contract Law' (2003) 19 *Journal of Contract Law* 155; Bridge, 'Does Anglo-Canadian Contract Law Need', above n 8, 409; Johan Steyn, 'Contract Law: Fulfilling the Reasonable Expectations of Honest Me' (1997) 113 *Law Quarterly Review* 433, 441; Stephen M Waddams, 'Codification, Law Reform and Judicial Developments' (1996) 9 *Journal Contract Law* 192, 194; Stephen M Waddams, 'Good Faith, Unconscionability and Reasonable Expectations' (1995) 9 *Journal Contract Law* 55; The Hon Mr Justice Steyn, 'The Role of Good Faith and Fair Dealing in Contract Law: A Hair-Shirt Philosophy?' [1991] *Denning Law*

adversarial model[37] and undermines the freedom and certainty of contract.[38] Significantly, the relevance of the classical approach has been openly questioned following the *Renard Constructions* case, which has emerged with greater optimism concerning good faith application.

Aside from the judicial bias towards the classical approach in Australia, the apparent obstacles in harmonising a consistent application of good faith obligation in commercial contracts stem from the unresolved issues related to the operation of contractual good faith obligation. As far as good faith is an implicit term in contracts, the unresolved issues[39] encompass the following:

(1) What is the definition of good faith?
(2) Can good faith be implied as a matter of law or fact or some form of hybrid combination, and if so can it be justified on both grounds?
(3) What is the test? Is it the reasonable expectations or legitimate interest of the contractual parties or community standards?
(4) Is the good faith obligation the same as an obligation to act reasonably?
(5) Is good faith the same as a fiduciary obligation?
(6) Is there a correlation between good faith and equitable and statutory unconscionability?

In addition to these issues, there is much doctrinal debate about the possible direction and approach (including from overseas) that the Australian High Court may adopt when it eventually faces the question of the applicability and relevance of good faith obligation in contract law.[40] While it is not the intention of this book to engage in speculative ventures about how the High Court will direct the application of good faith obligation, it is, however, possible to outline four main approach alternatives based on existing Australian legal precedents[41]:

(1) Alternative One: Incorporate a duty of good faith into a certain category of contracts as a matter of law or as an inherent aspect of all contracts;
(2) Alternative Two: Incorporate a duty of good faith as a matter of fact, with there being no general implication into all commercial contracts;

Journal 131, 133; Paul Finn, 'Commerce, The Common Law and Morality' (1989) 17 *Melbourne University Law Review* 87, 92–98; L J Priestley, 'Contract—The Burgeoning Maelstrom' (1988) 1 *Curent Law Journal* 15; John R Peden, *The Law of Unjust Contracts* (Butterworths, 1982) 28; Harvey McGregor, *A Contract Code: Drawn Up on Behalf of the English Law Commission* (Sweet & Maxwell, 1994) 40: comments in relation to the Contract Code that good faith is 'implicit in the Moorcock rule'.

[37] *Walford v Miles* [1992] 2 AC 128, 138.

[38] Hugh Collins, 'The Sanctimony of Contract' in Richard Rawlings (ed), *Law, Society and Economy, Centenary Essays for the London School of Economics and Political Science 1895–1995* (Clarendon Press, 1997) 63, 66.

[39] The unresolved issues indicated here will be elaborated and discussed in Chap. 5.

[40] These discussions will be raised in Chaps. 2 and 3.

[41] The numbering of the approaches presented here is purely for ease of reference in the present research and does not represent the order in which these approaches have been developed.

(3) Alternative Three: Reject the inclusion of a term of good faith as an inherent aspect of all contracts; or
(4) Alternative Four: To restrict the application of a duty of good faith specifically as a construction tool.

These four approach alternatives attract varying degrees of support by the Australian judiciary and contract law scholars. Based on existing precedents on the obligation of good faith in contractual performance and enforcement, alternative three enjoys only limited support.[42] There is some academic support for alternative four.[43] For example, Peden has been and continues to be a strong advocate of alternative four. She has suggested that a universal application of good faith can only operate consistently as a construction principle.[44] This suggestion of good faith as a process of construction has received mixed reception judicially,[45] although the argument has relevance and merit that will be explored further in chapter four. There is certainly a significant level of judicial support for alternative one.[46] However, alternative one's approach has also received tacit caution in the case of *Vodafone Pacific Ltd v Mobile*

[42] Carter and Peden, 'Good Faith in Australian Contract', above n 36; Robert McDougall, 'The Implied Duty of Good Faith in Australian Contract Law' (2006) 108 *Australian Construction Law Newsletter* 28; John W Carter, 'Good Faith in Contract: Why Australian Law is Incoherent?' (Research Paper No 14/38, Sydney Law School, 2014).

[43] Peden, *Good Faith in the Performance of Contracts*, above n 17; cf Paul Finn, 'Equity and Commercial Contracts: A comment' [2001] *AMPLA Yearbook* 414.

[44] Peden, *Good Faith in the Performance of Contracts*, above n 17, 140.

[45] *Vodafone Pacific Ltd v Mobile Innovations Ltd* [2004] NSWCA 15 [206]; *Paciocco v Australia and New Zealand Banking Group Ltd* [2015] FCAFC 50 [289]-[290]; *Mirvac (WA) Pty Ltd v Binningup Nominees Pty Ltd* [2020] WASC 28.

[46] Cf *Renard Constructions (ME) Pty Ltd v Minister of Public Works* (1992) 26 NSWLR 234; Other decisions that have followed approach one include (in no particular order): *Presmist Pty Ltd v Turner Corporation Pty Ltd* (1992) 30 NSWLR 478; *Hughes Bros Pty Ltd v Trustees of the Roman Catholic Church for the Archdiocese of Sydney* (1993) 31 NSWLR 91; *Service Station Association Ltd v Berg Bennett & Associates Pty Ltd* (1993) 117 ALR 393; *News Ltd v Australian Rugby Football League Ltd* (1996) 135 ALR 33; *Hughes Aircraft Systems International v Airservices Australia* (1997) 146 ALR 1; *Asia Pacific Resources Pty Ltd v Forestry Tasmania* (Unreported, Tasmanian Supreme Court (Full Court), 4 September 1997); *Alcatel Australia Ltd v Scarcella* (1998) 44 NSWLR 349; *Dalcon Constructions Pty Ltd v State Housing Commission* (1998) 14 BCLC 477; *Australis Media Holdings Pty Ltd v Telstra Corporation Ltd* (1998) 43 NSWLR 104; *WMC Resources Ltd v Leighton Contractors Pty Ltd* (1999) 20 WAR 489; *Advance Fitness v Bondi Diggers* [1999] NSWSC 264; *Australian Co-operative Foods Ltd v Norco Co-operative Ltd* (1999) 46 NSWLR 267; *Blackler v Felpure Pty Ltd* [1999] NSWSC 958; *K & S Freighters Pty Ltd v Linfox Transport (Aust) Pty Ltd* [1999] FCA 1325; *Shorrlong Pty Ltd v Northern Territory Housing Commission* [1999] NTSC 140; *Garry Rogers Motors (Aust) Pty Ltd v Subaru (Aust) Pty Ltd* (1999) ATPR ¶41–703; *Forklift Engineering Australia Pty Ltd v Powerlift (Nissan) Pty Ltd* [2000] VSC 443; *Far Horizons Pty Ltd v McDonald's Australia Ltd* [2000] VSC 310; *South Sydney District Rugby League Football Club Ltd v News Ltd* (2000) 177 ALR 611; *Thiess Contractors Pty Ltd v Placer (Granny Smith) Pty Ltd* (2000) 16 BCL 130; *Christopher John De Pasquale v The Australian Chess Federation Inc (AO 1325)* [2000] ACTSC 94; *Saxby Bridge Mortgages Pty Ltd v Saxby Bridge Pty Ltd* [2000] NSWSC 433; *Dickson Property Management Services Pty Ltd v Centro Property Management (Vic) Pty Ltd* (2000) 180 ALR 485; *Elfic Ltd v Macks* [2000] QSC 18; *Asia Television Ltd v Yau's Entertainment Pty Ltd* (2000) 48 IPR 283; *Howtrac Rentals Pty Ltd v Thiess Contractors (NZ) Ltd* [2000] VSC 415; *Walker v ANZ Banking Group Ltd (No 2)* (2001) 39 ACSR 557; *Commonwealth Bank of Australia*

Innovations Ltd where its appropriateness has been brought into question by the New South Wales (NSW) Court of Appeal, which noted the 'width and indeterminacy' of applying good faith in all commercial contracts.[47] With this judicial caution in mind, alternative two has increasingly generated judicial focus and interest, particularly in the state of Victoria.[48] Alternative two also allows the law to safeguard the

---

v Renstell Nominees Pty Ltd [2001] VSC 167; *Apple Communications v Optus Mobile* [2001] NSWSC 635; *Bamco Villa Pty Ltd v Montedeen Pty Ltd* [2001] VSC 192; *Radley Corporation Ltd v Suncorp Metway Ltd* [2001] VSC 272; *Edensor Nominees Pty Ltd v Anaconda Nickel Ltd* [2001] VSC 502; *NT Power Generation Pty Ltd v Power and Water Authority* (2001) 184 ALR 481; *LMI Australasia Pty Ltd v Baulderstone Hornibrook Pty Ltd* [2001] NSWSC 886; *Central Exchange Ltd v Anaconda Nickel Ltd* (2001) 24 WAR 382; *Central Exchange Ltd v Anaconda Nickel Ltd* [2002] WASCA 94; *Easts Van Villages Pty Ltd v Minister Administering the National Parks and Wildlife Act* [2001] NSWSC 559; *Automasters Australia Pty Ltd v Bruness Pty Ltd* [2002] WASC 286; *State of New South Wales v Banabelle Electrical Pty Ltd* (2002) 54 NSWLR 503; *Softplay v Perpetual* [2002] NSWSC 1059; *Wenzel v Australian Stock Exchange Ltd* [2002] FCAFC 400; *Royal Botanic Gardens and Domain Trust v South Sydney City Council* (2002) 186 ALR 289; *Overlook v Foxtel* (2002) Aust Contracts Rep 90–143; *Lay v Alliswell Pty Ltd* (2002) V ConvR ¶54–651; *Hudson Resources Ltd v Australian Diatomite Mining Pty Ltd* [2002] NSWSC 314; *Commonwealth Development Bank of Australia Pty Ltd v Cassegrain* [2002] NSWSC 965; *Cubic Transportation Systems, Inc v State of New South Wales* [2002] NSWSC 656; *GEC Marconi Systems Pty Ltd v BHP Information Technology Pty Ltd* (2003) 128 FCR 1; *Biscayne Partners Pty Ltd v Valance Corporation Pty Ltd* [2003] NSWSC 874; *Golden Sands Pty Ltd v Davegale Pty Ltd* [2003] VSC 458; *Esso Australia Resources Pty Ltd v Southern Pacific Petroleum NL* [2004] VSC 477; *Esso Australia Resources Pty Ltd v Southern Pacific Petroleum NL* [2005] VSCA 228; *Hoppers Crossing Club Ltd v Tattersalls Gaming Pty Ltd* [2005] VSC 114; *Pacific Brands Sports & Leisure Pty Ltd v Underworks Pty Ltd* [2005] FCA 288; *Australian Hotels Association (NSW) v TAB Ltd* [2006] NSWSC 293 (19 April 2006); *Meridian Retail Pty Ltd v Australian Unity Retail Network* [2006] VSC 223; *Maitland Main Collieries Pty Ltd v Xstrata Mt Owen Pty Ltd* [2006] NSWSC 1235; *Ingot Capital Investments v Macquarie Equity Capital Markets (No 6)* [2007] NSWSC 124; *Kellogg Brown & Root Pty Ltd v Australian Aerospace Ltd* [2007] VSC 200; *Farah Construction Pty Ltd v Say-Dee Pty Ltd* [2007] 230 CLR 89; *Sundararajah v Teachers Federal Health Ltd* [2009] NSWSC 1443, [31]; *United Group Rail Services Ltd v Rail Corporation of New South Wales* [2009] NSWCA 177; *Strzelecki Holdings Pty Ltd v Cable Sands Pty Ltd* [2010] WASCA 222; *Macquarie International Health Clinic Pty Ltd v Sydney South West Area Health Service* [2010] NSWCA 268; *Starlink International Group Pty Ltd v Coles Supermarket Australia Pty Ltd* [2011] NSWSC 1154; *AMC Commercial Leasing (NSW) Pty Ltd v Coade* [2011] NSWSC 932, [133–134]; *Cordon Investments Pty Ltd v Lesdor Properties Pty Ltd* [2012] NSWCA 184; *RPR Maintenance Pty Ltd v Marmax Investments Pty Ltd* [2014] FCA 409; *Bundanoon Sandstone Pty Ltd v Cenric Group Pty Ltd* [2019] NSWCA 87; *Heavy Plant Leasing Pty Ltd (in liq) v McConnell Dowell Constructors (Aust) Pty Ltd (No 2)*[2022] NSWSC 1775.

[47] *Vodafone Pacific Ltd v Mobile Innovations Ltd* [2004] NSWCA 15 [206]; some discussion and ramifications of this decision will be discussed in chapter five.

[48] E.g. *Esso Australia Resources Pty Ltd v Southern Pacific Petroleum NL* [2005] VSCA 228; *Tote Tasmania Pty Ltd v Garrott* [2008] TASSC 86; *Driveforce Pty Ltd v Gunns Ltd (No. 3)* [2010] TASSC 38; *Oliver v Commonwealth Bank of Australia* [2011] FCA 1440; *Trans Petroleum (Australia) Pty Ltd v White Gum Petroleum Pty Ltd* [2012] WASCA 165; *Specialist Diagnostic Services Pty Ltd (formerly Symbion Pathology Pty Ltd) v Healthscope Pty Ltd* [2012] VSCA 175; *Beerens v Bluescope Distribution Pty Ltd* [2012] VSCA 209; *Bytan Pty Ltd v BB Australia Pty Ltd* [2012] VSCA 233; *ACN 074 971 109 Pty Ltd v National Mutual Life Association of Australasia Ltd* [2013] VSCA 241; *Arhanghelschi v Ussher* (2013) ACSR 86; *Androvitsaneas v Members First Broker Network Pty Ltd* [2013] VSCA 212, [108]; *Aurizon Network Pty Ltd v Glencore Coal Queensland*

reasonable expectations of the contracting parties and foster a culture of contractual collaboration that could result in economic efficiency in contracting.[49]

In this respect, alternative two accords closely with the fundamental goal of good faith in that it renders contract law more adaptable to the demands of commerce and the reasonable expectations of the parties and the broader commercial community.[50] Reference to reasonable expectations, for example, has featured prominently in the observations of Steyn J who, in *First Energy (UK) Ltd v Hungarian International Bank Ltd*, states the following:

> A theme that runs through [the] law of contract is that the reasonable expectations of honest men must be protected. It is not a rule or principle of law. It is the objective which has been and still is the principal moulding force of our law of contract. ... [I]f the prima facie solution to a problem runs counter to the reasonable expectations of honest men, this criterion sometimes requires a rigorous examination of the problem to ascertain whether the law does indeed compel demonstrable unfairness.[51]

The concept of reasonable expectations has gained significant traction in contract law. Australian contract law, grounded in an objective contract theory, adheres to an external objective standard. Consequently, a party's reasonable expectations may be contravened if another party strictly follows the terms of a contract but acts in a way that was not reasonably anticipated of the parties. Accordingly, Lord Steyn recognises that reasonable expectations 'requires that the law … treat contractual obligations as defeasible or that a discretionary remedy should be denied.'[52]

A contractual obligation of good faith serves to protect and enforce reasonable expectations. Introducing an obligation of good faith can enhance the law's ability to honour the spirit of contracts, prioritising the reasonable expectations of contracting parties.[53]

However, the concept of reasonable expectations should be qualified and not be overly idealistic.[54] Contract law should reflect the views of ordinary, rational individuals, focusing on commercial pragmatism rather than abstract moral philosophy.[55] Good faith should aim to meet the reasonable expectations of the parties, rather than punish moral wrongdoings.[56]

Pty Ltd (2019) 1 QR 392; *Bensons Property Group Pty Ltd v Key Infrastructure Australia Pty Ltd* [2021] VSCA 69; *Hewlett Packard Pty Ltd v Subasic* [2021] ACTCA 3; *QNI Resources Pty Ltd v North Queensland Pipeline No 1 Pty Ltd* [2022] QCA 169 [116]; *Scanlan v 2–4 McCabe Pty Ltd* [2023] WASCA 135 [77]-[92].

[49] Brownsword, 'Positive, Negative, Neutral', above n 31.

[50] Edward Thomas, 'Good Faith in Contract: A Non-Sceptical Commentary' (2005) 11 *New Zealand Business Law Quarterly* 391, 393.

[51] *First Energy (UK) Ltd v Hungarian International Bank Ltd* [1993] Lloyd's Rep 194, 196.

[52] Steyn, 'The Role of Good Faith and Fair Dealing', above n 2, 223.

[53] Brownsword, 'Positive, Negative, Neutral', above n 31, 27.

[54] Steyn, 'The Role of Good Faith and Fair Dealing', above n 2, 222.

[55] Ibid 223; Duncan Kennedy, 'Form and Substance in Private Law Adjudication' (1976) 89 *Harvard Law Review* 1685, 1721.

[56] *Co-operative Insurance Society Ltd v Argyll Stores Ltd* [1997] 3 All ER 297, 305 (per Lord Hoffmann).

Reasonable expectations can may breached when a party attempts to regain opportunities lost upon entering the agreement.[57] A clearly defined obligation of good faith can prevent this by limiting a party's discretion to actions within the justified expectations at the point of the contract's formation.[58] Additionally, good faith may require parties to act reasonably if unforeseen events occur, ensuring fair distribution of unexpected contractual gains or losses.

1.3 Objective of This Book

The existing legal literature on good faith obligation tends to take the position either in favour of the development of good faith in contract law or against it.[59] The problem with this is that the commentators cannot agree on everything and an impasse is formed in the academic debate.[60] Moreover, the lack of a High Court decision on the role of good faith obligation in Australian contract law contributes to the existing conceptual quagmire. Amidst the various academic discourse, there has been no effort to reconcile the different perspectives and examine the actual function of good faith obligation within an adversarial context of contract law. This is important, as

[57] Steven J Burton, 'Breach of Contract and the Common Law Duty to Perform in Good Faith' (1980) 94 *Harvard Law Review* 369, 373.

[58] Elisabeth Peden, 'The Meaning of Contractual "Good Faith"' (2002) 22 *Australian Bar Review* 235.

[59] E.g. Eileen Webb, 'The Scope of the Implied Duty of Good Faith—Lessons from Commercial and Retail Leasing Cases' (2001) 9 *Australian Property Law Journal* 1; Carlin, 'The Rise (and Fall?)', above n 29; Bill Dixon, 'Common Law Obligations of Good Faith in Australian Commercial Contracts—a Relational Recipe' (2005) 33 *Australian Business Law Review* 87; Angelo Capuano, 'Not Keeping the Faith: A Critique of Good Faith in Contract Law in Australia and the United States' (2005) 17(1) *Bond Law Review* 29; Robert McDougall, *The Implied Duty of Good Faith in Australian Contract Law* (2006) < http://www.austlii.edu.au/au/journals/NSWJSchol/2006/2.pdf ≥ ; Geoffrey Kuehne, 'Implied Obligations of Good Faith and Reasonableness in the Performance of Contracts: Old Wine in New Bottles' (2006) 33 *University of Western Australia Law Review* 63; Bill Dixon, 'What is the Content of the Common Law Obligation of Good Faith in Commercial Leases?' (2007) 14 *Australian Property Law Journal* 113; Elisabeth Peden, 'Implicit Good Faith'—or Do We Still Need an Implied Term of Good Faith?' (2009) 25 *Journal of Contract Law* 50; Tyrone Carlin and Louise Chau, 'Good Faith—Time to Put the Genie Back in the Bottle', (2009) 3(2) *Journal of Law and Financial Management* 22; Andrew Stewart, 'What's Wrong with the Australian Contract Law?' (2012) 29 *Journal of Contract Law* 74; Carter, 'Good Faith in Contract: Why Australian Law is Incoherent', above n 42.

[60] Howard Munro conducted a snapshot of the debates surrounding good faith in Australian contract law from various academics that reveals major differences in philosophical directions that the law in the area might take in the future: Howard Munro, 'The Good Faith Controversy in Australian Contract Law: A Survey of the Spectrum of Academic Legal Opinion' (2009) *The University of Queensland Law Journal* 167.

good faith obligation is part of the Australian contract landscape, despite its unsatisfactory developments.[61] In this respect, good faith has become a necessary part of contractual considerations in any contracting relationships. The objective of this book is to address the continued relevance and viability of good faith obligation within an Australian contract law context. This would offer an economically justifiable insight (rather than continuing the polarised debate on the value of good faith) in understanding if there is a role for good faith in commercial contract.

The good faith model based on either alternative two or four mentioned above is ideal, as they are both an adversarial model and a cooperative one.[62] This challenges the fundamental premise in common law contractual doctrine that contracting parties are always in an adversarial relationship.[63] Indeed, in specific commercial contractual scenarios, it would not be out of place for the parties to operate in a spirit of trust and cooperation.[64]

The traditional view of the common law is that it has only been concerned with matters of procedural fairness leaving substantive fairness for statutory regulation.[65] The notion of fairness in contracting is not concerned with the substance and outcome of the bargain. Interfering in the outcome of the contract is contrary to the inherent concept of freedom of contracting.[66] The idea of fairness must not involve interfering in the substance of the deal.[67] Be that as it may, Priestly JA has acknowledged that courts are increasingly treating contract cases individually with a focus on substantive fairness rather than on inflexible legal rules.[68] Brennan noted that existing contract law in their 'unqualified and unsupplemented' state reflects the 'laissez-faire values of a bygone age.'[69] It is for this reason that Sir Anthony Mason commented that the 'recognition of good faith and fair dealing would bring greater coherence and unity to

---

[61] *Hughes Aircraft Systems International v Airservices Australia* (1997) 76 FCR 151; *Pacific Brands Pty Ltd v Underworks Pty Ltd* [2005] FCA 288; *Esso Australia Resources Pty Ltd v Southern Pacific Petroleum NL* [2005] VSCA 228, [27] (per Warren CJ); Carter and Peden, 'Good Faith in Australian Contract', above n 36; Robert McDougall, 'The Implied Duty of Good Faith in Australian Contract Law' (2006) 108 *Australian Construction Law Newsletter* 28; Carter, 'Good Faith in Contract: Why Australian Law is Incoherent', above n 42.

[62] Cf Simon Whittaker and Reinhard Zimmermann, 'Coming to Terms with Good Faith' in Reinhard Zimmermann and Simon Whittaker (eds), *Good Faith in European Contract Law* (Cambridge University Press, 2000), 700.

[63] Mason, 'Contract, Good Faith and Equitable Standards', above n 10, 70.

[64] Pei Yee Woo, 'Protecting Parties' Reasonable Expectations: A General Principle of Good Faith' [2001] 1(2) *Oxford University Commonwealth Law Journal* 195, 197; John W Carter et al., 'Terms Implied in Law: "Trust and Confidence" in the High Court of Australia' (2015) 32 *Journal of Contract Law* 203.

[65] Robert Bradgate, 'Unreasonable Standard Terms' (1997) 60 *Modern Law Review* 582, 591.

[66] Patrick S Atiyah, *The Rise and Fall of the Freedom of Contract* (Oxford University Press, 1985) 213.

[67] Patrick S Atiyah and Stephen A Smith, *Atiyah's Introduction to the Law of Contract* (Oxford University Press, 6th ed, 2005) 297–298.

[68] *Renard Constructions (ME) Pty Ltd v Minister of Public Works* (1992) 26 NSWLR 234, 268.

[69] Gerard Brennan, 'Opening Address' (1990) 3 *Journal of Contract Law* 85.

the varied array of principles which are presently available.'[70] Conceivably, the broad principle of good faith might bestow an uncomfortable discretion on the judiciary, which can result in challenges around contractual independence and competitive dealings. These arguments, and others, will be examined throughout the course of this book. Any assessment of the relevance of the good faith obligation must necessarily involve a balancing exercise.

It would be a missed opportunity for this book if there were no discussion on the obligation of good faith that have been accepted elsewhere as part of the contract regime. This is particularly evident in civil law jurisdictions. It is not the intent of this book to provide a comprehensive exposition on the reception of good faith in civil law jurisdictions. However, there will be a limited focus on France and Germany as they are regarded as the archetypical European civil law jurisdictions, and a separate chapter will be dedicated to an examination of the application of good faith in China. China's approach in this area will provide critical insights for legal scholars and practitioners, not only for those involved in trade between Australia and China, but also in promoting the harmonisation of contract law internationally in the Asia–Pacific region.

Unlike the Australian approach, Chinese contract law has always embraced the concept of good faith as a fundamental principle. The principle of good faith (诚实信用) is prominently featured in the *Civil Code of the People's Republic of China.*[71] Article 7 of the *Civil Code* explicitly states that parties to civil legal relations shall conduct civil activities under the principle of good faith. This principle applies to all aspects of contractual relationships, from formation to performance and interpretation.

The Chinese approach to good faith is rooted in the country's socialist market economy and emphasises the balance between individual and collective interests.[72] Unlike the adversarial model prevalent in common law jurisdictions, Chinese contract law promotes a more cooperative approach to contractual relationships. The principle of good faith in Chinese law serves multiple functions, including as an interpretive tool for judges, a gap-filling mechanism, and a behavioural standard for contracting parties. In addition, Chinese courts have a tendency to interpret the good faith obligation broadly,[73] using it to impose additional duties on contracting parties, such as the duty to disclose material information, to cooperate, and to mitigate losses. However, the broad and flexible nature of the good faith obligation in Chinese law has also raised concerns about legal certainty and predictability—issues that have been frequently debated in the Australian context.

---

[70] Mason, 'Contract, Good Faith and Equitable Standards', above n 10, 94.

[71] 《中华人民共和国民法典》 [Civil Code of the People's Republic of China] (People's Republic of China) National People's Congress, Order No 45, 28 May 2020 ('*the Civil Code*').

[72] Mo Zhang, *Chinese Contract Law—Theory & Practice* (Brill, 2nd ed, 2020), 13–14.

[73] Liang Huixing, 'The Principle of Good Faith and Gap Filling' 91(2) *Chinese Journal of Law* 22, 23; Cui Jianyuan, *Analysis of New Contract Law Theory and Cases* (Jilin University Press, 1999), 26–8; Wang Liming, *Studies on Contract Law* (China Renmin University Press, 2002),163–64;

The contrast between the Chinese approach and the Australian position on good faith in contract law showcases the diverse ways legal systems balance parties' autonomy and fairness in contractual relationships. As Australian scholars and judiciary continue to debate the position of good faith in contract law, the Chinese experience offers valuable insights on the benefits and shortcomings in accessing a duty of good faith in Australian contract law.

Additionally, this book also considers economic and empirical methodology to appraise good faith's relevance. The use of economic principles are relevant for two main reasons. First, similar to economic principles, the law is concerned with the control of scarce resources in society; and second, economic theory plays a crucial role in shaping the law, particularly in managing limited resources, regulating behaviour and imposing penalties for non-compliance.[74] It helps predict rational responses to the law and create incentives for desired economic outcomes.[75]

Economic considerations are deeply intertwined with law making both judiciary and politically with direct links to various legal fields,[76] including trade practices law, corporate law, tax law, intellectual property law, and torts and contract law. The integration of economics and contract law is vital to the commercial sector. Evaluating the obligation of good faith can enrich the discussion and offer insights into how contract law should incorporate this obligation. From an economic perspective, efficiency and wealth maximisation are key factors in the development of contract law. In *Austotel Pty Ltd v Franklins Selfserve Pty Ltd*, Kirby P recognised this fact when he said

> [C]ourts should be careful to conserve relief so that they do not, in commercial matters, substitute lawyerly conscience for the hard-headed decisions of business people. ... The wellsprings of the conduct of commercial people are self-evidently important for the efficient operation of the economy.[77]

This, arguably, means that contract regulation is more aptly suited for economic analysis. Thus, the contractual obligation of good faith is an ideal subject for the application of economic principles.[78]

The other empirical element focuses specifically on the motivation of commercial parties and their legal advisors for the inclusion of good faith provisions in contracts. An understanding of how good faith is utilised in arm's length commercial contract will be made by analysing actual good faith contracting provisions and interviewing

---

[74] Frank Easterbrook, 'The Inevitability of Law and Economics' (1989) 1 *Legal Education Review* 1, 3.

[75] Thomas J Miceli, *The Economic Approach to Law* (Stanford University Press, 2nd ed, 2009) 1; Kevin McGuinness, 'Law and Economics—A Reply to Sir Anthony Mason CJ Aust' (1994) 1 *Deakin Law Review* 117, 119.

[76] Sir Ivor Richardson, 'Law and Economics—and Why New Zealand Needs It' (2002) 8 *New Zealand Business Law Quarterly* 151, 154; Richard A Posner, *Economic Analysis of Law* (Aspen Publishers, 8th ed, 2011) 24.

[77] (1989) 16 NSWLR 582, 585–586.

[78] Arlen Duke, 'A Universal Duty of Good Faith: An Economic Perspective' (2007) 33 *Monash University Law Review* 182, 202; John Smillie, 'Certainty and Civil Obligation' (2000) 9 *Otago Law Review* 633, 639.

legal practitioners and contracting parties regarding their advice and use of the obligation. The empirical methodology employed will be a case study approach using Public Private Partnerships (PPPs) to represent a type of arm's length commercial agreement that utilises good faith obligation in contractual performance and enforcement. An examination of the occurrence of specific good faith contracting provisions in PPPs allows a snapshot to be made of 'what' and 'how' good faith obligation manifests within a commercial contracting setting. Interview accounts taken from legal practitioners and consultants and contracting parties provides a contextual hands-on background into the utility of good faith provisions as to whether the continued validity of good faith obligation in practice can be supported.

There are only two main Australian papers to date, which have published empirical work evaluating good faith application. The first of these studies is Gava and Kincaid's work in 1996 where they reported the result of a survey of NSW barristers in relation to their attitudes regarding the use of cooperative and good faith provisions.[79]

Although the survey findings from the Gava and Kincaid analysis are relevant here, they also have two key constraints. First, the empirical data were derived over two decades ago and, as such, the verdict is still out concerning current attitudes to good faith contracting. The second limitation is that the research was directed towards legal practitioners—barristers practising in NSW. This represents an important omission because it excludes the views of other contract stakeholders, particularly commercial contracting parties. Contracts are still primarily a prominent aspect of commercial activity. It would not, therefore, be appropriate to only consider the views of the legal community in understanding the landscape of commercial contracting as they may run counter to the expectations of the key users of contractual instruments.

The other study is Carlin's empirical work on the approaches of the courts to good faith application where he surveyed case law in Australia using the Austlii database in 2005.[80] The findings suggest that the development of good faith obligation in contractual performance is haphazard, lacks coherence in attaining consistency in legal meaning and application, and is fragmented along jurisdictional lines.[81] This has had a damaging effect for contract users when pleading good faith obligation without any clear pathways as to how it is implied into contracts.[82] Carlin, rightly, views the uncertainty created by this body of law as unacceptable to the core users of contract—those engaged in commerce.[83]

The empirical component presented here is an illustrative example to complement the economic analysis of good faith's viability and is intended to demonstrate elements of commercial reality. Thus, this research, essentially, still maintains a

[79] John Gava and Peter Kincaid, 'Contract and Conventionalism: Professional Attitudes to Changes in Contract Law in Australia' (1996) 10 *Journal of Contract Law* 141.

[80] Tyrone Carlin, 'Good Faith in Contractual Performance—Smoke without Flame?' (2005) 4 (2) *Journal of Law and Financial Management* 18.

[81] Ibid 34.

[82] Ibid 34–35.

[83] Ibid 35.

conventional doctrinal legal research approach in case law analysis and legal theories at its core. Legal scholarship can utilise empirical data to enhance understanding of societal and economic functions at all levels, thereby refining the instrument of law.[84] This aligns with Seddon's conception of 'measured mutation' in Australian contract law,[85] reflecting a broader shift from rigid rules.[86] This distinction would not surprise business practitioners[87] and aligns with Finn J's view that empirical evidence precedes doctrinal matters.[88] While commercial contract law primarily aims to achieve individual goals, these objectives are understood within their specific context and the reasonable expectations of the commercial setting.

The legal analysis together with the economic and empirical methodological approach provides a unique contribution to Australian contract law scholarship—offering valuable insights on the viability of the obligation in Australia.[89] The various arguments for and against will be weighed and a conclusion will ultimately be drawn.

1.4 Research Question

Before proceeding to outline the structure of this book, it is pertinent to capture the research question. The key research question is

Does an obligation of good faith (be it an overriding obligation or as an implied term or as tool of construction) continue to be relevant and viable in arm's length commercial contract based on the reasonable expectations of the contracting parties?

To consider the above research question, the proposition outline in this book will be formulated in three main parts, which address the 'why,' 'what,' and 'how,' questions:

Part 1: Why does good faith matter? Is the historical concept of good faith relevant to commerce? Can the obligation of good faith, as it is approached internationally, benefit Australian contract law?
Part 2: What judicial approaches have been considered in applying good faith obligation? Is there a way forward in achieving judicial common ground?
Part 3: How should good faith obligation be considered economically? Does it have a place in commercial contracting practice?

---

[84] Collins, 'The Sanctimony of Contract', above n 38, 63–89, 69; Terry C Hutchinson and Kylie Burns, 'The Impact of "Empirical Facts" on Legal Scholarship and Legal Research Training' (2009) 43(2) *The Law Teacher* 153 <http://eprints.qut.edu.au/30075/1/c30075.pdf>.

[85] Seddon, 'Australian Contract Law', above n 17, 94.

[86] Peden, *Good Faith in the Performance of Contracts*, above n 17, 143.

[87] Seddon, 'Australian Contract Law', above n 17, 104.

[88] Finn, 'Boats Against the Current', above n 17.

[89] Stewart Macaulay, 'An Empirical View of Contract' (1985) *Wisconsin Law Review* 465; Carlin, 'Good Faith in Contractual Performance', above n 80.

Chapter 2
The Concept of Good Faith Obligation

2.1 Introduction

Priestley JA in *Renard Constructions (ME) Pty Ltd v Minister for Public Works* (*Renard Constructions*) said that the implication of good faith and fair dealing is a reflection of 'community expectations of contractual behaviour.'[1] Indeed, a good faith approach of holding contracting parties to their bargain is of considerable benefit to the wider community and intrinsic in the very nature of contract in our common law legal system.[2] Good faith is not a new phenomenon in contract law. The essence of a duty of good faith existed at least two thousand years ago in Roman law where it had been a central concept in consensual contracts. This concept allowed the Roman jurists to be kept abreast of contemporary developments in Roman commercial life.[3] Without this flexible standard, their task would have been very difficult, if not impossible, and Roman law might have become irrelevant for merchants throughout the ages. Although the Roman experience may not be directly relevant in solving the contemporary problems of bad faith conduct in modern contracts, Roman law provides a relevant insight into the source of the relationship between good faith and

---

[1] (1992) 26 NSWLR 234, 268.

[2] The underlying approach of our courts is to try, whenever possible, to uphold contracting bargains; for example they do not look to the adequacy of the consideration (e.g. in *Thomas v Thomas* (1842) 2 QB 851, 859; *Woolworths Ltd v Kelly* (1991) 22 NSWLR 189, 193–94), and they construe contracts in order to give them effect (e.g. in *Minshull v Minshull* (1737) 1 Atk 411, *Greater London Council v Conolly* [1971] 2 QB 100, *The Tropwind* [1982] 1 Lloyd's Rep 232: a general unwillingness to hold agreements void for uncertainty; particularly true of wholly or partially performed contracts: *Trentham (G Percy) Ltd v Archital Luxfer Ltd* [1993] 1 Lloyd's Rep 25, 27 as per Steyn L J); agreements to negotiate in good faith are not too uncertain: *Coal Cliff Collieries Pty Ltd v Sijehama Pty Ltd* (1991) 24 NSWLR 1; contrast *Walford v Miles* [1992] 2 AC 128 and *Cable & Wireless plc v IBM (UK) Ltd* [2002] EWHC (Comm) 2059.

[3] Reinhard Zimmermann, *The Law of Obligations: Roman Foundations of the Civilian Tradition* (Oxford University Press, 1996).

A. Wan and P. Guo, *Good Faith Obligation*, International and Comparative Law in the Asia Pacific, https://doi.org/10.1007/978-981-97-7035-9_2

commercial contracts. Roman law also survived the test of time by playing a vital role in the development of European legal systems.

In terms of considering the relevance of good faith, it is pertinent to consider where the obligation as a concept was derived and whether it is consistent with the adversarial classical approach of contract law in Australia. As such, the aim of this chapter is to provide this aspect of good faith's background as it not only allows the research to put in context the present situation, but also to assess future developments of the obligation within the ambit of Australian contract law. The legal theories advanced on the concept of good faith are numerous, and they deal with a range of issues depending upon national jurisdiction.[4] In this sense, a general examination of the global good faith position is appropriate as it puts the discussion within the sphere of a juridical concept. Seddon and Ellinghaus made similar observations when they suggested that there is ample justification that good faith obligation may be the most widely prescribed standard of conduct for contracting parties globally.[5]

The principle of good faith was a cornerstone of Roman commercial law, designed to foster collaboration for the mutual benefit of all contracting parties.[6] This differs from the moral notion of good faith found in canon law, aligning more closely with the utilitarian objective that had encouraged its incorporation into Roman law. Thus, from a theoretical standpoint, it is crucial to understand why good faith has been adopted

[4] Expositions and commentaries on good faith obligations can be seen in the following: Hugh Collins, 'Good Faith in European Contract Law' (1994) 14 *Oxford Journal of Legal Studies* 229; Peter D V Marsh, *Comparative Contract Law: England, France, Germany* (Gower, 1994) 51; E Allan Farnsworth, 'Good Faith in Contract Performance' in Jack Beatson and Daniel Friedmann (eds), *Good Faith and Fault in Contract Law* (Oxford University Press, 2001) 153, 156; Johan Steyn, 'Contract Law: Fulfilling the Reasonable Expectations of Honest Men' (1997) 113 *Law Quarterly Review* 433; Anthony Mason, 'Contract, Good Faith and Equitable Standards in Fair Dealing' (2000) 116 *Law Quarterly Review* 66; John W Carter and Elisabeth Peden, 'Good Faith in Australian Contract Law' (2003) 19 *Journal of Contract Law* 155; Johan Steyn, 'The Role of Good Faith and Fair Dealing in Contract Law: A Hair-Shirt Philosophy?' in Johan Steyn (ed), *Democracy Through the Law: Selected Speeches and Judgments* (Routledge, 2004) 213; Howard O Hunter, 'The Growing Uncertainty about Good Faith in American Contract Law' (2004) 20 *Journal of Contract Law* 50; Martijn W Hesselink, 'The Concept of Good Faith' in Arthur S Hartkamp et al. (eds), *Towards a European Civil Code* (Wolters Kluwer, 4th ed, 2010) 471; Emily Houh, The Doctrine of Good Faith in Contract Law: A (Nearly) Empty Vessel? (2005) *Utah Law Review* 1; Jori Manukka, 'Harmonisation of Contract Law: In Search of a Solution to the Good Faith Problem' (2005) 48 *Scandinavian Studies in Law* 229; Shannon K O'Byrne, 'The Implied Term of Good Faith and Fair Dealing: Recent Developments' (2007) 86(2) *The Canadian Bar Review* 193; Howard O Hunter, 'Good Faith and the Construction of Terms in Commercial Contracts: The American Perspective' (2009) 25 *Journal of Contract Law* 39; Colin Liew, 'A Leap of Good Faith in Singapore Contract Law' (2012) *Singapore Journal of Legal Studies* 416; Kah Leng Ter, 'Good Faith in the Performance of Commercial Contracts Revisited' (2014) 26 *Singapore Academy of Law Journal* 111; Anthony Gray, 'Developments in Good Faith in Canada, Great Britain and Australia' (2015) 55(3) *Canadian Business Law Journal* XX.

[5] Nicholas C Seddon and Manfred P Ellinghaus, *Cheshire and Fifoot's Law of Contract* (LexisNexis Butterworths, 8th Australian ed, 2002) 421; Nicholas C Seddon, Rick A Bigwood and Manfred P Ellinghaus, *Cheshire and Fifoot Law of Contract* (LexisNexis Butterworths, 10th Australian ed, 2012) 465.

[6] Raphael Powell, 'Good Faith in Contracts' (1956) 9 *Current Legal Problems* 16, 20–21.

in such a utilitarian manner and how this informs one of the foundational themes of European legal and political philosophies—the interplay between the theories of freedom and responsibility.[7] Contractual theory is fundamentally about individuals and their liberty to associate. Central to this concept is their obligation towards their contracting counterparts. Good faith arises from this dynamic, as it always pertains to another party where both contractual freedom and responsibility are key elements in all commercial contracts.

Under the common law jurisdiction, good faith has constantly generated concern about its paternalistic embrace of moral standards within the sphere of commercial contracting. For instance, in England, economic liberalism at the close of the eighteenth century thwarted Lord Mansfield's attempt to establish good faith as a universal rule to contracts.[8] Conversely in the United States (US), with an economy heavily grounded in liberalism, has embraced the principle of good faith. Good faith is also recognised as the *lex mercatoria* in the global landscape of international transactions marked by liberalism. This raises a logical question: why is this the case? Does the good faith clause enhance economic efficiency in contract law or does it act as a hindrance for commercial parties? From a relevance standpoint, it is important to shed light on these issues.

Priestley JA made reference to US case law and foreign good faith obligations to explain the role of good faith in Australia in his judgement in the *Renard Constructions*' case.[9] The comparative examination in this chapter is to ascertain the relevance of the good faith obligation by examining whether it would be appropriate for Australia to consider any of the extant global practices. It is the failure to properly address these issues that has resulted in good faith becoming entangled in theoretical debates.[10]

The discussion in this chapter is not intended to be a comprehensive exposition. It starts by considering the origins of good faith and how it has influenced English common law that Australian law follows. There is also a general discussion of good faith obligation in the European civil law system. This will only focus on France and Germany as they are regarded as archetypical European civil law jurisdictions.[11] The US experience will also be an important inclusion in this chapter due to their shared

[7] Franz Wieacker, 'Foundations of European Legal Culture' (1990) 28 *American Journal of Comparative Law* 1.

[8] Patrick S Atiyah, *The Rise and Fall of Freedom of Contract* (Clarendon Press, 1985) 168.

[9] (1992) 26 NSWLR 234, 263.

[10] Eileen Webb, 'The Scope of the Implied Duty of Good Faith—Lessons from Commercial and Retail Leasing Cases' (2001) 9 *Australian Property Law Journal* 1; Edward P Belobaba, 'Good Faith in Canadian Contract Law' in Law Society of Upper Canada (ed), *Commercial Law: Recent Developments and Emerging Trends* (Richard De Boo Publishers, 1985) 73; Elisabeth Peden, '"Implicit Good Faith"—or Do We Still Need an Implied Term of Good Faith?' (2009) 25 *Journal of Contract Law* 50; *Ng Giap Hon v Westcomb Securities Pte Ltd* [2009] 3 SLR(R) 518; Andrew Stewart, 'What's Wrong with the Australian Contract Law?' (2012) 29 *Journal of Contract Law* 74; *Yam Seng Pte Ltd v International Trade Corp Ltd* [2013] EWHC 111; John W Carter, 'Good Faith in Contract: Why Australian Law is Incoherent?' (Research Paper No 14/38, Sydney Law School, 2014).

[11] Peter De Cruz, *Comparative Law in a Changing World* (Routledge-Cavendish, 3rd ed, 2006) 47.

commonality with Australia in having a common law jurisdiction. In this respect, the American approach is also essential since good faith obligation is implemented in their contract law as a commercial norm. Further, this comparative examination will conclude in Chap. 3 with an examination of good faith application in China. These discussions will allow for an examination of whether it would be appropriate for Australia to follow any of the approaches taken on good faith obligation beyond its jurisdictional boundaries or develop its own theory within its legal system.

2.2 Historical Overview of Good Faith—From Ancient Roman Law to English Common Law

Essentially, the development of good faith in Australian law is heavily influenced by how good faith is seen under English law. English law traces its origins to the ancient Roman law of equality in exchange, which is where the concept of good faith originates.[12] The earliest example of equitable concepts influencing a legal system arose in Roman law, where those administering justice allowed the circumvention of any formal procedural restrictions to offer equitable access to justice where preventing a party from accessing justice would have otherwise been unfair. This, of course, parallels equity in English law. Roman law was characterised as 'liberalistic spirit' that ignored substantive inequality and mandated only procedural fairness.[13]

Legis actio (act or sue according to the law) is the first known procedure in Roman law,[14] and it was carried out in two oral stages. In the first stage, originally, a clergyman would make a determination on whether an action could be brought by the plaintiff and what type of action was required on the facts. Later, on the enactment of the *leges Liciniae Sextiae* in 367 BCE, ecclesiastics in these positions were replaced by praetors (elected magistrates).[15] During this first stage, the plaintiff would frame their claim in words which conformed with the set form required by the legal system, which the defendant then repeated. This formed the *legis actio* (legal action).[16] If the plaintiff departed from the set form in verbalising their claim, the claim itself would be rejected. The second stage of the procedure saw the *iudex* (private judge) consider evidence to decide the case within the parameters set by the praetor in the

[12] Pei Yee Woo, 'Protecting Parties' Reasonable Expectations: A General Principle of Good Faith' [2001] 1(2) *Oxford University Commonwealth Law Journal* 195.

[13] Zimmermann, *The Law of Obligations*, above n 3, 255–6.

[14] George Mousourakis, *A Legal History of Rome* (Taylor & Francis, 2007) 28, 32.

[15] Ibid 28.

[16] The *legis actio* is an ancient form of Roman civil procedure: Christopher G Paulus, 'Legis actio', in Hubert Cancik et al. (eds), *Brill's New Pauly: Encyclopaedia of the Ancient World* (2006) < http/ /:referenceworks. Brillonline.com/entries/brill-s-new-pauly/legis-actio-e700130 > .

first stage.[17] The praetor did not have authority to proceed with any action that have not been provided for by legislation. This constituted the old *ius civile* (or civil law).

Around the second-century BCE and third-century BCE,[18] the *legis actiones* were eventually supplemented by the formulary system. This system allowed parties to freely state the facts and the praetor would issue a procedural formula that described the facts, appointed the judge, outline the litigation programme and identified the claims and defences. The formulary system offered more flexibility than the *legis actio*.

Each year, a new praetor was appointed who would declare a decree on the formula's arrangement.[19] As a result, the formula underwent regular changes over time, as this edict offered an opportunity to expand the list of enforceable actions and develop the *ius honorarium* (praetorian law). Over several centuries, the praetors built up the *ius honorarium*, which was eventually codified during Emperor Hadrian's reign.[20] The *ius honorarium* supplemented and corrected the *ius civile* and could arguably be seen as an equivalent to equity in English law.[21] Both *ius honorarium* and equity in English law aimed to mitigate the formal requirements of form and doctrine, which often led to a contradiction between positive law and justice. This contradiction was encapsulated in the ancient Roman phrase, *summum ius, summa iniuria*.[22] Therefore, the roles of the praetor and the Chancellor under English law are analogous.[23]

The praetor could insert procedural exceptions could be inserted into the procedural formula.[24] This insertion of exceptions did not constitute the creation of new legal rights per se. A legal right was only recognised in Roman law legislation and was not at the praetor's discretion. However, the praetor did have the power to create new de facto rights by introducing creative remedies within the formula.[25]

---

[17] Robert W Lee, *The Elements of Roman Law* (Sweet & Maxwell, 4th ed, 1986) 10; Franz Wieacker, 'The Importance of Roman Law for Western Civilization and Western Legal Thought' (1981) 4(2) *Boston College International and Comparative Law Review* 257.

[18] Lee, *The Elements of Roman Law*, above n 17; Mousourakis, above n 14, 32.

[19] Wieacker, 'The Importance of Roman Law', above n 17.

[20] Zimmermann, *The Law of Obligations*, above n 3, 680.

[21] William W Buckland, *Equity in Roman Law: Lectures Delivered in the University of London, at the Request of the Faculty of Laws (1911)* (2009) 5; Fritz Pringsheim, 'The Inner Relationship Between English and Roman Law' (1933) 5 *Cambridge Law Journal* 347, 357.

[22] Roughly translated, *Summum ius, summa iniuria* means 'the greater the right, the greater the wrong.' When a great right (e.g. the right to life) is violated, it results in a great wrong; Marcus Tullius Cicero, *De officiis*, Book 1 (Walter Miller trans, 1913) 33 < http://www.constitution.org/rom/de_officiis.htm#book1 > .

[23] Roscoe Dorsey, 'Roman Sources of Some English Principles of Equity and Common Law Rules' (1938) 8 *American Law School Review* 1233, 1235.

[24] Zimmermann, *The Law of Obligations*, above n 3, 680.

[25] Mousourakis, *A Legal History of Rome*, above n 14, 65.

The *ius civile* was Roman law and as trade began to expand in the Mediterranean, it became necessary to recognise trade agreements[26] which led to the development of the *ius gentium* (law of nations).[27] Agreements in the *ius gentium* established a binding legal relation between the parties based on the commercial ethic and customs of the trade.[28] In this context, the concept of good faith or *bona fides* in the *ius gentium* presupposed not just fair conduct but, also, respect for the mercantile customs.[29] It is unclear when *bona fides* became an operative element of Roman law, but it was already incorporated into the *ius honorarium*[30] during the second-century BCE.[31] Although the true origin of *bona fides* remains a matter of speculation, the role of commerce as a real influence cannot be underestimated.[32] This role will be investigated in the ensuing analysis of the development of *bona fides* under the formulary system of procedure in Roman law.

2.2.1 Bona Fides Under the Formulary Procedure

The formulary system that existed during the third-century BCE was a turning point in the development of *bona fides* in Roman law as the praetor was granted more power to create a new action on that basis. Previously, the praetor's authority had been limited under the old *legis actio*.[33]

The expansion of Roman commercial life, undoubtedly, played a vital role in the progress of *bona fides* as a concept related to commercial dealings. The growing complexity of Roman economic life, both in its expansion of territories and commercial relations, with its foreign trading neighbours became the basis for reform in civil procedure. This resulted in the necessity to modify their strict and simple system of contracts to meet the exigencies of the emerging community of international merchants.[34] Furthermore, the introduction of a special praetor to adjudicate

---

[26] Martin Josef Schermaier, 'Bona Fides in Roman Contract Law' in Reinhard Zimmermann and Simon Whittaker (eds), *Good Faith in European Contract Law* (Cambridge University Press, 2000) 68.

[27] Robert W Dyson, *Natural Law and Political Realism in the History of Political Thought: From the Sophists to Machiavelli* (Peter Lang, 2005) vol 1, 127.

[28] David J Bederman, *International Law in Antiquity* (Cambridge University Press, 2007) 84.

[29] Adda B Bozeman, *Politics and Culture in International History: From the Ancient Near East to the Opening of the Modern Age* (Transaction Publishers, 2nd ed, 2010) 210.

[30] The *ius honorarium* was the law developed in edicts issued by the praetors during the Roman Empire, aiding, supplementing or amending existing rules or procedures of the *ius civile*: Adolf Berger, *Encyclopedic Dictionary of Roman Law*, (American Philosophical Society, 1991) vol 43 part 2, 529.

[31] Schermaier, 'Bona Fides in Roman Contract Law', above n 26, 74.

[32] Ibid 69.

[33] Ibid 70–77; Barry Nicholas, *An Introduction to Roman Law* (Oxford University Press, 1976) 23.

[34] In this regard, Sherman emphasised the importance of commerce in the development of Roman law: 'What changed Roman law from a local rigid formal law into a world-wide rational formless

disputes between foreigners, and between Roman citizens and foreigners, clearly indicated that the commercial transactions of foreign merchants had to be recognised by obtaining legal validity under Roman law.[35] It is not surprising that during this formative period of Roman law, the praetor was given more authority to adapt the old *ius civile* to newer types of transactions, such as sale and hire that imposed obligations on both parties.

In these commercial transactions, *bona fides* were independent sources of obligation before their recognition at civil law. The greater flexibility afforded by the formulary system enabled the praetor to transform *bona fides* from a social concept to a legal principle in the *ius civile*.[36] It should be borne in mind that claims based on bona fides had no statutory basis at that stage. Accordingly, the only route to enforce such a claim was through the praetor who had the power to create a new action. This meant an evolution from the previous situation where if the claim lay outside the *ius civile* then it could not be enforced. The formulary process essentially became the precondition to the development of the *bonae fidei iudicia*, or good faith actions.[37] Moreover, this system opened the gate for new equitable defences like *exceptio doli* (exception of fraud), which softened the strict application of actions other than *bona fides*, for example *stricti iuris* (strict law).[38]

---

jurisprudence? The answer is the growth of foreign trade and commerce': Charles Sherman, *Roman Law in the Modern World* (Baker, Voorhis & Company, 1937) section 43, 37; Simon Whittaker and Reinhard Zimmermann, 'Good Faith in European Contract Law: Surveying the Legal Landscape' in Reinhard Zimmermann and Simon Whittaker (eds), *Good Faith in European Contract Law* (Cambridge University Press, 2000) 18; Rudolph Sohm, James Ledlie, Gruber Crawford and Erwin Bernhard, *The Institutes: A Textbook of the History and System of Roman Private Law* (Clarendon Press, 2009) 246.

[35] William W Buckland, '*Culpa* and *Bona Fides* in the *Actio Ex Emptio*' (1932) 48 *Law Quarterly Review* 217, 228.

[36] Kaser succinctly describes the evolution of *bonae fidei:* 'From the beginning of the classical age, *bonae fidei iudicia* were accepted as part of the *ius civile* because it was thought that good faith was just as binding as a *lex*. The function of *bona fides* changed accordingly; *bona fides* was no longer needed as an independent source of obligation but it now provided a standard according to which the judge had to examine the legal relationship. The content of the obligation was now taken to comprise all that which had been informally agreed upon by the parties themselves, with regard to the source and content of obligation, but also that which—even failing such agreement—was to be regarded as being owed according to the concrete circumstances and in consideration of the local and general custom.': Max Kaser, *Roman Private Law* (Rolf Dannenbring trans, Butterworths, 2nd ed, 1968) 142–143.

[37] Schermaier, 'Bona Fides in Roman Contract Law', above n 26, 76.

[38] Carole Lewis, 'The Demise of the *exceptio doli* is there Another Route to Contractual Equity?' (1990) 107 *The South African Law Journal* 26, 30. It should be noted that in about 66 BCE bad faith was allowed to be relevant in *stricti iuris* action under the praetorian—*exceptio doli* (exception of fraud). Before the existence of this exception, the defendant in an action on a stipulation could not plead that his promise had been induced by the plaintiff's fraud; Whittaker and Zimmermann, 'Good Faith in European Contract Law', above n 35, 16: 'The *exceptio doli* was worded in the alternative: "*si in ea re nihil dolo malo AA factum sit neque fiat*" (if in this matter nothing has been done, or is being done, in bad faith by the plaintiff). It was particularly the second alternative (*neque fiat*—or is being done) that made the *exceptio doli* such a powerful instrument in bringing about a

In this sense, *bona fides* (which became a form of good faith actions) gave the judge the opportunity to assess and decide the case in accordance with what appeared to be fair and reasonable by allowing him to examine the legal relationship between the parties.[39] This extended the role of judges from applying legal rules in a purely formal manner to facts established before him in assessing its legal merits of the case.[40] Although the judge had to confine any adjudication of the case within the formula issued by the praetor, the substantive content of *bona fides* was developed by the judge's interpretation of what was required in the individual case.[41] Nevertheless, it should be noted that this discretion resting on the judge was dependent on whether or not the words *ex fide bona* were inserted into the formula issued by the praetor. This equitable function was, therefore, crucial to the evolution of good faith actions or *bona fides* in Roman law.

2.2.2 Development of Good Faith Obligation Under Bona Fide Actions

During the period of the formulary procedure system, there were no attempts by jurists to classify actions in the law as the actions were still individually judged.[42] However, as far as judicial discretion was concerned, actions based on good faith or *bona fides*, formed a distinctive group that was completely different from the others, namely *stricti iuris*.

Historical records show that some contracts required good faith (*bona fides*), while others followed strict law (*stricti iuris*).[43] Contracts requiring good faith fide obligations included *tutela* (guardianship), *mandatum* (mandate), *emptio venditio* (sale), and *locatio conductio* (hire of goods or services).[44] Unilateral contracts like the *stipulatio* (where the promisor was strictly bound to the promise) followed *stricti iuris*.[45]

---

just solution, for it invited an answer which located *dolus* not so much in personal misconduct, but rather in an inequity or injustice that would flow from the action being allowed to succeed.'.

[39] Reinhard Zimmermann, *Roman Law, Contemporary Law, European Law: The Civilian Tradition Today* (2001) 83.

[40] 'Before the introduction of the *bonae fidei iudicia*, the judge was confined to determining whether the claim asserted under the procedural formula did or did not exist': Schermaier, 'Bona Fides in Roman Contract Law' above n 26, 84; Kaser, *Roman Private Law*, above n 36, 142.

[41] Peter Stein, *Fault in the Formation of Contract in Roman Law and Scots Law* (Oliver and Boyd, 1957) 8.

[42] Kaser, *Roman Private Law*, above n 36, 142.

[43] William W Buckland and Peter Stein, *A Text-Book of Roman Law: From Augustus to Justinian* (Cambridge University Press, 3rd ed, 2007) 413.

[44] Marcus Tullius Cicero, *De officiis*, Book 3, (Walter Miller trans, 1913) 70 < http://www.constitution.org/rom/de_officiis.htm#book3 > .

[45] Mousourakis, *A Legal History of Rome*, above n 14, 67.

Actiones stricti iuris (action at law in strict right) required jurors to consider and deal with the legal formula strictly, taking into account only what was explicitly stated.[46] In contrast, *actiones bonae fidei* allowed jurists to use their discretion, considering all the facts of the case, irrespective of whether they were specified or not.[47] This meant judges could look at the parties' intentions and consider any reasonable defences, even if they were not mentioned in the formula, allowing the application of good faith where the situation deemed it relevant.[48]

The judge of a dispute involving this type of contract could take into account any arrangements between the parties in assessing the defendant's duty to perform. Cicero gives us an example of how *bona fides* enabled the judge to alter the seller's duties according to the requirements of good faith. He cites a case where a demolition order had been decreed on a property whose owner had sold without divulging that fact to the buyer.[49] The seller, in fact, had known about this order when he advertised the house for sale. However, the seller was not in breach of the *ius civile* for not disclosing this order to the buyer. Under early Roman civil law, the seller was not liable for defects which he had not denied. An express warranty was not necessary during this early period of Roman law.[50]

In this case, the *actio ex empti* (action against seller) directed the judge to determine the case according to the requirement of good faith. Accordingly, the judge was able to order the defendant to compensate the plaintiff for the amount lost because of his silence. It is, perhaps, not surprising that subsequent developments of *bona fides* in case of sales enabled the jurists to free buyers from the harsh principle of *caveat emptor* (let the buyer beware).[51]

In a bona fide action, the defendant could also produce any defence to the claim involving good faith. On the other hand, in *stricti iuris* actions, he was required to produce his defences to the claim through an independent *exceptio*. The absence of a good faith element in these actions excluded any consideration of factors that would make the enforcement of contract substantially unfair. The issue was simply whether or not the defendant was liable in law. Therefore, a counterclaim arising from the same contract was impossible in these actions. However, in sales transactions, good faith allowed the judge to consider a counterclaim and 'condemn the defendant only for differences between the two claims.'[52] This emphasised the fact that good faith required the judge to look carefully at the legal relationship between parties rather than simply applying the law in a purely formal manner. Sohm describes sale as a '*bonae fidei negotiant,* [that is] both parties are bound, not merely to what they

---

[46] Buckland and Stein, *A Text-Book of Roman Law*, above n 43, 679.

[47] This power was granted by the praetor by appending the clause *ex fide bona* to the formula.

[48] Mousourakis, *A Legal History of Rome*, above n 14, 67.

[49] Stein, *Fault in the Formation of Contract,* above n 41, 8.

[50] Whittaker and Zimmermann, 'Good Faith in European Contract Law', above n 34, 16–17.

[51] Ibid.

[52] Ibid 17.

expressly undertook to do, but to do all that is involved in the requirements of good faith.'[53]

In purely commercial relationships, the application of *bona fides*, like sale under Roman law, indicated clearly that good faith was not a wholly moral concept as there was little to suggest that Roman lawyers were concerned with ethical principles in their treatment of good faith.[54] Rules derived from *bona fides* included prevailing standards of equity such as 'fairness, uprightness, playing the game, doing in given circumstances what a self-respecting man would do.'[55] For example, the protection for a buyer against latent defects in an ordinary sale was not initially available in the *actio empti,* which was a *bona fides* action.[56] However, liability in the law of sale was extended gradually by progressive interpretation of *bona fides* in relation to the seller's duties. The honest seller was only liable for reduction of the price due to defects of the sold object. However, the dishonest seller was liable for consequential damages. The qualification of *bona fides*, therefore, emphasises the precise standard of behaviour that was required by the seller.[57]

The obligation of good faith found in the *bona fides* helped the Roman jurists maintain their law in line with new developments in commercial life. Good faith in Roman law was characterised by a utilitarian character, as *bona fides* were invoked in the formula, not as a source of obligation, but in order to enlarge the discretion of the judge in arriving at his judgement.[58] Without this flexible notion of good faith, that task would have been very difficult, if not impossible, and the law would have become irrelevant to the needs of merchants throughout the ages.[59] In such a way, *bona fides* were one of the most fruitful agents in the development of contract law.

The significance of *bona fides* gradually reduced from the end of the classical period. This change came in around 130 CE with the final codification of the praetorian edict by Iulianus. This edict stagnated the praetors' creativity as the once flexible *ius honorarium* no longer allowed for discretion.[60] The *ius civile* and *ius honorarium* were merged, and the formulary procedure was replaced by the imperial *cognitio extra ordinem.*[61] By the end of the third-century BCE, this was the preferred procedure,[62] emphasising *aequitas* (equity), *humanitas* (humanity) and *benignitas* (fairness) over *bona fides.*[63]

Nonetheless, by the time the imperial *cognitio extra ordinem* emerged as the preferred process, a general body of rules had already taken shape out of the numerous

---

53 Sohm, Ledlie, Crawford and Bernhard, *The Institutes,* above n 34, 396–397.

54 Powell, 'Good Faith in Contracts', above n 6, 20.

55 Buckland, '*Culpa* and *Bona Fides*', above n 35, 228.

56 Zimmermann, *The Law of Obligations*, above n 3, 311.

57 Schermaier, 'Bona Fides in Roman Contract Law', above n 26, 82.

58 Schermaier, 'Bona Fides in Roman Contract Law', above n 26, 81–82.

59 Whittaker and Zimmermann, 'Good Faith in European Contract Law', above n 34, 18.

60 Zimmermann, *The Law of Obligations*, above n 3, 127.

61 A proceeding before an imperial magistrate rather than before the praetor and *iudex*; Ibid 681.

62 Mousourakis, *A Legal History of Rome*, above n 14, 128.

63 Cf Berger, *Encyclopedic Dictionary of Roman Law*, above n 30.

decisions based on *bona fides*. Despite this, a body of rules based on *bona fides* had already formed, aiding the adaptation of Roman law into modern legal systems.[64] The historical presence of *bona fides* in Roman law has been essential for incorporating good faith obligations in contemporary contract law.

2.2.3 Good Faith in the Ius Commune

The *Corpus Iuris Civilis* (Body of Civil Law) was developed during the Roman Empire's post-classic era under Emperor Justinian,[65] transitioning legal procedures to *cognitio extra ordinem*—a centralised system before an imperial magistrate. This period saw the principle of good faith gain substantive meaning, guiding party conduct beyond the old procedural characteristic of *bonae fidei iudicia*.

In continental Europe, Justinian law, known as *ius commune* (common law), became universally applicable in the absence of special regional laws[66] and was integral to Europe's Christian culture in the fourteenth century.[67] Medieval jurists recognised good faith and equity in contracts, describing three types of conduct expected of parties.[68]

First, parties were required to keep their promises, a principle rooted in faith and equity, applicable under the *ius gentium* (a law binding upon all peoples).[69] This principle, grounded in religion, differed from Roman law, which only considered some contracts binding by consent.[70] Canonists viewed all promises as binding on the promisor's conscience, equating any breach as akin to violating God's laws.[71]

Second, good faith did not encourage contracting parties to mislead or take advantage of each other. It enables victims to obtain remedies for deceit or fraud (*dolus*). *Dolus* could be causal, leading someone into a contract they otherwise would not have entered, or incidental, resulting in someone contracting under less favourable terms. Causal fraud allowed the victim to void the contract, while incidental fraud entitled them to damages.[72]

---

[64] Schermaier, 'Bona Fides in Roman Contract Law', above n 26, 88.

[65] The name *Corpus Juris Civilis* occurs for the first time in 1583 as the title of a complete edition of the Justinianic code by Dionysius Godofredus: Wolfgang Kunkel, *An Introduction to Roman Legal and Constitutional History* (J M Kelly trans, Oxford University Press, 2nd ed, 1973) 157.

[66] Wieacker, 'Foundations of European Legal Culture', above n 7, 6.

[67] Peter Stein, *Roman Law in European History* (Cambridge University Press, 1999) 74.

[68] James Gordley, 'Good Faith in Contract Law in the Medieval *Ius Commune*' in Reinhard Zimmermann and Simon Whittaker (eds), *Good Faith in European Contract Law* (Cambridge University Press, 2000) 93.

[69] Ibid 95.

[70] Ibid 99.

[71] Powell, 'Good Faith in Contracts', above n 6, 20.

[72] Zimmermann, *The Law of Obligations*, above n 3, 671.

Third, good faith required parties to act honestly within their transactions, reflecting the belief of medieval jurists that every contract had natural terms to be observed in good faith and equity according to the *ius gentium*.[73]

In the fourteenth century, Italian jurist Baldus further developed the concepts of good faith and equity by drawing on Aristotle and Thomas Aquinas works.[74] Aristotle's distributive justice recognised fair wealth distribution, while commutative justice regulated transactions.[75] Aquinas classifications of contracts as acts of either liberality (e.g., donations) or commutative justice (e.g., sales and leases).[76]

Baldus took it further and argued that good faith and equity prevented unjust enrichment at another's expense, forming the basis of commutative justice. For instance, his principle of natural equity and good faith allowed for remedies in cases of unjust pricing.[77] He reasoned that every contract must have a *causa* (reason)—either liberality or the receiving of something in return.[78] He, then, surmised that contracts without a *causa* were unenforceable under any law, including canon law.[79]

Baldus's theories heavily influenced late fourteenth-century scholarship[80] and were adopted by the Late Scholastics in sixteenth- and seventeenth-century Spain. They explored duties arising from equity and good faith, though they did not tie their conclusions to Roman texts much like Baldus.[81]

Although the notion of equality in exchange is less prominent today, Baldus's work significantly shaped the historical development of good faith in contract law. His definitions helped resolve individual cases and enhanced the understanding of good faith and equity in contemporary contract law.[82]

2.2.4 Development of Good Faith in English Law

It is fundamental that the development of good faith within English law is primarily attributable to the Court of Chancery, which had sought rules to mitigate the harshness of the common law where they would be too strict or unfair in certain situations.[83] This

---

[73] Gordley, 'Good Faith in Contract Law', above n 68, 103.

[74] Aristotle, *Nicomachean Ethics*, Book V, 2 (Ross, W D trans) < http://classics.mit.edu/Aristotle/nicomachaen.5.v.html > .

[75] Aristotle, *Nicomachean Ethics*, Book IV (Ross, W D trans), 1. < http://classics.mit.edu/Aristotle/nicomachaen.4.iv.html > .

[76] Gordley, 'Good Faith in Contract Law', above n 68, 107.

[77] James Gordley, *The Philosophical Origins of Modern Contract Doctrine* (Oxford University Press, 1993) 56, 67.

[78] Gordley, 'Good Faith in Contract Law', above n 68, 112.

[79] Gordley, *The Philosophical Origins*, above n 77, 56.

[80] Stein, *Roman Law in European History*, above n 67, 73.

[81] Gordley, *The Philosophical Origins*, above n 77, 39.

[82] Gordley, 'Good Faith in Contract Law', above n 68, 117.

[83] Patricia Loughlan, 'The Historical Role of Equitable Jurisdiction' in Patrick Parkinson (ed), *The Principles of Equity* (Law Book Co, 2nd ed, 2003) 3, 9.

is a natural consequence of early ecclesiastical chancellors importing the obligation of good faith inherent in canon law into the Court of Conscience.[84] Good faith and conscience inevitably lie deepest in the foundations of equity:

> The chancellor was an ecclesiastic, and probably carried with him into chancery the principles and theories of the ecclesiastical court. It is notorious that the ecclesiastical court did assume jurisdiction over *laesio fidei* [the breach of faith]. What more natural than that the chancellor should have proceeded upon the ground of breach of faith? ... I do not think it necessary to base the chancellor's jurisdiction on breach of faith alone; but that he did enforce gratuitous promises cannot be doubted.[85]

Despite this, the Court of Chancery was neither the first nor the sole court to adopt good faith obligation in England. King Henry II, known for his conflicts with bishops and the clergy, surprisingly appointed prelates from the church as justices.[86] Although these clerical justices had limited familiarity with canon law, Henry II's decision was pivotal in embedding the Roman canon law concept of *bona fides* into the common law system. In this regard, even a basic familiarity with canon law would encompass some comprehension of how the concept of *bona fides* from Roman law relate to Christian conscience.[87]

The clergy who served as judges in the royal courts were consequently able to utilise their understanding of canon law to the ambiguous and contradictory assortments of custom, tribal and feudal rules that constituted English law during that period.[88] The influence of canon law introduced Roman principles of *aequitas*[89] and *bona fides* into the nascent common law.

However, by the reign of King Edward II, conscience and good faith have ceased to be significant considerations in legal decisions. Canon law and civil law have stopped influencing English law by the end of the thirteenth century,[90] and any equitable notions within common law were extinguished. This shift was evident in *Le Walays v Melsamby*, where Chief Justice Bereford was reminded by counsel that he must not let conscience interfere with the law.[91] The assumption, therefore, became adversarial and that everyone entering into a contract would protect their own interests and 'if he were outwitted or even defrauded, he was without redress.'[92]

---

[84] John Baker, *An Introduction to English Legal History* (LexisNexis Butterworths, 4th ed, 2005) 123; Willard T Barbour, 'The History of Contract in Early English Equity' in Paul Vinogradoff (ed), *Oxford Studies in Social and Legal History* (Clarendon Press, 1914) vol IV, 158.

[85] Barbour, 'The History of Contract in Early English Equity', above n 84, 163.

[86] Frederick Pollock and Frederick Maitland, *The History of English Law Before the Time of Edward I* (Liberty Fund, New ed, 2010) 132.

[87] John F O'Connor, *Good Faith in English Law* (Dartmouth Publishing, 1990) vol 2, 2.

[88] Sir William Holdsworth, *A History of English Law* (Methuen & Company, 1972) vol 2, 177.

[89] This is the legal concept of equity and fairness: Quentin Skinner, *Visions of Politics* (Cambridge University Press, 2002) 49; George Mousourakis, *The Historical and Institutional Context of Roman Law* (2003) 28, 32–35.

[90] Holdsworth, *A History of English Law,* above n 88, 177.

[91] *Le Walays v Melsamby* Year Books 1 & 2 Edward II (vol 17, 1903), xix.

[92] Year Books 12 Edward II (vol 65, 1950), iv.

This stance reflected the common law's fear that notions of conscience and good faith were subjective and could lead to arbitrary interference from the law.[93]

In contrast, continental Europe's recognition of *aequitas* provided a remedy for the injustices of *ius strictum*. Consequently, *bona fides* dominated relations between merchants during the eleventh and twelfth centuries and, thus, the concept of good faith established itself as an essential form of medieval and early mercantile law.[94]

The royal courts were not interested in articulating a flexible action for enforcing informal contracts. There is no doubt that commercial activities were still primitive and property, not contracts, appeared to be the real concern of the royal courts. According to Glanville: 'It is not the custom of the court of the Lord King to protect private agreements, nor does it even concern itself with such contracts as can be considered to be like private agreements.'[95]

Under the writ system, the contractual remedies were Covenant, Debt, Detinue, and Account. An executory agreement was not sufficient to be brought under these actions. For instance, the action of Covenant was extremely formal where an obligation was evidenced by writing under seal. Detinue and Account were based upon real contract.[96] This seems to suggest that the writ of debt could be used as a basis for developing a contractual liability in an informal contract, to fill gaps created by the formalities of the writ system. However, the essence of this action was that the defendant had possessed something that belonged to the plaintiff: 'It claims restitution not the performance of an undertaking.'[97] Moreover, it had inherited a procedural problem by allowing defendants to wage their law. Accordingly, an action of debt was not fruitful in an executory agreement.[98]

Nevertheless, the absence of a general doctrine in the Royal courts with which to enforce parole agreements (informal agreements) at that stage did not mean that no other means existed to fill the obvious gaps in the common law. Good faith in the canonist sense was readily employable to fill these gaps. For instance, the Church courts in England were willing to enforce simple promises at a time when common law courts issued writs of prohibition to prevent recourse to Church courts. In his essay on early English equity, Holmes J said.

> But if the King failed, the church stood ready. For a long time, and with varying success, it claimed a general jurisdiction in case of *laesio fidei*. ... The clerical Chancellors seem for a time to have asserted successfully in a different tribunal, the power of which they had been shown as ecclesiastics to enforce contracts for which the ordinary King's Courts afforded no remedy.[99]

---

[93] Barbour, 'The History of Contract in Early English Equity', above n 84, 156.

[94] Whittaker and Zimmermann, 'Good Faith in European Contract Law', above n 34, 17.

[95] E Allan Farnsworth, 'The Past of Promise: An Historical Introduction to Contract' (1969) 69 *Columbia Law Review* 576, 588.

[96] James B Ames, 'Parol Contracts Prior to Assumpsit' (1895) 8 *Harvard Law Review* 252.

[97] Frederick Pollock, 'Contracts in Early English Law' (1893) 6 *Harvard Law Review* 389, 398.

[98] David J Ibbetson, *A Historical Introduction to the Law of Obligations* (Oxford University Press, 2001) 141.

[99] Oliver W Holmes, 'Early English Equity' (1885) II *Law Quarterly Review* 162, 171–174.

It is in this respect that the ecclesiastical courts employed the notion of good faith, although in the religious sense, to enforce informal contracts that were unenforceable under the inflexible rules of the common law. This inevitably led to an increase in ecclesiastical jurisdiction on contract law.[100] Ecclesiastical courts would enforce a contract in an action where a sworn promise—with words to the effect of 'by my faith'—could be derived from the agreement.[101] The basic requirement of good faith is that each party should keep his word. This, of course, does not mean that every promise should be enforced. However, although the difficult question of the propriety of enforcing simple promises was a central problem in canon law, it did not cause much difficulty for the English Church courts. The requirement of an oath or pledge of faith 'took an agreement out of the area of the *nadum pactum*.'[102] The extensive use of the oath was recognised to bind informal commercial agreements at that time.[103] In effect, then, a person would treat another's promise as having value only because of the promisor's oath that performance would be forthcoming in good faith. This basic function of good faith played a vital role in liberalising the law of contract during the subsequent development of commercial contracts. Sir William Holdsworth explained that

> the canonist's view that faith should be kept, in whatever form the promise was expressed, helped forward the development of forms of commercial contract which were quite unknown to the civil law; it assisted the legislature to deal adequately with the new forms of fraud and sharp practice rendered possible by a more elaborate organisation of commerce; and thus it contributed to enforce those high standards of good faith and fair dealing which are the very life of trade.[104]

The rigid common law led to the development of equitable jurisdiction in the fourteenth century, initially managed by the Court of Requests. Evidence of Chancery as a separate Court of Equity did not appear before 1340.[105] And subsequently, during the fourteenth and fifteenth centuries, equitable principles initially seen in common law courts started to be incorporated by the Chancellor and Chancery.[106]

During the fifteenth and early sixteenth centuries, the Court of Chancery was perceived as a Court of Conscience rather than a Court of Equity, as it later came to be known. Petitions during that time would make appeal to the Chancellor. This would include persons who had acted in good faith, which enable him to enforce contracts according to good faith and conscience even if the ordinary legal formalities had not been satisfied.[107]

---

[100] Ibid.

[101] Richard H Helmholz, *Roman Canon Law in Reformation England* (2004) 25.

[102] Richard H Helmholz, 'Assumpsit and *Fidei Laesio*' (1975) 91 *Law Quarterly Review* 406, 409.

[103] Ibid 406.

[104] Sir William Holdsworth, *A History of English Law*, vol 5 (1972) 81.

[105] O'Connor, *Good Faith in English Law*, above n 87, 5.

[106] Holdsworth, *A History of English Law*, above n 88, 346.

[107] Barbour, 'The History of Contract in Early English Equity', above n 84, 182; A W Brian Simpson, *A History of the Common Law of Contract: The Rise of the Action of Assumpsit* (Clarendon Press, 1996) 397.

Whether the Court of Chancery recognised good faith as a ground for enforcing informal contracts is a moot point. Furthermore, it would be far too simplistic to claim that a coherent vision of good faith existed in the Chancery. It must not be overlooked that during this early period of equity in English law there was, to some extent, overlap between faith in the religious sense and good faith in the legal sense. This basis could explain why it is extremely difficult for historians of contract law to identify the ground upon which the Chancery enforced informal contracts.[108] However, this ambiguity in Chancery practice does not mean that good faith was not approved and adopted by the Chancellors in the fifteenth century. As Powell said

> In the fifteenth century, the use of the words 'good faith and conscience' was probably necessary, not only to catch the eye of the Chancellor but also to put in his hands the key with which he could without qualms open his court to the petitioner.[109]

Therefore, it is entirely plausible to suppose that good faith was, to a considerable extent, the impetus for a very important development in the common law—the articulation of an adequate theory of contract.[110] For instance, the extension of assumpsit from a pure action in tort to the arena of contracts clearly indicates the pressure that the common law judges were under to develop a general contractual remedy. It is true that there were also further factors other than simply their concern with good faith.[111] However, we cannot dismiss the influence of good faith entirely from the development of assumpsit in contractual liability. Helmholz, who strongly suggested a connection between the growth of assumpsit and *Fidei Laesio,* concluded that 'the evidence seems, therefore, to point to a more direct connection between the canon law and the growth of assumpsit than has previously been thought.'[112] This finding should not disturb historians of contract law if accounts were taken of the fact that the canonists' conception of good faith influenced the law of promises in England.

From the late eighteenth century, the Court of Chancery was in decline in the stead of formalism's increasing favour.[113] Equity had hardened into rigid principles as it transformed from a discretionary jurisdiction to one reliant on precedent. Traditional equitable doctrines concerning penalties, forfeitures, mortgages, and unconscionable contracts were neglected.[114] Despite this, an emerging principle of good faith in contract law became evident in the in the latter half of the eighteenth century which aimed to ensure fair exchanges in contracts.[115] The idea of good faith was, therefore, congruent with the emergent sense of morality.[116] In 1766, Lord Mansfield CJ suggested that good faith had a general application to all contracts:

---

[108] Barbour, 'The History of Contract in Early English Equity', above n 84, 167.

[109] Powell, 'Good Faith in Contracts', above n 6, 22.

[110] O'Connor, *Good Faith in English Law*, above n 87, 18.

[111] Powell, 'Good Faith in Contracts', above n 6, 23.

[112] Helmholz, 'Assumpsit and *Fidei Laesio*', above n 102, 429.

[113] Atiyah, *The Rise and Fall of Freedom of Contract*, above n 8, 392.

[114] Ibid 394.

[115] Ibid 168.

[116] Ibid.

> The governing principle is applicable to all contracts and dealings. Good faith forbids either party by concealing what he privately knows, to draw the other into a bargain, from his ignorance of those facts, and his believing to the contrary. But either party may be innocently silent, as to grounds open to both, to exercise their judgement upon.[117]

Lord Mansfield was, therefore, prepared to restrict the operation of the doctrine of *caveat emptor* by referring to a general principle of good faith.[118] The sentiments of Mansfield were shared by Lord Kenyon in *Mellish v Motteux* where he opined that in 'contracts of all kinds, it is of the highest importance that courts of law should compel the observance of honesty and good faith.'[119] Similar views were endorsed during the early nineteenth century. In *Lumley v Wagner*, Lord St Leonards LC, sitting in the Lord Chancellor's Court, observed:

> Wherever this court has not proper jurisdiction to enforce specific performance, it operates to bind men's consciences, as far as they can be bound, to a true and literal performance of their agreements, and it will not suffer them to depart from their contracts at their pleasure, leaving the party with whom they have contracted to the mere chance of any damages which a jury may give. The exercise of this jurisdiction has, I believe, had a wholesome tendency towards the maintenance of that good faith which exists in this country to a much greater degree perhaps than in any other.[120]

However, from the mid to late nineteenth century, the principle of good faith was overshadowed by legal developments that reflected laissez-faire economics and contractual autonomy.[121] Shift was influenced by the political economy of the 1820s and 1830s,[122] which valued the freedom of competent parties to negotiate their agreements.[123] One of the basic elements in the classical theory of contract is the assumption that actors in contracts are fully knowledgeable and act rationally to further their economic self-interests. Thus, when contracts are made there is an assumption that each party has the right to enforce what he or she has bargained for and any attempts to intervene with the content of the contract must be rejected, as Jessel J emphasised in 1875:

> [I]f there is one thing which more than another public policy requires it is that men of full age and competent understanding shall have the utmost liberty of contracting, and that their contracts when entered into freely and voluntarily shall be held sacred and shall be enforced by Courts of justice.[124]

---

[117] *Carter v Boehm* (1766) 3 Burr 1905, 1910.

[118] Atiyah, *The Rise and Fall of Freedom of Contract*, above n 8, 164.

[119] (1792) 170 ER 113, 113–114.

[120] (1852) 42 ER 687, 693.

[121] Reziya Harrison, *Good Faith in Sales* (Sweet & Maxwell, 1997) 7.

[122] Atiyah, *The Rise and Fall of Freedom of Contract*, above n 8, 467.

[123] Dame Sian Elias, 'Opening Address to the 10th Annual Journal of Contract Law Conference' (2000) 6 *New Zealand Business Law Quarterly* 79.

[124] *Printing & Numerical Registering Co v Sampson* (1875) LR 19 Eq. 462, 462.

As a consequence, this common law idea that parties negotiating a contract were dealing at arm's length prevailed.[125] As such, the principle of *caveat emptor* established itself as an essential assumption at common law and, with it, the scales had tipped strongly against general standards of fairness in favour of predictability.[126] Incremental changes were preferred over overarching principles, which rendered general obligation of good faith obsolete[127] and an outdated form of moralistic ideals that were not inline with commercial contracting attitudes.[128]

The merger of the common law and equitable jurisdictions under the *Judicature Act 1873* likely accelerated these developments.[129] Many common law judges struggled to understand and apply equitable notions of good faith, leading them to disregard these principles. By the time the Act was passed, equity had already suffered approximately a century of decline.[130]

Good faith became a matter of mere marginal interest in England as a result of the prevailing school of thought.[131] It has been recognised that

> [w]ith the exception of Raphael Powell's inaugural lecture in 1956, good faith in contract was not a topic addressed by academics or textbook writers; nor was a violation of the principle of good faith a matter openly pleaded or addressed in litigation.[132]

Brownsword's 'pragmatic thesis' would further suggest that the English common law is more than capable of providing piecemeal solutions without the need for the application of a good faith obligation or principle.[133] These include estoppel, misrepresentation, duress, frustration, and the like.[134]

The debate on good faith did not reach maturity until the latter part of the twentieth century. This evolution was primarily driven by both Steyn J and Bingham LJ's judgement in *Banque Keyser Ullmann SA v Skandia (UK) Insurance Co Ltd*[135] and *Interfoto Picture Library Ltd v Stiletto Visual Programmes Ltd*,[136] respectively.

---

[125] *Banque Keyser Ullmann SA v Skandia (UK) Insurance Co Ltd* [1987] 2 All ER 923, 943 (per Steyn J).

[126] Horst K Lücke, 'Good Faith and Contractual Performance' in Paul Finn (ed), *Essays on Contract* (Law Book Co, 1987) 157.

[127] Atiyah, *The Rise and Fall of Freedom of Contract*, above n 8, 168.

[128] Ibid.

[129] Harrison, *Good Faith in Sale*, above n 121, 9.

[130] Atiyah, *The Rise and Fall of Freedom of Contract*, above n 8, 393.

[131] Roger Brownsword, Norma J Hird and Geraint Howells, 'Good Faith in Contract: Concept and Context' in Roger Brownsword, Norma J Hird and Geraint Howells (eds), *Good Faith in Contract: Concept and Context* (Dartmouth Publishing Co, 1999) 2.

[132] Andrew Grubb and Michael P Furmston, *The Law of Contract* (LexisNexis Butterworths, 1999) 68.

[133] Roger Brownsword, 'Two Concepts of Good Faith' (1994) 7 *Journal of Contract Law* 197.

[134] Roger Brownsword, 'Positive, Negative, Neutral: The Reception of Good Faith in English Contract Law' in Roger Brownsword, Norma J Hird and Geraint Howells (eds), *Good Faith in Contract: Concept and Context* (Dartmouth Publishing Co, 1999) 13, 21.

[135] [1987] 2 All ER 923.

[136] [1988] 1 All ER 348.

In the *Banque Keyser* case, Steyn J examined a claim of good faith in an insurance contract. His Honour acknowledged the long-standing principle that an insurance contract for insurance is a particular category of contract that necessitates disclosure in good faith:

> That principle, Lord Mansfield CJ said, is applicable to all contracts. To that extent Lord Mansfield CJ's generalised statement has not prevailed. Admittedly, there are other contracts which are sometimes described as contracts of the utmost good faith, such as contracts of suretyship, partnership and salvage, but the principles of disclosure applicable to those contracts cannot be equated with those applicable to contracts of insurance.[137]

Importantly, Steyn J held that the remedy for a breach of utmost good faith in insurance contracts was not limited to contract avoidance and return of premiums. It could include a claim for damages if the insured could prove that the lack of good faith disclosure induced them to enter into the contract and that damages were the only effective remedy.[138] Although the House of Lords later overturned this point, it sparked greater interest in using good faith obligation as a basis for claiming damages akin to contractual remedies.[139]

In the case of *Interfoto Picture Library Ltd v Stiletto Visual Programmes Ltd*, the English Court of Appeal was tasked with deciding on the validity of a particularly onerous clause. This clause obligated a photo library customer to pay a hefty holding fee for photographs returned past the due date.[140] The photo library, however, failed to bring this clause to the customer's attention at the time when the transaction occurred. Allusions to obligations of good faith were made by Bingham LJ in the course of his judgement:

> In many civil law systems, and perhaps in most legal systems outside the common law world, the law of obligations recognises and enforces an overriding principle that in making and carrying out contracts parties should act in good faith. This does not simply mean that they should not deceive each other, a principle which any legal system must recognise its effect is perhaps most aptly conveyed by such metaphorical colloquialisms as 'playing fair', 'coming clean' or 'putting one's cards face upwards on the table'. … English law has, characteristically, committed itself to no such overriding principle but has developed piecemeal solutions in response to demonstrated problems of unfairness. Many examples could be given. Thus equity has intervened to strike down unconscionable bargains. Parliament has stepped in to regulate the imposition of exemption clauses and the form of certain hire-purchase agreements. The common law also has made its contribution, by holding that certain classes of contract require the utmost good faith, by treating as irrecoverable what purport to be agreed estimates of damage but are in truth a disguised penalty for breach, and in many other ways.[141]

---

[137] [1987] 2 All ER 923, 943.

[138] Ibid 923, 947.

[139] *Banque Financière de la Cité SA (formerly Banque Keyser Ullmann SA) v Westgate Insurance Co (formerly Hodge General & Mercantile Co Ltd)* [1990] 2 All ER 947, 959; John Birds, *Birds' Modern Insurance Law* (9th ed, 2013) 140.

[140] [1988] 1 All ER 348, 357 (per Bingham LJ).

[141] [1988] 1 All ER 348, 352–353; cf *National Westminster Bank plc v Rabobank Nederland* [2007] EWHC 1056 (Comm).

Bingham LJ considered that a legal system based on good faith obligation would necessitate the photo library to explicitly alert the customer to the substantial fee. However, English law would instead examine the nature of the transaction at hand and the parties to determine what notice was provided and whether it would be just under all circumstances to enforce the bargain. Interestingly, Bingham LJ also acknowledged that the English approach would likely produce a similar outcome to the civil law principle of good faith.[142] Indeed, the court found that while there was a contract, the photo library had not done enough to highlight the clause to the customer, rendering it unenforceable.[143]

These decisions sparked debate in England about whether common law should shift from its piecemeal approach to a unified obligation of good faith. Libertarians, advocating for freedom of contract and classical contract law, resisted this shift.[144] Lord Ackner's comments in *Walford v Miles* exemplify this stance, arguing that an obligation to negotiate in good faith conflicts with the adversarial nature of contractual negotiations.[145] Long-standing principles of contract were thought to be undermined as a good faith obligation contradicts the classical law of contract allowing parties to contract to maximise their own interests and, effectively, compete with contracting parties to arrive at an outcome which benefits them most. This sentiment on the sanctity of contracts has not lost its place in modern cases involving contractual disputes.[146] There is nothing wrong with this view as long as the essence of classical contract theory remains valid. However, the developments in contracts during the twentieth century have brought several cases to courts in which the ideal conditions of classical contract theory are difficult to appreciate. For instance, the emergence of standard form contracts as a preferred model of contracting between commercial enterprises and consumers has enabled the stronger party to engineer the content of such contracts in their favour, leaving the courts helpless to deal with the unfairness of such contractual provisions. Strictly speaking, the common law courts are not entirely powerless in dealing with unfair contracts and are often able to apply existing rules in contract law to reach what they perceive as fair results; the absence of a general principle of good faith makes such tasks extremely difficult in certain areas where courts have no option other than to accept the rigidity of contract law and leave the matter for the legislature to intervene.[147] For example, in *Mackay v Scottish Airways Ltd*,[148] which concerned the validity of an exemption clause excluding

---

[142] [1988] 1 All ER 348, 357.

[143] Ibid 348, 352 (per Dillon LJ).

[144] Elias, 'Opening Address', above n 125, 79.

[145] [1992] 1 All ER 453, 460.

[146] In *EFT Commercial Ltd v Security Change* (1992) SC 414, 424: Lord President Hope said that 'it is the function of the court to enforce contracts according to the bargain which the parties have made for themselves. It is not for the court to interfere in order to modify a bargain which one of the parties later considers to be unfair.'.

[147] A prime example is the *Unfair Contract Terms Act 1977*.

[148] (1948) SC 254.

the airline's liability to pay damages for the death or injury of a passenger during carriage, Lord President Cooper observed:

> The remarkable feature of these conditions is their amazing width, and the effort which has evidently been made to create a leonine bargain under which the aeroplane passenger takes all the risks and the company accepts no obligations, not even to carry the passenger or his baggage nor even to admit him to the aeroplane. It was not argued that the conditions were contrary to public policy, nor that they were so extreme as to deprive the contract of all meaning and effect as a contract of carriage; I reserve my opinion upon these questions.[149]

In the case of the *Unfair Contract Terms Act 1977*, it was a consumer protection legislation designed to safeguard against abusive terms in various consumer contracts by subjecting the contractual clauses to a test of 'reasonableness'.[150] The test of reasonableness is closely associated with the good faith obligation.[151] However, in relation to the *Unfair Contract Terms Act 1977*, it did not generate a vigorous debate about the possibility of introducing broad general principles such as good faith or the doctrine of unconscionable conduct into English contract law. This subject was continually ignored among English lawyers during the 1970s and 1980s until the European Union (EU) dramatically changed this state of affairs. The EU introduced the principle of good faith in the EC Directive[152] on Unfair Terms in Consumer Contracts (Regulations of 1999 in the UK).[153] A term will be unfair when 'contrary to the requirements of good faith it causes a significant imbalance in the parties' rights and obligations arising under the contract, to the detriment of the consumer.'[154] The EU directive affects consumer contracts[155] as well as a certain class of commercial

[149] Ibid 254, 263.

[150] Section 2(2) *Unfair Contract Terms Act 1977*; case examples include *Stewart Gill Ltd v Horation Myer Ltd* [1992] QB 600, [1992] 2 All ER 257 (Court of Appeal); *George Mitchell (Chesterhall) Ltd v Finney Lock Seeds Ltd* [1983] 2 AC 803, [1983] 2 All ER 737 (House of Lords).

[151] *Socimer International Bank Ltd v Standard Bank Ltd* [2008] 1 Lloyd's Rep 558, 582; *Yam Seng Pte Ltd v International Trade Corp* [2013] EWHC 111.

[152] Directive 93/13 [1993] OJ L95/29.

[153] See comments on this legislation: Peter Duffy, 'Unfair Contract Terms and the Draft EC Directive' (1993) *Journal of Business Law* 67; Meryll Dean, 'Unfair Contract Terms: The European Approach' (1993) 56 *Modern Law Review* 581; Chris Willett, 'Good Faith in Consumer Contracts: Rule, Policy and Principle' in Angelo D M Forte (ed), *Good Faith in Contract and Property Law* (Hart Publishing, 1999) 181; *Director-General of Fair Trading v First National Bank Plc* [2002] 1 Lloyd's Rep 489.

[154] UK SI 1999/2083 Reg 5(1).

[155] The principle of good faith in Directive 93/13/ on Unfair Terms in Consumer Contracts (art 3): In the UK, this directive is given effect under the *Unfair Terms in Consumer Contracts Regulations 1999* (SI 1999/2083). Regulation 5 provides '(1) A contractual term which has not been individually negotiated shall be regarded as unfair if, contrary to the requirement of good faith, it causes a significant imbalance in the parties' rights and obligations arising under the contract, to the detriment of the consumer.' See also Directive 97/7/ on Distance Selling, implemented in the UK by the *Consumer Protection (Distance Selling) Regulations 2000*, (SI 2000, No 1334), which imposes a duty on suppliers to provide consumers with adequate information 'with due regard … to the principles of good faith in commercial transactions' (reg 7(2)).

agency contracts.[156] In respect of commercial agency contracts, the common law does not generally have categories of agency contracts, so this is an alien super-imposition upon the common law. Under this European directive, a commercial agent is a

> self-employed intermediary who has continuing authority to negotiate the sale and purchase of goods on behalf of another person (the principal), or to negotiate and conclude the sale and purchase of goods on behalf of and in the name of that principal.[157]

It includes agents who have no authority to contract as well as those who have; however, it does not include agents authorised for a single transaction only and does not include an intermediary who purchases for resale. Where the directive applies, there is imposed in every such contractual relationship mutual obligations to act in good faith,[158] which are mandatory[159] and cannot be contracted out of. In addition, the directive gives the agent an action for common law damages where the agency is terminated in breach of contract.

This directive is aimed at protecting commercial agents operating in the EU. In such a situation, the directive will apply as mandatory law in an English court (or any other court in the EU), irrespective of the parties' choice of law to govern the contract.[160] Apart from that, a choice of English law in a contract that falls within the definition of a commercial agency contract would attract the application of this law as part of English law, and the good faith duties would, under this law, appear to be mandatory, so long as the forum hearing the case (whether in the UK or elsewhere) gives effect to the parties' choice of English law clause.

These external developments have made the question of good faith inescapable in the UK.[161] It is also interesting to note that good faith has been described as a virus, which has been transplanted into UK laws by EU legislation:

> Good faith is irritating British law. … [T]he (in)famous European Consumer Protection Directive 1994 [1999 Regulations] transplanted the continental principle of *bona fides* directly into the body of British contract law where it has caused a great deal of irritation. ... The infecting virus had already earlier found inroads into the common law of contracts, especially in the United States where the *Uniform Commercial Code* and the *Restatement (2d) of Contracts* provide for a requirement of good faith in the performance and enforcement of contracts.[162]

---

[156] Directive 86/653/ on Self-employed Commercial Agents. This is implemented in the UK through the *Commercial Agents (Council Directive) Regulations 1993* (SI 1993/3053).

[157] *Commercial Agents (Council Directive) Regulations 1993*, reg 2(1).

[158] Ibid reg 2(1) regs 3(1), 4(1).

[159] Ibid reg 5(1).

[160] C-381/98, *Ingmar GB Ltd v Eaton Leonard Technologies Inc* < http://curia.europa.eu/jcms/jcms/j_6/ >.

[161] E.g. O'Connor, *Good Faith in English Law*, above n 89; Jack Beatson and Daniel Friedmann (eds), *Good Faith and Fault in Contract Law* (Oxford University Press, 2001); Harrison, *Good Faith in Sales* (1997), above n 123; Brownsword, Hird and Geraint Howells (eds), *Good Faith in Contract*, above n 131.

[162] Gunther Teubner, 'Legal Irritants: Good Faith in British Law or How Unifying Law ends up in New Divergences' (1998) 61 *Modern Law Review* 11, 11.

It would seem as though the above author has overlooked the fact that Scots law, as a facet of British law, is immune from the good faith virus as its concept has more historical roots in Scots law than English law.[163] The real concern for opponents of the good faith principle in English law is not with its potential role in consumer contracts, but rather how it will affect commercial contracts in general.

2.2.4.1 Position of Good Faith Obligation Under Present Common Law Theories

There is at present no separate principle of general good faith in contracting at arm's length under English common law. There are only notions of good faith that are incorporated into specific legal doctrines such as dishonesty in contract formation, fiduciary relationships, and utmost good faith contracts.[164] A brief summary comparing good faith obligation and contracting under existing law is necessary to highlight the differences.

(a) *Dishonesty in Contract Formation*

Contracting principles relating to misrepresentation, duress, undue influence, unconscionable dealing, and other similar acts concern the conduct of the contracting parties at the pre-contractual stage of contract making. The notion of good faith is inherent in these principles and may be difficult to differentiate at times as they overlap.

A dishonest act such as fraudulent misrepresentation would result in the contract becoming voidable, ab initio, at the option of the innocent party. The notion of good faith, however, is not concerned with conduct that invalidates the formation of contracts, which is also distinguishable from the principle of unconscionability.[165] Good faith obligation concerns promises relating to the negotiation and finalisation of contracts.[166] It includes preliminary agreements to negotiate or to negotiate in good faith, letters of intent, heads of agreements, and finalising agreements that are incomplete or made subject to contract. Thus, the notion of good faith has wider connotation than merely prohibiting dishonest conduct in contracting under existing legal principles.

[163] Thomas B Smith, *A Short Commentary on the Law of Scotland* (W Green & Sons, 1962) 297–298; Ole Lando and Hugh Beale (eds), *The Principles of European Contract Law, Part I and II* (Kluwer Law International, 1999) 58.

[164] Sara M Mitchell and Emilia J Powell, *Domestic Law Goes Global: Legal Traditions and International Courts* (Cambridge University Press, 2011) 41–42; Ewan McKendrick, *Contract Law: Text, Cases and Materials* (Oxford University Press, 6th ed, 2014) 505; *Mid Essex Hospital Services NHS Trust v Compass Group UK and Ireland Ltd (T/A Medirest)* [2013] EWCA Civ 200.

[165] Stephen M Waddams, 'Good Faith, Unconscionability and Reasonable Expectations' (1995) 9 *Journal of Contract Law* 55, 55; unconscionability will be discussed separately in Chap. 5.

[166] Mason, 'Contract, Good Faith and Equitable Standards', above n 4, 82; Lindy Willmott, Sharon Christensen and Desmond Butler, *Contract Law* (Oxford University Press, 4th ed, 2013) 15.

(b) *Fiduciary Relationships*

The concept of good faith may be confused with the honesty required for contracting parties in a fiduciary relationship. Examples of such contracts include contracts involving a trust or fiduciary relationship between partners, principal and agent, and others of a comparable nature. Equity expects specific standards of conduct from persons who are not considered to be at arm's length in their relationship with another.[167]

A fiduciary relationship obliges a party to act for the benefit of another person where that party has a responsibility to act in the interests of the other party.[168] In fiduciary relationships, the duty to act honestly means subordinating one's own interests to those of the other party.[169]

Good faith obligation is distinguishable from the duty of honesty or good faith imposed on the parties to fiduciary relationships. Good faith obligation concerns a contractual relationship at arm's length and deals with commercial relationships that are adversarial in nature with no obligation on the contracting parties to subordinate their respective interests to those of the other party.[170] In this regard, the contracting parties are allowed to advance their own respective interests. Further discussion on this distinction will be made in Chap. 5.

(c) *Utmost Good Faith*

English law prefers to designate specific contracts as contracts *uberrimae fidei* or utmost good faith, rather than recognising a general duty of good faith in every contractual relationship.[171] The *uberrimae fidei* principle requires full pre-contractual disclosures of material facts relating to the risk to be insured.[172] To this extent, the good faith requirement goes beyond the normal requirement of honesty and fair dealing in common law.[173]

It is not within the scope of this book to study this theory in detail. However, utmost good faith is relevant when considering good faith obligation in the negotiation of contracts. The theory of utmost good faith recognises an obligation based upon the

---

[167] Paul Finn, *Fiduciary Obligations* (Law Book Co, 1977) 78.

[168] Paul Finn, 'The Fiduciary Principle' in Timothy G Youdan (ed), *Equity, Fiduciaries and Trusts* (Law Book Co, 1989) 2; Paul Finn, '"Good Faith, Unconscionability and Fiduciary Duties" in Energy Law'90: Changing Energy Markets—the Legal Consequences' (Paper presented at the 9th Advanced Seminar on Petroleum, Mineral, and Energy Resources Law Proceedings, London, 22–27 April 1990) 105.

[169] Peter Watts, *Bowstead and Reynolds on Agency* (Sweet & Maxwell, 19th ed, 2012) para 1–001.

[170] Atiyah, *The Rise and Fall of Freedom of Contract*, above n 8, 402.

[171] E.g. the *Marine Insurance Act 1906*: Section 17 reads 'A contract of marine insurance is a contract based upon utmost good faith.'.

[172] Howard H Bennett, 'Mapping the Doctrine of Utmost Good Faith in Insurance Contract Law' (1999) *Lloyd's Maritime and Commercial Law Quarterly* 165, 187–193.

[173] Angelo D M Forte, 'Good Faith and Utmost Good Faith' in Angelo D M Forte (ed), *Good Faith in Contract and Property Law* (Hart Publishing, 1999) 77.

pre-contractual relations between the contracting parties. By contrast, the common law does not impose a general duty of disclosure in ordinary contractual relations.[174]

There is, perhaps, a loose assumption shared by judges and commentators that an insurance contract, unlike other types of commercial contracts, has an exceptional nature that imposes a positive duty of disclosure and utmost good faith requiring disclosure of all material facts.[175] Lord Mansfield's opinion that is most often quoted to support this assumption is as follows:

> Insurance is a contract upon speculation. The special facts upon which the contingent chance is to be computed lie most commonly in the knowledge of the insured only. The underwriter trusts his representation and proceeds in the confidence that he does not keep back any circumstance in his knowledge to mislead the underwriter into a belief that the circumstance does not exist, and to induce him to estimate the risk as if it did not exist. Keeping back such circumstance is a fraud, and therefore, the policy is void.[176]

In isolation, this passage supports the departure of insurance contracts from the general common law rules, which applied to all types of contract at the formation stage. Consequently, it supports the existence of a broad duty of disclosure and establishes the rule that a mere non-disclosure of a material fact without an inquiry into good faith is an invalidating factor.

There is no doubt that the protection of the insurance industry justified the existence of this exceptional approach in insurance contracts by English judges. For instance, Scrutton LJ once stated that

> The underwriter knows nothing of the particular circumstances of the voyage to be insured. The assured knows a great deal, and it is the duty of the assured to inform the underwriter of everything that he is not taken as knowing, so that the contract may be entered into on an equal footing.[177]

Nevertheless, a careful reading of what Lord Mansfield actually said in *Carter v Boehm* supports a more rational principle in contract law than merely an exceptional rule for a particular type of contract. In *Carter v Boehm,* the plaintiff obtained a policy of insurance indemnifying his brother, Governor of Fort Marlborough in Sumatra, against loss of the fort to a foreign enemy. The insurers sought to avoid the policy, claiming that certain material facts regarding the security of the fort, which was supposedly vulnerable to foreign attack, and the insured's fear of an invasion were not disclosed at the time of the formation of the policy. Two letters evidenced the insured's fear.

The first was a letter from the Governor to his brother, the plaintiff. This letter clearly indicated that there was a possibility of an attack on the settlement by the French. The second letter was from the Governor of the East India Company, indicating the weakness of the settlement and its exposure to a European enemy. Although

---

[174] Patrick S Atiyah and Stephen A Smith, *Atiyah's Introduction to the Law of Contract* (Oxford University Press, 6th ed, 2005) 247.

[175] Forte, 'Good Faith and Utmost Good Faith', above n 173, 82.

[176] *Carter v Boehm* (1766) 97 ER 1162, 1184.

[177] *Greenhill v Federal Insurance Co* (1927) 1 KB 65, 76.

this was an insurance case, Lord Mansfield understood that he applied a general contract rule:

> The governing principle is applicable to all contracts and dealings. Good faith forbids either party, by concealing what he privately knows, to draw the other into a bargain from his ignorance of that fact and his believing the contrary.[178]

This understanding of good faith as a valuable principle for all contracts had an important impact on the final outcome of this case. It seems likely that Lord Mansfield was aware of the fact that good faith could not be easily pigeonholed for a particular type of contract. Thus, he did not apply good faith in a purely technical way, to justify full disclosure by the insured without an inquiry into the good faith requirement.

Accordingly, the existence of a duty to disclose, and indeed of any other duties that are manifested by good faith, could be justifiably applied to any contract. His approach towards disclosure in *Carter v Boehm* was more rational than his successors. For example, there was no doubt of the materiality of the concealed facts in the letters sent by the governor to his brother and the company. However, materiality was not the cornerstone for establishing a duty to disclose in good faith but that the defendant should not have to prove that there were material facts concealed from him during the formation of contract. There must also have been a justifiable reliance by the defendant on good faith disclosure. The plaintiff in that case did not breach the requirements of good faith. According to Lord Mansfield:

> The underwriter knew the insurance was for the governor. He knew the governor must be acquainted with the state of the place. He knew the governor could not disclose it, consistent with his duty. He knew the governor, by insuring, appreciated, at least, the possibility of an attack. With this knowledge, without asking a question, he underwrote. By so doing, he took the knowledge of the state of the place upon himself. It was a matter as to which he might be informed in various ways.[179]

This rational approach towards the existence of good faith disclosure by Lord Mansfield is not surprising. Good faith does not mean that each party is allowed to expect from the other full disclosure of every material fact without any reasonable inquiry. Every party, even under good faith, must take care of themselves and should not unjustifiably rely on the good faith of the other. His Lordship's approach to the facts of this case clearly demonstrates a high degree of awareness of the implications of good faith in contracts.[180] Be that as it may, the issue is whether the reference by Lord Mansfield to good faith was reciprocal and intended as a general and independent duty in contracting.[181]

The subsequent cases did not support such a wide application of good faith and took the view that Lord Mansfield's statement was confined to the prevention of fraud

---

[178] 3 Burr 1905, 97 ER, 185.

[179] Ibid 187–188.

[180] See an invaluable analysis of *Carter v Boehm* in Eric M Holmes, 'A Contextual Study of Commercial Good Faith Disclosure in Contract Formation' (1978) 39 *University of Pittsburgh Law Review* 381.

[181] Nigel G Rein, 'Utmost Good Faith in Marine Insurance' (1999) 10 *Insurance Law Journal* 145, 146.

and misrepresentation. In *Mellish v Motteux*,[182] the plaintiffs agreed to purchase a brig from the defendant. The defendant knew that the brig contained latent defects, and relied upon the rule of *caveat emptor* to deny any obligation to disclose these defects. Further, a term of the sale was that the ship was to be sold 'with all faults' and without warranty. The court found an obligation to disclose faults that were known to the seller that could not be reasonably discovered by the buyer. Lord Kenyon said that '[I]n all contracts of all kinds, it is of the highest importance that the courts of law should compel the observance of honesty and good faith.'[183]

Lord Kenyon made reference to good faith as justification for the need for disclosure. In this sense, good faith was merely intended to support a specific duty that subsisted independently as there was a pre-contractual relationship requiring disclosure of the defects. This duty of disclosure found by Lord Kenyon was overruled in the subsequent case of *Baglehole v Walters*.[184]

The duty of disclosure before the formation of an insurance contract remains the main issue under the theory of utmost good faith. Once the contract is concluded, the duty of utmost good faith is confined to an obligation not to act fraudulently.[185] There is an obligation of good faith or honesty upon insured persons when they submit their claims.[186] The insured is also bound by a duty as an implication from the insurance relationship and the duty of disclosure only arises because of it.[187] A duty of disclosure is not imposed merely because the particular relationship requires good faith.[188]

Good faith obligation (as opposed to utmost good faith) is not concerned with specific pre-contractual relations between the contracting parties. Rather, it concerns the making and performance of commercial dealings at arm's length and involves the notions of honesty, fairness and reasonableness.[189]

---

182 (1792) Peake 156, 170 ER 113.

183 Ibid 113, 113–114.

184 (1811) 3 Camp 154, 170 ER 1338.

185 Semin Park, *The Duty of Disclosure in Insurance Contract Law* (Dartmouth Publishing, 1997) 223; See also Howard H Bennett, 'Utmost Good Faith, Materiality and Inducement' (1996) 112 *Law Quarterly Review* 405.

186 Scott Henchliffe, 'Insurance Claims: Fraud and the Duty of Utmost Good Faith' (1997) 8 *Insurance Law Journal* 210, 228.

187 John G Fleming, 'Insurer's Breach of Good Faith—A New Tort?' (1992) 108 *Law Quarterly Review* 357; cf insurance contracts are governed by statute that requires utmost good faith to be implied, for example in Australia under ss 13 and 14 of the *Insurance Contracts Act 1984* (Cth); *Zurich Australia Insurance Ltd v St Andrew's War Memorial Hospital* [1998] QSC 209, [37], [40].

188 Atiyah and Smith, *Atiyah's Introduction*, above n 174, 247.

189 Lücke, 'Good Faith and Contractual Performance', above n 128, 161; *Socimer International Bank Ltd v Standard Bank Ltd* [2008] 1 Lloyd's Rep 558, 582; *Yam Seng Pte Ltd v International Trade Corp Ltd* [2013] EWHC 111.

2.3 Good Faith in the Civil Law Jurisdictions of Europe

The civil law systems within Europe are also familiar with the obligation of good faith.[190] The majority of the continental civil codes incorporate the concept of good faith.[191] Good faith obligation has been used in the European codified systems to support development by the courts of doctrines not expressly included in the civil codes.[192] The civil law concept of good faith encompasses 'all the variety of instances when one party has abused the social practice of making promises.'[193] In this section, the discussion covers only French and German contract law as they are regarded as representative of the archetypical European civil law jurisdictions.[194]

2.3.1 *Good Faith Under French Contract Law*

Despite the generality of the formula of art 1134(3) of the *French Civil Code*, which provides in its declaration that all contracts must be performed in good faith (*bonne foi*), French law remains hesitant in its approach to good faith. This is, even, considering that art 1135 also contains a general statement:

> *Les conventions obligent non seulement à ce qui y est exprimé, mais encore à toutes les suites que l'équité, l'usage ou la loi donnent à l'obligation d'après sa nature* [Agreements are binding not only as to what is therein expressed, but also as to all the consequences which equity, usage or statute give to the obligation according to its nature][195]

Although good faith is not defined in the *French Civil Code*, it seems to impose a minimum obligation of honest conduct where the duties are not prescribed by contract or by law.[196] In principle, where no preliminary agreement exists, French law supports freedom of negotiations.[197] However, parties may not break negotiations 'without legitimate reason', 'abusively' or in 'bad faith.'[198] French courts will impose liability where one party enters into negotiations without having any intent to contract, yet creates a reasonable expectation in the other party that a contract will be forthcoming

---

[190] Jan H Dalhuisen, *Dalhuisen on Transnational and Comparative Commercial, Financial and Trade Law*, vol 1 (Hart Publishing, 4th ed, 2010) 284.

[191] Edward Thomas, 'Good Faith in Contract: A Non-Sceptical Commentary' (2005) 11 *New Zealand Business Law Quarterly* 391, 407.

[192] Waddams, 'Good Faith, Unconscionability and Reasonable Expectations', above n 165, 57.

[193] Collins, 'Good Faith in European Contract', above n 4, 250.

[194] De Cruz, *Comparative Law in a Changing World*, above n 11, 47.

[195] Bénédicte Fauvarque-Cosson and Denis Mazeaud (eds), *European Contract Law Materials for a Common Frame of Reference: Terminology, Guiding Principles, Model Rules* (European Law Publishers, 2008) 525.

[196] Powell, 'Good Faith in Contracts', above n 6, 30.

[197] Parties may conduct parallel negotiations with third parties or solicit opposing offers without notifying their counter-parties.

[198] Cass Civ 1, April 12 1976, Bull Civ I, no 122.

such that the other party incurs substantial pre-contractual expenses.[199] This may be the case if a party enters into negotiations for the sole purpose of preventing the injured party from negotiating with a third party or obtaining from the injured party certain confidential information.[200] Liability will also be imposed on bad faith negotiations when, for example, negotiating on the basis of an over-inflated price while simultaneously discussing a significantly lower price with third parties.[201] The further along the negotiation process, the more likely it is that a French court deems the party, breaking off the negotiations, to be acting in bad faith.

It should be noted that French law does not impose pre-contractual liability for breach of contractual obligations but does so on the basis of tort. The conditions for establishing tortious liability under art 1382 of the *French Civil Code* are similar to the elements of common law tort, whereby the plaintiff must establish fault, causation and compensable damages.[202] In the performance of contract, there are at least two main applications of the good faith principle.

The first is the duty of loyalty,[203] which is divided into two categories: *obligation de moyens* (a promise to do his or her best, such as the promise of a doctor to do his or her best to cure his or her patient) and *obligation de résultat* (a promise to realise something, such as the promise to build a house). If the promise is to do your best (*obligation de moyens*), the promisee is required to prove both the omission and negligence of the promisor. If it is a promise to do something specific, then the fault liability is assumed. This reference is to import the notion of fault from tort to contract under French jurisdiction. The difficulty is to prove that a fault is made by the promisor during the attempt to perform his or her best. The French courts do this by comparing the promisor's behaviour with the behaviour of the *bonus pater familias*, or the custom of the transaction.[204] That is, they ask, whether the promisor took the usual precautions? Or, did the promisor do what is normally done in similar circumstances in order to avoid injury to the promisee? The desire here is to protect the reasonable expectations of the contracting parties.[205] Therefore, contracting parties can expect to obtain the outcomes contemplated as resulting from the contract negotiations and must avoid any behaviour that would be an impediment to performance.

---

[199] Barry Nicholas, *The French Law of Contract* (Clarendon Press, 2nd ed, 1992) 53.

[200] Saul Litvinoff, 'Good Faith', (1997) 71 *Tulane Law Review* 1645.

[201] Cass Civ 1, January 6, 1998, JCP 1998 II 10,066.

[202] French law looks for very substantial deviation from pre-contractual reliance in order to establish a basis for liability in tort (art 1382) or for deceit (arts 1110 and 1116); cf Case C-334/00, *Fonderie Officine Meccaniche Tacconi SpA v Heinrich Wagner Sinto Maschinenfabrik GmbH (HWS)* ECJ, September 17 2002 < http://curia.europa.eu/jcms/jcms/j_6/ > .

[203] This duty was recognised by the Cassation case laws: Cass 8.4.1987, *Bull*, III, 53, *RTD Civ* 1988, 122 noted by Mestre J; Cass 5.6.1968, *D*, 1970, 453 noted by Jestaz; then several statutes implemented the doctrine for consumers (art 1244–1, L 9.7.1991—Cooling off period; art 331–1, L 31.12.1989).

[204] Pierre Garello, 'The Breach of Contract in French Law: Between Safety of Expectations and Efficiency' (2002) 22 *International Review of Law and Economics* 407.

[205] Ibid.

The second is the duty of cooperation[206] or a duty to disclose, for example, in utmost good faith contracts. This duty to disclose (*obligation d'information*) is now routinely applied by French courts in contracts where there are elements of fiduciary obligations.[207]

French law utilises the concept of good faith to avoid burdensome conditions in contracts.[208] It limits its application to specific areas through the established theory of abuse of rights (*abus de droit*).[209] The *abus de droit* includes the absence of cooperation. This stems from the political doctrine of solidarism, which was formulated by Léon Bourgeois in his work *Solidarité*,[210] and this was extended to 'Contractual solidarism' by Durkheim and Duguit, among others.[211] The doctrine reconciles stability and legal certainty with principles of solidarism, proportionality, and coherence. It allows judges to adjust imbalanced relations, requiring parties to collaborate and assist each other, based on an obligation of good faith and loyalty.[212]

The arbitral award in *Klöckner v Cameroon* illustrates this. Here, relying on what is considered a general principle of French law, the majority boldly stated.

> We assume that the principle according to which a person who engages in close contractual relations, based on confidence, must deal with its partner in a frank, loyal and candid manner is a basic principle of French civil law, as is indeed the case under the municipal codes which we know of.[213]

A further arbitral decision given by the International Court of Arbitration, applying French law, confirms this. It states that the duties of confidentiality and information

---

[206] Alberto M Musy, 'The Good Faith Principle in Contract Law and the Precontractual Duty to Disclose: Comparative Analysis of New Differences in Legal Cultures' (2001) 1(1) *Global Jurist* 1535, 1535–1536: referenced that this is specifically related to certain contracts, similar to the common law, utmost good faith contracts—cites François Terre, Philippe Simler and Yves Laquette, *Droit Civil: Les Obligations* (6th ed, 1996) 350.

[207] Examples of such decisions are*: Cass Civ 1 a sez, 24 nov 1976, Bull civ, I, n.370, D, 1977, IR, p.88; Cass Civ, 1 a sez, 15 apr 1975, D, 1976, 514; Cass com 23 maggio 1989, JCP, 1989, ed E, I, 18,761; Cass com, 4 dic 1990, Contrats, Concurrence, Consommation, febbraio 1991, n.28, 4; Cass com, 18 ott 1994, D 1995, 180* noted by Christian Atias, *French Civil Law* (Trans Alain A Levasseur) (2002).

[208] Muriel Fabre-Magnan, 'Duties of Disclosure and French Contract Law: Contribution to an Economic Analysis' in Jack Beatson and Daniel Friedmann (eds), *Good Faith and Fault in Contract Law* (Oxford University Press, 2001) 99.

[209] Nicholas, *The French Law of Contract,* above n 199, 153.

[210] Jack E S Hayward, 'The Official Social Philosophy of the French Third Republic: Leon Bourgeois and Solidarism' (1961) 6(1) *International Review of Social History*, 19, 32; Paul Rabinow, *French Modern: Norms and Forms of the Social Environment* (University of Chicago Press, 1995) 168.

[211] Robert N Bellah (ed), *Emile Durkheim on Morality and Society* (1973) 63.

[212] Bojinca Moise, 'Solidarism as Theoretical Foundation of Good Faith' (Paper presented at the 4th Year of the International Conference: Days of Law (COFOLA 2010), Czech Republic, 2010). < http://dvp.sehnalek.cz/files/prispevky/05_obcan/Bojinca_Moise_(4721).pdf ≥ .

[213] *Klöckner v Cameroon* (1986)1 ICSID Rev—FILJ 89; Georges R Delaume, 'The Myth of the Lex Mercatoria and State Contracts' in Thomas E Carbonneau (ed), *Lex Mercatoria and Arbitration: A Discussion of the New Law Merchant* (Juris Publishing, 1998) 122.

are considered as stemming from the general duty of good faith, which is understood as cooperation.[214]

The obligation of good faith under the *French Civil Code* is widely expressed and not specifically defined. In this sense, French judges are allowed to exercise wide discretion in applying good faith such as imposing extensive duties of disclosure.[215] This has impacted the application of good faith in French law as its meaning is open to further interpretation by the judiciary. Without a definition of good faith, the obligation seems undeveloped under French law.[216] French jurists are somewhat uncertain about the idea of good faith and even those who support the obligation have warned about good faith being an 'absolute altruism negating one's own'.[217] Jourdain explained good faith as follows:

> In the end, good faith remains a hazy notion, which is expressed effectively only when it runs into the legal mould of other concepts with more precise contents. This congenital weakness stems from the vague nature of a notion which in practice remains essentially moral and which has been made into a norm of behaviour governing pre-contractual relations. But if the notion of good faith appears to be of somewhat restrained utility as an instrument of legal technique, no one would contest that the idea of good faith inspires many actual solutions to legal problems. For this reason, should one at least raise it to the rank of a general principle of law? The debate on this question though, remains open.[218]

Good faith under French law is, therefore, approached as a broad principle and, in practice, has not advanced beyond the concept of implied terms under the common law.[219] The French experience provides an illustration that if good faith is not defined with specificity, it will attract inconsistency in application.

2.3.2 Good Faith Under German Contract Law

The most well-known code provision dealing with the obligation of good faith is art 242 of the *German Civil Code* (*Burgerliches Gesefzbuch*—'BGB'). Firstly, it imposes an obligation of performance according to the requirements of good faith (*Treu* and *Glauben*)[220]—the connotation of 'faith and fidelity.'[221] Art 242 has been

---

[214] This is award n.12127 in (2008) 33 Yb Comm Arb'n 82.

[215] Christophe Vigneau, 'The Obligation of Good Faith in France' (2010) 32 *Comparative Labor Law and Policy Journal* 593, 594; Atiyah and Smith, *Atiyah's Introduction*, above n 174, 269; Fabre-Magnan, 'Duties of Disclosure', above n 212, 99.

[216] O'Connor, *Good Faith in English Law*, above n 87, 95.

[217] Whittaker and Zimmermann, 'Good Faith in European Contract Law', above n 34, 38.

[218] Ibid 38–39.

[219] Articles 1134 and 1135 consider good faith as a broad concept rather than a criterion for contractual agreement; John N Adam, 'The Economics of Good Faith in Contract Law' (1995) 8 *Journal of Contract Law* 126, 135; Rene David, *French Law, Its Structure, Sources and Methodology* (Trans Michael Kindred) (Louisiana State University Press, 1972), 76.

[220] Whittaker and Zimmermann, 'Good Faith in European Contract Law', above n 34, 7, 18.

[221] Lücke, 'Good Faith and Contractual Performance', above n 126, 155.

used extensively to imply contractual terms to particularise an incomplete contractual obligation. This obligation includes duties to ensure transactional success, protect the other party's legal interests, and to make important disclosures that will impact on contractual decisions.[222] This approach resembles common law's implied terms but is broader, encompassing duties for both parties to cooperate and avoid jeopardising the transaction's success.[223] The resemblance, however, is stronger with some of the functions of good faith performance in American contract law as originally identified by Summers.[224]

Secondly, in instances where the contract is silent, German courts impose post-contractual duties of good faith, which serves as in internal restriction on legal rights in situations where they are exercised illegitimately. This is best described by the maxim, *venire contra factum proprium*—acting contrary to one's own prior conduct. This principle under German law, underpins sub-doctrines like the forfeiture of rights[225] and the enforcement of contracts despite non-compliance with formal requirements,[226] especially when reliance was induced or formalisation prevented by one party. The common law contains functional equivalents to these doctrines in estoppel, laches and consideration.

Thirdly, the German doctrine of *culpa in contrahendo* (fault in negotiating) concerns the conduct of the parties during negotiation.[227] The core idea of the

---

[222] German courts have relied on art 242 BGB to create additional duties for the parties that were not expressed in statute or the contract. Article 242 BGB is translated as '[Performance in accordance with good faith]—the obligator is obliged to effect performance as required by good faith with regard to business custom' (An obligator is a party who is required to perform some obligation); cf Werner F Ebke and Matthew W Finkin, *Introduction to German Law* (Kluwer Law International, 1996) 176; John P Dawson, 'Unconscionable Coercion: The German Version' (1976) 89 *Harvard Law Review* 1041, 1124.

[223] E.g., BGHZ 16, 4, 10 (1954)—duty of fashion tailor not to compete with contractual partner, a fashion designer, by marketing designs for personal profit; this case closely resemble the classic American case of *Wood v Lucy, Lady Duff Gordon*, 222 NY 88, 118 NE 214 (1917); BGHZ 67, 34, 35 (1976)—duty of the seller of land to agree to unproblematic modification of contract if necessary for buyer to get building permit; BHHZ 93, 29, 39 (1984)—duty of manufacturer to respect the dealer's interests in an automobile dealer franchise.

[224] Summers' case groups included evasion of the spirit of the deal, lack of diligence and 'slacking' off, interfering with or failure to cooperate in the other party's performance—Robert S Summers, '"Good Faith" in General Contract Law and Sales Provisions of the Uniform Commercial Code' (1968) 54 *Virginia Law Review* 195.

[225] E.g. BGHZ 43, 289, 292 (1965)—forfeiture of right of appeal; BGHZ 84, 280, 281 (1982)—partial forfeiture of alimony; BGHZ 105, 290, 298 (1988)—forfeiture in the context of a construction contract.

[226] Purchases of real estate requires authorisation under German law (art 313 BGB)—this requirement may be overridden by good faith only under exceptional circumstances; the application of the formal requirement must lead to not only a hard, but an unbearable result for the party relying on the validity of the contract—e.g., BGHZ 16, 334, 336 (1955); BGHZ 48, 396, 399 (1967); BGHZ 85, 315, 318 (1982); BGHZ 92, 164, 171–2 (1984).

[227] Friedrich Kessler and Edith Fine, 'Culpa in Contrahendo, Bargaining in Good Faith and Freedom of Contract: A Comparative Study' (1964) 77 *Harvard Law Review* 401, 402.

doctrine is the blameworthy conduct of the parties.[228] This doctrine was originally formulated by Jhering in the nineteenth century.[229] He postulated that contractual *diligentia* (carefulness) is owed not only when the contract has come into existence but also when it is still in *statu nascendi* (in the condition of being born).[230] The theory of *culpa in contrahendo* deals with breaches of pre-contractual duty entitling the injured party to claim damages.[231] It is based upon the provisions of the BGB and a general doctrine of liability developed by the German courts and scholars.[232]

Fourthly, and of note also, is the fact that art 242 may be relied upon without the need for it to be specifically pleaded. The judge under such circumstances is only called upon to determine if contractual performance has been in good faith. This functions to allow for good faith to act as a trigger for judicial law making and the pursuit of substantive fairness in favour of the weaker parties. The German courts can also rely on art 242 to create additional duties for the parties that were not expressly provided for in the statute or in the contract. This modification to art 242 has been made to settle the economic and social problems that arose after the two world wars and the reunification of Germany; it also evolved to keep pace with society's temporal changing social and moral attitudes.[233] Therefore, art 242 is regarded as a universal application to solve contractual problems occurring between contracting parties.[234] Schlechtriem commented that.

> You can find a source (be it a court decision or a scholarly theory) for every solution imaginable or wanted, BGB Article 242 [German civil code good faith provision] serving as the legal anchor to even the wildest propositions and results.[235]

This provision had a profound effect on the development of German contract law by courts that created a number of obligations to ensure a loyal performance of a contract such as a duty of the parties to cooperate, to protect each other's interests and to give information.

---

[228] Ibid 448.

[229] Rudolf von Jhering, 'Culpa in contrahendo, oder Schadensersatz bei nichtigen oder nich zum Perfektion gelangten vertragen' (1861) 4 *Jahrbücher für die Dogmatik des heutigen römischen und deutschen Privatrechts* 1, cited in Kessler and Fine, above n 231, 401.

[230] Zimmermann, *The Law of Obligations*, above n 3, 244.

[231] Werner F Ebke and Bettina M Steinhauer, 'The Doctrine of Good Faith in German Contract Law' in Jack Beatson and Daniel Friedmann (eds), *Good Faith and Fault in Contract Law* (Oxford University Press, 2001) 172.

[232] Gerhard Dannermann, *An Introduction to German Civil and Commercial Law* (The British Institute of International and Comparative Law, 1993) 32.

[233] See Hein Kötz, 'Towards a Europe Civil Code' in Peter Cane and Jane Stapleton (eds), *The Law of Obligations: Essays in Celebration of John Fleming* (Clarendon Press, 1998) 243, 244.

[234] Scott C Styles, 'Good Faith: A Principled Matter' in Angelo D M Forte (ed) *Good Faith in Contract and Property* (Hart Publishing, 1999) 157, 175.

[235] Peter Schlechtriem, *Good Faith in German Law and in International Uniforms Law* in Centro di studi e ricerche di diritto comparator e straniero, diretto da M.J. Bonell, Saggi, Conferenze e Seminari, No. 24 (Rome, February, 1997), < http://www.cisg.law.pace.edu/cisg/biblio/schlechtriem16.html >.

The judicial requirement of good faith in Germany is clearly and profoundly influenced by its economic culture. German business has been characterised by enduring cooperative relations under a private law system that applies the principle of good faith to react to the commercial risks involved.[236] The German theory of good faith has been formulated to supplement the provisions of the BGB. However, even though good faith is mentioned and has a central role to play, there is no widely accepted, formal definition of good faith. This shows that judges in a civil law system, like Germany, are given licence to engage in the creative interpretation of good faith, tailoring a specific meaning to each instance in which it arises.

The above discussion shows that good faith obligation is widely recognised in civil law countries throughout all phases of a contract, from negotiation to performance, and enforcement, allowing both parties to rely on it.[237] Despite its broad recognition, good faith has generally not been defined in the civil law codes but has developed through judicial interpretation on a case-by-case basis.[238]

2.4 Good Faith Under American Commercial Law

In the US, the obligation of good faith is a core principle in contract law. Initially, the recognition of the duty of good faith in contractual disputes was not swiftly adopted in the US courts.[239] However, the concept of good faith was incorporated into the *Uniform Commercial Code* (*UCC*) and subsequently adopted by the American Law Institute as part of the *Restatement (Second) of Contracts* (*Restatement*). This constituted a turning point in the developments of the good faith principle in the US; the American courts have traditionally recognised the principle in accordance with its application under the common law of each state.[240] Since the middle of the

---

[236] Teubner, 'Legal Irritants', above n 162.

[237] Paul J Powers, 'Defining the Undefinable: Good Faith and the United Nations Convention on the Contracts for the International Sale of Goods' (1999) 18 *Journal of Law and Commerce* 333, 338.

[238] Woo, 'Protecting Parties', above n 12, 221.

[239] Harold Dubroff, 'The Implied Covenant of Good Faith in Contract Interpretation and Gap-Filling: Reviling a Revered Relic' (2006) 80 *St John's Law Review* 559, 564.

[240] The adoption of good faith in the *UCC* should not be treated as the starting point of the history of good faith in American commercial law, because we cannot ignore the importance of early modern cases that dealt explicitly with good faith in commercial contracts, e.g. *Thomas v Fleury* 26 NY 26 (NY, 1862); *Baltimore & Ohio Railroad Co v Brydon* 3A 306, (Md, 1886); *Doll v Noble* 22 NE 406 (NY, 1889); *George W Crouch v Max L Gutmann*, 134 NY 45 (NY, 1892); *Genet v President of Delaware & H Canal Co* 32 NE 1078 (NY, 1893); *Whitson Trustee* v *Neilson and Co* (1828) 6 S 579; *Loudenback Fertilizer Co v Tennessee Phosphate Co* 121 F 298 (6th Cir, 1903); *New York Central Ironworks Co v United States Radiator Co* 66 NE 967 (1903); *Wood v Lucy, Lady Duff-Gordon* 118 NE 214 (NY, 1917); *Kirk La Shelle Co v Paul Armstrong Co* 188 NE 163 (NY, 1933); *Uproar Co v National Broad Co* 81 F 2d 373 (1st Cir, 1936); *Eline Realty Co v Foeman* 252 SW 2d 15, 18 (KY, 1952); *Brown v Superior Court* 2 12 P 2d 878 (Cal, 1949); *Matzen v Horwitz* 228 P 2d 841 (Cal Ct App, 1951); *Comunale v Traders & General Insurance Co* 328 P 2d 198 (Cal, 1958). For the

twentieth century, it has attracted the attention of American legal scholars to employ the good faith concept particularly in commercial cases.[241] Llewellyn stated during the New York Law Revision Commission's hearing in 1954 that 'good faith has been a part of mercantile obligation since American law began.'[242]

The codification of a duty of good faith is recognised under the *UCC* and the *Restatement* in relation to the performance and enforcement of contracts. The duty is described as a cornerstone of American law.[243]

All American states except for Louisiana[244] have adopted the *UCC*, which provides that an 'obligation of good faith in its performance and enforcement' is expected in every contract.[245] This should not be surprising given that Karl Llewellyn (the Chief draftsman of the *UCC*) was familiar with, and influenced by, German law.[246] Llewellyn's admiration of flexible doctrines such as commercial reasonableness, good faith and unconscionability was consistent with his vision of commercial law.[247] One of his goals was to reform contracts by discarding obsolete formalism and instituting modern flexibility. Kamp, in his analysis into the history of the *UCC*, described Llewellyn's contract law whereby 'it is easy to get into a contract, but hard to get out of one.'[248] This, of course, does not mean that all of Llewellyn's ideas were adopted in the *UCC*. As it stands, the *UCC* is the product of hard compromise among a broad range of legal participants. Speaking to the Tennessee bar in 1952, Llewellyn himself acknowledged the extent of his compromises:

---

influence of New York state cases on good faith in American jurisdiction, see Farnsworth, 'Good Faith in Contract Performance', above n 4, 153, 155; Seth W Goren, 'Looking for Law in all the Wrong Places: Problems in Applying the Implied Covenant of Good Faith Performance' (2003) 37 *University of San Francisco Law Review* 257, 260–64; Troy A Weigand, 'The Duty of Good Faith and Fair Dealing in Commercial Contracts in Massachusetts' (2004) 88 *Massachusetts Law Review* 174, 176.

241 Dubroff, above n 239, 561.

242 Karl N Llewellyn, *State of New York Law Revision Commission Report: Hearing on the Uniform Commercial Code* (1954), 115.

243 E Allan Farnsworth, 'Ten Questions about Good Faith and Fair Dealing in United States Contract Law' [2002] *AMPLA Yearbook* 1, 2.

244 Louisiana has only adopted select parts of the *UCC* because its commercial law is based on civil law and the Napoleonic Code rather than common law.

245 *UCC*, s 1–203.

246 Ralph J Mooney, 'Hands across the Water: The Continuing Convergence of American and Australian Contract Law' (2000) 23(1) *University of New South Wales Law Journal* 1, 25.

247 Llewellyn succeeded in giving the *UCC* open-ended standards over firm rules. The *UCC* is not an attempt to provide an exclusive statement of law, rather, it has directed courts to supplement rules with general legal and equitable principles. For an analysis of Llewellyn's vision of commercial law, see Imad D Abyad, 'Commercial Reasonableness in Karl Llewellyn's Uniform Commercial Code Jurisprudence' (1997) 83 *Virginia Law Review* 429; Gregory E Maggs, 'Karl Llewellyn's Fading Imprint on the Jurisprudence of the Uniform Commercial Code' (2000) 71 *University of Colorado Law Review* 541.

248 Allen R Kamp, 'Uptown Act: A History of the Uniform Commercial Code: 1940–49' (1998) 51 *Santa Monica University Law Review* 275, 303.

> I am ashamed of [the *UCC*] in some ways, there are so many pieces that I could make a little better; there are so many beautiful ideas I tried to get in that would have been good for the law, but I was voted down. A wide body of opinion has worked the law into some sort of compromise after debate and after exhaustive work. However, when you compare it with anything that there is, it is an infinite improvement.[249]

The principle of good faith, championed by Llewellyn, is integral to the *UCC*. Though the *UCC* is not a comprehensive codification of commercial law, it explicitly includes a duty of good faith, referenced in over 50 provisions.[250] This duty limits discretionary powers such as the option to expedite at will (s 1–208), the right to rectify a defective delivery of goods (s 2–508), and the obligation of a merchant buyer to salvage goods that have been rejected (s 2–603). While not covering all commercial transactions and leaving some issues to common law, the *UCC* imposes good faith obligations to ensure fairness and reasonableness in commercial dealings.

Good faith is defined in the *UCC* to mean 'honesty in fact'[251] and 'observance of reasonable commercial standards of fair dealing.'[252] 'Honesty in fact' is frequently referred to as the 'pure heart and empty head' test as it requires only honesty in action without malice, deceit or ulterior motive.[253] Hunter noted that the explicit incorporation of commercial reasonability is intended to clarify possible areas of confusion under the *UCC*.[254] The distinction made in the *UCC* between 'honesty in fact' and 'fair dealing' is a significant one. Further discussion of this distinction will be made in Chap. 5 when considering the content of the good faith obligation.

Overall, the jurisprudential concept of good faith, at the heart of the *UCC*, is to determine whether the contracting parties had acted 'reasonably' and in conformity with the 'law merchant' and customs and usage.[255] Llewellyn designed the good faith obligation legal machinery under the abandoned s 59, which provides for the submission of a wide range of questions to merchant jurors on the motion of either contracting parties.[256] These jurors are expected to be lay specialists with business experience. In this sense, good faith performance requires an objective standard connected to commercial reasonableness.[257] In the absence of the merchant juries under the abandoned s 59, the issue has largely been reduced to theoretical debate as

---

[249] Karl N Llewellyn, 'Why a Commercial Code?' (1953) 22 *Tennessee Law Review* 779, 784.

[250] See E Allan Farnsworth, 'Good Faith Performance and Reasonableness under the Uniform Commercial Code' (1963) 30 *University of Chicago Law Review* 666.

[251] *UCC*, s 1–201.

[252] Ibid (20).

[253] James Nehf, 'Bad Faith Breach of Contract in Consumer Transactions' in Roger Brownsword, Norma J Hird and Geraint Howells (eds), *Good Faith in Contract: Concept and Context* (Dartmouth Publishing Co, 1999) 122.

[254] Hunter, 'The Growing Uncertainty', above n 4, (Footnote 2).

[255] James Q Whitman, 'Commercial Law and the American Volk: A Note on Llewellyn's German Sources for the Uniform Commercial Code' (1987) 97 *Yale Law Journal* 156, 158: Llwellyn 'believe[s] that finding the "immanent law" of the transaction somehow corresponded to deciding whether the parties had acted "reasonably" and in conformity with "the law merchant."'.

[256] Whitman, 'Commercial and the American Volk', above n 255, 171.

[257] Farnsworth, 'Good Faith Performance', above n 250, 671.

to what good faith should and should not entail.[258] As a result, very little consensus has been achieved on this matter.[259]

In 1981, the American Law Institute adopted Summers' approach in s 205 of the *Restatement*. Section 205 of the *Restatement* provides that every contract 'imposes upon each party a duty of good faith and fair dealing in its performance and enforcement.'[260] This section is described as 'one of the truly major advances in American contract.'[261] The *Restatement* would extend to contracts not covered under the *UCC*.[262] The *Restatement* has been described as a cross between a statute and Halsbury's Law of England.[263] While the *Restatement* has no statutory force, it is nevertheless persuasive and is well respected by judges,[264] and thus has application as an authoritative statement by the American courts.

Summers' '*Restatement*/excluder-analysis' introduces the concept of contractual good faith as an 'excluder,' that is, as a concept 'which has no general meaning or meanings of its own, but which serves to exclude many heterogeneous forms of bad faith.'[265] Good faith is simply defined as a negative corollary of bad faith.[266] Summers' articulation of good faith is made out by identifying what bad faith conduct is,[267] which he had taken from an expansive review of the then existing body of good faith cases.

In Burton's 'foregone opportunities' approach,[268] the basic premise is that contracts often involve an uneven distribution of 'discretion in performance' among the contracting parties to the extent that a weaker party might require some protection against the stronger party's assigned discretion.[269] The good faith obligation addresses this issue by affording protection where its application in a given set

[258] Whitman, 'Commercial Law and the American Volk', above n 255, 158, 174.

[259] Steven J Burton, 'Breach of Contract and the Common Law Duty to Perform in Good Faith' (1980) 94 *Harvard Law Review* 369; Steven J Burton, 'Good Faith Performance of a Contract within Article 2 of the Uniform Commercial Code' (1981) 67 *Iowa Law Review* 1; Steven J Burton, 'More on Good Faith Performance of a Contract: A Reply to Professor Summers' (1984) 69 *Iowa Law Review* 497; Mark Snyderman, 'What's so Good about Good Faith? The Good Faith Performance Obligation in Commercial Lending' (1988) 55 *University of Chicago Law Review* 1335; Robert S Summers, 'The General Duty of Good Faith—Its Recognition and Conceptualization' (1982) 67 *Cornell Law Review* 810.

[260] It should be noted that this, like the *UCC*, only applies to contractual performance and enforcement and not to contract negotiation.

[261] Summers, 'The General Duty of Good Faith', above n 259, 810.

[262] Farnsworth, 'Good Faith in Contract Performance', above n 4, 156. Farnsworth suggested that s 205 of the *Restatement* may cover areas not covered by the *UCC*, e.g. in the case of *Dalton v Education Testing Service* 87 NY 2d 384 (NY, 1995).

[263] L J Priestley, 'A Guide to a Comparison of Australian and United States Contract Law' (1989) 12 *University of New South Wales Law Journal* 4, 8.

[264] Ibid.

[265] Summers, '"Good Faith" in General Contract Law', above n 224, 201.

[266] Ibid 200–201.

[267] Ibid 204.

[268] Burton, 'Breach of Contract', above n 259.

[269] Ibid 380–384.

of circumstances is reliant on the legitimacy of the exercise of that discretion.[270] The contracting parties are not allowed to exercise their discretionary power under the contract to obtain or recapture additional benefits that they might have missed when they concluded their bargain.[271] This theory is very much derived from a cost perspective and the contractual expectation interest.[272]

Good faith in the enforcement of contracts imposes a restriction on the parties to the extent that 'an enforcement term may only be invoked only if … the term would advance the purpose for which it was included in the agreement without imposing … costs on the non-enforcing party.'[273] In the US, the general duty of good faith is confined to the performance and enforcement of contracts and does not extend to negotiations. American courts have generally declined, apart from very specific circumstance,[274] to enforce a general obligation of good faith preventing a party from breaking off negotiations.[275] The obligation of good faith has also been used in the US to facilitate the re-negotiation of long-term contracts following a change of circumstances.[276]

The infusion of the good faith obligation in the US is not without its objections. The abandonment of Llewellyn's merchant jurors has led to the development of various legal theories, which have not produced uniformity in the application of reasonableness. This has fundamentally led to the view that the market is a better place to work out commercial standards and that the courts should leave the market alone until they know more than the contracting parties concerning the factors that influence contracts.[277] In view of the US scenario, Australia should not follow the American example by engaging and becoming entangled in theoretical debates. This aspect of the discussion will be expanded further in Chap. 5.

---

[270] Ibid 382–383.

[271] Ibid 378, 386.

[272] Ibid 403; Steven J Burton, 'Good Faith Performance', above n 259, 30.

[273] Eric G Andersen, 'Good Faith in the Enforcement of Contracts' (1988) 73 *Iowa Law Review* 299, 301.

[274] E.g. in an agreement to enter into negotiation: *Howtek v Relisys* 958 F Supp 46 (DNH 1997); cf *Channel Home Centers v Grossman* 755 F 2d 291 (3rd Cir 1986); G Richard Shell, 'Opportunism and Trust in the Negotiation of Commercial Contracts: Towards a New Cause of Action' (1991) 44 *Vanderbilt Law Review* 222, 243.

[275] E Allan Farnsworth, 'Precontractual Liability and Preliminary Agreements: Fair Dealing and Failed Negotiations' (1987) *Columbia Law Review* 217, 239.

[276] Howard O Hunter, 'Commentary on "the Renegotiation of Contracts"' (1988) 13 *Journal of Contract Law* 205, 207.

[277] Snyderman, 'What's so Good about Good Faith?', above n 329.

2.5 Chapter Summary

The amount of judicial and academic interest in this area of good faith obligations in contract is overwhelming. The objections raised against the introduction of the good faith obligation under the 'repugnancy' and 'pragmatic' theories do not deny the existence of the problems that arise under the present legal contracting principles in Australia.

The European good faith approaches, such as those in France and Germany discussed in this chapter, have been developed for a codified system, which is fundamentally different from the common law system in Australia. Their notion of good faith complements the provision of their Codes and cannot be easily replicated in Australia. The French experience indicates that the notion of good faith does not succeed where it has been defined too widely. In the US, failure to implement commercial norms has resulted in an entangled theoretical debate. The concern in Australia is that the introduction of good faith would also trudge these paths of entangled legal debates.

In the next chapter, the utilisation of good faith obligation in China will be explored. With China being Australia's largest two-way trading partner, it is important for both Chinese and Australian commercial parties to have greater mutual understanding of both countries' contracting regimes which will only strengthened economic competitiveness and assist in commercial contract drafting. This presents fertile ground for greater academic discussions that will mutually benefit both Australian and Chinese academics and legal practitioners. China has a longstanding background with good faith obligation[278] and this discussion would provide useful insight into its operation in Chinese jurisdiction. This is another ray of enlightenment (much like what has been considered so far in this chapter) in the evolution of good faith obligation in Australia.

278 Xu Wang, 'Fundamental Principles of China's Contract Law' (1999) 13 *Columbia Journal of Asian Law* 1, 17.

Chapter 3
The Obligation of Good Faith in Chinese Contract Law

3.1 Introduction

Good faith is regarded as one of the fundamental and general principles in the 1999 *Contract Law of the People's Republic of China* ('the 1999 CCL').[1] Chinese academics and courts have generally accepted and embraced the principle of good faith as an indispensable principle of the 1999 CCL.[2] It is, therefore, of great importance to understand the meaning, functions, and scope of the obligation of good faith before considering the application of it in practice.

3.2 Good Faith as a Principle of Modern Contract Law: Historical Development and Systemic Evolution

The development of the good faith principle in modern Chinese contract law can be categorised into three distinct phases. Initially, good faith was elevated from a traditional moral concept to a formal legal principle, marking its incorporation into the legal framework. Following this, the principle was integrated more deeply into specific areas of contract law, enhancing the distinctiveness of departmental laws. Most recently, with the transition from specific contract laws to the civil code, there has been a notable enhancement in the structural significance of good faith. This enhancement is crucial for the systemic coordination required in codification. Additionally, the Civil Code has introduced minor revisions to the good faith

---

[1] 《中华人民共和国合同法》 [Contract Law of the People's Republic of China] (People's Republic of China) National People's Congress, Order No 15, 15 March 1999 ('the 1999 CCL').

[2] Chunlin Leonhard, 'A Legal Chameleon: An Examination of the Doctrine of Good Faith in Chinese and American Contract Law' (2009) 25 *Connecticut Journal of International Law* 305 ('A Legal Chameleon') 309.

A. Wan and P. Guo, *Good Faith Obligation*, International and Comparative Law in the Asia Pacific, https://doi.org/10.1007/978-981-97-7035-9_3

rules, which have subsequently received greater attention and application in judicial interpretations than previously observed.

3.2.1 Good Faith in the 1986 GPCL: Legalisation of Traditional Moral Concepts

Post-1949, following the establishment of the People's Republic of China, the government initiated regulations for contractual activities.[3] However, comprehensive legislation in contract law did not materialise until in the 1980s.[4] During this era, China developed three different contract systems based on the subject, region, and object: the 1981 *Economic Contract Law of the People's Republic of China* ('the 1981 ECL'),[5] the 1985 *Law of the People's Republic of China on Economic Contracts Involving Foreign Interest* ('the 1985 FECL'),[6] and the 1987 *Law of the People's Republic of China on Technology Contracts* ('the 1987 TCL').[7,8] These laws catered respectively to domestic business transactions, foreign economic activities, and intellectual property transactions, collectively forming a 'three pillar' legal framework. These laws were acting as transitional laws during China's early economic reforms and market liberalisation,[9] aiming to address the then-legal vacuum in Chinese contract law.[10]

As specific areas of law, like contract law, began to mature and establish their own distinct legislations, broader issues in civil activities started to emerge, highlighting the urgent need for overarching legal provisions.[11] In response, the 1986 *General*

---

[3] Bing Ling, *Contract Law in China* (Sweet & Maxwell Asia, 2002) 11–12.

[4] Ibid.

[5] 《中华人民共和国经济合同法》 [Economic Contract Law of the People's Republic of China] (People's Republic of China) National People's Congress, Order No 12, 13 December 1981 ('the 1981 ECL').

[6] 《中华人民共和国涉外经济合同法》 [Law of the People's Republic of China on Economic Contracts Involving Foreign Interest] (People's Republic of China) Standing Committee of the National People's Congress, Order No 22, 21 March 1985 ('the 1985 FECL').

[7] 《中华人民共和国技术合同法》 [Law of the People's Republic of China on Technology Contracts] (People's Republic of China) Standing Committee of the National People's Congress, Order No 53, 23 June 1987 ('the 1987 TCL').

[8] Liu Chuntian, 'Regarding Intellectual Property as the First Property Rights Is a Discovery in Civil Law' [2015] (10) *Intellectual Property* 3, 4.

[9] Larry A DiMatteo and Lei Chen, 'History of Chinese Contract Law' in Larry A DiMatteo and Lei Chen (eds), *Chinese Contract Law: Civil and Common Law Perspectives* (University Press, 2018) 3, 5.

[10] Xiaoyang Zhang, *Chinese Civil Law for Business* (Open University of Hong Kong Press, 1st ed, 2013) 193.

[11] Jiang Ping, 'Introduction' in Department of Civil Law, China University of Political Science and Law (ed), *Speech on the General Principles of the Civil Law of the People's Republic of China* (China University of Political Science and Law Press, 1986) 1, 6–7.

Principles of the Civil Law of the People's Republic of China ('the 1986 GPCL')[12] was adopted during the Fourth Session of the Sixth National People's Congress. The 1986 GPCL was established in response to the urgent demand for economic system reform, drawing from several specific laws such as the Economic Contract Law, Inheritance Law, Trademark Law, and Patent Law.[13] Its enactment laid down fundamental principles and systems essential for regulating China's socialist market economic relations.[14]

The provisions concerning contracts within the GPCL are categorised into two main sections. The first section includes general provisions that are applicable not only to contracts but also to other areas. Specifically, Articles 3–7 outline the core principles of China's civil law, which serve as the guiding framework ('Class (纲)') for the specific systems and norms ('Order (目)') within civil law. These principles are essential as they underpin and influence the detailed legal systems and standards.[15] Other provisions also cover subjects including civil legal acts, and civil rights. A special section (Sect. 3.2) is more specific and is located in the civil liability chapter (Chap. 6). It specifies the responsibilities parties face when contract breaches occur, outlining how civil liabilities should be addressed.[16]

During this transformative period, marked by the enactment of Article 4 of the 1986 GPCL, the principle of good faith was elevated from a mere societal moral standard to a foundational principle of civil law.[17] This elevation underscored the principle's fundamental value within the civil domain of Chinese society and its applicability across all norms of civil law, including contract law.[18] Notably, prior legislations such as the 1981 ECL and the 1985 FECL did not explicitly mention 'good faith.' It was only with the introduction of the 1986 GPCL that 'good faith' was formally incorporated into Chinese legal text,[19] establishing it as a core principle in civil law. Article 4 of the 1986 GPCL explicitly states that 'civil activities shall

---

12 《中华人民共和国民法通则》 [General Principles of the Civil Law of the People's Republic of China] (People's Republic of China) National People's Congress, Order No 37, 4 December 1986 ('the 1986 GPCL').

13 Tong Rou, 'General Principles of Civil Law—An Important Milestone in The Construction of Democracy and Legal System in China' in Tong Rou (ed), *A Brief Introduction to the General Principles of the Civil Law of the People's Republic of China* (China University of Political Science and Law Press, 1987) 1, 5.

14 Ibid 1.

15 Zhang Xinbao and Cai Chaoxiong, 'An Overview of Some Basic Problems of Civil Law' in Tong Rou (n 13) 7, 15.

16 The 1986 GPCL, above n 12, 111–16.

17 Tong Rou, 'General Principles of Civil Law—An Important Milestone in The Construction of Democracy and Legal System in China' in Tong Rou, above n 13, 1, 6; Shi Yue and Yang Zhenshan, 'Basic Principles' in China University of Political Science and Law, above n 11, 14, 27.

18 Xu Guodong, *The Interpretation of the Basic Principles of Civil Law—Centered on the Legal Analysis of the Principle of Good Faith* (China University of Political Science and Law Press, 2001), 35.

19 Lou Jianbo and Liu Yan, 'The Limitation of the Principle of Freedom of Contract and Its Relationship with the Principle of Good Faith' [1995] (06) *Peking University Law Journal* 35, 42.

follow the principles of voluntariness, fairness, compensation of equal value, and good faith.' Subsequently, the 1987 TCL adhered to this principle, applying good faith specifically in the formation of technology contracts.[20] Additionally, Article 14 of the same law mandates that 'Intermediaries providing services for the conclusion of technology contracts shall abide by the relevant provisions of this Law, follow the principle of good faith, and may charge reasonable fees.' Although not explicitly cited in earlier laws, the principle of good faith had already begun to influence legal practices as seen in the 1985 FECL, which included provisions on the suspension of contract performance and restrictions on remedies for breach of contract,[21] reflecting the practical application of the good faith principle.[22]

3.2.2 *Good Faith in the 1999 CCL: Specialisation and Concretisation in Uniform Contract Law*

Although the three pillars of Chinese contract law established in the 1980s functioned effectively in safeguarding party interests, ensuring transactional order, and fostering the growth of the market economy, by the 1990s, these laws no longer met the evolving legal needs of Chinese society.[23] Moreover, the inconsistencies among the three existing contract laws highlighted the necessity for a more contemporary, business-oriented, and systematic approach to contract law.[24] This need led to the adoption of the 1999 CCL during the Second Session of the Ninth National People's Congress. The 1999 CCL is a unified piece of legislation that harmonises and codifies the previous contract laws relating to specific contracts which became invalid at the time of its publication.[25] It replaced the earlier segmented contract laws and marked a significant shift towards the codification and harmonisation of contract regulations.[26]

The 1999 CCL introduced substantial modifications to the contract law landscape in China. According to Mo Zhang, three key changes are most noteworthy: firstly, the 1999 CCL represents a blend of civil and common law principles, although it remains predominantly influenced by civil law roots; secondly, it is designed to be more aligned with the principles of a market economy than its predecessors; thirdly, the 1999 CCL integrates certain rules from relevant international treaties and

[20] The 1987 TCL, above n 7, stipulates that 'The conclusion of a technology contract must adhere to the principles of voluntariness and equality, mutual benefit and compensation, and honesty and creditability': at art 4.

[21] E.g. excessive or low liquidated damages should be adjusted; the aggrieved party shall not be entitled to claim compensation for the enlarged loss if it fails to take measures to prevent the enlarged loss, etc.: see Lou Jianbo and Liu Yan, above n 19, 42–3.

[22] Ibid 42–3.

[23] Ibid 25.

[24] Larry A DiMatteo and Lei Chen, 'History of Chinese Contract Law' in DiMatteo and Chen (n 9) 5.

[25] Ibid.

[26] Zhang, above n 10, 194.

conventions, reflecting China's commitment to fulfilling its international obligations and aligning with global legal standards.[27] Liang Huixing also notes that despite some existing deficiencies, the 1999 CCL represents a significant advancement towards a unified and modern contract law framework that is both reflective of China's realities and consistent with international standards.[28]

The advancement of the 1999 CCL in establishing rules based on the principle of good faith represents a significant historical milestone. This legislation not only adopts good faith as its legislative guiding principle[29] but also explicitly articulates and refines good faith norms within contract law through five distinct clauses.[30] The 1999 CCL positions the good faith principle at the core of its framework, affirming its foundational status within the general provisions of contract law. It incorporates the good faith principle throughout the lifecycle of a contract, from formation and performance to modification, termination, interpretation, and the assignment of responsibilities, ensuring that the good faith principle underpins all contractual obligations and contract applicable rules.[31] This emphasis on the good faith principle is a logical progression in China's economic reforms, which have transitioned the economy from state-planned directives towards a system that prioritises individual transactions and contractual autonomy. The 1999 CCL significantly enhances the autonomy of contracting parties and shifts away from administrative contracts towards regulated contractual agreements,[32] highlighting the importance of constructing robust good faith norms within this framework.

Specifically, the 1999 CCL clarifies in its General Provisions that good faith is an independent and fundamental principle exclusive to contract law. Article 6 of the 1999 CCL specifically mandates that 'The parties shall follow the principle of good faith in exercising their rights and performing their obligations.' This provision marks a departure from Article 4 of the 1986 GPCL, as it applies directly and exclusively to contractual matters, unlike the rationale in the 1986 GPCL that the application of good faith in contract law is seen as an extension of civil law.[33] Zheng Qiang views Article 6 as a completion of the modernisation of good faith obligation within Chinese contract law.[34] Article 6 not only solidifies the legal status of the good faith principle within the contract law framework by establishing it as a general

---

[27] Mo Zhang, *Chinese Contract Law—Theory & Practice* (Brill, 2nd ed, 2020), 13–14.

[28] Liang Huixing, 'Uniform Contract Law: Successes and Shortcomings' [1999] (03) *China Legal Science*, 25–9.

[29] Chen Nianbing, 'On the Principle of Good Faith—An Analysis from the Perspective of Norms' [2003] (06) *Science of Law (Journal of Northwest University of Political Science and Law)* 59, 62.

[30] Luo Peixin, 'Good Governance Relies on Good Law: A Discussion on Social Credit Legislation' [2016] (12) *Law Science* 104, 105.

[31] Jiao Fumin, 'Good Faith Principle Perfecting Chinese Contract Law' [2002] (04) *Hebei Law Science* 35, 37.

[32] Jianhua Zhong and Guanghua Yu, 'China's Uniform Contract Law: Progress and Problems' (1999) 17 *UCLA Pacific Basin Law Journal* 1, 31.

[33] Zheng Qiang, *A Study on the Principle of Good Faith in Contract Law: A Legal Interpretation of the Empire Provision* (Law Press (China), 2000), 63.

[34] Ibid.

principle[35] but also mandates its compulsory application.[36] Furthermore, the general provisions grant the judicial organ a degree of discretion to accommodate the unique socio-economic circumstances of China, such as its vast territory, the unbalanced economic and cultural development, and the appearance of new types of civil cases.[37] This flexibility is reflective of the international evolution of the good faith principle, aligning China's contract law with global legal development.

The 1999 CCL transcends merely requiring parties to a contract follow the good faith principle in an abstract sense; it extends the principle to the entire spectrum of contractual relationships.[38] The law delineates a comprehensive system of obligations influenced by this principle, encompassing pre-contractual, contractual, incidental, and post-contractual obligations.[39]

This approach assists in regulating the conduct of the parties to a contract. For instance, Article 42 of the 1999 CCL mandates that parties must adhere to their contractual obligations during the contracting process; failure to do so causes the violating party to bear liability for breaching the good faith principle. Article 92 specifies that, in addition to fulfilling explicitly agreed-upon obligations, parties are also required to perform incidental obligations such as notification, assistance, and confidentiality, in accordance with the good faith principle. Moreover, Article 60(2) stipulates that obligations of the contract persist even after the termination of the contract, necessitating the performance of post-contractual obligations. Furthermore, Article 125 boldly positions the good faith principle as a legal basis for the interpretation of contractual terms. As such, the 1999 CCL articulates multiple scenarios where the good faith principle directly applies, empowering judges to reference these specific norms when adjudicating cases without having to refer to the good faith principle.[40]

3.2.3 Good Faith in the Civil Code and Its Supporting Judicial Interpretations: The Rise of Structural Status and the Precise Adjustment of Content

The concept of good faith in the Civil Code of China and its judicial interpretations reflects a significant evolution in its structural role and the precision of its content

---

[35] Ibid.

[36] Chen Nianbing, above n 29, 62.

[37] Wang Liming and Xu Chuanxi, 'Fundamental Principles of China's Contract Law' (1999) 13(1) *Columbia Journal of Asian Law* 1, 17.

[38] Luo Peixin, above n 30, 105.

[39] Chen Nianbing, above n 29, 62.

[40] Li Xie, 'On the Typology of the Principle of Good Faith Again: With Reference to the Traditional Thought of Abstract Concept' [2013] (05) *Journal of Southwest University of Political Science and Law* 68, 76.

within the legal framework. Historically, China's civil law system was loosely codified under the 1986 GPCL, adopting a piece-meal legislative approach whereby 'making one part as the part mature.'[41] Codifying a comprehensive Civil Code that encompasses various legal domains including contract law has been challenging and protracted.[42] Despite initiating civil law codification attempts in 1954, 1962, 1979, and 2001, none of the attempts were successful.[43] It was not until October 2014 that compiling a Civil Code was prioritised. This push was made in the Fourth Plenary Session of the 18th Central Committee of the Communist Party of China, which mandated the compilation of the Civil Code within five years.[44]

This led to the adoption of a 'two-step' approach.[45] The first step was the enactment of the 2017 *General Provisions of Civil Law of the People's Republic of China* ('the 2017 GPCL'),[46] which was regarded as the prelude to the codification of the Civil Code.[47] It replaced the 1986 GPCL and served as the foundational framework for the forthcoming comprehensive Civil Code.[48] The second step was the compilation of the *Civil Code of People's Republic of China* (*'the Civil Code'*)[49] itself following the promulgation of the 2017 GPCL, which was finally adopted at the third session of the 13th National People's Congress and promulgated in 2020.[50]

The method of compiling the Civil Code in China is unique. Rather than constructing a new code from scratch, the process involves a deep and comprehensive integration of existing civil laws. This method allows for the creation of a standardised and logically structured organic code system, reflecting a sophisticated blend of historical legal principles and modern legislative requirements.[51] Within

---

[41] Yang Lixin, '40 Years of Chinese Civil Law: From Quasi-Codification to Codification' [2023] (12) *Chinese Rule of Law* 14, 14–15.

[42] Peng Guo, Shu Zhang, and Lixuan Li, 'CISG and Chinese Contract Law Reform in the New Chinese Civil Code: Impacts, Interactions and Implications' (2021) 37(3) *Journal of Contract Law* 192, 195.

[43] China's top legislature made it clear that the previous two failed to achieve practical results due to various reasons. After careful study of the last two times, it was decided to formulate separate civil laws separately in accordance with the working idea of 'mature one, through one,' and then compile the civil code when conditions were ripe: see Zhang Dejiang, *Report on the Work of the Standing Committee of the National People's Congress* (the Fifth Session of the Twelfth National People's Congress, 3 March 2017).

[44] Yang Lixin, above n 41, 14–15.

[45] Zhang Dejiang, above n 43.

[46] 《中华人民共和国民法总则》 [General Provisions of the Civil Law of the People's Republic of China] (People's Republic of China) National People's Congress, Order No 66, 15 March 2017 ('the 2017 GPCL').

[47] Zhu Guangxin, 'Codification of Civil Law: Unified Recodification of Civil Special Law' [2017] (6) *Journal of Comparative Law* 169.

[48] Peng Guo, Shu Zhang, and Lixuan Li, above n 42, 196.

[49] 《中华人民共和国民法典》 [Civil Code of the People's Republic of China] (People's Republic of China) National People's Congress, Order No 45, 28 May 2020 ('the Civil Code').

[50] Ibid.

[51] Xie Hongfei, 'Legislative Technology and Institutional Arrangement of Contract General of Civil Code' [2017] (06) *Henan Social Sciences* 28, 29.

the Civil Code, the contract-related norms are organised into two main sections: the general provisions found in Book One and contract norms located in Book Three. These sections incorporate and build upon the principles and clauses established by the 1999 CCL, particularly the integration of five good faith clauses.

In the Civil Code, the influence and integration of the 1999 CCL is far deeper when compared to the 1986 GPCL. An example of this is Article 7 of the Civil Code, which significantly elevates the principle of good faith from its previous status under the 1986 GPCL. Article 7 recognises good faith as a foundational civil law principle, applicable universally across all civil activities. The clause states that 'The parties to civil legal relations shall conduct civil activities under the principle of good faith, adhere to honesty, and fulfil their promises.' This clause in the Civil Code is not merely a continuation of the principles outlined in Article 4 of the 1986 GPCL. Rather, it is an enhancement and expansion of Article 6 of the 1999 CCL as indicated by their similarities.[52] Additionally, unlike the 1986 GPCL which lacked an independent rule for interpretation, the Civil Code introduces Article 142. This article, used for interpreting the expression of will in civil matters, aligns more closely in purpose, wording, and norms with Article 125 of the 1999 CCL.

During the drafting of the Civil Code, there was significant debate regarding how to maintain the structural integrity of the contract law framework. This debate was fuelled by the introduction of the 2017 GPCL which overlapped considerably with the existing 1999 CCL. This overlap presented a codification dilemma: reducing provisions to avoid duplications might compromise the comprehensive nature of the legal system, especially when contract law was codified independently; yet repeating them would obviously contravene basic legislative principles.[53] The central issue in this dilemma was whether Book Three of the Civil Code should establish an autonomous contract law system that is akin to the 1999 CCL, or whether it should integrate fully into the broader structure of the Civil Code.[54] The resolution of this issue was crucial because the structural organisation of the Civil Code not only addresses the regulation of social relations under civil law but also enhances the interpretative clarity and logical coherence of the legal norms.[55] Ultimately, the Civil Code adopted divergent approaches to the incorporation of good faith: while the specific clause related to the good faith principle regulating contract behaviour was not included in the contract code, the rule of using good faith to interpret the meaning of a contract was incorporated.

In addition to Article 6, the Civil Code has preserved four specific rules from the 1999 CCL concerning good faith in the Contracts Book. However, significant revisions have been made to the contract interpretation rules, both in terms of the system

---

[52] Han Shiyuan, 'Codified Contract Law: New Progress, New Problems and Countermeasures' [2021] (06) *Research on Rule of Law*, 5.

[53] Xie Hongfei, above n 51, 29.

[54] Bing Ling, 'The New Contract Law in the Chinese Civil Code' (2020) 8(3) *The Chinese Journal of Comparative Law* 558, 562.

[55] Zhou Hailin, 'Interpretation Path Based on the Structure of the Civil Code' [2022] (03) *Journal of CUPL* 76.

and content. Originally, the Rule of Interoperation of the 1999 CCL under Article 125 of, the most central rules of contract law, was positioned in the final chapter as part of the 'other provisions.'[56] In contrast, Article 466 of the Civil Code has systematically advanced and elected this rule to the general section of the contract code, signifying its importance by designating it as a general provision.[57] The modifications to the contract interpretation rules introduced in the Civil Code are extensive, impacting four key areas: the legislative intent behind contract interpretation, the hierarchical order of interpretation rules, the inclusion of a method to interpret by nature, and the adaptation of interpretation rules across different texts. Meanwhile, the remaining three articles concerning fault in contracting, the obligation of strict performance and good faith, and the rules post-contract termination have seen no substantial changes.

Following the enactment of the Civil Code, the Supreme People's Court of China has issued a series of judicial interpretations addressing various aspects of the Civil Code.[58] To guide the application of the Civil Code, particularly the contract law part, the *Interpretation by the Supreme People's Court of Several Issues Concerning the Application of Title One General Provisions of Book Three Contracts of the Civil Code of the People's Republic of China* ('judicial interpretation')[59] was issued on 4 December 2023, specifically addresses the general provision of the Contract Book. This judicial interpretation emerged from two foundational elements[60]: firstly, it builds upon two previous judicial interpretations of the 1999 CCL,[61] summarising experiences from judicial practices and incorporating findings from theoretical research in contract law; secondly, between 2021 and 2023, the drafting group engaged extensively in brainstorming sessions, revisions, and discussions before the Judicial Committee of the Supreme People's Court approved the final

---

56 Sun Meng, 'Probe Into The Rules Of Contracts Interpretation' [2013] (10) *Citizen and Law* 22, 24.

57 Tian Ye, 'The Amendment and Judicial Application of Contract Interpretation Rules in Civil Code' [2020] (09) *Academic Journal of Zhongzhou* 55.

58 E.g. the time effect, the General Provisions Book, the Property Rights Book, the Guarantee System, the Book of Marriage and Family, and Inheritance Book.

59《最高人民法院关于适用〈中华人民共和国民法典〉合同编通则若干问题的解释》[Interpretation by the Supreme People's Court of Several Issues Concerning the Application of Title One General Provisions of Book Three Contracts of the Civil Code of the People's Republic of China] (People's Republic of China) Supreme People's Court, Judicial Intrepretation No 13, 4 December 2023 ('Judicial Interpretation').

60 Yang Lixin, 'Significant Progress of The Interpretation of the General Principles of Chapter of Contract of Civil Code in the Perfection of the Rule of Contract' [2024] (04) *Journal of Law Application* 24.

61《最高人民法院关于适用〈中华人民共和国合同法〉若干问题的解释(一)》[Interpretation I of the Supreme People's Court of Several Issues Concerning the Application of the Contract Law of the People's Republic of China] (People's Republic of China) Supreme People's Court, Judicial Interpretation No 19, 19 December 1999 ('*Interpretation I of the CCL*');《最高人民法院关于适用〈中华人民共和国合同法〉若干问题的解释(二)》[Interpretation II of the Supreme People's Court of Several Issues Concerning the Application of the Contract Law of the People's Republic of China] (People's Republic of China) Supreme People's Court, Judicial Interpretation No 5, 24 April 2009 ('*Interpretation II of the CCL*').

draft.[62] The judicial interpretation introduces distinct features, such as clarifying legal terminology, guiding contractual behaviours and judgements, and enhancing judicial procedures. These developments mark a significant milestone in the evolution of China's civil judicial interpretation, reflecting a more sophisticated application of legal principles.[63]

The judicial interpretation comprises 69 articles, with nine specifically dedicated to the principle of good faith. These address various aspects:

- Article 1—the interpretation of contracts,
- Article 5—the impact of fraud or coercion on the conclusion of contracts by third parties,
- Article 7—the processes involved in negotiating and concluding contracts
- Article 16—how breaches of mandatory contract provisions are handled,
- Article 24—the restitution of benefits from contracts deemed void or revoked,
- Article 59—ascertaining the moment when the rights and obligations from a contract terminate,
- Article 62—calculating the losses incurred by the non-defaulting party,
- Article 65—determining liquidated damages, and
- Article 67—penalties concerning deposits.

These articles underscore the judicial interpretation's emphasis on good faith, demonstrating a precise application of this principle in varied contractual situations.

3.3 The Principle of Good Faith: Definition, Function and Scope of Application

The principle of good faith is a foundational principle in Chinese civil law.[64] As stipulated in Article 6 of the 1999 CCL, 'the parties shall abide by the good faith principle in exercising their rights and performing their obligations.' This principle is so central that it is often referred to as the 'imperial principle' within Chinese Contract Law.[65]

While the CCL does not explicitly define good faith, scholarly consensus views it as an amalgamation of legal and moral standards. It was argued that good faith

[62] The Supreme People's Court, in addition to conducting extensive and in-depth argumentation and soliciting opinions in the local people's courts at all levels, has also conducted dozens of theoretical discussions in the civil law theoretical circles and relevant ministries and commissions, discussed and demonstrated article by article, and published it through the Internet, extensively soliciting opinions for revision, and has also passed the record review of the legislature.

[63] Meng Qinguo, 'The Historical Progress of the Civil Judicial Interpretations—The Commentary on the Highlights of the Judicial Interpretations of the General Principles of the Contracts of the Civil Code by the Supreme People's Court' (2024) 39(02) *Journal of Shanghai University of Political Science and Law(The Rule of Law Forum)* 42.

[64] See The 1986 GPCL, above n 12, art 4; The 2017 GPCL, above n 46, art 7.

[65] Ling, above n 3, 50.

encompasses honesty, trustworthiness, and good-will; it demands that parties respect truth, fulfil promises, avoid fraud, and exercise their rights and obligations with good-will, avoiding any evasion of legal and contractual duties; it also involves balancing conflicting interests and collaborating to meet the reasonable expectations of all parties involved.[66] The good faith principle's ambiguity is argued to allow flexible application.[67] However, concerns were raised over the potential for judicial overreach and the unpredictability of outcomes due to the broad discretionary powers it confers the judges.[68]

Chinese academics further define the function of the good faith principle from various perspectives. Wang summarises five functions of the principle of good faith: (1) filling in the gaps in laws and contracts; (2) establishing rules for conduct; (3) balancing the interests both between the parties, and between the parties and the society; (4) interpreting law and contracts; and (5) reducing transaction costs and enhancing efficiency.[69] Liang lists three functions, including (1) guiding the parties to perform their rights and obligations; (2) interpreting, evaluating and supplementing legal activities; and (3) interpreting and supplementing the law.[70] Other academics have also given similar explanations of the functions of the principle of good faith, including gap-filling, providing judicial discretion, and balancing the interests between different parties.[71]

In addition to its role as a foundational principle of contract law under Article 6 of the 1999 CCL, good faith underpins the doctrine of *culpa in contrahendo* as outlined in Article 42. Article 60 imposes an obligation to adhere to good faith during the performance phase of a contract, while Article 92 mandates that parties act in accordance with good faith upon the termination of a contract. Furthermore, Article 125 mandates that any discrepancies within the contract be interpreted with the consideration of good faith principle. It was argued by Xu that although the CCL does not explicitly recognise the doctrine of change of circumstances as a derivative of good faith, this principle has been adopted by the Supreme People's Court ('SPC') in practice.[72]

The SPC has also reinforced the principle of good faith in its judicial interpretations, such as requiring its application in the adjustment of liquidated damages as

---

[66] Liang Huixing, 'The Principle of Good Faith and Gap Filling' 91(2) *Chinese Journal of Law* 22, 23; Cui Jianyuan, *Analysis of New Contract Law Theory and Cases* (Jilin University Press, 1999), 26–8; Wang Liming, *Studies on Contract Law* (China Renmin University Press, 2002) 163–64; Ling, above n 3, 52–4.

[67] Liang Huixing above n 66, 23–6.

[68] See Leonhard, above n 2, 306–9 for a more detailed summary of the critics.

[69] Wang Liming, above n 66, 169–76.

[70] Liang Huixing, above n 66, 25.

[71] Zheng Qiang, above n 33, 40.

[72] Wang Liming and Xu Chuanxi, above n 37, 17–22; Wang Liming (n 66) 176–8.

stipulated in contracts,[73] and in determining what constitutes a 'reasonable period' for inspection.[74]

Thus, it can be concluded that the principle of good faith acts as a pervasive and overarching guideline applicable at every contractual stage, encompassing pre-contractual negotiations, formation, execution, termination, and post-contractual obligations, as well as in the interpretation of contracts. This perspective is endorsed by scholars such as Jiang,[75] Wang, and Xu,[76] who affirm the extensive influence of good faith in contract law.

3.4 Application of the Good Faith Principle in China's Judicial Practice

Given the fundamental role of the good faith principle in Chinese contract law, this section delves into a selection of the Supreme People's Court decisions that demonstrate the application of this principle. Although China follows a civil law system and does not adopt the doctrine of precedent under the common law system, decisions published by the SPC often guide lower courts in deciding similar cases. This section also includes cases from lower courts that the SPC has chosen to publish as guiding cases which illustrate the application of the good faith principle.[77] Predominantly, these cases were decided in the last ten years (2013–2023), reflecting recent judicial trends.[78]

According to the different roles the good faith principle may play in contractual disputes, the cases are divided into the following categories:

(1) general application of the principle of good faith;
(2) application of pre-contract obligation and liability for contracting negligence;
(3) application of contractual obligations and liability for breach of contract;

---

[73] *Interpretation II of the CCL*, above n 61, art 29.

[74] 《关于审理买卖合同纠纷案件适用法律问题的解释》 [Interpretation of the Supreme People's Court on Issues Concerning the Application of Law for the Trial of Cases of Disputes over Sales Contracts] (People's Republic of China) Supreme People's Court, Interpretation No 8, 10 May 2012, art 17.

[75] Jiang Ping, *A Detailed Explanation of Contract Law* (China University of Political Science and Law Press, 1999) 6–8.

[76] Wang Liming and Xu Chuanxi, above n 37, 17–22; Wang Liming, above n 66, 176–8.

[77] See《最高人民法院印发〈关于案例指导工作的规定〉的通知》[Notice of the Supreme People's Court on Issuing the Provisions on Case Guidance] (People's Republic of China) Supreme People's Court, Notice No 51, 26 November 2010, art 7 which stipulates that the lower courts should refer to the guiding cases when dealing cases involving similar situations.

[78] These cases can be found on the following websites: Supreme People's Court of the People's Republic of China, 'China Guiding Cases' < http://www.court.gov.cn/shenpan-gengduo-77.html > ; Supreme People's Court of the People's Republic of China, 'China Judgements Online' < https://wenshu.court.gov.cn/ > ; Peking University Centre for Legal Information, 'Judicial Cases Database of China' < https://pkulaw.com/english > .

(4) application of modification, invalidation, rescission, and termination of the contract;
(5) application of application of post-contract responsibility; and
(6) other application.

3.4.1 General Application of the Principle of Good Faith

3.4.1.1 Application as a Tool of Contract Interpretation

Under Article 125 of the 1999 CCL, the principle of good faith guides the interpretation of contract clauses. An illustrative case is *Qinhuangdao Qiuran Property v Geshan Construction Group.*[79] Here, the contract stipulated that payment of 85% of the completed part should occur within ten days after the tenth floor's completion, or on the 10 December 2018 per the Lunar Calendar, or if construction was delayed or stopped for reasons not attributable to Geshan. Disputes arose over the interpretation of these terms. Qiuran interpreted the clause to mean as they would only pay 85% either when Geshan completed the tenth floor, or, if not completed, on the aforementioned date on the condition that such delay was not caused by Geshan. However, the court ruled that payment should be made under three independent circumstances: (1) the tenth-day post-completion of the tenth floor, (2) on 10 December 2018 as per the Lunar Calendar, or (3) if there was a delay not caused by Geshan. This interpretation was affirmed by the SPC and was held to be 'consistent with the good faith principle and the concept of fairness' under Art 125, contrary to Qiuran's restrictive interpretation which imposed an unreasonable expectation on Geshan. Nor did Qiuran notify Geshan of their unreasonable understanding of the clause.

In *Huaihua Fuda Property Development v Huaihua Kailedi Hotel,*[80] the lease agreement stipulated that Fuda, the property owner, would not introduce any competitors to Kailedi in the same business sector during the lease term. The interpretation of 'introduce' was contested. The SPC ruled that, in accordance with the nature of the contract[81] and Kailedi's reasonable expectations, the word 'introduce' should be construed to mean that Fuda must not actively seek any competitors of Kailedi and should ensure that future leases excluded Kailedi's competitors. This interpretation upheld Kailedi's subsequent termination of the lease since Fuda had agreed to the relevant clause but later failed to prevent competitors from renting space.

---

[79] *Qinhuangdao Qiuran Property Development Co Ltd v Geshan Construction Group Co Ltd,* Supreme People's Court, Civil Retrial No 2023, 23 August 2021.

[80] *Huaihua Fuda Property Development v Huaihua Kailedi Hotel,* Supreme People's Court, Civil Retrial No 399, 9 September 2015.

[81] Kailedi's lease agreement was significant for both parties in this case, as when the lease contract was signed, the 24-level building was only leased out for 2–3 levels, and Kailedi's leased 9 levels of this building.

In the case of *Lu'an Huayu Property Development v Zhang Yu*,[82] Huayu borrowed RMB 50 million from Zhang, securing the loan with a property purchase and buyback agreement. The terms stated that 'when Huayu intends to buy back the property purchased by Zhang within one month, it should pay 52.5 million; in two months, 55.5 million; in three months, 57.5 million; ... when Zhang received the payment, the parties should then terminate the property purchase agreement and de-register the intended purchase.' Huayu later refused to repurchase the property, arguing that the clause granted them a discretionary right to decide whether to buy back the property. However, the SPC found that the real intention behind the agreement was to secure the repayment of the debt, not to provide Huayu with a discretionary buyback option. The court held that without explicit representation to show that the buyback was discretionary, interpreting the clause as such would contravene fundamental civil law principles including autonomy, fairness, equal value, equal compensation, and good faith. Therefore, such an interpretation was unacceptable.

In *A Company v Shanxi B Company*,[83] the parties entered into an intermediary contract that included a no liability clause, which stated that 'A company shall not be liable for the advice or work provided to Shanxi B Company.' The SPC held that while the intermediary's primary duty is to report truthfully, the clause exempting it from liability for 'work' should be interpreted as excluding responsibility for the outcomes of transactions to which the intermediary services were directed, rather than absolving the intermediary from all its contractual and statutory obligations, including the duty to report truthfully. This interpretation aligns with the purpose of the intermediary contract, the customary practices in trading, and the principle of good faith.

In *Anhui Rice Industry Co Ltd v Anhui Agricultural Science and Technology Co Ltd*,[84] the central issue was whether the repeated use of specific plant new product and new variety rights by Anhui Agricultural Science and Technology for commercial purposes constituted a breach of contract.[85] The SPC noted that resolving this dispute hinged on the interpretation of the licensing terms granted by the rice industry company to the agricultural technology company. The court held the meaning should be determined in accordance with the *Seed Law of the People's Republic of China*

[82] *Lu'an City Huayu Property Development Co Ltd v Zhang Yu—Appeal on the Debt Transfer Dispute*, Supreme People's Court, Civil First Branch Final No 144, 20 December 2013.

[83] *A Company v Shanxi B Company—Dispute over Intermediary Contract*, Supreme People's Court, Civil Final no 402, 18 September 2019.

[84] *Anhui Rice Industry Co Ltd v Anhui Agricultural Science and Technology Co Ltd—Dispute over Infringement of the Right to New Plant Varieties*, Supreme People's Court, Intellectual Property Civil Final No 605, 5 December 2023.

[85] The *Seed Law* and relevant judicial interpretations stipulate that no unit or individual shall produce, reproduce or sell the reproduction materials of the authorised varieties without the permission of the owner of the new variety rights. Production, reproduction and sales activities beyond the permitted scale, or production and reproduction activities beyond the agreed area, constitute a competition between breach of contract and infringement, and the variety owner has the right to choose to file an infringement lawsuit and investigate the tort liability of the act.

('*Seed Law*')[86] and the language employed in several contracts between the parties combined with the relevant clauses, the clauses' nature and purpose, customary practices, and the principle of good faith.

In *Shanghai Biotech Co Ltd v Zhuhai Co Ltd & Zhuhai International Holding Co Ltd*,[87] the dispute was about determining which products were included in the calculation of sales profits for the purpose of paying technology royalties. The contract stated that 'Party A shall pay Party B a technology royalty of 5% of the sales profit every year' following formal production. The Technology Development Contract did not explicitly mention 'recombinant human insulin API' and 'recombinant human insulin injection.' The SPC held that in determining whether these products were included under the royalty calculation, it was essential to consider the contract's terms, the contract's purpose, customary transaction practices, and the good faith principle, in accordance with Article 125 of the 1999 CCL. This approach would clarify the true meaning of the contractual clause.

3.4.1.2 Application as a General Principle

In addition to the application of the good faith principle in specific contract-related scenarios, the SPC also considers good faith as a general guiding principle in determining general issues of contract law. In *Xinjiang Eagle Property Development Co Ltd v Nantong Fourth Construction Group Co Ltd*,[88] the issue at hand was Eagle Property's refusal to pay Nantong, which led Nantong to stop their performance. Subsequently, Eagle Property sued Nantong for breach of contract, seeking damages and the continuation of performance. The SPC ruled that Eagle Property's claims were not supported both by the facts and law. Moreover, their actions contravened the principles of good faith and social public order as outlined in Articles 7 and 8 of the 2017 GPCL.

In *Qingdao Wanhe Thermal Power Co Ltd v Qingdao Houhai Thermal Power Co Ltd & Anor*,[89] the parties reached a settlement agreement reached during the appeal of a prior dispute. Although the settlement was not enforced as a judgement in the original proceedings, the SPC held it represented the mutual consent between the parties, and parties were obligated to honour this agreement in accordance with the principle of good faith. When one party failed to perform under the terms of the

[86] 《中华人民共和国种子法》 [Seed Law of the People's Republic of China] (People's Republic of China) Standing Committee of the National People's Congress, Order No 34, 8 July 2000 ('*Seed Law*').

[87] *Shanghai Biotech Co Ltd v Zhuhai Co Ltd & Zhuhai International Holding Co Ltd—Retrial Review*, Supreme People's Court, Civil Complaint No 1690, 30 March 2021.

[88] *Xinjiang Eagle Property Development Co Ltd v Nantong Fourth Construction Group Co Ltd*, Supreme People's Court, Civil Final No 133, 30 November 2017.

[89] *Qingdao Wanhe Thermal Power Co Ltd v Qingdao Houhai Thermal Power Co Ltd & Anor—Appeal on the Contract Dispute*, Supreme People's Court, Civil Second Branch No 364, 7 July 2016.

settlement, the complying party was entitled to initiate a new lawsuit based on the settlement agreement.

In the case of *Zhongning Rural Credit Cooperation Association v Xing Xuehua*,[90] the issue arose when the Zhongning Association transferred a debt claim against its debtor to Xing without disclosing that the claim was subject to ongoing litigation. Subsequently, when Xing delayed the payment for the transaction, Zhongning Association notified the court of its intent to enforce the claim after its restructuring. This notification led the court to terminate the enforcement proceedings, effectively making Xing's ability to pursue the debtor impossible. The SPC found that the Zhongning Association's termination of the enforcement proceedings was not executed in good faith, as their action significantly increased Xing's risk associated with the debt transfer transaction, and was deemed excessive as a legal defence to Xing's delayed payment. Consequently, the court held that Zhongning Association had breached its contractual obligations to Xing.

In *Xinjiang Huacheng Anju Real Estate Development Co Ltd v China Railway Construction Bridge Engineering Bureau Group Co Ltd*,[91] the Supreme People's Court intervened to amend invalid contractual provisions in their contract on the principle of good faith. In the second instance, Huacheng Company contended that the contract was invalid due to its own unlawful bidding practices. The SPC held this claim was a breach of the fundamental principle of honesty and credit, considering it a malicious and dishonest defence behaviour intended solely to maximise its own benefits at the expense of others. This behaviour was viewed as detrimental to the stability of civil legal relations.

In the landmark case *Beijing Longchang Weiye Trade Co Ltd v Beijing Urban Construction Heavy Industry Co Ltd*[92] (Guiding Case No. 166 by the Supreme People's Court), both parties initially resolved a sales contract dispute through a settlement during the second instance. The terms of the settlement specified that 'if the defendant fails to pay the amount determined in the settlement agreement in time, the plaintiff can recover from the defendant the liquidated damages agreed in the settlement agreement of 800,000 yuan.' Subsequent to this agreement, the plaintiff withdrew protective measures previously placed against the defendant, demonstrating trust and compliance with the agreed terms. However, the defendant did not fulfil the payment obligations stipulated in the settlement agreement. In response, plaintiff not only sought the enforcement of the original civil judgement but also to file a separate lawsuit for the agreed liquidated damages of 800,000 RMB. The defendant contended that the stipulated liquidated damages were excessively high and sought a reduction, claiming the amount was obviously unfair.

---

[90] *Zhongning County Rural Credit Cooperation Association v Xing Xuehua—Retrial on the Auction Contract Dispute*, Supreme People's Court, Civil Retrial No 1077, 16 May 2015.

[91] *Xinjiang Huacheng Anju Real Estate Development Co Ltd v China Railway Construction Bridge Engineering Bureau Group Co Ltd*, Supreme People's Court, Civil Final No 347, 30 April 2019 ('*The Huacheng Anju Case*').

[92] *Beijing Longchang Weiye Trade Co Ltd v Beijing Urban Construction Heavy Industry Co Ltd—Appeal on Contract Dispute*, Second Intermediate People's Court of Beijing Municipality, People's Republic of China, Civil Final No 8676, 31 October 2017.

The second instance court upheld the validity of the settlement agreement, affirming that it represented the genuine intentions of both parties and did not contravene any compulsory legal provisions, ruling that both parties should performance in good faith. The court emphasised that the plaintiff had acted in accordance with the agreement by cancelling the protective measures, demonstrating good faith. Conversely, the defendant's failure to perform the subsequent obligations in the settlement agreement constituted bad faith, which is a clear breach of the good faith principle.

3.4.2 Application of Pre-contract Obligation and Liability for Contracting Negligence

The Supreme People's Court has recognised that implied duties may arise from the principle of good faith during the pre-contractual phase. In *Hubei Jinhua Co Ltd v Wuhan Haoyu Realestate Consulting Co Ltd*,[93] the SPC emphasised that parties are expected to act in good faith throughout the negotiation process prior to the formation of a contract. In this particular case, Haoyu was appointed as the agent responsible for selling all the real estate properties in a project developed by Jinhua. The Court found that due to the nature of the relationship envisaged between the parties, Haoyu's ability to undertake sales activities was dependent on Jinhua's duty to provide accurate property details, a duty that stems from the good faith principle. It was later revealed that there were significant discrepancies between the information Jinhua disclosed before the contract was finalised and the actual condition of the properties. These discrepancies were only discovered in post-contractual exchanges. The SPC ruled that Jinhua was responsible for Haoyu's inability to sell the properties as per the agreement due to the undisclosed facts.

In *Ning v Zhongrong*,[94] the court examined the obligation to disclose under the principles of good faith. The first instance questioned whether there was an obligation to disclose based on the contractual terms, while the second instance focused on the rule of evidence, particularly the difficulty in proving intentional concealment of facts that contravene good faith principles. The judgement in the first instance found that the trust company failed to meet its disclosure obligations, not because the transfer contract explicitly required it, but due to lack of evidence confirming whether the trust company and the capital company were aware or should have been aware of the actual financial and business status of the company, or whether they intentionally provided false or concealed information. The evidence presented during the application for retrial was insufficient to challenge this finding. Therefore, the Supreme People's Court concluded that, notwithstanding the absence of an explicit contractual clause,

[93] *Hubei Jinhua Industry Co Ltd v Wuhan Haoyu Real Estate Consulting Co Ltd—Retrial of the Commercial Estate Sale Agency Dispute*, Civil Retrial No 143, 30 April 2014.

[94] *Ning v Zhongrong—Partnership Agreement Dispute Civil Application for Retrial Review*, Supreme People's Court, Civil Final Complaint No 994, 14 December 2022.

relevant parties are still expected to perform disclosure obligations in accordance with good faith principles.

In *Dalian Azimut Yacht Company v Gu & Li*,[95] the Supreme People's Court held that liability for contracting negligence is based on the breach of the good faith principle during the contract negotiation process. The court held that if such a breach leads to the contract being declared void, invalid, rescinded, or ineffective, the aggrieved party is entitled to compensation for the loss of trust interests. This includes the costs incurred during the contracting process and the potential benefits that would have been obtained upon contract performance. However, the compensation should not surpass the foreseeable loss due to contract breach at the time the contract was signed. In this specific instance, Li had formally notified the intention to terminate the contract prior to the Yacht Company fulfilling its obligations. Despite this, the Yacht Company proceeded to purchase the yacht and incurred related taxes and fees, subsequently seeking compensation from Gu and Li for the resale loss of the yacht and other related costs such as parking, custody, and exhibition fees over five years. The first instance court ruled that the Yacht Company's actions were primarily driven by its own marketing needs rather than by contractual obligations, thus denying their claims for compensation. The Supreme People's Court upheld this decision, finding no error in the first instance court's judgement.

In *A Finance Company v Shanghai B Bank*,[96] the Shanghai High People's Court found that the defendant, serving as an underwriter, breached the good faith principle by transferring short margin loans while being aware of undisclosed material adverse information. The bank had transferred these financial instruments to a finance company in the interbank bond market before commencing its duties as the lead underwriter, without proving the effectiveness of its internal isolation mechanisms. This action suggested a conflict of interest and indicated that the bank prioritised its own interests over its duties by misusing the information. Consequently, the court held the bank had contravened the good faith principle by improperly transferring the short margin loans.

In *A Property Management Co v B Bank Qingdao Branch & C Commercial Co*,[97] the Supreme People's Court ruled, guided by the principle of good faith, that the provisions agreed upon between the developer and the buyer in a commercial housing pre-sale contract do not legally bind the property management company. The court ruled that it was inappropriate for the developer and the buyer to disregard the property company's rights and interests during the pre-sale, especially when they were aware of an existing property service contract. The court noted that the developer, having previously signed a property service contract, breached good faith by allowing in the commercial housing pre-sale contract for the buyer to choose their

---

[95] *Dalian Azimut Yacht Co Ltd v Gu & Li—Retrial of the culpa in contrahendo dispute*, Supreme People's Court, Civil Complaint No 299, 9 April 2022.

[96] *A Finance Company v Shanghai B Bank—Tortious Liability Dispute*, High People's Court of Shanghai Municipality, People's Republic of China, Civil Final No 962, 27 October 2022.

[97] *A Property Management Co v B Bank Qingdao Branch & C Commercial Co—Service Contract Dispute*, Supreme People's Court, Civil Retrial No 223, 28 June 2023.

own property management service to oversee the property and its ancillary facilities. Additionally, the principle of contract relativity reinforces that such terms cannot impose obligations on the property management company, and the owner is still bound by the initial property service contract.

3.4.3 Application of Contractual Obligations and Liability for Breach of Contract

3.4.3.1 To Instruct the Parties in the Performance of the Contract

The principle of good faith not only underpins the formation of contracts but also guides their execution by the involved parties. In *Lou Xibiao v Yili Xinlei Construction Co Ltd*,[98] the SPC held that parties are required to fulfil their contractual duties in adherence to good faith. Lou's failure to perform his contractual obligations was seen as both a breach of the contract and a violation of the good faith principle. Consequently, it was ruled that the parties must continue the performance of the original contract.

During the performance of a contract, parties are bound by duties derived from the good faith principle. These duties may include providing proper notice, offering necessary assistance, or maintaining confidentiality, depending on the contract's nature, purpose, and customary practices.[99] For instance, in the case of *Pan v Si County Rural Commercial Bank Co*,[100] Pan was induced into depositing a substantial sum in exchange for an immediate 16% interest payment, promised by an individual later found had involvement in financial fraud. If Pan had adhered to the obligations of good faith by reporting this suspicious offer to the bank or the police as outlined in art 60 of the 1999 CCL, the subsequent loss suffered due to financial fraud could have been avoided. Therefore, Pan's neglect of the good faith obligation should be considered when assessing damages.

In *Guangdong Zhende Pharmaceutical Co Ltd v Hunan Hengsheng Pharmaceutical Co Ltd*,[101] Zhende was the distributor contracted to sell a specified quantity of goods provided by Hengsheng. The dispute arose over whether the sales target should be calculated across different categories of goods rather than as a total

[98] *Lou Xibiao v Yili Xinlei Residential Property Construction Co Ltd—Retrial of the Sale Contract Dispute*, Supreme People's Court, Civil Retrial No 1057, 28 September 2014.

[99] The 1999 CCL, above n 1, art 60.

[100] *Pan Shouxiang v Anhui Si County Rural Commercial Bank Co—Appeal on the Deposit Contract Dispute*, Supreme People's Court, Civil First Branch Final No 238, 27 November 2014.

[101] *Guangdong Zhende Pharmaceutical Co Ltd v Hunan Hengsheng Pharmaceutical Co Ltd—Appeal on the Deposit Contract Dispute*, Supreme People's Court, Civil Retrial No 115, 29 June 2016.

amount. The SPC found that Hengsheng only specified the categorisation requirement upon deciding to terminate the contract, which contradicted its earlier acceptance of Zhende's sales records from previous years. This retrospective stipulation by Hengsheng was ruled as a breach of the good faith obligations outlined in Article 60.

In *Nanjing Baoqing Yinlou Chain Development Co Ltd, Jiangsu Chuangyu Industry and Trade Co Ltd & Nanjing Baoqing Yinlou Jewelry Co Ltd*,[102] the High People's Court of Jiangsu Province emphasised the importance of operating in good faith within a franchise agreement. It was noted that the franchisee must adhere strictly to the contractual terms, and not infringe upon the intellectual property of the franchisor, or utilise franchise resources to establish outlets without prior authorisation. Specifically, the unauthorised employment of the franchisor's trade mark for business activities was identified as an act of trade mark infringement. Furthermore, the Court upheld that the franchisor is entitled to retain absolute control over its franchise resources. Therefore, Chain Development was prohibited from opening stores or using business resources linked to the 'Baoqing' series of registered trade marks owned by Nanjing Yinlou Jewelry without formal approval. Any use of these trade marks or related business resources would need to pay the licensing fees as stipulated in the franchise agreement.

In *GuoHua Life Insurance Co Ltd v He & Wang*,[103] the court emphasised the principle of utmost good faith in insurance contracts. The principle of good faith requires the insurance applicant to fully disclose all relevant information about the insured subject matter, allowing the insurer to accurately assess the risk and determine appropriate premiums. Conversely, insurers are responsible for clearly presenting and explaining the contract terms, particularly focusing on any clauses that exempt the insurer from liability. Given that insurance contracts are professional and technical which often presented in standardised forms of insurance policy, this requirement is essential to ensure that the insurer fully understands the terms, especially those related to exemptions.

3.4.3.2 To Deal with Failure to Perform the Contract for Any Reason

When the performance of a contract failes for some particular reason, the parties should engage in good faith interactions. In *Hebei Zhuolong Property Development v Jiangsu Construction & Engineering Group*,[104] the SPC ruled that if parties find

[102] *Nanjing Baoqing Yinlou Chain Development Co Ltd, Jiangsu Chuangyu Industry and Trade Co Ltd & Nanjing Baoqing Yinlou Jewellery Co Ltd—Retrial of Franchise Contract Dispute*, High People's Court of Jiangsu Province, People's Republic of China, Intellectual Property Civil Final No 0154, 30 July 2014.

[103] *GuoHua Life Insurance Co Ltd v He & Wang*, Second Intermediate People's Court of Beijing Municipality, People's Republic of China, Civil Final No 7960, 3 September 2020.

[104] *Guangdong Zhende Pharmaceutical Co Ltd v Hunan Hengsheng Pharmaceutical Co Ltd—Appeal on the Deposit Contract Dispute*, Supreme People's Court, Civil Retrial No 115, 29 June 2016, above n 101.

themselves unable to continue with contract performance, they must negotiate in good faith to form a new agreement. Should these negotiations fail, it becomes necessary for the parties to make prompt and responsible decisions to mitigate the losses incurred by both sides.

In the case of *Zeng v Wuhan Fitness Management Co Ltd*,[105] the court held that under Article 509 of *the Civil Code*, parties bound by a service contract are required to adhere to the good faith principle. This involves fulfilling duties of notification, assistance, and confidentiality, which must align with the contract's nature, purpose, and customary trading practices. Specifically, if a contract explicitly states the performance location, the business operator must deliver goods or services at this designated place. Should circumstances such as relocation or store closure arise, altering the original environment and location agreed upon from the beginning of the contract, and subsequently increasing the performance costs for the consumer, the latter is entitled to reject any changes to the performance location and may legally request contract to be terminated.

3.4.3.3 Liability for Breach

The good faith principle is useful in determining the occurrence of a breach of contract. In *Ziyun Government v Shunxing Property Co Ltd*,[106] the agreement between the parties stipulated that if the government intended to utilise a portion of the land developed by Shunxing, the subsidy provided by the government should be calculated based on the actual development costs incurred. Despite Shunxing's final cost claim being substantially higher than anticipated, the agreed subsidy reflected the mutual consent at the time of contract signing and should be honoured in accordance with the principle of good faith. The government's refusal to pay the agreed subsidy amounted to a breach of contract as well as a breach of the principle of good faith and strict compliance.

Article 114 of the 1999 CCL mandates that agreements on liquidated damages should be respected under the good faith principle.[107] Nonetheless, courts possess the discretionary power to adjust these damages in special circumstances, taking into account various factors under the good faith and fairness principles.[108] This

[105] *Zeng v Wuhan A Fitness Management Co Ltd—Case of Service Contract Dispute*, Wuhan Qiaokou District People's Court of Hubei Province, People's Republic of China, Civil First No 109, 15 December 2021.

[106] *Ziyun Miao and Buyi Autonomous County People's Government of Guizhou Province v Guizhou Ziyun Shunxing Property Co Ltd—Appeal on Contract Dispute*, Supreme People's Court, Civil Final No 440, 7 November 2016.

[107] *Hunan Province No 3 Construction Engineering Co Ltd v Xiangxi Autonomous City Xinhui Real Estate Development Co Ltd—Retrial on the Construction Engineering Project Contract Dispute*, Supreme People's Court, Civil Retrial No 1472, 30 June 2017; *Weifang Shengda Real Estate Development Co Ltd v Wang Gen Zhao—Retrial on the Residential Property Pre-sale Contract Dispute*, Supreme People's Court, Civil Retrial No 3103, 28 February 2017.

[108] See *Interpretation II of the CCL*, above n 61, art 29.

was evident in the case of *Huaihua Highway & Bridge Construction Corporation v Hunan Tanheng Expressway Development Co Ltd*,[109] where the SPC noted that the primary purpose of damages, which is compensation rather than punishment, had already been fulfilled by other compensations awarded by a lower court. It was also held that the party suffering losses might have contributed to its own losses. Consequently, the excessively high and punitive liquidated damages initially agreed upon were deemed unreasonable and were adjusted accordingly.

3.4.3.4 Liability Exemption

In the case of *A Company v Shanxi B Company*,[110] the principle of good faith plays an important role in interpreting the extent of liability and exemptions applicable to the parties involved. Given that an intermediary's primary duty is to provide truthful reporting, any clause stating that the intermediary is not responsible for the 'work' should be interpreted in line with the objectives of the intermediary contract, customary trading practices, and the principle of good faith. This interpretation implies that the intermediary is exempt from liability for the outcomes of the transactions facilitated by its services, rather than being exempted from all contractual and statutory duties, including the essential obligation of truthful reporting. Should the exemption be misinterpreted as absolving the intermediary from all forms of contractual and statutory responsibilities, it would undermine the execution of the intermediary contract and burden the achievement of its objectives. Such an interpretation contravenes the statutory nature of the duty to report truthfully. Moreover, it conflicts with the agreement between the parties in this case, which includes a high incentive fee on top of the regular remuneration.

3.4.4 Application of Modification, Invalidation, Rescission, and Termination of the Contract

3.4.4.1 Modification of the Contract

In *Wang Suiping v Wang Yongqin & Anor*,[111] the court applied the principle of good faith to determine the validity of the modification of terms of a contract through particular means. The evidence, which included recording materials and WeChat chat records, indicated that the party being recorded was unaware of and did not consent

[109] *Hunan Huaihua Highway Bridge Construction Corporation v Hunan Tanheng Expressway Development Co Ltd—Appeal on the Debt Contract Dispute*, Supreme People's Court, Civil Final No 504, 22 December 2017.

[110] *A Company v Shanxi B Company*, above n 83.

[111] *Wang Suiping v Wang Yongqin & Anor*, Guangzhou Intermediate People's Court of Guangdon Province, People's Republic of China, Civil Final No 18160, 7 November 2022.

to the recording being used to alter the performance period of the contract. The court determined that changing a written contract through unauthorised recording, particularly in the presence of intermediary personnel, contradicted common sense and the principles of fairness and good faith. Consequently, the recordings could not be deemed as forming a supplementary agreement to modify the contract.

(a) *Invalidation of the Contract*

In *Xinjiang Huacheng Anju Real Estate Development Co Ltd v China Railway Construction Bridge Engineering Bureau Group Co Ltd*,[112] the issue at hand was a party's knowledge of its prior actions that would invalidate a contract, yet still pushing forward with the contract signing for their self-interest. The Supreme People's Court found that this behaviour breached the principle of good faith and therefore did not uphold their claim that the contract was invalid.

The primary purpose of the contract invalidation mechanism is to prevent the execution of void contracts from harming national, societal, and third-party interests, and to preserve legal order and public morality. In this case, Huacheng Company, having acted in bad faith by conforming the contract's invalidity, sought to obtain benefit improperly from its own wrongful actions. Supporting Huacheng's appeal would allow it to evade its contractual obligations from unlawful conduct and gain unfair advantages, thereby undermining the objectives of the contract invalidating mechanism. Consequently, the court ruled that Huacheng Company's actions in negotiating substantive contract terms with Railway Construction before the bidding process violated the *Tendering and Bidding Law*, and its claim for contract invalidation was rejected due to the breach of the principle of good faith.

In *Dazhuang Village Committee v Zibo Huixing Transport Co Ltd*,[113] the contract was deemed invalid, leading the court determines the law based on the principle of good faith. The court follows this principle when determining the extent of damage compensation, which was confined strictly to actual losses incurred. The court also clarified that the actual loss did not encompass the loss of benefits that would have been indemnified. In addition, the court highlighted the necessity of fully considering the degree of fault of both parties involved in the contracting process to align with the principles of fairness and justice, ensuring the responsibility is apportioned reasonably. Only the parties found to be at fault are liable for compensation. In cases of compensation arising from invalid contracts, the principle of fault liability is applied, and the extent of each party's fault is used to determine the division of liability.

[112] *Xinjiang Huacheng Anju Real Estate Development Co Ltd v China Railway Construction Bridge Engineering Bureau Group Co Ltd* (n 91).

[113] *Zibo Gaoqing County Luhu Sub-district Dazhuang Village Committee of Shandong Province v Zibo Huixin Transport Co Ltd—Dispute Over the Land Least Contract*, Zibo Intermediate People's Court of Shandong Province, People's Republic of China, Civil Final No 880, 28 March 2023.

(b) *Rescission of the Contract*

In *Tan v Chang & Chang*,[114] one party was aware that the other party intended to cultivate crops that were prohibited in the Yellow River siltation area but proceeded to forming in a land subcontract regardless, breaching the principle of good faith. The silt back areas of the Yellow River are critical for water source conservation, enhancing flood resistance, and supplying flood control materials, thus have specific land use restrictions. The contractor, by concealing that the land was located in the silt back area and knowing the subcontractor's intentions to plant high-stalk crops, violated both the honesty and credit principle stipulated in the *Civil Code* and the objectives of the *Yellow River Protection Law* which aim to ensure the river's stability. The subcontractor sought to rescind the subcontract, and the claim was upheld by the people's court.

In *You Co Ltd v Zhong International Trading Co Ltd*,[115] the relationship between the parties was governed by an exclusive distribution agreement, which the court held imposed obligations on the parties to maintain good faith throughout the contract term to ensure cooperation. The court emphasised that contracts should not be terminated capriciously, as such actions could cause the other party incur performance costs. The court acknowledged the validity of termination clauses that reflect the true intentions of the parties, provided they comply with mandatory laws and administrative regulations. This approach respects the parties' freedom to shape their contractual rights according to personal and economic needs within international trade contexts. Nevertheless, the court stressed the importance of modesty in determining the right to terminate contracts to prevent arbitrary decisions and maintain the stability of contractual performance.

(c) *Termination of the Contract*

In cases involving breaches of contracts, parties are expected to act in good faith to resolve disputes before proceeding to terminate the contract. Both cases, *Tangshan Xindaihe Real Property Development Co Ltd v Tangshan Kangtai Construction & Engineering Co Ltd*[116] and *Yinchuan Xinhua Commercial Group Co Ltd v Ningxia Great World Industrial Co Ltd*[117] demonstrate the necessity for parties to engage in good faith consultations to address disputes prior to making claims for damages or terminating the contract.

---

[114] *Tan v Chang & Chang—Disputes over Land Management Rights*, Liaocheng Intermediate People's Court of Shandong Province, People's Republic of China, Civil Final No 3926, 28 March 2023.

[115] *You Co Ltd v Zhong International Trading Co Ltd—Appeal on Contract Dispute*, High People's Court of Beijing Municipality, People's Republic of China, Civil Final No 726, 2 February 2023.

[116] *Tangshan Xindaihe Real Estate Development Co Ltd v Tangshan Kangtai Construction & Engineering Co Ltd—Retrial of the Contract of the Transfer of the Land Use Right*, Supreme People's Court, Civil Retrial No 35, 26 November 2015.

[117] *Yinchuan Xinhua Commercial Group Co Ltd v Ningxia Great World Industrial Co Ltd—Retrial of the Property Lease Contract Dispute*, Supreme People's Court, Civil Retrial No 116, 28 September 2020.

If the conditions stipulated by law or the contract for termination are not satisfied, any attempts to terminate the contract are likely to be rejected by the courts on grounds of lacking good faith. In *Zhongyi Huahai v Fugu Hongsheng Colliery & Ors*,[118] Zhongyi Huahai unilaterally terminated the contract on the ground that the joint investment in collieries could not be fulfilled. However, the SPC found that the joint investment project was ready for registration and that the reluctance of Zhongyi Huahai to proceed was influenced by a downturn in the coal market. The SPC ruled that the colliery companies were not in breach of contract and that the termination by Zhongyi Huahai did not satisfy any legal condition and violated the principle of good faith. Such action would impose undue hardship on the other parties. Similarly, in *Chengdu Hexin Zhiyuan Real Estate Consulting Co Ltd v Sichuan Nanbu Jinli Real Estate Development Co Ltd*,[119] where the parties had contractually limited their right to terminate, the SPC highlighted held that the parties were required to act in good faith and did not possess discretionary rights to terminate the contract arbitrarily the importance of due to the legal relationship, shared interests, and mutual trust between the parties.

3.4.5 Application in Post-contractual Responsibility

In the case of *Shijiazhuang Zexin Amino Acid Co Ltd & Anor v Beijing Junde Tongchuang Biotechnology Co Ltd*,[120] the dispute centred around the infringement of technical secrets. The Beijing Company, as the holder of these technical secrets, permitted the Shijiazhuang company to utilise these secrets through a strategic cooperation agreement and a processing agreement. The objective was to fully leverage the commercial potential of the technical secrets and to foster a mutually beneficial collaboration with the Shijiazhuang Company. The Supreme People's Court noted that even after the expiration of the confidentiality period stipulated in the technical secret licensing agreement, the termination of the licensee's confidentiality obligations does not occur automatically unless explicitly stated otherwise in the agreement. Furthermore, the court held that the licensee continues to bear a general passive non-action obligation under tort law, as well as a confidentiality obligation that is based on the principle of good faith.

[118] *Zhongyi Huahai Import & Export Co Ltd v Fugu County Miaogoumen Village Hongsheng Colliery & Ors—Appeal on the Contract Dispute*, Supreme People's Court, Civil Second Branch Final No 129, July 2015.

[119] *Chengdu Hexin Zhiyuan Real Estate Consulting Co Ltd v Sichuan Nanbu Jinli Real Estate Development Co Ltd—Appeal on the Agency Contract Dispute*, Supreme People's Court, Civil First Branch Final No 226, 29 June 2016.

[120] *Shijiazhuang Zexin Amino Acid Co Ltd & Anor v Beijing Junde Tongchuang Biotechnology Co Ltd*, Intellectual Property Civil Final No 621, 18 December 2021.

3.4.6 *Other Application*

3.4.6.1 Application in the Assignment of Contractual Rights and Obligations to a Third Party

In a series of cases involving Cai Fuying,[121] it was held the assignment of contractual rights and obligations to a third party should adhere to the principle of good faith. Specifically, if parties attempt to assign their debts to a third party to evade fulfilling their financial obligations under the original contract, such assignments might be deemed invalid. In this instance, Cai Fuying sought to enforce a judgement debt against a company named Fanrong, which had tried to transfer its property rights to a shell company and subsequently to third parties. These third parties contested the enforcement of Cai's judgement debt, asserting that the property rights had been transferred. The SPC determined that the transactions between Fanrong, its shell company, and the third parties were fraudulent and aimed at evading the judgement debt. Consequently, the court ruled that these parties had not acted in good faith, and their claims should be dismissed.

3.4.6.2 Application in the Context of Unjust Enrichment

In *Jiangsu Suzhong Construction Co Ltd v Xinjiang Shuiqingmuhua Property Investment Co Ltd*,[122] the parties had initially entered into a main contract and subsequently reached a further agreement on payment terms and liabilities. However, when the main contract was later invalidated, the SPC, following the principle of good faith, held that the subsequent agreement regarding payment and liabilities should be treated as the parties' arrangement concerning obligations in the situation of restitution to prevent unjust enrichment of one party due to the absence of a valid main contract.

Similarly, in *Lin Jinfang & Ors v Hainan Tianjing Farm Co Ltd & Ors*,[123] the parties had agreed to invest in several farms with the expectation of future profits from their joint venture. The collaboration, however, did not materialise, and the contract was subsequently terminated. The SPC ruled that, since the investors would

[121] *Wang Shuijing v Cai Fuying—Claim Raised by the Third Party on the Enforcement of Judgment of the Debt Dispute*, Supreme People's Court, Civil First Branch Final No 166, 14 November 2014; *Guo Ziyan v Cai Fuying—Claim raised by the Third Party on the Enforcement of Judgment of the Debt Dispute*, Supreme People's Court, Civil First Branch Final No 200, 15 November 2014; *Lin Shuni v Cai Fuying—Claim raised by the Third Party on the Enforcement of Judgment of the Debt Dispute*, Supreme People's Court, Civil First Branch Final No 201, 14 November 2014.

[122] *Jiangsu Suzhong Construction Group Co Ltd v Xinjiang Shuiqingmuhua Property Investment Co Ltd—Appeal on the Construction and Engineering Contract Dispute*, Supreme People's Court, Civil Final No 733, 28 June 2017.

[123] *Li Jinfang & Ors v Hainan Tianjing Farm Co Ltd & Ors—Appeal on the Joint Venture and Cooperation on Development of Property Contract Dispute*, Supreme People's Court, Civil Final No 517, 23 January 2017.

not receive the anticipated benefits under the contract, allowing the farms to merely return the initial investment without any interest would result in unjust enrichment. This would violate the principle of good faith. Therefore, the farms were required to refund not only the principal amount but also the accrued interest.

3.5 Analysis and Evaluation

The general principle of good faith is a cornerstone in the development of reliable and trustworthy contractual dealings. Although its incorporation into the complexities of the Chinese Civil Code brings about significant benefits, it also encounters notable challenges.

One of the main advantages of applying the good faith principle in China is its role in enhancing trust and reliability within commercial transactions. It compels parties to maintain honesty, transparency, and integrity during all phases of a contract—from negotiation through to execution and termination. This not only aids in creating favourable conditions for business collaborations but also supports economic stability and growth. Additionally, by integrating good faith into contractual engagements, China demonstrates its dedication to aligning its legal frameworks with international norms and best practices. This commitment helps bolster China's image as a dependable participant in global commerce.

The implementation of the principle of good faith is, however, not without hurdles. A significant challenge is the inherent vagueness of the good faith concept. Unlike some Western jurisdictions where the doctrine is clearly defined and codified, Chinese law tends to rely on broader judicial interpretations, which can lead to inconsistent applications and a degree of uncertainty.

To thoroughly assess the application of the general principle of good faith in the Chinese Civil Code, it is crucial to examine the distribution and typicality of relevant cases, as well as the judiciary's adherence to legal principles. For instance, cases like *Beijing Longchang Weiye Trade Co Ltd v Beijing Urban Construction Heavy Industry Co Ltd*[124] offer valuable insights into how courts emphasise honesty in resolving contract disputes, reflecting the judicial commitment to uphold contract voluntariness and honesty. However, the distribution of cases across different issues may be uneven, potentially skewing the understanding and application of the good faith principle in certain contexts. Moreover, in some instances where laws are cited without thorough reasoning, or where there is a low degree of alignment with the cases at hand, it reflects a superficial application of legal principles by the courts.

Issues also arise when appellate courts amend substantive aspects of judgements without referencing the pertinent substantive law provisions, relying instead on procedural statutes. This indicates potential gaps or ambiguities in the judicial application of contract law, suggesting a need for a more robust application and

[124] *Beijing Longchang Weiye Trade Co Ltd v Beijing Urban Construction Heavy Industry Co Ltd*, above n 92.

interpretation of legal standards. Cultural and contextual factors also play a role in how the good faith principle is perceived and enforced in China. Traditional values such as loyalty and harmony may influence interpretations of what constitutes good faith, potentially leading to deviations from Western legal interpretations. Moreover, challenges such as limited judicial resources, complex procedures, and bureaucratic inefficiencies can impede the effective enforcement of good faith obligations, leading to procedural delays and uncertainties.

Addressing these challenges requires ongoing efforts to clarify and standardise the application of the good faith principle through legislative reforms and judicial training. Enhancing the clarity, consistency, and enforcement mechanisms of good faith in the Chinese Civil Code is essential for ensuring that it effectively promotes fairness and integrity in commercial dealings.

In summary, while the integration of the good faith principle in the Chinese Civil Code marks a positive development towards fostering fair commercial practices, its application remains a dynamic and intricate aspect of the legal landscape that requires continuous scrutiny and enhancement.

3.6 Chapter Summary

The theories of good faith advanced in chapters two and three so far have either been foreign to Australian law or they have too widely defined the scope or definition of good faith. In either case, the introduction of good faith would be hampered by an attempt to implement irrelevant or impractical theories into the Australian business environment. A proposal for an Australian good faith approach must be compatible with existing legal principles.

How, then, should good faith proceed in an Australian commercial environment? A limited or confined application of good faith would be more practical for commercial purposes and more effective in practice. An overriding notion of good faith that requires contracting parties at arm's length to have regard for the interest of the other party is difficult to apply in practice, unlike in China. The extent of good faith in that context would not be easy to ascertain given the adversarial context of the Australian contracting environment.

It is for these reasons that an approach must be taken to recognise and apply good faith based on the reasonable expectations of the contracting parties. The focus in the following chapters will be to identify the shortfall in the present legal principles and the ensuing business difficulties. The aim will also be to ascertain whether the scope and relevance of good faith application can be more precisely articulated or defined.

Part II

Chapter 4
Good Faith in the Australian Context

4.1 Introduction

The aim of this chapter is to provide an overview of the development of good faith in Australia. In Chap. 2, the importance of good faith obligation as a concept has been recognised historically in its ability to provide courts with a basis with which new rules can emerge to deal with developments in commerce that cannot be satisfactorily resolved under existing rules. This has led to the development of positive law to meet the progressive need of commercial life both within civil and common law jurisdictions.[1] In this way, Seddon and Ellinghaus' assertion that good faith represents the most widely prescribed standard of conduct globally for contracting parties seems justified.[2]

Australia's commercial law is based, primarily, on the English common law system. Like the English common law, Australian law contains piecemeal principles and doctrines of law and equity that have already performed similar functions as the obligation of good faith.[3] These notions of good faith are incorporated into

[1] See the analysis of the historical role of the development of bona fides or good faith actions in English law and its influence on the European civil law in Chap. 2 and the comparative analysis of good faith obligation in China in Chap. 3.

[2] Nicholas C Seddon and Manfred P Ellinghaus, *Cheshire and Fifoot's Law of Contract* (LexisNexis Butterworths, 8th Australian ed, 2002) 421; Nicholas C Seddon, Rick A Bigwood and Manfred P Ellinghaus, *Cheshire and Fifoot: Law of Contract* (LexisNexis Butterworths, 10th Australian ed, 2012) 465.

[3] Michael Bridge, 'Does Anglo-Canadian Contract Law Need a Doctrine of Good Faith?' (1984) 9 *Canadian Business Law Journal* 385, 409; Johan Steyn, 'Contract Law: Fulfilling the Reasonable Expectations of Honest Me' (1997) 113 *Law Quarterly Review* 433, 441; Stephen M Waddams, 'Codification, Law Reform and Judicial Developments' (1996) 9 *Journal Contract Law* 192, 194; Stephen M Waddams, 'Good Faith, Unconscionability and Reasonable Expectations' (1995) 9 *Journal Contract Law* 55; Johan Steyn, 'The Role of Good Faith and Fair Dealing in Contract Law: A Hair-Shirt Philosophy?' [1991] *Denning Law Journal* 131, 133; Paul Finn, 'Commerce, The Common Law and Morality' (1989) 17 *Melbourne University Law Review* 87, 92–98; L J Priestley, 'Contract—The Burgeoning Maelstrom' (1988) 1 *Current Law Journal* 15; John R Peden, *The*

A. Wan and P. Guo, *Good Faith Obligation*, International and Comparative Law in the Asia Pacific, https://doi.org/10.1007/978-981-97-7035-9_4

specific legal doctrines under common law and are not generally regarded as a separate or new legal principle that warrants recognition as an explicit duty.[4] This is also the underlying sentiment in Australia. For example, Gummow J observed in *Service Station Association Ltd v Berg Bennett & Associates Pty Ltd* (*SSA*)[5] that the origin of good faith did not appear to differ from an implied obligation of cooperation.[6] He remarked that to recognise a separate obligation of good faith in Australian contract law required a 'leap of faith.'[7] Gummow J's statements encapsulate the main argument against having a separate good faith regime in Australia. That is, good faith adds little value to the already established common law principles, which has sufficiently infused contract law without the need for an implication of a good faith obligation.[8]

Nevertheless, the reception of good faith obligation in Australian contract law remains positive, in the light of Priestley JA's decision in the *Renard Constructions (ME) Pty Ltd v Minister for Public Works* (*Renard Constructions*) case.[9] The manner in which *Renard Constructions* has achieved widespread acceptance allows good faith obligation to gain traction in Australian contract law with an emerging line of judicial authority affirming good faith as an implied duty.[10] This has attracted

---

Law of Unjust Contracts (Butterworths, 1982) 28; Harvey McGregor, *A Contract Code: Drawn Up on Behalf of the English Law Commission* (Sweet & Maxwell, 1994) 40: comments in relation to the Contract Code that good faith is 'implicit in the Moorcock rule'; Roger Brownsword, 'Two Concepts of Good Faith' (1994) 7 *Journal of Contract Law* 197, 198; Michael Bridge, 'Good Faith in Commercial Contracts' in Roger Brownsword, Norma J Hird and Geraint Howells (eds), *Good Faith in Contract: Concept and Context* (Dartmouth Publishing Co, 1999) 139; John W Carter and Elisabeth Peden, 'Good Faith in Australian Contract Law' (2003) 19 *Journal of Contract Law* 155.

[4] Except in a contract of insurance; Lord Mansfield made a commentary about elevating good faith to the level of general principles in contract law but it never developed any further: *Carter v Boehm* (1766) 97 ER 1162, 1164; Sara M Mitchell and Emilia J Powell, *Domestic Law Goes Global: Legal Traditions and International Courts* (2001) 41–42; Ewan McKendrick, *Contract Law: Text, Cases and Materials* (Oxford University Press, 6th ed, 2014) 505; *Mid Essex Hospital Services NHS Trust v Compass Group UK and Ireland Ltd (T/A Medirest)* [2013] EWCA Civ 200.

[5] (1993) 117 ALR 393.

[6] Ibid 405–406.

[7] Ibid 406.

[8] E.g. Paul Finn, 'Equity and Commercial Contracts: A Comment' [2001] *AMPLA Yearbook* 414; Tyrone Carlin, 'The Rise (and Fall?) of Implied Duties of Good Faith in Contractual Performance in Australia' (2002) 25 *University of New South Wales Law Journal* 99; Carter and Peden, 'Good Faith in Australian Contract,' above n 5; Elisabeth Peden, 'Implicit Good Faith—or Do We Still Need an Implied Term of Good Faith?' (2009) 25 *Journal of Contract Law* 50; contrast Priestley, 'The Burgeoning Maelstrom,' 15.

[9] (1992) 26 NSWLR 234; Leading contract law academics like John Carter and Andrew Stewart have described good faith obligations in contractual performance and enforcement as the most important unresolved issue in Australian contract law—John W Carter and Andrew Stewart, 'Interpretation, Good Faith and the "True Meaning" of Contracts: The Royal Botanic Decision' (2002) 18 *Journal of Contract Law* 182, 190.

[10] E.g. in no particular order: *Presmist Pty Ltd v Turner Corporation Pty Ltd* (1992) 30 NSWLR 478; *Hughes Bros Pty Ltd v Trustees of the Roman Catholic Church for the Archdiocese of Sydney* (1993) 31 NSWLR 91; *Service Station Association Ltd v Berg Bennett & Associates Pty Ltd* (1993) 117 ALR 393; *News Ltd v Australian Rugby Football League Ltd* (1996) 135 ALR 33; *Hughes Aircraft Systems International v Airservices Australia* (1997) 146 ALR 1; *Asia Pacific Resources Pty Ltd*

both critics and supporters, as evidenced by the extensive commentary written on

v Forestry Tasmania (Unreported, Tasmanian Supreme Court (Full Court), 4 September 1997); *Alcatel Australia Ltd v Scarcella* (1998) 44 NSWLR 349; *Dalcon Constructions Pty Ltd v State Housing Commission* (1998) 14 BCLC 477; *Australis Media Holdings Pty Ltd v Telstra Corporation Ltd* (1998) 43 NSWLR 104; *WMC Resources Ltd v Leighton Contractors Pty Ltd* (1999) 20 WAR 489; *Advance Fitness v Bondi Diggers* [1999] NSWSC 264; *Australian Co-operative Foods Ltd v Norco Co-operative Ltd* (1999) 46 NSWLR 267; *Blackler v Felpure Pty Ltd* [1999] NSWSC 958; *K & S Freighters Pty Ltd v Linfox Transport (Aust) Pty Ltd* [1999] FCA 1325; *Shorrlong Pty Ltd v Northern Territory Housing Commission* [1999] NTSC 140; *Garry Rogers Motors (Aust) Pty Ltd v Subaru (Aust) Pty Ltd* (1999) ATPR ¶41–703; *Forklift Engineering Australia Pty Ltd v Powerlift (Nissan) Pty Ltd* [2000] VSC 443; *Far Horizons Pty Ltd v McDonald's Australia Ltd* [2000] VSC 310; *South Sydney District Rugby League Football Club Ltd v News Ltd* (2000) 177 ALR 611; *Thiess Contractors Pty Ltd v Placer (Granny Smith) Pty Ltd* (2000) 16 BCL 130; *Christopher John De Pasquale v The Australian Chess Federation Inc (AO 1325)* [2000] ACTSC 94; *Saxby Bridge Mortgages Pty Ltd v Saxby Bridge Pty Ltd* [2000] NSWSC 433; *Dickson Property Management Services Pty Ltd v Centro Property Management (Vic) Pty Ltd* (2000) 180 ALR 485; *Elfic Ltd v Macks* [2000] QSC 18; *Asia Television Ltd v Yau's Entertainment Pty Ltd* (2000) 48 IPR 283; *Howtrac Rentals Pty Ltd v Thiess Contractors (NZ) Ltd* [2000] VSC 415; *Walker v ANZ Banking Group Ltd (No 2)* (2001) 39 ACSR 557; *Commonwealth Bank of Australia v Renstell Nominees Pty Ltd* [2001] VSC 167; *Apple Communications v Optus Mobile* [2001] NSWSC 635; *Bamco Villa Pty Ltd v Montedeen Pty Ltd* [2001] VSC 192; *Radley Corporation Ltd v Suncorp Metway Ltd* [2001] VSC 272; *Edensor Nominees Pty Ltd v Anaconda Nickel Ltd* [2001] VSC 502; *NT Power Generation Pty Ltd v Power and Water Authority* (2001) 184 ALR 481; *LMI Australasia Pty Ltd v Baulderstone Hornibrook Pty Ltd* [2001] NSWSC 886; *Central Exchange Ltd v Anaconda Nickel Ltd* (2001) 24 WAR 382; *Central Exchange Ltd v Anaconda Nickel Ltd* [2002] WASCA 94; *Easts Van Villages Pty Ltd v Minister Administering the National Parks and Wildlife Act* [2001] NSWSC 559; *Automasters Australia Pty Ltd v Bruness Pty Ltd* [2002] WASC 286; *State of New South Wales v Banabelle Electrical Pty Ltd* (2002) 54 NSWLR 503; *Softplay v Perpetual* [2002] NSWSC 1059; *Wenzel v Australian Stock Exchange Ltd* [2002] FCAFC 400; *Royal Botanic Gardens and Domain Trust v South Sydney City Council* (2002) 186 ALR 289; *Overlook v Foxtel* (2002) Aust Contracts Rep 90–143; *Lay v Alliswell Pty Ltd* (2002) V ConvR ¶54–651; *Hudson Resources Ltd v Australian Diatomite Mining Pty Ltd* [2002] NSWSC 314; *Commonwealth Development Bank of Australia Pty Ltd v Cassegrain* [2002] NSWSC 965; *Cubic Transportation Systems, Inc v State of New South Wales* [2002] NSWSC 656; *GEC Marconi Systems Pty Ltd v BHP Information Technology Pty Ltd* (2003) 128 FCR 1; *Biscayne Partners Pty Ltd v Valance Corporation Pty Ltd* [2003] NSWSC 874; *Golden Sands Pty Ltd v Davegale Pty Ltd* [2003] VSC 458; *Esso Australia Resources Pty Ltd v Southern Pacific Petroleum NL* [2004] VSC 477; *Esso Australia Resources Pty Ltd v Southern Pacific Petroleum NL* [2005] VSCA 228; *Hoppers Crossing Club Ltd v Tattersalls Gaming Pty Ltd* [2005] VSC 114; *Pacific Brands Sports & Leisure Pty Ltd v Underworks Pty Ltd* [2005] FCA 288; *Australian Hotels Association (NSW) v TAB Ltd* [2006] NSWSC 293 (19 April 2006); *Meridian Retail Pty Ltd v Australian Unity Retail Network* [2006] VSC 223; *Maitland Main Collieries Pty Ltd v Xstrata Mt Owen Pty Ltd* [2006] NSWSC 1235; *Ingot Capital Investments v Macquarie Equity Capital Markets (No 6)* [2007] NSWSC 124; *Kellogg Brown & Root Pty Ltd v Australian Aerospace Ltd* [2007] VSC 200; *Farah Construction Pty Ltd v Say-Dee Pty Ltd* [2007] 230 CLR 89; *Sundararajah v Teachers Federal Health Ltd* [2009] NSWSC 1443, [31]; *United Group Rail Services Ltd v Rail Corporation of New South Wales* [2009] NSWCA 177; *Strzelecki Holdings Pty Ltd v Cable Sands Pty Ltd* [2010] WASCA 222; *Macquarie International Health Clinic Pty Ltd v Sydney South West Area Health Service* [2010] NSWCA 268; *Starlink International Group Pty Ltd v Coles Supermarket Australia Pty Ltd* [2011] NSWSC 1154; *AMC Commercial Leasing (NSW)*

the subject.[11] In view of the widespread acceptance of *Renard Constructions*, the question remains as to whether the 'controversy' is a mere storm in a teacup?[12] The answer to this question, at times, depends on which side of the fence one sits on. Be that as it may, the current judicial approach to the duty of good faith in Australia is that it is implied, with the accepted view pointing to an implication into a certain class of contracts as a matter of law.

In line with the objective of this book to appraise the relevance and viability of good faith as a contractual term, this chapter intends to provide an overview of the judicial developments of good faith obligation that is currently premised on implied terms following the *Renard Constructions* decision. Essentially, it is the intention of this chapter to consider whether the framework of bringing good faith obligation into a contractual undertaking under implied terms is appropriate or not? If so, should it be implied in law or in fact? Or should it instead be applied as a principle of construction of contract, rather than implied terms? And, lastly, this chapter will consider whether the concept of good faith obligation should be extended to pre-contractual negotiations. The reason for considering pre-contractual negotiation is that modern commercial contracts require, in many instances, complicated and lengthy negotiations, which tend to demonstrate the insufficiency of existing contract law governing the different stages of contractual negotiation. In this respect, Sir Anthony Mason has strongly argued for the inclusion of good faith at the negotiation stage of contracting as a means of redressing this deficiency.[13]

Pty Ltd v Coade [2011] NSWSC 932, [133–134]; *Cordon Investments Pty Ltd v Lesdor Properties Pty Ltd* [2012] NSWCA 184; *RPR Maintenance Pty Ltd v Marmax Investments Pty Ltd* [2014] FCA 409.

[11] E.g. Eileen Webb, 'The Scope of the Implied Duty of Good Faith—Lessons from Commercial and Retail Leasing Cases' (2001) 9 *Australian Property Law Journal* 1; Adrian Baron, '"Good Faith" and Construction Contracts—From Small Acorns Large Oak Grow' (2002) 22 (1) *Australian Bar Review* 54; Carlin, 'The Rise (and Fall?)', above n 8; Carter and Stewart, 'Interpretation,' above n 9; Carter and Peden, 'Good Faith in Australian Contract,' above n 3; Adam Wallwork, 'A requirement of good faith in construction contracts?' (2004) 20 *Building and Construction Law* 257; Bill Dixon, 'Common Law Obligations of Good Faith in Australian Commercial Contracts—a Relational Recipe' (2005) 33 *Australian Business Law Review* 87; Angelo Capuano, 'Not Keeping the Faith: A Critique of Good Faith in Contract Law in Australia and the United States' (2005) 17(1) *Bond Law Review* 29; Robert McDougall, *The Implied Duty of Good Faith in Australian Contract Law* (2006) http://www.austlii.edu.au/au/journals/NSWJSchol/2006/2.pdf ; Geoffrey Kuehne, 'Implied Obligations of Good Faith and Reasonableness in the Performance of Contracts: Old Wine in New Bottles' (2006) 33 *University of Western Australia Law Review* 63; Bill Dixon, 'What is the Content of the Common Law Obligation of Good Faith in Commercial Leases?' (2007) 14 *Australian Property Law Journal* 113; Peden, 'Implicit Good Faith,' above n 8; Tyrone Carlin and Louise Chau, 'Good Faith—Time to Put the Genie Back in the Bottle' (2009) 3(2) *Journal of Law and Financial Management* 22; Andrew Stewart, 'What's Wrong with the Australian Contract Law?' (2012) 29 *Journal of Contract Law* 74; John W Carter, 'Good Faith in Contract: Why Australian Law is Incoherent?' (Research Paper No 14/38, Sydney Law School, 2014).

[12] 'Burgeoning maelstrom' is a term of reference used in Priestley, 'The Burgeoning Maelstrom,' 15.

[13] Anthony Mason, 'Contract, Good Faith and Equitable Standards in Fair Dealing' (2001) 116 *Law Quarterly Review* 66, 82.

In considering these matters, this chapter does not deal with the legal standard of good faith obligations in regards to its operation and application. Rather, this will be provided separately in Chap. 5 that includes a comparative analysis of how American contract law has dealt with the basis of good faith application, which has become a central pillar of their contract regime.

4.2 Judicial Developments of Good Faith in Australia

4.2.1 An Implied Term Approach

The main mechanism for the imposition of good faith obligation in Australia has been the implied contractual term. Implied terms, generally, operate within the confines of two categories that are quite distinct.[14] The first category covers implied terms concerning the actual intention of the parties, which is consistent with the classical model of contract law. These are commonly known as terms implied in fact,[15] the implication being made ad hoc. A court, however, still exercises caution when implying a term into a contract and will not simply do so because it may appear reasonable. The key element is that it must provide business efficacy to the operation of the contract.[16] The Privy Council set out the five requirements in *BP Refinery (Westernport) Pty Ltd v Shire of Hastings* ('*BP Refinery*') to be satisfied to enable the implication of a term on the basis of business efficacy.[17] The five requirements are that the term must (1) be reasonable and equitable; (2) be necessary to give business efficacy to the contract, so that no term will be implied if the contract is effective without it; (3) be so obvious that 'it goes without saying'; (4) be capable of clear expression; and (5) not contradict any express term of the contract.[18] The approach of *BP Refinery* was affirmed by Kirby J in *Roxborough v Rothmans of Pall Mall Australia Pty Ltd*[19] as being 'inherent in the economic freedom to which the law of contract gives effect.'[20]

---

[14] This does not suggest that there may not be considerable overlap between the two categories as demonstrated by the decision of Finn J in *Hughes Aircraft Systems International v Airservices Australia* (1997) 146 ALR 1 discussed below.

[15] Lindy Willmott, Sharon Christensen and Desmond Butler, *Contract Law* (Oxford University Press, 2nd ed, 2005) 256.

[16] Cf *Secured Income Real Estate (Australia) Ltd v St Martins Investment Pty Ltd* (1979) 144 CLR 596.

[17] (1977) 180 CLR 266.

[18] This was approved by the High Court of Australia in a number of decisions, probably the most well known being *Codelfa Constructions Pty Ltd v State Railway Authority of New South Wales* (1982) 149 CLR 337.

[19] (2001) 185 ALR 335.

[20] Ibid [161].

The concept of economic liberty, referenced by Kirby J, typically reveals itself through comprehensive contractual terms that aim to explicitly govern every facet of the contractual relationship. The strong correlation between terms implied in fact and the parties' actual, but unexpressed, intentions allows for minimal flexibility,[21] making it difficult to meet the five prerequisites of applying good faith obligation.[22] The main challenge is that a term cannot be implied in fact if it contradicts an explicit term in the contract.[23]

By contrast, the second category of implied terms, being terms implied by law, arises on the basis of an imputed intention, regardless of the contracting parties' actual intent.[24] These terms are imposed on the contracting parties as a matter of law, such that the contract term is implied as a legal incident of a particular class of contract.[25]

In order for a contractual term to be implied as a matter of law, a two stage test must be satisfied. The first stage requires that there must be an identifiable class of contractual relationships, for example, contracts between employer and employee, sale of goods,[26] landlord and tenant, and contracts of carriage by sea. The nature of these classes of contracts may incorporate relational characteristics; however, that is by no means a governing criteria. It seems conceivable that the classes of contracts in which the law will imply terms by law are not closed.[27] The second stage requirement is to satisfy the test of necessity.[28] This test originates from the decision in *Liverpool City Council v Irwin.*[29] In that case, Lord Wilberforce held that the obligation 'should be read into the contract as the nature of the contract itself implicitly requires, no more, no less: a test, in other words of necessity.'[30] In Australia, necessity is understood to mean that 'unless such a term [is] implied, the enjoyment of the rights conferred by the contract would or could be rendered nugatory, worthless, or, perhaps, be seriously undermined.'[31] Wider policy reasons

[21] Alexander F H Loke, 'Fiduciary Duties and Implied Duties of Good Faith in Contractual Joint Ventures' [1999] *Journal of Business Law* 538, 547.

[22] *Overlook v Foxtel* (2002) Aust Contracts Rep 90–143, [60].

[23] Noted by Lord Browne-Wilkinson in the Privy Council judgment of *Dymocks Franchise Systems (NSW) Pty Ltd v Todd* [2004] 1 NZLR 289, [54].

[24] *Breen v Williams* (1996) 186 CLR 71, 103.

[25] *Australis Media Holdings Pty Ltd v Telstra Corporation Ltd* (1998) 43 NSWLR 104, 122–123.

[26] Now codified by statute.

[27] *Castlemaine Tooheys Ltd v Carlton & United Breweries Ltd* (1987) 10 NSWLR 468, 487 (Hope JA).

[28] *Esso Australia Resources Ltd v Plowman* (1995) 183 CLR 10, 30 (Mason CJ).

[29] [1977] AC 239.

[30] [1977] AC 239, 254.

[31] *Byrne v Australian Airlines Ltd* (1995) 185 CLR 410, 450 (McHugh and Gummow JJ); *Breen v Williams* (1996) 186 CLR 71, 103 (Gaudron and McHugh JJ), 24 (Gummow J). An alternative way of describing the test of necessity is whether the term sought to be implied is necessary in contracts of the class to which the subject contract belongs in the sense that, without it, the whole basis of the contracts in the class would be rendered futile: *Castlemaine Tooheys Ltd v Carlton & United Breweries Ltd* (1987) 10 NSWLR 468, 488 (Hope JA, Samuels and Priestly JJA agreeing).

have also been seen to support the implication of a contractual term as a matter of law.[32] Nevertheless, it has been recognised that the narrower test of necessity is better equipped to address 'the broad range of instances where the issue of such implication ordinarily arises' in good faith obligation.[33]

4.2.1.1 The Distinction and Issues Relating to Implication By Law and Fact

The distinction between the two types of implied terms—those implied in fact and those implied by law—is important when considering the implied obligation of good faith in the performance and enforcement of commercial contracts. There is disagreement among scholars regarding whether the good faith obligation should be actualised through a term implied in law or, rather, if it is better suited to be implied in fact.

Prima facie, it seems a term implied in law would be more appropriate for the governance of the duty of good faith where it is intended to be implied in all contracts.[34] When a term is implied by law, it is connected to a certain class of contracts. In the case that there is an express contractual term that is inconsistent with statute—including a term implied by law—statute often prevails and the express term in the contract may be found to be void. This would not affect the operation of the contract as a whole. In this category, it is presumed that the implied term is incorporated into all contracts of the same class. Nonetheless, exclusion of the implied term of good faith is still achievable where the contract clearly stipulates that exclusion.[35] This is because a term implied in fact cannot invariably be subsumed into all contracts universally. The duty of good faith, therefore, would rarely find itself called upon if it were implied in fact.

The problem with an implication by law approach, in relation to the implication of a term of good faith, is that it does not take into account the circumstances of the parties or the provisions of the contract (beyond clear exclusions). The only concession is that the parties are presumed to have intended to include the specific implied term (for example, good faith obligation) in a particular type of contract. This all or nothing approach is problematic as the context of the contractual terms is not taken into consideration. As a result, by implying the obligation in this manner, the duty of good faith exists as a duty at large with minimal context in which to determine the contracting parties' intention.

---

[32] Policy reasons have been expressly articulated in the past, e.g. in *Lister v Romford Ice* [1957] AC 555, 576–579; *Simonius Vischer & Co Holt & Thompson* [1979] 2 NSWLR 322, 348. In the context of good faith, Finn J has expressly acknowledged that considerations of public policy can and does have an overt role to play in some instances: *Hughes Aircraft Systems International v Airservices Australia* (1997) 146 ALR 1, 39.

[33] *Hughes Aircraft Systems International v Airservices Australia* (1997) 146 ALR 1.

[34] Jeannie M Paterson, 'Good Faith in Commercial Contracts? A Franchising Case Study' (2001) 29 *Australian Business Law Review* 270, 273.

[35] *Castlemaine Tooheys Ltd v Carlton & United Breweries* (1987) 10 NSWLR 468.

The business efficacy requirement associated with terms implied in fact, likewise, presents an impediment to the implied good faith obligation. The challenges arise when a term cannot be implied if the contract would remain effective without it,[36] or where the term is so obvious or self-evident that it goes without saying, or where the term presumption of the term is inconsistent with the contract as a whole.[37] This predicament was foreseen by Priestley JA in *Renard Constructions* and can be a significant obstacle.[38] It will also be similarly difficult to satisfy the business efficacy requirements where the contract can operate in circumstances that allow the contracting parties to perform their obligations in their own interests.[39] As such, it is, perhaps, not surprising that the implication of good faith obligation has arisen through implication by law simply because of the 'difficulty of complying with the criteria for an implication in fact.'[40]

Despite this, some scholars argue the inverse; that the implied duty of good faith should be implied in fact as the court's expectation of the parties' conduct under this obligation diverges depending on the case at hand.[41] This is distinguished from the approach discussed above contending that the obligation of good faith should be implied at law, which would not hold the circumstances of each matter in as high a regard should the term be implied in fact. This is due to the lack of reliance on the intentions of the parties for terms implied at law.[42] In this circumstance, the terms of a particular contract are extraneous to the assessment of whether a good faith obligation is implied. Here, the implication would be broad as it may be interpreted without regard to the agreement or the intention of the parties to the agreement. Discretion would be limited in making a determination on the extent to which the parties are bound by the duty of good faith.[43]

This sensitivity to the contractual provisions, more than just focusing on clear words of exclusion, allows the contracting parties' reasonable expectations to be the central focus and allows judges to define the good faith duty as the facts require.[44] The ambit of the good faith obligation would arise out of the specific terms and

---

[36] E.g. *South Sydney District Rugby League Football Club Ltd v News Ltd* (2000) 177 ALR 611.

[37] E.g. *Saxby Bridge Mortgages Pty Ltd v Saxby Bridge Pty Ltd* [2000] NSWSC 433.

[38] Demonstrated in *Christopher John De Pasquale v The Australian Chess Federation Inc* (AO 1325) [2000] ACTSC 94; in *Overlook v Foxtel*, Barrett J dismissed the suggestion that an implied term of good faith arose on the grounds of presumed intention or business efficacy: [60].

[39] Elisabeth Peden, *Good Faith in the Performance of Contracts* (LexisNexis Butterworths, 2003) 132.

[40] *Central Exchange Ltd v Anaconda Nickel Ltd* [2002] WASCA 94, [52] (Steytler J).

[41] Paterson, 'Good Faith in Commercial Contracts,' above n 34, 273.

[42] Marcel Gordon, 'Discreet Digression: The Recent Evolution of the Implied Duty of Good Faith' (2007) 19 *Bond Law Review* 26, 31.

[43] Ibid.

[44] Cf Paul Finn, 'Good Faith and Fair Dealing: Australia' (Paper presented at the Commercial Good Faith Conference, Auckland, New Zealand, 2 September 2005): Finn considers the reasonable expectations approach as the greatest merit in unpacking the context of a contractual relationship.

circumstances of each case, rather than relying on the ambiguity associated with an implication in fact.[45]

Nevertheless, there are limitations to this argument. As discussed above, the conduct of expected of the parties when observing their duty of good faith can significantly vary depending on the specific context and facts of the matter. For instance, the conduct required to fulfil an implied term of reasonable care and skill in accordance with an employment contract[46] or a contract for architectural supervision[47] will rest on the circumstances of each case. Although a good faith obligation implied at law may not give regard to the intentions of the parties, it may still necessitate different types of conduct depending on the fact scenario.

It is obvious that both arguments for the classification of an implied duty of good faith in contract possess benefits and drawbacks. However, incorporating an implied obligation of good faith into Australian law—by either means of classification—is problematic. These obstacles will be further considered in Part II C of this chapter.

Before proceeding with the discussion on the problems associated with the implied term approach, it is important to review the development of good faith obligation thus far. In order to do that, it is relevant to begin at the source of how good faith obligation was introduced in Australian contract law in the *Renard Constructions* case. Specifically, it is the revised test of necessity in the decision of the *Renard Constructions* case that allowed Priestley JA to use implied terms as the vehicle for an obligation of good faith to operate in the exercise of contractual rights.

4.2.2 *The Significance of Renard Constructions*

The *Renard Constructions* case dealt with the exercise of the rights of satisfaction and termination under an industry-based standard form construction contract. In that case, the New South Wales (NSW) Minister for Public Works (the principal) awarded Renard Constructions (the contractor) two similar contracts for construction work under the standard form NPWC Edition 3 (1987).[48]

The rights of satisfaction and termination were contained in the 'Default Clause' of the contracts—clause 44.1—that prescribed a procedure in which the principal may terminate the contract upon default by the contractor. This clause provided that if the contractor defaulted in the performance of any condition or refused to comply with any direction, the principal could call upon the contractor to show cause. The contractor had to give a response that was to the satisfaction of the principal. The principal could only be satisfied with the contractor's response if it described the action necessary to remedy the default. Nothing less would suffice. If the contractor

[45] Gordon, above n 42, 31–32.

[46] *Harmer v Cornelius* [1843–1860] All ER 624.

[47] *Bagot v Stevens Scanlan & Co* [1964] 3 All ER 577.

[48] It stands for National Public Works Council (Australia), *General Conditions of Contract* (3rd ed, 1987).

could not remedy the default, the contract conferred on the principal the discretion to take over the whole, or any part, of the work and to exclude the contractor from the site.

Following the granting of two extensions of time for the principal to complete the work, a show cause notice was issued. Ten days later, the contractor received notification from the principal's authorised officer that the principal would finish the work that was left, and that the contractor would be excluded from entering the construction site. This decision was largely based upon misleading, incomplete and prejudicial information supplied to the authorised officer. At the time, the authorised officer was under a mistaken view as to the date of completion due to the failure of the materials to be supplied by the principal until a much later date. In the days following the show cause notice, the contractor responded by increasing the size of its work force, employed its workers for extended hours, and engaged an experienced foreman to complete the work in a timely manner. The authorised officer was unaware of these facts when excluding the contractor from the construction site and assuming responsibility for the remainder of the project. As the contractor had taken steps to expedite the completion of the work, it regarded the principal's conduct in terminating the contract as repudiatory. The contractor commenced arbitration proceedings where an award was eventually made in their favour against the principal for acting unreasonably.

The principal, then, appealed the arbitration award to the NSW Supreme Court. On appeal, Cole J remitted the matter for the arbitrator to issue an award in favour of the principal and, in doing so, held that the arbitrator's award be set aside. Cole J's conclusion hinged on the fact that the relevant subclause did not impose an implied obligation on the principal to reasonably exercise their discretion in taking over from the contractor to complete the work, and exclude the contractor from the construction site.[49]

The contractor, then, appealed to the Court of Appeal where it was held in the contractor's favour. Priestley JA's decision was premised on the ground of contractual construction[50] and expressed the view that the show cause procedure required the principal to act in good faith or reasonably in terminating the contract.[51] Three separate judgements were delivered, and, although all three judges agreed on the outcome and the orders to be made, they were divided in their reasoning. In relation to the issue of good faith obligation, the judgement of Priestley JA was the only judgement that dealt instructively with its adoption as an implied duty.

---

[49] *Minister of Public Works v Renard Constructions (ME) Pty Ltd* (Unreported, New South Wales Supreme Court, Cole J, 26 October 1989); (1992) 26 NSWLR 234, 255.

[50] (1992) 26 NSWLR 234, 272.

[51] Ibid 264–269.

4.2.2.1 Priestley JA's Judgement

Priestley JA held that the principal had not acted reasonably when issuing the show cause notice. The principal had a duty to act reasonably when considering the contractor's response to the show cause notice and when considering whether any power (e.g., takeover) should be exercised.[52] In addressing the implied obligation of reasonableness, Priestley JA examined the two classes of implied contractual terms, being implications in fact (or implications ad hoc) and implications in law.[53]

When considering implication in fact, Priestley JA cited the High Court decision in *Meehan v Jones*[54] and the decision of the NSW Court of Appeal in *Progress & Properties (Straithfield) Pty Ltd v Crumblin*[55] (*Progress & Properties*) as authority for the approach. These cases, on reflection, did not present very compelling authorities for Priestley JA's judgement. The High Court in *Meehan v Jones* was divided over the implied obligation: Mason and Wilson JJ supported an implied obligation of honesty but saw no need for a duty to act reasonably—a duty commonly seen as an integral part of an implied duty of good faith.[56] Conversely, Gibbs CJ agreed on an obligation of honesty but opposed a duty of reasonableness based on the business efficacy rule. Murphy J opposed both duties, and Aickin J passed away before a judgement was delivered. *Progress & Properties* merely recognised the division in authority in *Meehan v Jones* and leaned towards an implied duty of reasonableness. Therefore, these cases weakly support an implication of reasonableness, especially where a sale completion is contingent upon the securing of satisfactory finance. At most, they suggest that implication in fact is not excluded in such circumstances. His Honour was, however, satisfied that all the criteria for an implication in fact or ad hoc had met the business efficacy test for the implication of terms:

> For myself, I cannot see why a term should not be implied at both stages; that is, it seems to me relatively obvious that an objective and reasonable outsider to this contract upon reading subclause 44.1 would assume without serious question that the principal would have to give reasonable consideration to the question whether the contractor had failed to show cause and then, if the principal had reasonably concluded that the contractor had failed, that reasonable consideration must be given to whether any power and if any which power should be exercised.[57]

---

[52] Ibid 257.

[53] In adopting the terminology of implication ad hoc, Priestley JA referred to the article by Horst K Lücke, 'Ad Hoc Implications in Written Contracts' (1973–1976) 5 *Adelaide Law Review* 32.

[54] (1982) 149 CLR 571.

[55] (1984) 3 BPR 9496.

[56] Apart from *Renard Constructions*, the cases that follow include *Vodafone Pacific Ltd v Mobile Innovations Ltd* [2004] NSWCA 15; *JK Keir Pty Ltd v Priority Management Systems Pty Ltd* [2007] NSWSC 789 per Rein AJ at [27]; *Mangrove Mountain Quarries Pty Ltd v Barlow* [2007] NSWSC 492 per Windeyer J at [27]; *Nauru Phosphate Royalties Trust (Receivers and Managers appointed) & Business Australia Capital Mortgage Pty Ltd v Nauru Phosphate Royalties Trust* [2008] NSWSC 916 per Einstein J at [43].

[57] (1992) 26 NSWLR 234, 257.

Further, Priestley JA said, in relation to the application of the business efficacy test, that:

> The question of 'effectiveness' will only come up when a dispute has arisen about the way the contract is to work, and one party is saying that a term needs to be implied which will produce what that party claims is a fair (or reasonable, or proper, or just) way of resolving the dispute, and the other party is saying that the contract can work (which implicitly means 'for practical purposes' or fairly, reasonably, properly or justly) without the claimed implied terms.[58]

In resolving the question of 'effectiveness,' Priestley JA favoured the implication of reasonableness:

> One way of explaining this view is to say that no contractor in his senses would enter into a contract under which such a thing could happen. The reasonable contractor, the reasonable principal and the reasonable looker-on would all assume that such could not come about except with good reason.[59]

Thus, it seems that the manner in which Priestley JA applied the business efficacy test assumed that the parties were reasonable persons. The more likely inference, however, would be that the exercise of the wide power under the default clause would be constrained by prevailing industry practices, as ascertained by the arbitrator. The difficulty in implying prevailing industry practices is that they would fail the efficacy test as a term implied in fact under the common law.

In the NSW Supreme Court decision of *Hughes Bros Pty Ltd v Trustees of the Roman Catholic Church for the Archdiocese of Sydney* (*Hughes Bros*), Giles J found no implication of reasonableness under a bankruptcy clause, which gave a contracting party the discretion to terminate the contract in the event action for winding up commenced against the other contracting party. Accordingly, Giles J held that the unambiguous words of a contract must be given effect notwithstanding its appearance of capriciousness or unreasonableness; it also represented the principle of an unfettered discretion in the exercise of contractual rights.[60] Priestley JA disagreed with this view.[61] He thought that Giles J should have implied an obligation to act reasonably, on grounds similar to those applying to the default clause.[62] His justification was:

> I find it hard to think that either a contractor would agree to giving a principal the unqualified right … in the event that a third party instituted a groundless proceeding or that the principal would have the likelihood to insist on such a completely unqualified right. … [B]ut I also feel sure that the principal would tell the contractor that the contractor could rely on the principal not to exercise it except for a good commercial reason—why should a reasonable business man insist on anything more?[63]

---

[58] Ibid 257.

[59] (1992) 26 NSWLR 234, 258.

[60] *Hughes Bros Pty Ltd v Trustees of the Roman Catholic Church for the Archdiocese of Sydney*, (Unreported, NSW SC, Giles J, 21 September 1989) BC 8,901,683, 15.

[61] (1992) 26 NSWLR 234, 255, 259, 260.

[62] Ibid 259.

[63] Ibid.

Priestley JA further saw no reason why the terms implied in fact or ad hoc would not also be implied by law as a necessary incident of this form of contract.[64] This conclusion was reached on two bases.

The first drew support from legislative analogy. They are Acts of Parliament (the judgement made reference to the *CISG*, the *Trade Practices Act 1974* (Cth), the *UCC* and various NSW legislative provisions[65]), which imposed terms upon particular classes of contract because 'it was thought the terms were needed to make the contracts work more fairly between the parties.'[66]

In the statutory analogy, Priestley JA claimed support for his notion of good faith as.

> the kind of reasonableness [that] ... seems ... to have much in common with the notions of good faith which are regarded in many of the civil law systems in Europe and in all States in the United States as necessarily implied in many kinds of contract.[67]

Priestley JA went on to say that people have generally 'grown used to the courts applying standards of fairness to contract which are wholly consistent with the existence in all contracts of a duty upon the parties of good faith and fair dealing in its performance.'[68] However, the concept of good faith found in the legislation mentioned in Priestley JA's judgement, while based on the underlying idea of fairness, focused mainly on the content of the agreement. While it is appropriate to suggest that contracts are read in the light of legislation and that the increasing trend in legislation is to impute fairness in contracts, none of the Australian legislation listed in the judgement truly considered the behaviour of the parties after the formation of the contracts or how the contracts should be construed.

Second, Priestley JA considered the contract in question to be 'an example of a wider and common class of contract ... in which one party promises to build a work of some size for the other party,'[69] which relied on the implied reasonableness by law as a necessary incident of that class of contracts. In this respect, he considered that the word 'necessity' should not be used in the absolute sense that a contract could not have worked without the implied term. The notion of necessity being central to such implication:

> In all [classes of contracts] it would have been possible for the main purposes of the contracts to have been attained without the implications the judges have held they include. The rules

---

[64] (1992) 26 NSWLR 234, 260–261; even if construction contracts could not be categorised as a class of contract, Priestley J A was of the view that an implied obligation of reasonableness arose being a hybrid of fact and law: (1992) 26 NSWLR 234, 262–263.

[65] NSW legislation listed in Renard, which gave the courts power to reopen and sometimes rewrite unconscionable transactions, such as the *Moneylenders and Infants Loan Act 1905* (NWS), *Usury Bills of Lading and Written Memoranda Act 1902* (NSW), *Hire Purchase Act 1960* (NSW), *Industrial Arbitration Act 1959* (NSW) s 88F, *Contracts Review Act 1980* (NSW), *Credit Act 1984* (NSW).

[66] (1992) 26 NSWLR 234, 263.

[67] Ibid 263–264.

[68] Ibid 268.

[69] Ibid 261.

> in regard to each of them have come into existence not because in the particular cases giving rise to recognition of the implication it has been thought that it would be impossible for such contracts to be made and carried out without the implication, but because the court decided it would be better or more appropriate or more reasonable in accordance with the contemporary thinking of the judges and parties concerned with such contracts that the term should be implied than it should not. The idea is conveyed I think by Holmes' phrase, 'the felt necessity of time', where necessity has the sense of something required in accordance with current standards of what ought to be the case, rather than anything more absolute.[70]

Priestley JA's consideration of an implication by law for the specific class of contracts in the case would seem to dictate the scope of the implied duty of reasonableness or good faith.[71] As such, the suggestion is that any implication by law should be circumscribed to the class of contract described, where there are discretionary powers invested in one contracting party, and only in those types of clauses. If this is the correct interpretation of the decision, then the implied term by law approach prescribed would be very narrow.

Priestley JA also turned to the argument provided in *Gullett v Gardner*[72] when considering the discretionary powers of the contracting party as to whether or not the class of contract described was a proper one for the purposes of implication by law. Dixon J, in *Gullett v Gardner*, implied a term based on the intention of the parties by stating that the 'intention is to be derived from what they [the contracting parties] have said and done, and what each party to the contract had the right to expect, but it does not necessarily mean an enquiry into their actual mental state.'[73] In this regard, Priestley JA reasoned that if the contracting parties' mental state was not a consideration, then the court would be able to attach the implied obligation 'either implication by law rather than ad hoc, at least as a hybrid between the two.'[74] Respectfully, there might have been a misinterpretation of the High Court's ruling in *Gullett v Gardner*. Dixon J did not equate the absence of enquiry into the parties' mental state by ignoring their actual intentions. Instead, his Honour assessed the parties' intentions using objective evidence, rather than considering any subjective elements. Therefore, the implication in *Gullett v Gardner* was made in fact, not by law.

It can be seen from the above discussion that Priestley JA's judgement sat more comfortably with an implication in fact rather than an implication in law. The consideration of implication by law was less convincing and, within the context of *Renard Constructions*, its validity was restricted to a narrow ambit of the specific class of contract. The implication of reasonableness allowed the court to control the exercise of rights under the default clause on a basis that was objectively considered fair and reasonable. This notion of reasonableness was how Priestley JA regarded as being in common with good faith obligation.[75] Therefore, if an approach is to be drawn from

---

[70] Ibid 262.

[71] Ibid.

[72] (1948) 22 *Australian Law Journal* 151.

[73] Cf Ibid 155; also quoted by Priestley J A in (1992) 26 NSWLR 234, 263.

[74] (1992) 26 NSWLR 234, 263.

[75] Ibid.

Renard Constructions on the implied duty of good faith, it is that the implication of the duty ought to be considered as an implication in fact, based on the intention of the parties.

4.2.2.2 Handley and Meagher JJA's Judgement

Handley JA's judgement, likewise, implied a requirement of reasonableness in the exercise of the contractual power as a matter of construction,[76] even though Priestley JA did not think that the distinction between construction and implication was particularly important. Priestley JA observed that 'questions of construction and different kinds of implication tend to blur together.'[77] It has been contended, in this respect, that Priestley JA went beyond the mere construction of the contract to imply an obligation of reasonableness.[78]

Meagher JA, however, took a different view regarding the imposition of reasonableness on the principal's power, which can be used as a guide if the relevant matters are known, rather than a strict obligation.[79] According to Meagher JA, the concept of reasonableness has been interpreted as the balancing of the interests of the principal against those of the contractor, and for this reason, the principal should not be forced to have regard to any interests except its own.[80]

The three judges of the Court of Appeal were in disagreement regarding the implication of the 'additional' duty to act reasonably. However, they were unanimous in limiting the exercise of rights of the principal under the default clause. Meagher JA found for the contractor on the ground that the principal's decision was based upon the fundamental misunderstanding of relevant facts. The default clause provided that the action to take over the work could only be taken if the principal was not satisfied with the show cause by the contractor. This was unable to be satisfied through the principal's own fault because of prejudice and misinformation.[81] It is submitted that Meagher JA may have confused the contractual requirement for the termination (or the absence of satisfaction) with a test of satisfaction. Meagher reached this conclusion by imposing upon the principal an obligation that required more than mere honesty, namely that the dissatisfaction by the principal required an objective consideration of the factual background. Honest dissatisfaction would not have satisfied the objective test. Could it have been that Meagher JA was considering the test of necessity for the implication of the terms? A duty to act reasonably would not meet the necessity test unless Priestley's JA's reformulation of necessity is accepted.

---

[76] Ibid 280.

[77] Ibid 255.

[78] Francis Johns, 'Building Contracts—Good Faith—Quantum Meruit Claim' (1992) 5(3) *Journal of Contract Law* 269, 270.

[79] (1992) 26 NSWLR 234, 275; cf *Armstrong v Victoria (No 2)* (1957) 99 CLR 28, 88–89.

[80] (1992) 26 NSWLR 234, 275.

[81] Ibid 276.

Priestley and Handley JJA both concluded that the exercise of rights under the default clause was not absolute. The duty to act reasonably required the principal to objectively justify the exercise of the right in accordance with common standards prevailing in the industry. The test of satisfaction by the principal also required the imposition of an implied objective standard of conduct.

4.2.3 Rise of the Implied Duty Following Renard Constructions

According to Priestley JA in *Renard Constructions*, the notion of good faith is equated with the conception of reasonableness and the way it is imputed contractually is through implied term, either in fact (or ad hoc) or in law.[82] Therefore, the decision of *Renard Constructions* represents a radical new shift in the application of the good faith obligation that would elicit an imminent judicial response. The Court of Appeal decision of *Hughes Bros*[83] provided such an opportunity. This case was very similar to the facts in *Renard Constructions'* and affected another standard form construction contract. The dispute involved another set of arguments relating to an assertion of rights explicitly conferred by the contract, the principal being subject to an implied duty to act reasonably regarding a bankruptcy clause. The interesting point in this case was that in *Hughes Bros*, Kirby P sat with Meagher and Priestley JJA, where Meagher JA opposed the majority decision in *Renard Constructions*. This was notwithstanding Kirby P's previous assertions in defence of the freedom of commercial contractual relationships and emphasised the significance of commercial entities being able to set their own terms without undue influence.[84]

The disputed clause in *Renard Constructions* differed from that in dispute in *Hughes Bros* and would have allowed Kirby P to hold that *Renard Constructions* was restricted to the particular clause litigated. Instead, his Honour argued that it was his 'judicial duty' to follow *Renard Constructions*, thus reinforcing the legitimacy and applicability of *Renard Constructions*.[85] In short, *Hughes Bros* upheld *Renard Constructions* which, per se, is a decision on the extent to which the exercise of powers expressly conferred by contract can be tempered by the implication of a term requiring reasonableness. Following *Hughes Bros*, a number of decisions that

---

[82] Ibid 263–269.

[83] (1993) 31 NSWLR 91.

[84] *Austotel Pty Ltd v Franklins Selfserve Pty Ltd* (1989) 16 NSWLR 582, 586: Kirby P's famous admonition against judges substituting the world view generated by their overly tender consciences for the decisions made by hard-headed business people; see also *State Rail Authority of NSW v Heath Outdoor Pty Ltd* (1986) 7 NSWLR 170, 177; *Trawl Industries of Australia v Effem Foods Pty Ltd* (1992) 27 NSWLR 326, 332: it was noted that courts should be upholders and not destroyers of commercial bargains.

[85] (1993) 31 NSWLR 91, 93: Kirby P stated that he applied the doctrine only out of duty and that he felt bound to do so even if he disagreed with the doctrine.

have adopted a good faith position tended to trace their authority back to *Renard Constructions*—particularly one implied by law.

For example, in the case of *Hughes Aircraft Systems International v Airservices Australia* (*Hughes Aircraft*),[86] Hughes, the unsuccessful tenderer, in a two-party bid for a contract by the Civil Aviation Authority (CAA) claimed that the award made to Thompson Radar Australia Corporation Ltd (Thompson) was not conducted fairly and in accordance with defined procedures and criteria. Hughes argued that the CAA should have evaluated the bids fairly, ensuring equal opportunities to both Hughes and Thompson as it was contractually bound to do so.

Hughes' contention that this term formed part of the contract was sustained on three grounds. Firstly, the term was explicitly stated; secondly, it was implied ad hoc; and thirdly, it should be implied in law, either discretely or imputed as a general obligation of good faith and fair dealing.[87] Finn J rejected the express term argument but indicated the term should be implied ad hoc due to the 'overwhelming' duty in this case.[88] This should effectively make the discussion for the third proposition unnecessary. However, Finn J still deemed it appropriate on the submission that the proposed term was an implication in law of a general implied duty of good faith and fair dealing. His Honour observed:

> I should add that … I consider a virtue of the implied duty to be that it expresses in a generalisation of universal application, the standard of conduct to which all contracting parties are to be expected to adhere throughout the lives of their contracts.[89]

Finn J's remaining commentary focused on two primary themes, namely (1) a neo internationalist reasoning for embracing the obligation of good faith and (2) the fact that one of contracting parties was a government entity. He suggested that adopting a good faith approach from foreign jurisdictions could be beneficial for domestic contract law. With respect, this was fundamentally centred on a value judgement rather than on any systematically developed legal precedent. In the latter, Finn J observed that the CAA was a government instrumentality. This was of importance to his Honour's conclusion that the contract should be implied with the standards of good faith and fairness. Finn J recognised that the parties' status or purpose in contracting was relevant when considering whether a term would be implied as a direct result of a specific, definable category of contractual relationship.[90] While this case concerned a government agency, Finn J indicated that this principle could apply more broadly. In particular, those contracting in commercial relationships might reasonably expect parties to behave in a way that is consistent with an implied duty of good faith. This

---

[86] (1997) 146 ALR 1.

[87] Ibid 34.

[88] Ibid 35.

[89] Ibid 37.

[90] Ibid 40 (Finn J referred to *Scally v Southern Health and Social Services Board* [1992] 1 AC 294, 307).

suggests that the duty may also be presumed in relational contracts.[91] The judgement also suggested that Finn J implied a term of good faith, both in fact and law.

In addition to *Hughes Aircraft*, a number of cases continued to defer to *Renard Constructions* on the basis of precedent. One of these decisions was the Victorian case of *Far Horizons Pty Ltd v McDonald's Australia Ltd*.[92] This case involved a McDonald's franchise, where Byrne J stated that:

> As I indicated to counsel in argument, I do not see myself as at liberty to depart from the considerable body of authority in this country which has followed the decision of the New South Wales Court of Appeal in *Renard Constructions (ME) Pty Ltd v Minister for Public Works*. I proceed, therefore, on the basis that there is to be implied in a franchise agreement a term of good faith and fair dealing which obliges each party to exercise the powers conferred upon it by the agreement in good faith and reasonably, and not capriciously or for some extraneous purpose. Such a term is a legal incident of such a contract.[93]

The case of *Burger King Corporation v Hungry Jack's Pty Ltd* ('*Burger King*')[94] also followed this trend. In this case, the NSW Court of Appeal[95] stated that '[a] review of cases … indicates that courts in various Australian jurisdictions have, for the most part, proceeded upon an assumption that there may be implied, as a legal incident of a commercial contract, terms of good faith and reasonableness.'[96]

The *Burger King* case concerned a dispute over the termination of its development agreement with Hungry Jack. This agreement required Hungry Jack to open new restaurants annually. However, one clause stipulated that Burger King's approval was needed for new franchises.[97] Burger King refused to give the approval needed for Hungry Jack to comply with this requirement, which it was entitled to do under the agreement. As a result, two notices of default were served on Hungry Jack's, which was later followed by a notice of termination.

The NSW Court of Appeal accepted that it was necessary to imply a requirement of reasonableness and good faith into the restaurant development agreement between Burger King and Hungry Jack's so as to avoid Burger King, 'for the slightest of breaches, bringing to an end the very valuable rights which [Hungry Jack's] had under the Development Agreement.'[98]

Their Honours in *Burger King* concluded that while the obligation was not limited to standard form contracts, it would be more readily implied in such cases, particularly where the contract contained a general power of termination.[99] Common in the

---

[91] This issue is considered further in Chaps. 5 and 6; cf Dixon, 'Common Law Obligations of Good Faith in Australian Commercial Contracts,' above n 11.

[92] [2000] VSC 310.

[93] Ibid [120].

[94] [2001] NSWCA 187.

[95] Comprising of Sheller, Beazley and Stein JJA.

[96] [2001] NSWCA 187 [159].

[97] Ibid [55].

[98] Ibid [183].

[99] Ibid [163].

judicial understanding of the scope of good faith obligation is the recognition of its ability to curb unrestricted power.[100]

The decision in *Burger King* (at least in NSW) supports the existence of an implied term at law of a good faith obligation in commercial contracts.[101] Therefore, and consistent with *Renard Constructions*, *Burger King* demonstrated that such a term would be more readily applied where the contract in question provided broad powers of termination. The court assessed Burger King's behaviour against what an honest person would regard as fair dealing.[102] As such, the application of good faith extended beyond internal norms and considered external norms, thus resembling Brownsword's good faith regime.[103] Additionally, although the court framed its decision as a matter of law, the language of the decision suggested an implication based on fact.[104]

In the case of *Commonwealth Bank of Australia v Renstel Nominees Pty Ltd*,[105] an unsuccessful attempt was made to distinguish *Renard Constructions* in the implication of good faith as a matter of law. The issue was whether the Commonwealth Bank may be entitled to summarily cancel an overdraft facility that would require immediate repayment of the same by its customer (Renstel). Renstel argued that in exercising the discretion to cancel the overdraft, the bank was under an implied obligation of reasonableness and good faith. The Commonwealth Bank maintained that such an implication did not apply where the contract authorised the Bank to call up the overdraft upon demand. The Commonwealth Bank was unsuccessful in attempting to distinguish the nature of the right under an obligation of good faith, from the exercise of its discretion to terminate the overdraft facility.

Gzell J in *Commonwealth Bank of Australia v Spira*[106] ruled that a term of good faith was implied into a loan facility agreement by law. In *Hunter Business Finance v*

---

[100] Paterson, 'Good Faith in Commercial Contracts,' above n 34, 270: she argues that good faith should not be used to restrict the exercise of express rights; this was affirmed in Finkelstein J's judgement in *Garry Rogers Motors Aust Pty Ltd v Subaru (Aust) Pty Ltd* (1999) ATPR ¶41–703, 43–014.

[101] Although Burger King demonstrated the application of the obligation of good faith to commercial contracts, there is no reason to think that the decision will be so limited. The decision did not discuss the application of good faith in non-commercial contracts, but rather confirmed its application to commercial contracts.

[102] [2001] NSWCA 187 [189].

[103] Brownsword, 'Positive, Negative, Neutral: The Reception of Good Faith in English Contract Law' in Roger Brownsword, Norma J Hird and Geraint Howells (eds), *Good Faith in Contract: Concept and Context* (Dartmouth Pub Co, 1999) 15, 34: While industry norms may be recognised by the regime, they are not crucial to its understanding of good faith. Instead, the regime attempts to create particular markets and prescribed cooperative ground rules for the ways parties should act and, certainly, may extend beyond recognised industry standards.

[104] This was similarly noted by Gzell J in *Commonwealth Bank of Australia v Spira* [2002] NSWSC 905, and in later decisions such as *Vodafone Pacific Ltd v Mobile Innovations Ltd* [2004] NSWCA 15, [190]; *Oliver v Commonwealth Bank of Australia* [2011] FCA 1440, [30–34]; *Alstom Ltd v Yokogawa Australia Pty Ltd (No 7)* [2012] SASC 49.

[105] [2001] VSC 167.

[106] [2002] NSWSC 905.

Australian Business and Equipment Finance,[107] he similarly found the term implied into the terms of engagement of several finance brokers. His Honour ruled that the finance brokers breached their duty of good faith by taking and duplicating files from Hunter Business Finance for use in their new venture.[108] In *Biscayne Partners Pty Ltd v Vallance Corporation Pty Ltd*,[109] Einstein J ruled that Holly Vallance's management agreement included an implied term that she and her management company would act in good faith in exercising and performing their rights, powers, and obligations as outlined in the management agreement. The context of the contract involved a type of long term personal services agreement between a manager and an artist/performer (in this case, Holly Vallance). It was held that an implied term of such a contract that contained an exercise of a specific termination clause must be adhered to under a good faith obligation.

The evolution of the implication by law of the good faith obligation has, to an extent, proceeded into the territory of an application in all contracts as a legal incident. This signifies a shift from the prior stance on the implication of good faith obligation which was confined to specific types or classes of contract based on necessity or mutual understanding in certain contractual relationships. In *Garry Rogers Motors (Aust) Pty Ltd v Subaru (Aust) Pty Ltd*[110] ('*Garry Rogers*'), the court took this approach and was prepared to imply good faith obligation in a dealership agreement and, perhaps, in all commercial agreements. Finkelstein J, citing *Renard Constructions*, stated that 'recent cases make it clear that in appropriate contracts, perhaps even all commercial contracts, such a term will ordinarily be implied; not as an ad hoc term (based on the presumed intention of the parties) but as a legal incident of the relationship.'[111] Similarly, in *Overlook Management BV v Foxtel Management Pty Ltd*[112] ('*Overlook*'), a case concerning arrangements between Foxtel, a pay television provider, and one of its television content providers, Barrett J stated that '[a]n additional term implied by law into commercial contracts is a term requiring the exercise of good faith in the performance of the contract. This is now in this State [New South Wales] a legal incident of every such contract.'[113]

In the same case, Barret J held that the duty required an 'adherence to standards of conduct which are honest, as well as being reasonable having regard to the parties' interests.'[114]

> Viewed in this way, the implied obligation of good faith underwrites the spirit of the contract and supports the integrity of its character. A party is precluded from cynical resort to the black letter. … The duty is not a duty to prefer the interests of the other contracting party. It

---

[107] [2003] NSWSC 122.

[108] Ibid [73].

[109] [2003] NSWSC 874.

[110] (1999) ATPR 41–703.

[111] Ibid 43–014.

[112] [2002] NSWSC 17.

[113] Ibid [62].

[114] Ibid [64]; citing Sir Anthony Mason's formulation in: Mason, 'Contract, Good Faith and Equitable Standards,' above n 13, 69.

is, rather, a duty to recognise and to have due regard to the legitimate interests of both the parties in the enjoyment of the fruits of the contract as delineated by its terms.[115]

Notwithstanding, *Overlook* may be seen as a high water mark for the recognition of the implied obligation of good faith by law in Australia following the precedent set in *Renard Constructions*. In other state jurisdictions, the judicial sentiment expressed in *Overlook* has not been widely endorsed.[116]

The NSW Court of Appeal decision of *Vodafone Pacific Ltd v Mobile Innovations Ltd*[117] ('*Vodafone*') took a more cautious approach on the implied obligation of good faith. Giles JA, with Sheller and Ipp JJA concurring, concluded that the law does not yet recognise commercial contracts as a class inherently carrying an implied term of good faith. While affirming that courts could imply such a term, Giles JA rejected the idea of implying it into all commercial contracts due to the 'width and indeterminacy'[118] of such a class.[119] Giles JA was also less sure that the implication of the term must necessarily be one implied by law.[120]

In essence, the decision in *Vodafone* represents a turning point, amidst the vigorous and seemingly universal application of good faith obligations in all contracts. As a result, the language of the courts (even in NSW) when recognising the implied obligation of good faith, have now tended to be tempered with its inclusions as part of the contractual bargain and its expressed terms.[121] The manner in which good faith obligation is implied in Australia is not consistent and tends to vary between Australian state and federal jurisdictions, which can be seen in the following figure generally (Fig. 4.1).[122]

There is little doubt that the development of the implied obligation of good faith has been significant since the *Renard Constructions* decision. There is also generally good support, both judicially as evident above and also among legal academics, for good faith to exist as a principle of contract law in Australia.[123] The obligation is not,

---

[115] [2002] NSWSC 17 [67].

[116] E.g. *Varangian Pty Ltd v OFM Capital Ltd* [2003] VSC 444; *GEC Marconi Systems Pty Ltd v BHP Information Technology Pty Ltd* [2003] FCA 50; *Pacific Brands Sport & Leisure Pty Ltd v Underworks Pty Ltd* [2005] FCA 288; *Trans Petroleum (Australia) Pty Ltd v White Gum Petroleum Pty Ltd* [2012] WASCA 165, [152–154]; *Beerens v Bluescope Distribution Pty Ltd* [2012] VSCA, [57], [160].

[117] [2004] NSWCA 15.

[118] Ibid [204–206].

[119] Ibid [189].

[120] Ibid [191].

[121] E.g. in *Macquarie International Health Clinic Pty Ltd v Sydney South West Area Health Service* [2010] NSWCA 268, [12–15]; *Starlink International Group Pty Ltd v Coles Supermarket Australia Pty Ltd* [2011] NSWSC 1154; *Aquila Coal Pty Ltd v Bowen Central Coal Pty Ltd* [2011] QSC 264, [90], [93], [95], [105–107]; *Cordon Investments Pty Ltd v Lesdor Properties Pty Ltd* [2012] NSWCA 184, [144].

[122] Alicia Hill, 'Good Faith: Enforcement in Australia' (2013) 11(3) *International Journal of Franchising Law* 1, 13 http://www.mcw.com.au/Content/Attachment/Good%20faith%20-%20Enforcement%20in%20Australia.pdf .

[123] Carlin, 'The Rise (and Fall?),' above n 8, 122.

	Term implied in Law (following *Renard Constructions*' approach)	Term implied in fact or ad hoc
New South Wales	✓	
Victoria		✓
Queensland	✓	
South Australia	✓	
Western Australia	✓	
Tasmania		✓
Federal Court	✓	

Fig. 4.1 Implied term of good faith

however, without its critics. Much of the criticism has centred predominantly on the theoretical inconsistency of the judicial approach utilising implied term as the vehicle in the application of good faith. For example, Carlin refers to the development of implied terms for applying good faith obligation as 'tortured' where 'the hallmark [of good faith] … seems to have been misconstruction heaped upon misconstruction.'[124] Carter and Stewart[125] criticised the notion of equating good faith with an implied term of reasonableness, arguing that imposing an objective standard of reasonableness in this way risks changing agreements that was never intended and overshadowed other well-established legal principles. Peden also criticised the NSW Court of Appeal for failing to distinguish between good faith and objective reasonableness, and the finding that good faith is a term implied by law in all contracts.[126] Peden consistently maintained that such an implication of good faith is incompatible with Australian contract law.[127]

Judicial dissent has also emerged, albeit limited in numbers, where judges have disagreed with the approach taken in the leading cases. In the case of *GSA Group v Siebe plc*,[128] the court was critical of the imposition of an obligation of good faith being imposed on contracting parties 'who are quite able to look after their own interests … especially where all of the parties are wealthy, experienced, commercial entities.'[129] Such parties are thoroughly entitled to take an adversarial position to one another under the circumstance and, therefore, an imposition of good faith would be unnecessary or inappropriate.

[124] Ibid.

[125] Carter and Stewart, 'Interpretation,' above n 9.

[126] Elisabeth Peden, 'Incorporating Terms of Good Faith in Contract Law in Australia' (2001) *Sydney Law Review* 222; cf Carter and Peden, 'Good Faith in Australian Contract,' above n 3.

[127] Peden, 'Incorporating Terms of Good Faith,' above n 126; Peden, *Good Faith in the Performance of Contracts*, above n 39, 132.

[128] (1993) 30 NSWLR 573.

[129] Ibid 579.

In the Federal Court decision of *Service Station Association Ltd v Berg Bennett & Associates Pty Ltd*[130] ('*SSA*'), Gummow J found there was no authority binding the court to support an implication of an obligation of good faith:

> Anglo-Australian contract law as to the implication of terms has heretofore developed differently, with greater emphasis upon specifics, rather than the identification of a genus expressed in wide terms. Equity has intervened in matters of contractual formation by the remedy of rescission, upon the grounds mentioned earlier. It has restrained freedom of contract by inventing and protecting the equity of redemption, and by relieving against forfeitures and penalties. To some extent, equity has regulated the quality of contractual performance by the various defences available to suits for specific performance and for injunctive relief. In some, but not all, of this, notions of good conscience play a part. But it requires a leap of faith to translate these well-established doctrines and remedies into a new term as to the quality of contractual performance, implied by law.[131]

What Gummow J meant by 'a leap of faith' was that although his Honour recognised that good faith could be seen as informing a range of remedies and principles, it would be a stretch to translate these 'well-established doctrines and remedies' into a single doctrine of law.

The approach of Gummow J in *SSA* was followed by Heerey, Whitlam, and Weinberg JJ in *Wenzel and Rough v Australian Stock Exchange Ltd*,[132] where the Federal Court held that a term of good faith and fair dealing was not implied into admission agreements for the Australian Securities Exchange and expressed support for the view that there was no such generally applicable implied term under Australian law. Hansen J in *Playcorp Pty Ltd v Taiyo Kogyo Ltd*[133] also found that a requirement of good faith was not implied into a distribution agreement for the supply of toys. His Honour stated that:

> The term [sought to be implied] is of such width and uncertainty as, in the circumstances, to belie its implication as a matter of law. The present is a commercial contract between two independent parties providing for the international sale of goods. Each party is a substantial organisation well able to attend to its own interests. It is not a contract under which, relevantly, one party is to consider whether, and how, to exercise a power that will affect the ability of the other party to have the benefit of the contract, as, for instance, in *Renard Constructions*. ... And it is not a contract in which, relevantly to the present issue, there is a need to imply a term of good faith.[134]

4.2.3.1 Trend Towards Implication in Fact

Following the decision in *Vodafone*, a growing body of case law has started to emerge that demonstrates in their rationale and conclusion that implication in fact rather than by law is the better approach. It also seems to represent a pragmatic and useful method in dealing with an obligation of good faith.

---

130 (1993) 117 ALR 393.

131 Ibid 406–407.

132 [2002] FCAFC 400.

133 [2003] VSC 108.

134 Ibid [267].

The implied requirement of good faith was considered favourably in this manner by Buchanan JA in the Victoria Court of Appeal's decision of *Esso Australia Resources Pty Ltd v Southern Pacific Petroleum NL*[135] ('*Esso*') where his Honour appeared to accept that an obligation of good faith could be implied into some contracts. His Honour, however, expressed some reluctance 'to conclude that commercial contracts are a class of contracts carrying an implied term of good faith as a legal incident ... so that an obligation of good faith applies indiscriminately to all the rights and power conferred by a commercial contract.'[136] His Honour did recognise that it might 'be appropriate in a particular case to import such an obligation to protect a vulnerable party from exploitative conduct which subverts the original purpose for which the contract was made.'[137] In the particular case, his Honour did not need to consider whether such a term should be implied into the agreement under consideration and stated that, 'even if such an obligation was imposed ... it was not breached.'[138]

Warren CJ, who agreed with Buchanan JA, made further observations, while acknowledging that 'there has been clear recognition of the doctrine of good faith,'[139] pointed out that 'where commercial leviathans are contractually engaged, it is difficult to see that a duty of good faith will arise'[140] and 'courts have, more often than not, decided these matters on other bases and thereby avoided the conceptual difficulty ... of a duty of good faith.'[141] The court, similarly, made the observation that the duty of good faith was reserved for cases where it can 'protect a vulnerable party from exploitative conduct which subverts the original purpose for which the contract was made.'[142] Buchanan JA further added that 'implication in this fashion is perhaps ad hoc implication [or implied in fact] ... rather than implication as a matter of law.'[143] This decision seems to have struck a chord with judges wary of the implications of a universally applicable duty of good faith and fair dealing.[144]

The decision of *Council of the City of Sydney v Goldspar Australia Pty Ltd*[145] provided another good example of the implication of good faith in fact rather than by law. Gyles J, having considered the considerable array of authorities and academic

135 [2005] VSCA 228 (15 November 2005).

136 Ibid [25].

137 Ibid.

138 Ibid [27].

139 Ibid [2].

140 Ibid [4].

141 Ibid [2].

142 Ibid [25].

143 Ibid.

144 Examples of some of the cases that have adopted this position: *Australian Hotels Association (NSW) v TAB Ltd* [2006] NSWSC 293 (19 April 2006); *Meridian Retail Pty Ltd v Australian Unity Retail Network* [2006] VSC 223 (21 June 2006); *Maitland Main Collieries Pty Ltd v Xstrata Mt Owen Pty Ltd* [2006] NSWSC 1235 (23 November 2006); *Ingot Capital Investments v Macquarie Equity Capital Markets (No 6)* [2007] NSWSC 124 (30 March 2007); *Kellogg Brown & Root Pty Ltd v Australian Aerospace Ltd* [2007] VSC 200.

145 [2006] FCA 472.

views, decided to concentrate solely on the contractual provision in question. His Honour considered this in the context of the 'particular circumstances of the case' to determine whether a duty of good faith ought to be implied or not.[146] The approach suggests that his Honour took a contextual position in favour of implication in fact.

In the subsequent decision of *Australian Hotels Association (NSW) v TAB Ltd* ('*Australian Hotels*'),[147] Bergin J held that commercial contracts were not a class of contracts into which an obligation of good faith was implied by law. Her Honour referred to Buchanan JA and Warren CJ's judgement in *Esso*[148] in which she expressed reluctance to imply good faith where 'commercial leviathans' were involved: whether 'an obligation is implied ... will depend upon the terms of the particular contract, and the other matters to which it is permissible to have regard.'[149] The preference in this case is again leaning on an implication in fact.

The case of *Maitland Main Collieries Pty Ltd v Xstrata Mt Owen Pty Ltd* ('*Maitland*') points to a similar preference.[150] This case involved the construction of a rail link between Xstrata's Mt Owen mine to the main railway line, which crossed an area that could result in subsidence from underground mining proposed by Maitland. Maitland sought certain guarantees from Xstrata to alleviate these concerns, which culminated in the parties signing a deed. The deed was imprudently brief in its content and disputes inevitably arose on its meaning before long. This led, as a consequence, to Maitland seeking a declaration that the deed contained an implied term requiring Xstrata to 'act reasonably and in good faith in the performance of its obligations' and that they have breached this implied term.

Bergin J followed her own decision in *Australian Hotels*. Her Honour explained that the presence or absence of a duty to act reasonably and in good faith 'will depend on the nature of the obligations in the contract. ... Commercial contracts are not a class of contracts that have an implied obligation of good faith.'[151] She further stated that the duty may be justifiably implied as a matter of construction, in the light of the contracting parties' intention. Bergin J declined to acknowledge the duty of good faith as a broad duty at large, beyond the scope of the specific contractual clauses.

Maitland demonstrated the suitability of approaching the obligation of good faith by implication in fact. Her Honour has been sensitive to the contracting party intentions, which resulted in a more practical and commercially realistic outcome. This is an approach that has been seen in a number of cases in recent years when construing good faith obligations in contractual enforcements.[152]

---

[146] Ibid [168].

[147] [2006] NSWSC 293.

[148] Ibid [75].

[149] Ibid [77–78], [80].

[150] [2006] NSWSC 1235.

[151] Ibid [56].

[152] *Insight Oceania Pty Ltd v Philips Electronics Australia Ltd* [2008] NSWSC 710; *Starlink International Group Pty Ltd v Coles Supermarket Australia Pty Ltd* [2011] NSWSC 1154; *Aquila Coal Pty Ltd v Bowen Central Coal Pty Ltd* [2011] QSC 264, [95]; *Oliver v Commonwealth Bank of*

4.2.3.2 Problems with the Implied Term Approach

It has been asserted that if good faith obligations were to be recognised as a universal term expressing 'the standard of which all contracting parties are to be expected to adhere throughout the lives of their contracts,'[153] then its ability to contract out of an obligation of good faith should be limited or precluded.[154] Unfortunately, implied terms under existing law does not extend to accommodate this. Parties can exclude terms implied by law through an express provision in their contract.[155] The *BP Refinery* criterion would not be satisfied.

Further, if the duty of good faith is solely treated as an implied contractual term, its scope would be significantly restricted. It is entirely possible that the duty may also apply to pre-contractual negotiations under this obligation. This issue is considered further below under Part IV.

(a) Issues with the Term Implied in Law

Leaving aside terms that are implied by statute, the usual way in which terms are implied in law are those that are implied as an incident of a particular class of contracts.[156] This would not support the view that good faith obligation can function as a doctrine applicable in all contracts. Good faith obligation implied in law also expresses a presumption of intention irrespective of the contractual context simply because the contract falls within the relevant class.

The High Court, however, has approved a test where the implication of a particular term must be necessary to prevent the enjoyment of rights conferred under the contract from being 'rendered nugatory, worthless or, perhaps, [being] seriously undermined.'[157] The new term must be essential or necessary for the reasonable

Australia [2011] FCA 1440; *Trans Petroleum (Australia) Pty Ltd v White Gum Petroleum Pty Ltd* [2012] WASCA 165, [152, 154]; *Beerens v Bluescope Distribution Pty Ltd* [2012] VSCA 209.

[153] E.g. in *Hughes Aircraft Systems International v Airservices Australia* (1997) 76 FCR 151, 193 (Finn J); see also *Garry Rogers Motors (Aust) Pty Ltd v Subaru (Aust) Pty Ltd* [1999] FCA 903; *Alcatel Australia Ltd v Scarcella* (1998) 44 NSWLR 349, 366. The courts have subsequently distanced themselves from such statements: *CGU Workers Compensation (NSW) Ltd v Carlos Garcia* (2007) 69 NSWLR 680, 704–705; *Australian Hotels Association (NSW) v TAB Ltd* [2006] NSWSC 293 [78]; *Insight Oceania Pty Ltd v Philips Electronics Australia Ltd* [2008] NSWSC 710.

[154] This also supports the argument that good faith is inherent in all common law principles: Carter and Peden, 'Good Faith in Australian Contract,' above n 3; Peden, 'Implicit Good Faith,' above n 8. See also Jeannie M Paterson, 'Implied Fetters on the Exercise of Discretionary Contractual Powers' (2009) 35(1) *Monash University Law Review* 45, 67.

[155] Willmott, Christensen and Butler, *Contract Law*, above n 15, [8.720]; *Commonwealth Bank of Australia v Spiral* (2002) 174 FLR 274, [146]; Bill Dixon, 'Common Law Obligations of Good Faith in the Performance and Enforcement of Joint Ventures of a Non-Fiduciary Nature' in William D Duncan (ed), *Joint Ventures Law in Australia* (The Federation Press, 3rd ed, 2012) 131–132.

[156] Paul Finn, 'Good Faith and Fair Dealing: Australia' (2005) 11 *New Zealand Business Law Quarterly* 378, 383.

[157] *Byrne v Australian Airlines Ltd* (1995) 185 CLR 410, 450 (per McHugh and Gummow JJ).

performance of the contract and also relevant to the specific type of contract.[158] Once implied in law, it applies to that category or class of contract.

Meeting the necessity test can be challenging in a detailed commercial contract involving experienced contracting parties. This was evident in *Burger King* where it was contended that two terms, framed within the notion of good faith and reasonableness should be implied in law.[159] Despite the court acknowledging that there was no pertinent category of contract to imply these terms, they were still implied notwithstanding.[160] This highlights the law's desire for a uniform, universal set of terms which would be perfectly assumed in all contracts, as well as implying certain terms only to specific classes of contract.[161] Interestingly, one contract law textbook dedicated a whole subsection under implied terms to universal terms.[162] Both the duty to cooperate and the duty of good faith have been favoured among some scholars as highly desirable contenders for a universal implication at law.[163] Acceptance of the notion of a universal implied term of good faith is not widely accepted following the *Vodafone* case. Giles JA rejected the contention that commercial contracts were a class of contracts capable of justifying a term of good faith implied in law.[164] Perhaps the broad and indeterminate nature of commercial contracts discouraged Giles JA and others in the judiciary from setting this down as legal precedent.

(b) Issues with the Term Implied in Fact

A major issue with the term implied in fact is that a duty of good faith would not apply universally. Introducing the good faith obligation this way would fail to meet the *BP Refinery* criterion in most instances, as previously mentioned. Peden highlighted the uncertainty in definitioning and applying the tests of business efficacy and obviousness as outlined by *BP Refinery*.[165] In *Renard Constructions*, Priestley JA acknowledged the challenges of applying a good faith obligation as a term implied in fact or ad hoc. Are contracting parties obligated by good faith as a necessity to ensure business efficacy to the contract, or is it so obvious that it goes without saying,[166] given that the contract may still function even if the parties fulfil their obligations and act in their own interests?[167] Peden is right in that the tests are notoriously flexible

[158] Cf *Breen v Williams* (1996) 186 CLR 71.

[159] The court also implied, in addition, the standardised term of cooperation: [2001] NSWCA 187, [183].

[160] [2001] NSWCA 187, [183].

[161] See Michael Bryan and Manfred P Ellinghaus, 'Fault Lines in the Law of Obligations: *Roxborough v Rothmans of Paul Mall Australia Ltd*' (2000) 22 *Sydney Law Review* 636, 651.

[162] Nicholas C Seddon and Manfred P Ellinghaus, *Cheshire and Fifoot's Law of Contract* (LexisNexis Butterworths, 9th Australian ed, 2008) 442–460.

[163] Bryan and Ellinghaus, above n 161.

[164] *Vodafone Pacific Ltd v Mobile Innovations Ltd* [2004] NSWCA 15, [191].

[165] Peden, 'Incorporating Terms of Good Faith,' above n 126, 230.

[166] (1992) 26 NSWLR 234, 256.

[167] Ibid 258.

and, at worst, may conceal policy judgements in which the court can select as to whether a term of good faith ought to be implied.[168]

Be that as it may, as a general principle of contract law, the tests for implication in fact have always been unduly flexible, not just in relation to good faith obligation. In this sense, implication is just as acceptable in this context as it is in any other. The main advantage that implication in fact has over implication in law is that it focuses judicial attention in the right areas, that is, the facts of the case, the contractual provisions and the intentions of the contracting parties. This provides relevant context in which to define good faith and as such provides a stable basis within contract law to develop a good faith obligation. In regards to the relevance of the tests, judicial authority will eventually determine that.

Australian courts typically hold the view that the majority of contracts can function without the requirement of good faith obligation. In *Saxby Bridge Mortgages Pty Ltd v Saxby Bridge Pty Ltd*, Simos J rejected the implication of a term of good faith to incorporate a new company, citing the lack of necessity and obviousness in the contract.[169] In his *obiter dictum*, he observed that the likelihood of implying good faith is reduced when a contract is thorough or comprehensive.[170] For example, in *Chan v Ng*, a term of good faith was not implied in a land sale agreement because the contract was purely transactional, with no basis for such an obligation.[171] Had the contract been relational, an implication may have been found to flow from the agreement. According to Associate Judge Doogue, the criteria set out in *BP Refinery* would not likely have been satisfied, except perhaps the fifth criterion.

Arguably, it is intrinsic to a term of good faith that it cannot be expressed clearly and, as such, an undefined term would struggle to meet the *BP Refinery* criterion requiring specific formulation of terms.[172] Substantiating this argument, Tipping J in *Dovey v Bank of New Zealand* posited that, in order to satisfy the *BP Refinery* test, a term must be both capable of clear expression and be uncontroversial.[173] In *Hungry Jack's Pty Ltd v Burger King Corporation*,[174] Rolfe J interrogated whether a term of reasonableness could be implied into the contract. However, determining the meaning and context of reasonableness relies on judicial assessment, which may not align with the contracting parties' views. Therefore, Rolfe J held that it was difficult, if not impossible, to clearly express reasonableness where implied terms

---

168 Peden, *Good Faith in the Performance of Contracts*, above n 39, 72–91.

169 [2000] NSWSC 433, [62–64].

170 See *Codelfa Construction Pty Ltd v State Rail Authority of New South Wales* (1982) 149 CLR 337.

171 (High Court, Auckland, CIV 2007-404-6226, 28 March 2008), [34], [37], [41]; see also *Walton Mountain Ltd v Apple New Zealand Ltd* (2004) 5 NZCPR 241.

172 *CGU Workers Compensation (NSW) Ltd v Carlos Garcia* (2007) 69 NSWLR 680, 706; [2007] NSWCA 193, [143] (per Mason P, with whom Hodgson and Santow JJA agreed): failure to satisfy the business efficacy requirement is relevant basis for rejecting the implied duty of good faith in statutory contract.

173 [2000] 3 NZLR 641, 654.

174 [1999] NSWSC 1029.

are concerned.[175] If courts hesitate to recognise reasonableness in this context, it is likely that good faith will receive similar treatment, given it is less acquainted with the common law. Accordingly, incorporating an obligation of good faith through an implied term in fact would go against established rules of implication.[176]

The *Renard Constructions* decision did not resolve the issue concerning the legal approach to be followed when imposing good faith that incorporates reasonableness in the exercise of contractual rights. The different approaches taken by the three judges in the *Renard Constructions* case have been considered in subsequent cases without settling the debate. In some cases, the court has applied the construction of contract approach; whereas others have followed the implied term position, either in fact or in law.[177] In dealing with the issue, the courts have also indistinguishably used the terms reasonableness, good faith, and fair dealing.

Peden is, perhaps, the most prominent opponent of the introduction of a good faith obligation through implied terms. She concludes:

> No terms are implied into all contracts. If the courts want the notion of good faith to apply in all situations, what they should be looking to do is use good faith as a principle or tool of construction. That is, to construe all contracts on the basis that there is an expectancy of good faith in all terms. ... Unlike terms implied in fact or law, which apply specifically to a contract or class of contracts, rules of construction apply generally to all contracts.[178]

Peden's views align with those who advocate that the good faith obligation should serve a broader purpose beyond treating it as a mere implied term. Good faith could be used, instead, as a conceptual basis for interpreting and constructing contracts.[179] It is, therefore, appropriate to examine, in the subsequent section, what has been labelled the 'constructivist' approach.[180]

4.3 Good Faith as a Rule of Contractual Construction

The proposition has been put forth that the duty of good faith in contracts cannot be established by the common law courts unless it is incorporated as an implied term. In *GEC Marconi Systems Pty Ltd v BHP Information Technology Pty Ltd*, Finn J opined:

> There is not yet agreement in this country as to the province of good faith in contract law. ... Part of our difficulty arises from the fact that, express or implied term apart, we have no other available common law device for imposing obligations on parties that are contractual

---

[175] Ibid [432].

[176] See generally Peden, 'Incorporating Terms of Good Faith,' above n 126.

[177] Peden, *Good Faith in the Performance of Contracts*, above n 39, 14.

[178] Peden, 'Incorporating Terms of Good Faith,' above n 126, 230.

[179] Edward Thomas, 'Good Faith in Contract: A Non-Sceptical Commentary' (2005) 11 *New Zealand Business Law Quarterly* 391, 394.

[180] Paula Baron, 'Resistance: A Consideration of the Opposition to a Duty of Good Faith in Australian Commercial Contracts' (2005) 11 *New Zealand Business Law Quarterly* 408, 424.

in character. We do not have the facility, for example, to treat the duty as simply a mandatory rule of contract law as do many European legal systems.[181]

Finn J's rationale is reductive. As some scholars argue, common law courts are in fact able to introduce an obligation of good faith into contract law without imposing a strict proposition on how terms are to be implied. Conventional judicial procedure could accommodate good faith as a general principle applicable to all contracts[182] by adopting it as a rule of construction.[183]

Existing, well-established rules of construction within contract law may provide guidance to execute this broader principle. For instance, words are generally given their ordinary meaning[184]; the contract is construed as a whole[185]; courts will avoid unreasonable interpretations that defy commercial common sense[186]; and the matrix of the contractual facts will be considered by the court to realise an appropriate applicable construction.[187] Importantly, the rules of construction extend beyond interpreting words that rest in a written agreement. They also help to determine the parties' intentions, to contextualise contracts, and even to rescue incomplete contracts.[188]

---

[181] Federal Court of Australia, NG 733 of 1997, 12 February 2003 [920].

[182] Thomas, 'Good Faith in Contract: A Non-Sceptical Commentary,' above n 179, 395.

[183] Peden, 'Incorporating Terms of Good Faith,' above n 126, 224.

[184] *Investors Compensation Scheme Ltd v West Bromwich Building Society* [1998] 1 All ER 98, 115 (per Lord Hoffmann); *Benjamin Developments Ltd v Robert Jones (Pacific) Ltd* [1994] 3 NZLR 189; *Yoshimoto v Canterbury Golf International Ltd* [2001] 1 NZLR 523; *Mount Joy Farms Ltd v Kiwi South Island Co-operative Dairies Ltd* (Court of Appeal, CA 297/00, 6 December 2001); *Mannai Investment Co Ltd v Eagle Star Life Assurance Co Ltd* [1997] 3 All ER 352; *Codelfa Construction Pty Ltd v State Rail Authority of New South Wales* (1982) 149 CLR 337, 352; *Maggbury Pty Ltd v Hafele Australia Pty Ltd* (2001) 210 CLR 181, 185, 188; *Zurich Insurance (Singapore) Pte Ltd v B-Gold Interior Design & Construction Pte Ltd* [2008] 3 SLR(R) 1029, 1063; *Jireh International Pty Ltd t/a Gloria Jean's Coffee v Western Exports Services Inc* [2011] NSWCA 137; see David McLauchlan and Matthew Lees, 'Construction Controversy' (2011) 28 *Journal of Contract Law* 101.

[185] *Inglis v John Buttery & Co* (1878) 3 App Cas 552, 577; *Shore v Wilson* (1842) 8 ER 450, 529; *SGS (NZ) Ltd v Quirke Export Ltd* [1988] 1 NZLR 52, 58 (per Somers J); *Chartbrook Ltd v Persimmon Homes Ltd* [2009] 1 AC 1101, 1119–1120; *Byrnes v Kendle* (2011) 243 CLR 253, 285; *Westfield Management Ltd v AMP Capital Property Nominees Ltd* (2012) 293 ALR 241, 250; John W Carter, *The Constructions of Commercial Contracts* (Hart Publishing, 2013) § 633; John W Carter, 'Context and Literalism in Construction' (2014) 31(1) *Journal of Contract Law* 100.

[186] *The Antaios* [1984] 3 All ER 229, 233 (per Lord Diplock); *The Fina Samco* [1995] 2 Lloyd's Rep 344, 350 (per Neill L J).

[187] *Prenn v Simmonds* [1971] 1 WLR 1381, 1384; *L Schuler AG v Wickman Machine Tool Sales Ltd* [1974] AC 235; *Boat Park Ltd v Hutchinson* [1999] 2 NZLR 74; *Pyne Gould Guinness Ltd v Montgomery Watson (NZ) Ltd* [2001] NZAR 789.

[188] *Mackay v Dick* (1881) 6 App Cas 251, 263; *Hart v MacDonald* (1910) 10 CLR 417; *Trollope & Colls Ltd v North West Metropolitan Regional Hospital Board* [1973] 1 WLR 601, 609; *Hughes Bros Pty Ltd v Trustees of the Roman Catholic Church for the Archdiocese of Sydney* (1993) 31 NSWLR 91, 104 (per Meagher JA); *Presmist Pty Ltd v Turner Corporation Pty Ltd* (1992) 30 NSWLR 478, 484 (per Cole J); *Equitable Life Assurance Society v Hyman* [2002] 1 AC 408, 459; *Attorney General of Belize v Belize Telecom Ltd* [2009] 1 WLR 1998, 1994; Peden, 'Incorporating Terms of Good Faith,' above n 126; Peden, *Good Faith in the Performance of Contracts*, above n

Introducing a rule of law through construction is not unprecedented, nor is it against the custom of the judiciary. Indeed, it has been seen before where the doctrine of frustration evolved from being based on an implied term to what is now viewed as a matter of construction.[189] As Lord Reid emphasised in *Davis Contractors Ltd v Fareham Urban District Council*, frustration should not be dependent on the addition of an implied term, but rather it rests on a true construction of the contract.[190] In making an assessment of whether a contract is frustrated, principles of construction should be examined by the court, including how terms are formulated, the nature of the contract, and the surrounding circumstances in which the contract was made.

Frustration has evolved from an implied term to an independent common law rule, suggesting that good faith could follow a similar trajectory.[191] Other examples supporting good faith as a general contract principle include the requirement for reasonable time for performance and the doctrine of repudiation.[192]

Should the courts take on the constructivist approach with regard to the obligation of good faith, it is expected that good faith would become a term of the contract where a positive obligation demanding affirmative action is created.[193] Therefore, it is possible that the constructivist approach will encompass the implied term methodology. However, it should be noted that Giles JA criticised this view in *Vodafone*,[194] suggesting that construction merely places a gloss on an express term and cannot create standalone obligations which are not already found among the existing contractual terms. These concerns may be overstated, as implying a term in fact constitutes a form of constrution in itself.[195]

Sir Anthony Mason, who wrote the forward in Peden's book, made a comment about Peden's method in distinguishing construction from implied terms: 'it is this elusive distinction that underlies [Peden's] approach. Whether the distinction is as sharp as the author contends may be open to question.'[196]

In fairness, Peden recognises that 'the inference of the parties' intentions involved in construction and implication in fact are the same,' and with the construction method, 'the courts would merely be moving away from the use of the tests of implication that has been shown to be lacking.'[197] If the tests hold value in implication in fact to ascertain the contracting parties' intention, the construction method would equally have to devise a substitute methodology to discover and implement the

39, 24; Wayne Courtney and John W Carter, 'Implied Terms: What is the Role of Construction?' (2014) 31 *Journal of Contract Law* 151.

189 Thomas, 'Good Faith in Contract: A Non-Sceptical Commentary,' above n 179, 395.

190 [1956] 2 All ER 145, 153.

191 Gordon, above n 42, 40.

192 Thomas, 'Good Faith in Contract: A Non-Sceptical Commentary,' above n 179, 395.

193 Peden, 'Incorporating Terms of Good Faith,' above n 126, 232.

194 [2004] NSWCA 15, [206].

195 *Codelfa Construction Pty Ltd v State Rail Authority of New South Wales* (1982) 41 ALR 367, 376 (per Mason J).

196 Peden, *Good Faith in the Performance of Contracts*, above n 39, v.

197 Ibid 141.

parties' intention. Peden's analysis concedes that even in the construction approach, tests of some nature may be necessary to constrain contractual uncertainty. In this regard, Peden suggested the very tests used in implication in fact: 'to the extent that the "business efficacy" and "obviousness" tests help courts discover and implement the parties' intentions, there is no reason why they cannot be retained as tests of construction.'[198] Therefore, is the distinction between implication in fact and the constructivist approach merely a false dichotomy? Peden, in her conclusion, states that 'implication in fact is a rule of construction' and 'the tests of "business efficacy" and "obviousness" are guides to determining the intentions of the parties.'[199] This suggests that the construction approach is basically a form of implication in fact, which allows the contractual content to operate in context.[200]

Any sustainable doctrine of law should arise from existing legal principles, just as Peden has shown in the case of frustration and anticipatory breach.[201] It is the contention of this book that a good faith obligation can evolve from implication in fact to a constructivist approach to become an integral, independent rule of the common law as a function of the imputed intention of the parties.

If, under an obligation of good faith, a contract is required to include a standalone provision which expressly provides for the duty of good faith, it follows that a term should be incorporated into the contract as a natural consequence of that construction in any case. Peden underscores this reasoning as rational:

> Construction, in the interpretation sense, most simply provides the meaning of words. If taken even further, construction can be used to imply terms. This is 'implication by construction', and it is suggested that all these processes are informed by the general principle of good faith. … [T]he principle of good faith can be applied in construction that results in implying a new term. There is no need to imply in fact or in law a term that the parties should cooperate or act in good faith.[202]

Bergin J in *Maitland* flagged the duty of good faith as one that may be justified by construction. Before commenting on Bergin J's judgement, the decision of Pagone J in *Network Ltd v Speck*[203] ('*Network*') should be considered for comparison. In *Network*, the contracting parties agreed to enter a business arrangement framed under a Memorandum of Understanding (MOU), which was subject to an undertaking of final due diligence by the plaintiff. A deposit was subsequently paid, subject to the due diligence undertaking, and the MOU provided specific circumstances in relation to the expiry and termination of the agreement, when the defendant was obliged to repay

198 Ibid 147.

199 Ibid 152.

200 Ibid 141; cf *Codelfa Construction Pty Ltd v State Rail Authority of NSW* (1982) 149 CLR 337, 353 (per Mason J).

201 Peden, *Good Faith in the Performance of Contracts*, above n 39, 19–24.

202 Ibid 113–114, 140 (Peden goes on to suggest that 'the only situation when "good faith" needs to be implied as an actual term is when it is going to be used as a positive obligation requiring some positive action, independent of any terms.' In all other cases 'contractual rights would be construed to require them to be exercised in good faith').

203 [2009] VSC 235.

the deposit to the plaintiff. A further provision permitted the plaintiff to terminate the agreement only after providing notice that a material adverse circumstance (as defined under the MOU) had been discovered in the due diligence process.

When the plaintiff gave notice of the material adverse circumstance, the defendant contended that notice was ineffective as it was not given in good faith, but for the collateral purpose of either obtaining further indulgence or to re-negotiate the terms of the agreement that had been agreed to in the MOU. The plaintiff argued that the contractual provision expressly conferred on the plaintiff the power to determine the material adverse effect circumstance, and this was wholly for the plaintiff's benefit and capable of being exercised without qualification. This would essentially exclude the implication of good faith in the manner contended by the defendant.

Pagone J held that a construction of the MOU gave 'no weight to the careful balancing of rights and obligations between the parties ... that permitted a notice to be given.'[204] As the definition of 'material adverse effect' required the plaintiff to act reasonably, his Honour contended that the plaintiff's action be subjected to a standard of reasonableness and that this would include good faith in the wider sense.[205] The implication of good faith in this case, according to Pagone J, arose from the language of the contractual provision.[206] Citing Finkelstein J in *Garry Rogers*, his Honour held that an express obligation of reasonableness included good faith obligations of loyalty to the agreement, a duty not to act capriciously, and reasonableness in the promotion of legitimate interest.[207] These obligations arose by virtue of the express obligation to act reasonably, which in this case expanded to incorporate the wider good faith obligations.

This approach mirrors that of Bergin J in *Maitland*. Even though her Honour concluded that commercial contracts do not inherently attract an obligation of good faith, each clause of the Deed is examined individually as a matter of construction. This aligns with how Pagone J weighed the competing rights and obligations of the parties involved in *Network*. Consequently, in both *Maitland* and *Network*, it seems that the express term of the contract forms the foundation for implying the good faith obligation.

Therefore, there is room for the constructivist approach to afford the creation of a freestanding obligation of good faith when circumstances call for it. However, this does not warrant the universal application of a good faith obligation to all contracts. Some contracts do not require a separate term of good faith.

The constructivist approach would allow for a general application to be achieved by interpreting express terms in the light of the good faith obligations.[208] For instance,

---

[204] Ibid [17].

[205] Ibid [19].

[206] Ibid [21].

[207] Ibid.

[208] This is the methodology under which the doctrine of good faith predominantly operates in the US. It has been observed that 'courts generally utilise the good faith duty as an interpretive tool to determine "the parties"' justifiable expectations': *Duquesne Light Co v Westinghouse Electric Co*, 66 F3d 604, 617 (per Greenberg J) (US App, 1995).

the exercise of contractual powers could necessitate their execution in good faith, thereby preventing the undermining of positive obligations in the contract.[209] This approach aligns with the mutual intentions of the parties and integrates the good faith obligation within its contractual matters. A key benefit of this approach is its flexibility: good faith can be utilised as an independent obligation on a case-by-case basis or as a universally applicable approach when construing express terms.

However, this approach faces similar criticisms as the implied term methodology discussed above, such as the potential avoidance of the duty through express agreement. Similarly again, pre-contractual conduct is not likely to be influenced by a rule of construction.

The constructivist approach primarily applies to written contracts, precluding its effect on contracts containing an oral component. This limitation suggests the implied term methodology would be more effective for oral and partly oral contracts.

Critics contend that the constructivist approach unrealistically infers the intentions of the contracting parties. Giles JA indicated that making an implication of good faith in a contract suggests that the obligation is imposed by law, rather than construction which presumes the parties' intentions through a process of construction.[210] This is problematic because there is not always a manifest intention of good faith evident in the construction of a contract and, in applying the good faith obligation generally, the courts would then be required to interpret a contract to establish an obligation for the parties to act in good faith where there is no such intention between the parties. In this situation, it is arguable that courts would engage in a form of judicial activism by inserting a doctrine into a contractual relationship that never wanted to be bound by such an obligation. For example, if commercial parties intend an express right to be exercised at the parties' discretion,[211] the implication approach is better suited as it highlights that the common law deems good faith necessary, regardless of the contracting parties' explicit intentions.[212]

Despite these valid criticisms, one cannot disregard the fact that the courts' objective in construing any contract is to determine the parties' mutual intentions at the time of contracting.[213] In making this determination, it must be stressed that the court can still find that good faith obligations were intended to form part of the contract when the parties cannot produce evidence of their intention to exclude this obligation from their contract.

In *First Energy (UK) Ltd v Hungarian International Bank Ltd*, Steyn LJ highlighted that good faith reflects the 'reasonable expectations of honest' people, a theme pervasive in contract law.[214] One main facet of good faith is to uphold the

---

[209] Peden, 'Incorporating Terms of Good Faith,' above n 126, 232.

[210] [2004] NSWCA 15, [206].

[211] Kuehne, 'Implied Obligations of Good Faith,' above n 11, 96.

[212] Ibid.

[213] *River Wear Commissioners v Adamson* (1877) 2 App Cas 743; *Pioneer Shipping Ltd v BTP Tioxide Ltd, The Nema* [1981] 2 All ER 1030, 1035 (per Lord Diplock).

[214] [1993] 2 Lloyd's Rep 194, 196 (Nourse and Evans LJJ also agreeing); Waddams, 'Good Faith, Unconscionability and Reasonable Expectations,' above n 3; Steyn, 'Contract Law: Fulfilling the

parties' agreement and ensure contracts are interpreted commercially. This is linked with contractual fidelity and give effect to the contracting parties' intentions.[215] Notwithstanding, the courts still maintain a responsibility to ensure that the contract is construed in a commercially sensible way. This takes into account what is deemed commercially sensible within the context of the contractual instrument itself.[216] It allows for greater coherence in resolving one-off contractual disputes than the current approach in applying good faith using implied terms. There also seems to be a preference in decisions of the High Court for commercially sensible results.[217]

In this respect, the role of construction facilitates and determines the specific contract's scope and application. These matters are resolved using the 'perspective rule.'[218] This rule enables the interpretation of the contractual provisions to reflect what a reasonable person in the contracting parties' position would understand it within the context of the contractual instrument.[219]

Nevertheless, contracting parties may only deviate from *ex lege* principles, from which a significant part of contract law is derived, if they can prove there was an intention present at the time of contracting that is contrary to these longstanding principles.[220] This way, the autonomy of the parties is not compromised.[221]

While the obligation of good faith has no clear place within either of the two implied term categories already existing at law, the constructivist approach allows for general application and, further, it would not impact on the existing law relating to implied terms. Therefore, on balance, it is evident that if an obligation of good faith should be implemented, the constructivist approach is the better route to take, rather than recognising it as an implication.

This is not to say that the constructivist approach does not have certain drawbacks. However, the limitations of this approach pale in comparison with the implied term approach as the latter is likely to have a cascading effect on other areas of contract law. It is clear that if good faith is to become a standalone obligation in Australian contract law, it should be clearly expressed as a matter of principle.

Reasonable Expectations,' above n 3; Steven J Burton, 'Breach of Contract and the Common Law Duty to Perform in Good Faith' (1980) 94 *Harvard Law Review* 369, 371.

[215] Carter, *The Constructions of Commercial Contracts*, above n 185, §3–37.

[216] Ibid ch 1.

[217] E.g. *Ringstad v Gollin & Co Pty Ltd* (1924) 35 CLR 303, 316 (per Starke J); *J Kitchen & Sons Pty Ltd v Stewart's Cash & Carry Stores* (1942) 66 CLR 116, 124–125 (per Latham CJ and McTiernan J); *Gollin & Co Ltd v Karenlee Nominees Pty Ltd* (1983) 153 CLR 455, 464; *Concut Pty Ltd v Worrell* (2000) 176 ALR 693, 708–709; *International Air Transport Association v Ansett Australia Holdings Ltd* [2008] HCA 3, [8] (per Gleeson CJ).

[218] Carter, *The Constructions of Commercial Contracts*, above n 185, §4–22.

[219] See *Toll (FGCT) Pty Ltd v Alphapharm Pty Ltd* (2004) 219 CLR 165, 179; cf *Attorney General of Belize v Belize Telecom Ltd* [2009] 1 WLR 1988, 1994 (per Lord Hoffmann); Courtney and Carter, above n 188.

[220] Jack Beatson and Daniel Friedman, 'From Classical to Modern Contract Law' in Jack Beatson and Daniel Friedman (eds), *Good Faith and Fault in Contract Law* (Oxford University Press, 2001) 16.

[221] Brownsword, 'Positive, Negative, Neutral,' above n 103, 37.

In particular, further consideration is required to ascertain how pre-contractual negotiations—and the respective rights of the parties during pre-contractual negotiations—would be impacted by an obligation or principle of good faith. The consequences of the suggested good faith obligation are even more vague where no contract comes into existence during pre-contractual negotiations. These uncertainties will be explored in the next section.

4.4 Good Faith and Pre-contractual Negotiations

Sir Anthony Mason has argued for the inclusion of good faith at the negotiating stage of contracting:

> [I]t is in the area of contract negotiation perhaps more than anywhere else that a positive infusion of good faith doctrine may be desirable. This is particularly so in the case of letters of intent and heads of agreement which fall short of a binding contract. Neither contractual nor restitutionary remedies are entirely satisfactory. Estoppel can provide a solution in some but not all cases.[222]

It is this contention and submitted here that the notion of good faith can be utilised to give legal recognition to a pre-contractual relationship created by agreements made in the course of negotiation if the parties so intended.

Thomas J argues for a principle of good faith, proposes that it necessitates parties who are involved in contractual discussions genuinely pursued the contract and not to abandon the bargaining process for capricious or arbitrary reasons.[223] However, this does not clarify how this obligation would benefit the aggrieved party in situations where a contract fails to materialise. The obligation applies only after contractual formation, leaving a wronged party without a contractual basis to claim a breach of good faith when negotiations are terminated.[224] The reason for disregarding the conduct of the party ending 'negotiations' was the lack of recognition of any legal relations between the negotiating parties.[225] In this sense, the parties have an unfettered right to withdraw from the negotiation without liability until legal relations recognised under common law are created. Does this demonstrate the insufficiency of contract law to govern the different stages of contractual negotiation? Would an infusion of good faith obligation remedy this shortfall?

In many commercial transactions, the parties often engage in lengthy and complex negotiations at the pre-contractual stage and/or following the conclusion of an agreement. The focus has always been upon the validity of a concluded contract. Where

---

[222] Mason, 'Contract, Good Faith and Equitable Standards,' above n 13, 82.

[223] Thomas, 'Good Faith in Contract: A Non-Sceptical Commentary,' above n 179, 393.

[224] Pollock MR considered that it was not part of the business of the court to consider whether any party was to be blamed for withdrawing from the deal. It was irrelevant whether a party 'broke off negotiations for reasons good, bad, or indifferent'—*Chillingworth v Esche* [1924] 1 Ch 97, 103.

[225] *Chillingworth v Esche* [1924] 1 Ch 97, 112.

no contract is actually concluded, less attention has been focused upon the conduct of the parties to the failed negotiation.

The requirement of good faith should be applicable to complex commercial contracts that require progressive stages in their conclusion, as opposed to contracts that do not have such characteristics. This type of complex transaction often followed prior advanced negotiations in which parties enter into preliminary agreements pending further negotiations regarding matters of detail. An issue to be examined is whether the law enforces such preliminary agreements, particularly the obligation to negotiate in good faith the final terms of the contract at a later time. The conclusion of a contract does not necessarily end contractual negotiations as the parties may have agreed to negotiate further terms to supplement their concluded contract.[226] It is not uncommon in a lengthy contractual relationship for the parties to have agreed to re-negotiate some components of the original deal after a specified period.[227] These contractual obligations to negotiate are usually intended to fill certain matters in the contract, which it is impossible to finalise at the time of contracting. Are these sorts of terms legally binding? If so, are the parties bound to negotiate or re-negotiate in good faith? For example, the calling of tenders has replaced contractual negotiations in the making of many contracts.[228] If this line of thinking is right, tenders would involve more than a mere invitation to treat and as such the terms of the tendering procedure should be capable of being part of the terms of the contract. Further, pre-contractual relationship based on good faith is not foreign to the common law, for example, the doctrine of utmost good faith in insurance law.

4.4.1 Complexities in Contract Negotiations

It is a common practice to make promises to negotiate with a view to concluding an agreement.[229] In this respect, the business community has experienced considerable frustration in seeking to enforce express promises to negotiate (or continue to negotiate). The courts have refused to give legal effect to such pre-contractual promises even where there are express agreements by the parties.[230] Although it reflects commercial realities, the rules of offer and acceptance and the doctrine of

---

[226] *Mallozzi v Carapelli SpA* [1976] 1 Lloyd's Rep 407.

[227] *Queensland Electricity Generating Board v New Hope Collieries Pty Ltd* [1989] 1 Lloyd's Rep 205; *R&D Construction Group Ltd v Hallam Land Management Ltd* **[2009] CSOH 128.**

[228] Cf *MJB Enterprises Ltd v Defence Construction (1951) Ltd* (1999) 44 CLR (2d) 163 (Supreme Court of Canada); *Kinetic Construction Ltd v Regional District of Comox-Strathcona* (2004) BCCA 485 (British Columbia Court of Appeal); Janet McLean and Toni Ashton, 'Quasi-Markets and Pseudo-Contracts in the New Zealand Public Health System' (2001) 10(1) *Otago Law Review* 17, 28–29; Australian Audit Office, *Developing and Managing Contracts: Getting the Right Outcome, Paying the Right Price*, Department of Finance and Administration (2007) Part 2, 26–28.

[229] Farnsworth, 'Precontractual Liability,' above n 250; John W Carter, 'The Renegotiation of Contracts' (1998) 13 *Journal of Contract Law* 185.

[230] *Walford v Miles* [1992] 2 AC 128.

consideration provide a certain set of (fairly rigid) principles for contract formation that do not fit easily with the complexity of negotiations in many commercial transactions. This is because commercial parties in the course of lengthy negotiations appear to be willing to accept incomplete agreements and in many cases are not conscious about the legal implications of such agreements. What appears to be an unenforceable agreement from a lawyer's point of view may seem to involve some obligations and expectations from a commercial contracting party's point of view to preserve their negotiating positions.[231] Letters of intent and heads of agreements require the parties to honour stages previously achieved in the conclusion of their contract and to negotiate in good faith the terms of the final contract.[232] The parties bind themselves to that process in the hope of concluding a valid contract.[233] The courts, however, do not share the same views of such agreements commonly adopted by commercial parties.[234] Letters of intent are generally considered by commercial parties as forming a limited relationship. However, they are not legally binding contracts and in the absence of any midway category, they inevitably have no legal effect.[235]

A further difficulty relates to the lack of legal recognition for agreements that provide for the gradual development of business relationships.[236] In many cases, negotiations have taken the place of contractual terms as an instrument for the development of business relationships.[237] Notwithstanding, the court has also refused to give force to contractual terms to re-negotiate the adjustment of prices despite the parties intention to do so.[238] Contract law does not impose an obligation on the parties to re-negotiate their contract, even to resolve problems which are experienced in its performance.[239] The reason for this is because a promise to re-negotiate is regarded as uncertain and hence invalid.[240]

---

[231] John W Carter and Michael P Furmston, 'Good Faith and Fairness in the Negotiation of Contracts: Part I' (1994) 8 *Journal of Contract Law* 1, 8.

[232] *Coal Cliff Collieries v Sijehama Pty Ltd* (1991) 24 NSWLR 1; *Australia Media Holdings Pty Ltd v Telstra Corporation Ltd* (1998) 43 NSWLR 104.

[233] *Hillas & Co Ltd v Arcos Ltd* [1932] All ER 494, 505.

[234] S N Ball, 'Work Carried Out in Pursuance of Letters of Intent—Contract or Restitution?' (1983) 99 *Law Quarterly Review* 572, 580.

[235] Ibid.

[236] *Australia Media Holdings Pty Ltd v Telstra Corporation Ltd* (1998) 43 NSWLR 104.

[237] G Richard Shell, 'Opportunism and Trust in the Negotiation of Commercial Contracts: Towards a New Cause of Action' (1991) 44 *Vanderbilt Law Review* 221, 233.

[238] *Carr v Brisbane City Council* [1956] St R Qd 402.

[239] John W Carter, 'Problems in Enforcement—Part 1' (1992) 5 *Journal of Contract Law* 199, 201; David E Allen and Mary E Hiscock, *Law of Contract in Australia* (CCH Australia, 2nd ed, 1992) 553; *Baldwin v Icon Energy Ltd* [2015] QSC 12.

[240] *Courtney & Fairbairn Ltd v Tolani Brothers (Hotels) Ltd* [1975] 1 WLR 297, 301; *Walford v Miles* [1992] 2 AC 128; *Elizabeth Bay Developments Pty Ltd v Boral Building Services Pty Ltd* (1995) 36 NSWLR 709, 716.

4.4.2 Legal Position of Agreements to Negotiate

Under the law of contract, there is no liability for refusing to negotiate or terminating negotiations without any justification. The parties are free to terminate negotiations at any time without showing any cause. However, what if the parties wish to voluntarily restrict their freedom and agree to negotiate and to do so in good faith?

The courts in the UK and Australia have considered the validity of agreements to negotiate.[241] In the UK, the obiter dictum of *Hillas v Arcos* foreshadowed the recognition of an agreement to negotiate as a valid contract. However, this view was not followed in subsequent cases.[242] The unanimous decision of the House of Lords in *Walford v Miles* (*Walford*) sets the view of the English position that a duty to negotiate in good faith is inherently uncertain and practically unworkable.[243] Lord Ackner explained the nature of the uncertainty by asking rhetorically: 'how is a vendor ever to know that he is entitled to withdraw from further negotiations? How is the court to police such an "agreement"?'[244] This position was reaffirmed by the Privy Council when it observed that 'the principle that an alleged contract [to negotiate] is ineffective or unenforceable in law … is well established, and remains an important principle.'[245]

In Australia, the *Coal Cliff Collieries v Sijehama Pty Ltd* ('*Coal Cliff*') case constituted the main decision on the enforceability of good faith negotiation clauses and appeared to usher in the possibility of enforcing such negotiation clauses. *Coal Cliff* dealt with a preliminary agreement that sets out the basis of a proposed joint venture, which included a statement that 'the parties will forthwith proceed in good faith to consult together upon the formulation of a more comprehensive and detailed Joint Venture Agreement.'[246] In the end, the Court ruled that the agreement to negotiate was not legally binding. The acceptance to negotiate in good faith was qualified. Kirby P determined that the preliminary agreement was void for uncertainty—not in the promise to negotiate itself but rather in the incomplete nature of the preliminary agreement. The agreement lacked 'a readily ascertainable external standard for the court to use to add flesh to an agreement which is otherwise unacceptably

---

241 *Hillas & Co Ltd v Arcos Ltd* (1932) 147 LT 503; *Courtney & Fairbairn Ltd v Tolani Brothers (Hotels) Ltd* [1975] 1 WLR 297, 301; *Walford v Miles* [1992] 2 AC 128; *National Transport Co-operative Society Ltd v The Attorney General of Jamaica* [2009] UKPC 48; *Coal Cliff Collieries v Sijehama Pty Ltd* (1991) 24 NSWLR 1; *Elizabeth Bay Developments Pty Ltd v Boral Building Services Pty Ltd* (1995) 36 NSWLR 709; *Australia Media Holdings Pty Ltd v Telstra Corporation Ltd* (1998) 43 NSWLR 104; *United Group Rail Services Ltd v Rail Corporation of New South Wales* [2009] NSWCA 177; *Baldwin v Icon Energy Ltd* [2015] QSC 12.

242 E.g. *Courtney & Fairbairn Ltd v Tolani Brothers (Hotels) Ltd* [1975] 1 WLR 297, 301; *Walford v Miles* [1992] 2 AC 128; *National Transport Co-operative Society Ltd v The Attorney General of Jamaica* [2009] UKPC 48.

243 *Walford v Miles* [1992] 2 AC 128, 138.

244 Ibid.

245 *National Transport Co-operative Society Ltd v The Attorney General of Jamaica* [2009] UKPC 48, [61].

246 *Coal Cliff Collieries v Sijehama Pty Ltd* (1991) 24 NSWLR 1, 13.

vague or uncertain or apparently illusory'[247] such as an 'arbitration clause to permit a nominated external person … to settle any term upon which the parties could not themselves agree.'[248] This view is similar to that expressed by Lord Denning in the *Courtney & Fairbairn Ltd v Tolani Brothers (Hotels) Ltd* case[249] ('*Courtney*'), which was followed by *Walford*. The qualification makes an agreement to negotiate in good faith an intermediary process. The promise to negotiate then becomes of no real effect since a breach of the duty to negotiate would not entitle the innocent party to any remedy other than to seek arbitration. Notwithstanding, the judgement also holds some encouragement in that such agreements may under certain circumstances be enforceable. Kirby P suggested by way of obiter dictum that a promise to negotiate in good faith might be enforceable:

> I do not share the opinion of the English Court of Appeal that no promise to negotiate in good faith would ever be enforced by a court. I agree with Lord Wright's speech in *Hillas* that, provided there was consideration for the promise, in some circumstances a promise to negotiate in good faith will be enforceable, depending upon its precise terms.[250]

In *United Group Rail Services Ltd v Rail Corporation of New South Wales* case ('*United Group*'),[251] the NSW Court of Appeal considered whether *Coal Cliff* should guide the development of the law in Australia regarding the enforceability of agreements to negotiate as opposed to *Walford*, which the court did not find to be persuasive. The court held that a dispute resolution (ADR) clause requiring the parties to a complex commercial contract to 'meet and undertake genuine and good faith negotiations' was an enforceable obligation.[252] Allsop P, who gave the judgement of the Court of Appeal, held that.

> a promise to negotiate … genuinely and in good faith with a view to resolving claims to entitlement by reference to a known body of rights and obligations, in a manner that respects the respective contractual rights of the parties, giving due allowance for honest and genuinely held views about those pre-existing rights is not vague, illusory or uncertain.[253]

This view is contrary to the English decision in *Walford* insofar as it applies to the unenforceability of agreements to negotiate. However, it may be premature to declare that *Walford* is no longer applicable law in Australia as *United Group* dealt with ADR clause within a concluded contract regarding a process to be adopted by the contracting parties, rather than an agreement to finalise a contract on open terms. This was the conclusion of the Queensland Supreme Court in *ACMI (IO) Pty Ltd v Aquila Steel Pty Ltd,*[254] which also considered ADR provision requiring

---

[247] Ibid 27.

[248] Ibid 19.

[249] 'If they have left the price to be agreed by a third party as an arbitrator, it would have been different. But here it was to agree between the parties themselves': *Courtney & Fairbairn Ltd v Tolani Brothers (Hotels) Ltd* [1975] 1 WLR 297, 301.

[250] *Coal Cliff Collieries v Sijehama Pty Ltd* (1991) 24 NSWLR 1, 26.

[251] *United Group Rail Services Ltd v Rail Corporation of New South Wales* [2009] NSWCA 177.

[252] Ibid [5].

[253] (2009) 74 NSWLR 618, 639.

[254] [2009] QSC 139.

the contracting parties to negotiate and resolve any dispute in good faith. Douglas J refused to follow existing legal proposition that such a clause was illusory and conferred no legal rights.[255] He highlighted the distinctions between agreements to negotiate within dispute resolution and those found in preliminary agreements. For example, in *Walford*, the agreement was 'in effect ... an agreement to negotiate a further agreement.'[256]

This judicial approach is aligned with a liberal interpretation of ADR and promotes the public policy reasoning behind them.[257] This includes substantial savings in litigation costs and, from a public perspective, the freeing up of judicial resources.[258] Colman J also noted this position in England when he said, in terms also applicable to the Australian context: 'For the courts now to decline to enforce contractual references to ADR on the grounds of intrinsic uncertainty would be to fly in the face of ... public policy.'[259] Although not referred to in *United Group* or *ACMI(IO)* case, it appears that the High Court's decision in *Thorby v Goldberg*[260] offers further support for enforcing agreements to negotiate to resolve a dispute. In that case, the court dismissed an argument that a contract was uncertain for leaving essential matters to be agreed. Kitto J held that no future agreement was required. His Honour asserted that the rights of the parties had already been defined in the contract's terms and implied a term that they would 'negotiate reasonably' to ensure that their 'respective rights ... as defined are given effect.'[261] While ADR negotiation agreements are similar to the term implied by Kitto J, this argument is less likely to succeed in preliminary agreements where a greater consensus is needed between the parties regarding their respective rights.[262] Nevertheless, there is still

---

[255] E.g. Giles J had held that an agreement to negotiate in good faith to resolve a dispute would require 'conduct of unacceptable certainty': *Elizabeth Bay Developments Pty Ltd v Boral Building Services Pty Ltd* (1995) 36 NSWLR 709, 716; Hammerschlag J held that an ADR negotiation clause was uncertain because there was no 'objective yardstick by which to measure the good faith or otherwise of a negotiating party's stance': *Laing O'Rourke (BMC) Pty Ltd v Transport Infrastructure Development Corporation* [2007] NSWSC 723 [50]; the Federal Court also took the same view in *Jobern Pty Ltd v BreakFree Resorts (Victoria) Pty Ltd* [2007] FCA 1066; Handley JA's judgement in *Coal Cliff Collieries v Sijehama Pty Ltd* (1991) 24 NSWLR 1, 38–43.

[256] *Elizabeth Bay Developments Pty Ltd v Boral Building Services Pty Ltd* (1995) 36 NSWLR 709 [30].

[257] E.g. *Comandate Marine Corporation v Pan Australia Shipping Pty Ltd* (2006) 157 FCR 45, 87–93 (per Allsop P).

[258] Charles Thensted, 'Litigation and Less: The Negotiation Alternative' (1984) 59 *Tulane Law Review* 76; Carrie Menkel-Meadow, 'Introduction: What Will We Do When Adjudication Ends? A Brief Intellectual History of ADR' (1997) 44 *UCLA Law Review* 1613, 1619–1620; Vicki Donnenberg, 'Judicial Review of Arbitral Awards Under the Commercial Arbitration Acts' (2008) 30 *Australian Bar Review* 177, 178–179; Giles J's comments that 'mediation is a valuable means of resolution of disputes, and agreements to mediate should be recognised and given effect in appropriate cases': *Elizabeth Bay Developments Pty Ltd v Boral Building Services Pty Ltd* (1995) 36 NSWLR 709, 716.

[259] *Cable & Wireless plc v IBM (UK) Ltd* [2002] EWHC (Comm) 2059.

[260] (1964) 112 CLR 597.

[261] (1964) 112 CLR 597, 603 (McTiernan and Windeyer JJ also agreeing: 602, 616).

[262] *Coal Cliff Collieries v Sijehama Pty Ltd* (1991) 24 NSWLR 1, 39 (per Handley JA).

cause for optimism as *United Group* illustrates judicial willingness to look beyond the constraining approach of *Walford*.

4.4.3 Role of Good Faith in Agreement to Negotiate

Contract law is fundamentally about upholding 'a contract wherever possible to avoid the reproach of being the destroyer of bargains.'[263] It must also serve the marketplace and not simply 'exist to satisfy lawyer's desires for neat rules.'[264] With this in mind and to better understand the relevant issues, it is necessary to point out a number of observations regarding the role and meaning of good faith in commercial negotiations.

4.4.3.1 Difference between an Obligation to Negotiate in Good Faith and an Agreement to Contract

Coal Cliff illustrates this distinction. In that case, the negotiation agreement was made early, with significant terms still undecided, leading Kirby P to deem the negotiation clause unenforceable.[265] Such agreements are susceptible to being classified under the general prohibition in *Walford*.[266]

As noted earlier, the complexity of negotiating large commercial transactions always leaves negotiating parties with no choice other than to proceed with negotiations through an intermediate agreement as a basis for reaching a contract. The difficulty with such agreements under the common law is that they are neither contracts nor incomplete contracts that might be completed by the courts,[267] because the language used often does not express an intention to create a binding contract. *What courts have failed to recognise in these agreements is that the parties have contracted to negotiate, and not to reach a contract* (emphasis added). In essence, the obligation is confined to negotiating in good faith, rather than to ensure a specific outcome. It does not mandate the parties to reach an agreement by unspecified means.[268] The agreement simply obligates the parties to negotiate, not to agree, so the rule against agreements to agree does not apply. In *Ridgway v Wharton*, Lord Wensleydale said that the reason not to enforce agreements to agree is that 'it is absurd to say that a man enters into an agreement till the terms of that agreement are settled. Until those terms

[263] *Hillas & Co Ltd v Arcos Ltd* (1932) 147 LT 503, 514.

[264] *Coal Cliff Collieries v Sijehama Pty Ltd* (1991) 24 NSWLR 1, 22 (per Kirby P).

[265] Ibid 27.

[266] *Booker Industries* Pty Ltd *v Wilson Parking* (Qld) Pty Ltd (1982) 149 CLR 600, 604.

[267] E.g. through implied terms.

[268] Amy Schmitz, 'Confronting ADR Agreements' Contract / No Contract Conundrum with Good Faith' (2006) 56 *DePaul Law Review* 55, 83.

are settled, he is perfectly at liberty to retire from the bargain.'[269] As such, if a court cannot find an existing contract that satisfies the requirements of contract formation, that court will simply conclude that what the parties have agreed is not a contract but an agreement to agree—which cannot be enforced for lack of certainty in its terms. However, this does not mean an agreement to negotiate in good faith has the same effect as an agreement to agree. The obligation to engage in negotiation is designed to be effective even if the eventual contract fails since the negotiation process occurs before the performance of any specific contractual clause.[270] This may be likened to arbitration agreements, where the arbitration clause is deemed independent and separable from the primary contract.[271] Similarly, the obligation to negotiate, being distinct from the main agreement, should not be affected by any uncertainty.

The importance of the *Hillas v Arcos* case lies in Lord Wright's dictum regarding the possibility of enforcing an agreement to negotiate by virtue of its differences to an agreement to agree, which cannot generally be enforced under the common law. His Lordship suggested that:

> If, however, what is meant is that the parties agree to negotiate in the hope of effecting a valid contract, the position is different. There is then no bargain except to negotiate, and negotiations may be fruitless and end without any contract ensuing; yet even then, in strict theory, there is a contract (if there is good consideration) to negotiate, though in the event of repudiation by one party the damages may be nominal, unless a jury think that the opportunity to negotiate was of some appreciable value to the injured party.[272]

This modest attempt to recognise a contract to negotiate has been rejected by Lord Denning in *Courtney*. His Lordship stated that:

> If the law does not recognise a contract to enter into a contract (when there is a fundamental term yet to be agreed) it seems to me it cannot recognise a contract to negotiate. The reason is because it is too uncertain to have any binding force. No court could estimate the damages because no one can tell whether the negotiations would be successful or would fall through; or if successful, what the result would be. It seems to me that a contract to negotiate, like a contract to enter into a contract, is not a contract known to the law.[273]

The missing element in the statements of both Lord Wright and Lord Denning is the concept of good faith.[274] Without that concept, Lord Wright's suggestion may be regarded as bad law and Lord Denning's as extremely good law, especially in relation

---

[269] (1857) 10 ER 1287, 1313.

[270] Cf *Whitlock v Brew* (1968) 118 CLR 445, 461.

[271] See *Comandate Marine Corporation v Pan Australia Shipping Pty Ltd* (2006) 157 FCR 45, 102 (per Allsop P).

[272] *Hillas & Co Ltd v Arcos Ltd* (1932) 147 LT 503, 505; Lord Wright appeared to be aware of the inflexibility in English contract law to reflect the realities of contemporary commerce. It should be noted that in the Court of Appeal, Scrutton L J recognised some rigidity in the English law: 'I regret that in many commercial matters the English law and the practice of commercial men are getting wider apart, with the result that commercial business is leaving the courts and is being decided by commercial arbitrators with infrequent reference to the courts': [1932] 147 LT 503, 506.

[273] *Courtney & Fairbarn Ltd v Tolaini Bros (Hotels) Ltd* [1975] 1 All ER 716, 720.

[274] In *Mallozzi v Carapelli SpA* [1975] 1 Lloyd's Rep 229, Kerr J applied the view of Lord Wright in *Hillas* but based his judgement on the concept of *bona fide* or good faith as the cornerstone for

to the situation where one party may be used in bad faith during negotiations as a bridge to better deal. On the facts, no one could argue successfully that a contract existed between the parties in *Courtney*, but the all or nothing approach to contract formation under the common law put a huge burden on Mr Courtney, who had negotiated in good faith.[275] It is in cases like this where a contract to negotiate in good faith is the only option that could protect the reasonable expectations of the negotiating parties. It is also common in commercial negotiations that one party cannot keep all his or her cards away from the other party. Therefore, the notion of good faith must not be regarded as irrelevant to business dealings. Certainty of contract law should not be an obstacle to the recognition of a commercially sensible agreement to negotiate in good faith. More importantly, the meaning of good faith between commercial parties does not ignore the fact that each party acts for his or her self-interest. The requirements of good faith are not static in all circumstances or cases.

The notion of good faith in commercial negotiations also does not protect the disappointed party from the risk of losing a profitable contract, if negotiations break down. This risk is always a part of doing business and no matter how advanced the parties are in their negotiations, if they cannot reach a contract, each party is still free to withdraw from the bargain. However, preserving this freedom should not result in the parties being always without liability. What an obligation of good faith does is protect a negotiating party from the bad faith withdrawal of the other party by imposing a liability upon that party to pay for losses incurred during negotiations.

---

an agreement to negotiate. In his view, a term which stated that 'the parties will agree on the port of discharge when the ship passes through the Straits of Gibraltar' obligated the parties to at least negotiate bona fide (good faith) with the view to trying to reach an agreement; see also Anthony M Dugdale and Nigel V Lowe, 'Contracts to Contract and Contracts to Negotiate' (1976) *Journal of Business Law* 28.

[275] The facts of the *Courtney* case were that Mr Tolaini wanted to develop a site by building a motel, filling station and hotel. He got in touch with Mr Courtney, a property developer. Mr Courtney was well placed to obtain finance for the building development and at a meeting between the two it was agreed, informally, that Mr Courtney should find someone to provide finance for the project. Mr Tolaini was to develop the site for a motel and other buildings. But he was to employ Mr Courtney or his company for the construction work. After that meeting, Mr Courtney wrote a letter to Mr Tolaini emphasising that the reason for providing his service was 'to build the three projects.' Mr Tolaini accepted the terms of that letter. However, after Mr Courtney introduced a person who then provided finance for the projects, negotiations between the parties failed due to differences of opinion about the price. However, Mr Tolaini took advantage of the finance that Mr Courtney had made possible and employed other contractors. This, of course, does not mean that the defendant was acting in bad faith in his decision to break off negotiations. If negotiations failed due to disagreement after good faith efforts, it is unlikely that such a decision would amount to bad faith conduct. This point was not considered by the court because English law does not recognise a general principle of good faith in contracts. However, it is the contention here that the facts of the *Courtney* case do suggest that there was an element of good faith, which had been established between the parties and the plaintiff was entitled to recompense for his service during the period of negotiations.

In the US, the *Restatement* establishes that express agreements to negotiate in good faith are enforceable.[276] It asserts that 'bad faith in negotiation,' though not covered by art 205, 'may be subject to sanctions.'[277] The Second Circuit Court of Appeals supports the enforceability of clauses where 'the parties recognise the existence of open terms, even major ones, but, having agreed on certain important terms, agree to bind themselves to negotiate in good faith to work out the terms remaining open.'[278] The obligation here is 'only to negotiate in good faith towards conclusion within the agreed framework.'[279] The Second Circuit clarified that agreements requiring further negotiation do not typically 'do not create binding obligations'[280] but aim to 'limit the parties' discretion in the conduct of negotiations,'[281] without enforcing incomplete clauses. The court recognised that the obligation to negotiate should not be undermined by the uncertainty of the attached obligation. Therefore, an agreement to negotiate in good faith is not equivalent to an agreement to agree or enter into a contract. This approach ensures that negotiating parties are bound to act in good faith, providing structure and fairness in the negotiation process.

4.4.3.2 The Meaning of an Agreement to Negotiate in Good Faith

An agreement to negotiate in good faith is not an agreement to enter into a contract, nor does it restrict the negotiating parties' freedom from contract. The argument that both agreements have the same effect of enforcing negotiating parties to agree is plainly inadequate. The reason why the common law equates a contract to enter into a contract with a contract to negotiate is their fear of introducing an obligation to negotiate in good faith to commercial negotiations, which may disturb the inherent adversarial position of the parties under the classical theory of contract law. Lord Ackner said that the 'concept of a duty to carry on negotiations in good faith is inherently repugnant to the adversarial position of the parties when involved in negotiations.'[282] This objection is strongest in preliminary agreements where parties lack a strong contractual connection and are not restrained by a pre-existing contract. The basis for denying enforceability is 'the rule permitting a court to refuse its assistance

---

[276] Nili Cohen, 'Pre-contractual Duties: Two Freedoms and the Contract to Negotiate' in Jack Beatson and Daniel Friedmann (eds), *Good Faith and Fault in Contract Law* (Oxford University Press, 2001) 25, 40.

[277] American Law Institute, *Restatement (Second) of Contracts* (1981) § 205 cmt (c) http://www.lexinter.net/LOTWVers4/Restatement_(second)_of_contracts.htm.

[278] *Shann v Dunk* [1996] USCA2 372; 84 F 3d 73 (2nd Cir 1996) 11–12 (Leval J); as of 2007, this 'framework' for analysing preliminary agreements 'is followed in at least thirteen states, sixteen federal district courts and seven federal circuits': Alan Schwartz and Robert E Scott, 'Precontractual Liability and Preliminary Agreements' (1997) 20 *Harvard Law Review* 661, 663.

[279] *Shann v Dunk* [1996] USCA2 372; 84 F 3d 73 (2nd Cir, 1996) 12 (Leval J).

[280] Ibid.

[281] Jeannie M Paterson, 'The Contract to Negotiate' (1996) 10 *Journal of Contract Law* 120, 121.

[282] *Walford v Miles* [1992] 2 AC 128, 138.

to enforce a contract where to do so would be contrary to public policy.'[283] However, this objection fails because the parties have mutually agreed to limit their discretion in negotiations 'in a commercial context and for good consideration.'[284] Denying this right undermines party autonomy and freedom of contract, which respects the parties' competency and their 'utmost liberty of contracting.' The High Court in *Ringrow Pty Ltd v BP Australia Pty Ltd* stated that 'exceptions from freedom of contract require good reason to attract judicial intervention to set aside the bargains upon which parties of full capacity have agreed.'[285] This threshold is not met for express contracts to negotiate. Arguing against enforceability due to the adversarial nature of negotiations imposes irrelevant judicial opinions on proper negotiation conduct over the parties' wishes.

According to the good faith provisions under the *UNIDROIT Principles*,[286] the basic meaning of an obligation to negotiate in good faith is that each party should have an intention (not a duty) to reach a contract. This formula means that a degree of fault must be established on the part of the party who decides to break off negotiations without any reasonable disagreement.[287] Therefore, a party who negligently creates the expectation that a contract will be reached, but in reality is aware that a contract will not be reached, acts in bad faith if he or she continues the negotiations with the other party. The existence of good faith is vital to plug the gaps in contract law to deal with bad faith conduct in the absence of existing contractual obligations. If the law governing the parties' relationship does not recognise a duty to negotiate in good faith, an agreement to negotiate in good faith could help negotiating parties to avoid the rigidity of such law and a court should treat this agreement like any other agreement. To deny the enforceability of an agreement to negotiate in good faith is simply to ignore the parties' intention to create a legally binding relationship in their negotiations.

It must be kept in mind, however, that negotiating parties who enclose a good faith clause in their preliminary agreement must not rely on the basic general meaning of good faith in negotiations. In other words, it is for the parties themselves to decide what exactly they mean by negotiating in good faith. To reduce the chances of their agreement being found unenforceable, negotiating parties must clearly express their views regarding the fundamental issues in their process of negotiation. For example, to negotiate in good faith there must be a consideration (e.g. withdrawing a property from the market, not negotiating with third parties). Identifying the negotiators is crucial to avoid the clause being declared uncertain and to ensure it is commercially useful and enforceable. The Hong Kong case of *Hyundai Engineering & Construction*

---

[283] *Fitzgerald v FJ Leonhardt Pty Ltd* (1997) 189 CLR 215, 247 (per Kirby J).

[284] Jeff Cumerbatch, 'In Freedom's Cause: The Contract to Negotiate' (1992) 12 *Oxford Journal of Legal Studies* 586, 589.

[285] (2005) 224 CLR 656, 659.

[286] *UNIDROIT Principles*—The Principles of International Commercial Contracts (PICC) of 2010 is a document drawn up by UNIDROIT, which is intended to help harmonise international commercial contract law. Australia is a member state to the UNIDROIT.

[287] Article 2.1.15, *UNIDROIT Principles*.

Co Ltd v Vigour Ltd[288] highlights the risks of not properly identifying negotiators. Rogers VP in the Court of Appeal, applying *Walford*, found the clause unenforceable, noting the haphazard attempt to identify the negotiator without specifying a name or title.[289] Determining a time limit is crucial, similar to lock-out agreements where a party agrees not to negotiate with a third party.

Although lock-out agreements bear resemblance to agreements to negotiate, they are handled with more flexibility or leniently[290] and have been fundamentally endorsed in *Walford*. The rationale for this additional flexibility is not entire clear, but 'good commercial reasons' were mentioned by Lord Ackner as justification for lock-out agreements.[291] Considering that a time limit is deemed an 'essential characteristic' of a lock-out agreement,[292] it might also be prudent to impose time constraints on the negotiation obligation to ensure enforceability. Support for this view also appears in Hayne JA's judgement in *Con Kallergis Pty Ltd v Calshonie Pty Ltd* where his Honour distinguished *Walford* in contracts where there is a provision for 'an end to the negotiation other than the parties to it retreating to their offices to nurse their pride and their rejected bargaining position.'[293] Furthermore, in complex negotiations, it would be advisable for the parties to set up a mechanism through which to resolve any disagreement in good faith (for example, electing a third party to mediate, creating an arbitration clause). All of these steps will help courts to enforce an agreement to negotiate in good faith. Therefore, the meaning of good faith in negotiations is not legally static; rather it is a concept that derives its meaning from commercial practice between commercial parties. The notion that commercial parties may have no regard to good faith should be viewed with scepticism: 'The bully boy approach to the making of commercial contracts, which appears to have found favour with Lord Ackner, and which anything short of misrepresentation is to be viewed as legitimate, is a grotesque parody.'[294]

4.4.3.3 Is It Rational and Relevant to Have a Contract to Negotiate in Good Faith?

In the case of *Kevin A Copeland v Baskin Robbins USA*,[295] the Californian Court of Appeal, Second District, in recognising the validity of an agreement to negotiate the terms of a contract in good faith appears to concede that the modern nature of commercial negotiations makes it a commercially sensible agreement.

---

288 [2005] 3 HKLRD 723.

289 Ibid 731.

290 Nili Cohen, 'Pre-contractual Duties,' above n 276, 25, 43.

291 *Walford v Miles* [1992] 2 AC 128, 139.

292 Ibid 140.

293 (1998) 14 BCL 201, 212.

294 Angelo D M Forte, 'Good Faith and Utmost Good Faith' in Angelo D M Forte (ed), *Good Faith in Contract and Property Law* (Hart Publishing, 1999), 77, 100.

295 96 Cal App 4th 2d 1251 (2002).

> Gone are the days when our ancestors sat around a fire and bargained for the exchange of stone axes for bear hides. Today the stakes are much higher and negotiations are much more complex. Deals are rarely made in a single negotiating session. Rather, they are the product of a gradual process in which agreements are reached piecemeal on a variety of issues in a series of face-to-face meetings, telephone calls, e-mails and letters involving corporate officers, lawyers, bankers, accountants, architects, engineers and others. ... These slow contracts are not only time-consuming but costly. For these reasons, the parties should have some assurance.[296]

Therefore, commercial parties who face this complex reality of negotiations and high risks should have the freedom to make a contract that creates binding obligations during negotiations. Good faith was a well-known principle between merchants under Roman law and has been throughout the history of commercial law in Europe as discussed previously in Chap. 2. Good faith cannot simply be denied to have any role in the dealings between commercial parties in the twenty-first century and be treated as an unworkable concept in commercial law. Given its deep historical roots, an agreement to negotiate in good faith, which is mutually created by negotiating parties, is a workable agreement. It gives both parties an opportunity to negotiate and protects them from any opportunistic behaviour during negotiations.[297] Although parties in commercial negotiations are acting in arm's length relationships, the position of a negotiating party could be vulnerable in a lengthy and complex negotiation process. If the law is unlikely to offer any shields beyond the ordinary recognised protections during negotiations (fraud and misrepresentation) why should negotiating parties not have the option to increase their protection through a contractual agreement to negotiate in good faith? The absence of contract rules to deal directly with these concerns does not mean that contract law is hopeless in providing an acceptable solution for businesspersons in commercial negotiations. An agreement to negotiate in good faith is a contract, and it is a sensible contractual solution to overcome the vulnerability that might face commercial parties in complex business negotiations.[298]

Essentially, the starting point for considering the rationality of good faith in commercial negotiations is to ask a simple question: Do commercial parties resort to the notion of good faith in their negotiations of commercial contracts? If the answer is yes, then it is unfair to say that because we do not like that principle, any agreement that creates such an obligation to negotiate in good faith should be treated as unenforceable by the law. Commercial negotiations are conducted under the arm's length rule that makes any intervention by courts helpless to outlaw bad faith conduct by one party during negotiations. However, if the commercial parties decide to change the rules of the game, contract law must not be an obstacle to their introduction of an element of good faith into carrying out their negotiations.

---

[296] 96 Cal App 4th 2d 1251, 1263 (2002) (per Johnson PJ).

[297] Juliet P Kostritsky, 'Bargaining with Uncertainty, Moral Hazard, and Sunk Cost: A Default Rule for Precontractual Negotiations' (1993) 44 *Hastings Law Journal* 623, 636; Shell, 'Opportunism and Trust,' above n 238.

[298] See Jeannie M Paterson, 'The Contract to Negotiate in Good Faith: Recognition and Enforcement' (1996) 10 *Journal of Contract Law* 120; Jack O'Connor, 'The Enforceability of Agreements to Negotiate in Good Faith' (2010) 29(2) *University of Tasmania Law Review* 177.

The second point is that the analysis of good faith must not be reduced to two polarised positions. At one extreme, good faith is viewed as a major principle, which would change or challenge many settled rules in contract law and to be accepted a new theory of contract is needed to accommodate its existence in contract law.[299] At the other extreme, good faith is portrayed as non-rational, possibly altruistic, certainly embedded in morality, and such an obligation 'gave too much power to the individual judges freed from the disciplined traditions of contract law. Visceral justice was, and remains … an emotional spasm.'[300] Both views neglect the role of contract law in sustaining good faith, which has formed the underlying rationale for many contract law principles. These include misrepresentation, estoppel, forfeiture and waiver.

Good faith does not disturb the facts that parties in commercial negotiations are self-interested and that each party still has the right to walk away from a bad transaction. The degree of restriction of the freedom of the parties depends upon their intention. The parties may have intended that they be required to act honestly (subjective good faith) or honestly and reasonably (objective good faith).

In *Interfoto Picture Library Ltd v Stiletto Visual Programmes Ltd*, Bingham LJ examined good faith in the civil law systems and states:

> In many civil law systems, and perhaps in most legal systems outside the common law world, the law of obligations recognises and enforces an overriding principle that in the making and carrying out of contracts parties should act in good faith. This does not simply mean that they should not deceive each other, a principle which any legal system must recognise; its effect is perhaps most aptly conveyed by such metaphorical colloquialism as 'playing fair', 'come clean' or 'putting one's cards face upwards on the table'. It is in essence a principle of fair and open dealing.[301]

It is submitted that the scope of good faith as defined by Bingham LJ accurately reflects what is needed to overcome the difficulties presently experienced by the business community. It is not proposed here that good faith should be imposed upon negotiating parties as a matter of law. The obligation of good faith is recognised where the parties have expressly or by implication agreed to act in that manner. A duty of good faith represents an additional obligation voluntarily undertaken to restrict the inherent freedom of the parties during the negotiation.

The scope of the duty is likely to vary depending upon the stage of the negotiations, again depending on the intention of the parties. At an early stage of negotiation, the likelihood is that the parties intended that mere honesty is required. At a later stage, the parties may have intended to act reasonably to finalise an already concluded deal that is not complete in all respects.

Honesty in the exercise of discretion is subjective and does not oblige the parties to conclude a contract.[302] The negotiating parties are entitled to act according to their

---

[299] See Philip Girard, 'Good Faith in Contract Performance: Principle or Placebo?' (1983) 5 *Supreme Court Law Review* 309.

[300] Bridge, 'Good Faith in Commercial Contracts,' above n 3, 140; Bridge, 'Does Anglo-Canadian Contract Law Need,' above n 3.

[301] [1989] QB 433, 439.

[302] See Raphael Powell, 'Good Faith in Contracts' (1956) 9 *Current Legal Problems* 16, 23–24.

own interest, with no obligation to have regard to that of the other party. Good faith encompassing only honesty does not relinquish the right to act unreasonably. The parties may, if they so agree, retain the right to withdraw from the deal even beyond reaching an agreement on all terms until the contemplated contract is executed.[303]

Good faith has been utilised in an attempt to ensure performance of a promise where the law fails to give it legal force. The negotiating parties create a hypothetical relationship of good faith in substitution for formal legal relations in an endeavour to enforce their non-contractual promise. For example, in *Zurich Australia Insurance Ltd v St Andrew's War Memorial Hospital*, Chesterman J recognised this relationship: 'The duty is not to act in good faith. It is because the relationship between the insurer and the insured is one 'of the utmost good faith' that the duty to disclose arises.'[304]

As can be observed, reference to the duty of utmost good faith was made to identify the relationship justifying the specific obligation to disclose. A promise to negotiate is correspondingly the more specific duty that the parties intended to enforce under a relationship of good faith. Hence, the parties are to conduct their negotiations in a relationship of good faith.

Contemporary negotiations resemble any other business investment. The notion of good faith is called for to compel the negotiating parties to act honestly in exercising their inherent discretion to withdraw from the negotiations. The necessity for this limitation is to protect the venture in the negotiations as they progress. The parties may have reached an agreement on certain terms of their deal to be followed by further negotiations on other outstanding issues.

A partial agreement of that nature has no legal force under the common law, leaving the parties exposed to the commercial risk of wasted resources through the abuse of the absolute discretion to terminate the negotiations.

The absence of legal recognition for pre-contractual agreements has created 'an unacceptable discrepancy between the law and the confident assumptions of commercial parties.'[305] A voluntary agreement to negotiate necessarily implies honesty in the exercise of the discretion to withdraw from the negotiation. The implication of honesty is necessary to give the agreement business efficacy.

The issue of the uncertainty of the agreement to negotiate in good faith is caused by a lack of understanding of what the contracting parties mean by that term. The scope of good faith in contractual negotiation ought to reflect the usages of ordinary, right-thinking people.[306] The scope of good faith is judged by community standards.[307] In

---

[303] Cf *Masters v Cameron* (1954) 91 CLR 353, 355; *Attorney General of Hong Kong v Humphreys Estate (Queen's Gardens) Ltd* [1987] AC 114.

[304] [1998] QSC 209 [37].

[305] *Blackpool & Fylde Aero Club Ltd v Blackpool Borough Council* [1990] 1 WLR 1195, 1201.

[306] Christopher J F Boge, 'Does the Trade Practices Act Impose a Duty to Negotiate in Good Faith? Part II' (1998) 6 (2) *Trade Practices Law Journal* 68, 87.

[307] Christopher J F Boge, 'Does the Trade Practices Act Impose a Duty to Negotiate in Good Faith? Part I' (1998) 6 (1) *Trade Practices Law Journal* 4, 5.

developing the law, the judiciary should attempt to enforce what the society embraces as rules of conduct.[308]

Notwithstanding, commercial parties can still set out some of the characteristics of good faith to assist the court, which would make the requirement for a definition of good faith unnecessary to ensure enforceability.[309] Even in many US jurisdictions, courts are still 'reluctant to enforce ... agreements that call for good faith negotiations without setting clear parameters for what good faith means.'[310] In Australia, courts found difficulty in applying a good faith standard, as noted by Hammerschlag J, who stated there is no objective yardstick for determining breach in a simple agreement to negotiate in good faith.[311] To aid courts, parties should define 'good faith' by excluding certain bad faith behaviours,[312] such as conducting parallel negotiations or denying the other party the original bargain in ADR clauses.[313]

The reasons for the introduction of a pre-contractual relationship of good faith in the negotiation of contracts are even stronger than those that led to the recognition of the relationship of utmost good faith. The law ought to give effect to binding legal relations at the pre-contractual stage when the parties so intended it.

The enforcement of pre-contractual agreements has not yet been judicially considered. Notwithstanding that, specific performance would not be appropriate[314]; a breach of a mere agreement to negotiate would entitle the innocent party to damages for loss of a chance to successfully conclude the negotiation.[315]

Good faith in agreements to negotiate may extend to reasonableness when used as a mechanism for the variation of contractual terms. It may import into the negotiations an objective standard to be followed to achieve a successful outcome.

4.5 Chapter Summary

Notwithstanding the diverse views of the appellate courts, the contractual duty of good faith is here to stay, until the legislature or the High Court decides otherwise. It is not imposed on all contracts (except possibly in NSW) and depends on the objective intention of the parties and the contract's express language.

The law is unsettled, but if good faith is to be implied, it ought to be an implication in fact rather than by law. This approach allows case law to develop, providing

---

[308] F A Hayek, *Law, Legislation and Liberty* (Routledge, 1982) 88.

[309] See *Con Kallergis Pty Ltd v Calshonie Pty Ltd* (1998) 14 BCL 201.

[310] Schmitz, above n 269, 68.

[311] *Laing O'Rourke (BMC) Pty Ltd v Transport Infrastructure Development Corporation* [2007] NSWSC 723 [49]; *Baldwin v Icon Energy Ltd* [2015] QSC 12.

[312] Charles Knapp, 'Enforcing the Contract to Bargain' (1969) 44 *New York University Law Review* 673, 722.

[313] Cf *Butt v M'Donald* (1896) 7 QLJ 68, 70–71 (per Griffith CJ).

[314] Cf See Paterson, 'The Contract to Negotiate in Good Faith,' above n 300, 139.

[315] See *Chaplin v Hicks* [1911] 2 KB 786.

guidance on which contractual provisions will include a duty of good faith and its content, as noted by Warren CJ in *Esso*: 'if good faith is not readily capable of definition then [contractual] certainty is undermined.'[316] Implication in fact is clearly a useful and pragmatic approach as it offers a practical path that takes into consideration, not only the intention of the contracting parties but also the commercial purpose of the dealings.

Alternatively, a preferred approach would be the constructivist methodology that suggests that contractual discretions, powers, and rights may be exercised in good faith as an incidence of contractual construction. Zeller's comment on good faith as a state of mind is an example of this perspective. According to Zeller, good faith implication can be ascertained by the contracting parties 'state of mind': 'Therefore, a state of mind of parties will be translated into 'conduct' of parties. It is well established in our law that equity regulates the quality of contractual performance. It can also be argued that performance equates to conduct.'[317]

It has been shown that the obligation of good faith may be useful in negotiation agreements. Courts may use the obligation to enforce previously unenforceable agreements, aligning contract law more closely with commercial parties' expectations when contracting.

In general, the Australian courts have embraced the concept of good faith at common law, albeit, cautiously. However, in the absence of a binding High Court authority, the position is less clear on what the good faith standard is in the application of the obligation. As indicated in Chap. 1, there are still several significant unresolved issues as to what the applicable good faith standard is, which the next chapter deals with.

---

316 [2005] VSCA 228 [3].

317 Bruno Zeller, 'Good Faith—The Scarlet Pimpernel of the *CISG*' [2000] 7 *International Trade Business Law Annual* 2 http://CISGw3.law.pace.edu/CISG/biblio/zeller2.html .

Chapter 5
The Premise of Good Faith in Contractual Performance

5.1 Introduction

Good faith has always been regarded as a nebulous concept. When the contractual context changes, it can take on a new or expanded meaning.[1] Therefore, any attempt to explain the concept of good faith renders an explanation of the explanation necessary.[2]

One of the main objections to introducing an obligation of good faith is because of the difficulty in defining and applying it consistently. Good faith is often interpreted subjectively, so it is hard for courts to discern how much one party should sacrifice their own best interests to further the other party's to fulfil their obligation of good faith.[3] As such, it continues to be a contentious issue plaguing this area of contract law, particularly the lack of a uniform, consensus approach to the application of the good faith obligation by the judiciary.[4]

Despite this, for good faith obligation to remain relevant the modern role of good faith obligation should go beyond its historic function in providing equity for the enforcement of agreements.[5] Good faith obligation should be able to concern itself with its ability to limit, modify or otherwise give content to the express terms of

---

[1] Horst K Lücke, 'Good Faith and Contractual Performance' in Paul Finn (ed), *Essays on Contract* (Law Book Co, 1987) 160.

[2] *State v Robinson* (1893) 23 SW 1066, 1069.

[3] Michael Bridge, 'Does Anglo-Canadian Contract Law Need a Doctrine of Good Faith?' (1984) 9 *Canadian Business Law Journal* 385, 407.

[4] See Chap. 4; cf Anthony Gray, 'Good Faith in Australian Contract Law after Barker' (2015) 43 *Australian Business Law Review* 358.

[5] See Chap. 2 on the role of bona fides or good faith in Roman law; see also Martin Josef Schermaier, '*Bona Fides* in Roman Contract Law' in Reinhard Zimmermann and Simon Whittaker (eds), *Good Faith in European Contract Law* (Cambridge University Press, 2000) 68; James Gordley, 'Good faith in Contract Law in the Medieval *Ius Commune*' in Reinhard Zimmermann and Simon Whittaker (eds), *Good Faith in European Contract Law* (Cambridge University Press, 2000) 93.

A. Wan and P. Guo, *Good Faith Obligation*, International and Comparative Law in the Asia Pacific, https://doi.org/10.1007/978-981-97-7035-9_5

a contract.[6] These outcomes may seem unacceptable to common law lawyers as it impinges on contractual freedom, but at the same time, the absence of a general principle of good faith does not necessarily mean that the courts have no power to intervene where the minimum standards of decency and fair dealing are breached.[7] The generality of the principle of good faith in many international contract regulations seems to indicate that good faith cannot be analysed as a concrete rule, since it is incapable of having a definitive scope in its application despite its focus in protecting the reasonable or justified expectations of the contracting parties. For example, the Official Comment to art 205(a) of the *Restatement* states:

> The phrase 'good faith' is used in a variety of contexts and its meaning varies somewhat with the context. Good faith performance or enforcement of a contract emphasizes faithfulness to an agreed common purpose and consistency with the justified expectations of the other party; it excludes a variety of types of conduct characterized as involving 'bad faith' because they violate community standards of decency, fairness or reasonableness.[8]

This sums up the complexity of good faith and to attempt to define any concrete scope for its application in contracts is virtually futile. However, this problem does not exclude good faith from any utility in contract law. There is, perhaps, an analogy between a duty of care and the principle of good faith in the sense that the potential scopes of application of both concepts are incapable of conclusive definition.[9] Good faith is no different from many other principles, and therefore, the absence of a

---

[6] Mason J has canvassed the possibility that the 'legitimate expectations' of the parties might constrain an apparent unconstrained contractual right: *Meehan v Jones* (1982) 149 CLR 571, 589; some support may be derived from the Canadian Supreme Court decision of *Bhasin v Hrynew* [2014] SCC 71, [45]: '[contracting] parties may generally be assumed to intend certain minimum standards of conduct' (per Cromwell J).

[7] Common law courts, in the absence of a general principle of good faith, resort to specific doctrines in dealing with the question of fairness in contracts. E.g. the requirement of due notice and the interpretation of contract terms *contra proferentem* are used to deal with unfair contracts. Scott C Styles said in his analysis of the principle of good faith—'Naturally, the courts only invoked doctrines such as due notice or interpretation *contra proferentem* when they considered that the contract was in some sense unfair, but through fear of general principles the court could not bring themselves to admit that their underlying concern was really with basic contractual fairness': Scott C Styles, 'Good Faith: A Principled Matter' in Angelo D M Forte (ed), *Good Faith in Contract and Property Law* (Hart Publishing, 1999) 172. See the Court of Appeal decision in *Interfoto Picture Library Ltd v Stiletto Visual Programmes Ltd* [1989] QB 433.

[8] American Law Institute, *Restatement (Second) of Contracts* (1981) § 205 cmt (c) http://www.lexinter.net/LOTWVers4/Restatement_(second)_of_contracts.htm; Robert S Summers, 'The Conceptualisation of Good Faith in American Contract Law: A General Account' in Reinhard Zimmermann and Simon Whittaker (eds), *Good Faith in European Contract Law* (Cambridge University Press, 2000) 118.

[9] The existence of a duty of care does not depend upon the existence of certain circumstances where the courts can impose this duty between parties. Lord Keith in *Governors of the Peabody Donation Fund v Sir Lindsay Parkinson & Co Ltd* [1984] 3 All ER 529 warned against any definitive approach to the existence of such a duty: 'This is a temptation which should be resisted. The true question in each case is whether the particular defendant owed to the particular plaintiff a duty of care having the scope which is contended for, and whether he was in breach of that duty with consequent loss to the plaintiff. A relationship of proximity in Lord Atkin's sense must exist before any duty of care can arise, but the scope of the duty must depend on all the circumstances of the case. ... So in

definition does not deprive the concept of significance.[10] Although opponents of good faith in contract law have emphasised its lack of definition, the hostility towards the principle of good faith does not stop at this point.[11] It is the need for an element of certainty in commercial law that creates the real ground for the aversion among common law lawyers towards a good faith principle.[12]

This, of course, does not mean that in the absence of a general principle of good faith, courts cannot protect the reasonable or legitimate expectations of contracting parties. Nevertheless, the advantage of having a good faith principle in contract law is to provide a contemplated behavioural standard according to which contractual relationships should be conducted. In this sense, it can be argued that good faith brings community standards of decency and fair dealing into the law and also connects pragmatic developments in commercial practice with contract law. By way of example, the concept of 'community standards' has also been mentioned in European contract law[13] and the purpose for such a principle 'is to enforce community standards of decency, fairness and reasonableness in commercial transactions.'[14] This concept means that there are objective standards within a collection of values shared by a community, which contracting parties should respect in their dealings. Courts may interfere with the parties' freedom to contract if the behaviour of a contracting party is not in line with these standards. What gives such standards legal force is the principle of good faith. However, it must be stressed that the application of a good faith principle in contracts must be derived from the parties' agreements.

Following the discussion in Chap. 4, the immediate issue in this chapter concerns the applicable legal standards, which have remained unresolved and often divided judicial decisions. These unresolved issues are used as the basis from which to

---

determining whether or not a duty of care of particular scope was incumbent on a defendant it is material to take into consideration whether it is just and reasonable that it should be so.'; *Donoghue v Stevenson* [1932] AC 562, 534, 580. For a discussion, see Jane Stapleton, 'Duty of Care and Economic Loss: A Wider Agenda' (1991) 107 *The Law Quarterly Review* 249.

[10] The principle of good faith should not be treated as a rule that is capable of determinate application without recourse to any norm of behaviour; see generally Neil MacCormick, *Legal Reasoning and Legal Theory* (Oxford Scholarship Online, 2003); Duncan Kennedy, 'Form and Substance in Private Law Adjudication' (1976) 89 *Harvard Law Review* 1685; Louis Kaplow, 'Rules Versus Standards: An Economic Analysis' (1992) 42 *Duke Law Journal* 557.

[11] Joseph M Thomson, 'Good Faith in Contracting: A Sceptical View' in Angelo D M Forte (ed), *Good Faith in Contract and Property Law* (Hart Publishing, 1999), 63, 75.

[12] The position of common law lawyers opposed to the introduction of good faith in contract law should not be misunderstood as rejection of the idea of good faith and fair dealing in commercial contracts. It is rather about how courts should approach the question of fairness in contracts generally. E.g. it is always argued that the problem of unfairness in contracts must be tackled through the application of specific doctrines rather than restoring to a broad principle which could create an element of discretion in commercial cases: Roger Brownsword, 'Positive, Negative, Neutral: The Reception of Good Faith in English Contract Law' in Roger Brownsworth, Norma J Hird, and Geraint Howells (eds), *Good Faith in Contract: Concept and Context* (Dartmouth Publishing Co, 1999), 13.

[13] See discussion in Chap. 2.

[14] Ole Lando and Hugh Beale (eds), *The Principles of European Contract Law, Part I and II* (Kluwer Law International, 1999) 113.

explore the role of good faith in contractual performance. The issues remaining in dispute regarding the good faith standards are as follows: (1) defining good faith; (2) determining whether good faith is based on the reasonable expectations and/or legitimate interests of the contracting parties, community standards, or a general obligation to act reasonably, cooperatively and honestly; (3) ascertaining whether good faith should assume the same standard as is required of fiduciary obligations; and (4) understanding how good faith relates to equitable and/or statutory unconscionability.

It is necessary to unpack these issues in order to discuss the role that good faith plays in contractual performance. This will also be necessary to lay the groundwork in considering the continued relevance and viability of good faith obligation.

5.2 The Meaning of Good Faith

There is currently no universally accepted definition of the term good faith in Australia.[15] As seen in Chap. 2, the same it seems is experienced in other civil law jurisdictions where good faith is recognised in their respective contractual regimes.[16] The observation of White and Summers on the US *Uniform Commercial Code* (*UCC*) also cautioned anyone 'who is confident about the meaning of good faith.'[17] The inability to give an absolute definition for the principle of good faith in contracts that can clarify its application does not mean that no attempts should be made to find some sort of definitive test or standard, which could aid judges or arbitrators in applying the principle to contractual disputes. For example, as provided in international law under the *UNIDROIT Principles*, the idea that contracting parties must act in accordance with good faith and fair dealing seems to suggest that there must be a standard or test that takes into account their contractual relationships. Indeed, without such a standard or guidance for contracting parties, the principle of good faith may appear superfluous, which is evidently not the case.

From the literature survey, good faith has been described as being void of fixed meaning,[18] where the obligation takes on meaning according to context.[19] Perhaps, this can be explained by viewing good faith with other fundamental terms that are

[15] Elisabeth Peden, *Good Faith in the Performance of Contract* (LexisNexis Butterworths, 2003) 159; Adrian Baron, '"Good Faith" and Construction Contracts—From Small Acorns Large Oaks Grow' (2002) 22 (1) *Australia Bar Review* 54.

[16] See Chap. 2, particularly under civil law jurisdictions of Europe; Gordley, 'Good Faith in Contract Law', above n 7, 93; Terence R H Cole, 'Law—All in Good Faith' (1994) *Building & Construction Law Journal* 18, 19; Paul Finn, 'Commerce, the Common Law and Morality' (1989) 17 *Melbourne University Law Review* 87; Bridge, 'Does Anglo-Canadian Contract Law Need', above n 3, 407.

[17] Uniform Commercial Code, vol 1 (4th ed, 1995) 187 as referred to by Paul Finn, 'Equity and Commercial Contracts: A Comment' (2001) *AMPLA Yearbook* 414, 420.

[18] *Bropho v Human Rights and Equal Opportunity Commission* (2004) 204 Australian Law Reports 761, 783–785.

[19] E.g. as per Einstein J in *Aiton Australia Pty Ltd v Transfield Pty Ltd* (2000) 16 BCL 70 [156]; Roger Brownsword, Norma J Hird and Geraint Howells (eds), *Good Faith in Contract: Concept*

applied to human conduct such as honesty or malice. Good faith is, perhaps, 'better described than defined.'[20]

This chapter begins by considering the approach taken by the Americans on the issue of good faith standards. It provides a background from a common law jurisdiction from which to understand the issues associated with identifying the good faith standards experienced in Australia. The key American good faith provisions are found under the *Restatement* and the *UCC*.[21] Their respective conceptualisation of good faith is quite different. The *UCC* takes a definitional approach, whereas the *Restatement* does not.

Good faith is defined in s 1-203 of the *UCC* to mean 'honesty in fact in the conduct or transaction concerned.' There is also an exclusive definition of good faith concerning merchants, which is provided in art 2 (Sales), s 2-103 (1) (b).

> In this article, unless the context otherwise requires ... good faith in the case of a merchant means honesty in fact and the observance of reasonable commercial standards of fair dealing in the trade.

The definition, however, seems nebulous. Apart from the definition, good faith is also mentioned specifically 'in some fifty out of the four hundred sections of the code.'[22] For example, s 2-311(1) that expressly mentioned good faith in a specific fact situation such as in the sale contract whereby:

> An agreement for sale which is otherwise sufficiently definite (s 2-204(3)) to be a contract is not made invalid by the fact that it leaves particulars of performance to be specified by one of the parties. Any such specification must be made in good faith and within limits set by commercial reasonableness.

Good faith can be expressly or impliedly required of contracting parties. For example, s 2-601 grants buyers the right to handle incorrect deliveries by either rejecting all, accepting all, or accepting only certain parts of the delivery.

The *UCC* has two varying definitions of good faith. Farnsworth classified it in two manners: (1) good faith purchase and (2) good faith in performance or enforcement.[23] In the first and in a larger group of provisions, good faith is described as a 'state of mind' whereby:

> A party is advantaged only if he acted with innocent ignorance or lack of suspicion. This meaning of good faith is very close to that of lack of notice. ... In addition, the Code also uses good faith-as did prior law-in substantially the same sense in protecting others, the

and Context (Dartmouth Pub Co, 1999) 3; Johan Steyn, 'The Role of Good Faith and Fair Dealing in Contract Law: A Hair-Shirt Philosophy?' [1991] *The Denning Law Journal* 131, 140.

[20] Terminology used by Mahoney JA to describe unconscionability in *Antonovic v Volker* (1986) 7 New South Wales Law Review 151, 165 and referred to in Anthony Mason, 'Contract, Good Faith, and Equitable Standards in Fair Dealing' (2000) 116 *Law Quarterly Review* 66, 89.

[21] See Chap. 2. The *Restatement* is the *Restatement (Second) of Contracts.*

[22] E Allan Farnsworth, 'Good Faith Performance and Reasonableness under the Uniform Commercial Code' (1963) 30 *University of Chicago Law Review* 666, 667.

[23] Ibid 668.

> purchasers, and these situations will be included in this discussion under the generic term 'good faith purchase'.[24]

This approach considers only the parties' actual belief. In the second and in a smaller group of provisions, good faith is used to describe performance or enforcement as follows:

> In this sense good faith has nothing to do with a state of mind. ... Here the inquiry goes to decency, fairness or reasonableness, or notice. This sense of the term may be characterized as 'good faith performance' to distinguish it from 'good faith purchase' and is the sense in which 'good faith' is used in the general obligation of good faith. It is also the sense in which that term is used in a number of more specific sections ... resulting in an implied term of contract requiring cooperation on the part of one party to the contract so that another party will not be deprived of his reasonable expectations.[25]

The former approach considers only the actual belief of the parties, while the latter approach takes into account both the actual belief and the reasonableness of that belief and conduct. These contrasting perspectives have led to a lack of clarity in the definition of good faith in the *UCC*. Dobbins warned that this ambiguity can leave contracting parties unsure of their obligations, leading to contractual uncertainties.

US courts have taken liberties with the *UCC*'s vague terms, imposing varied liabilities on parties and sometimes even expecting them to act with integrity or in the best interest of both parties. They might even find that a moral obligation exists between the parties. The good faith obligation is, thus, divided in application.

The Official Comment and Reporter's Note of the *Restatement* suggests in s 205 that the phrase good faith can be used in a variety of contexts and that its meaning is dependent on such usage. Good faith, in this sense, is also said to raise the notion of 'faithfulness to an agreed common purpose and consistency with the justified expectations of the other party.' It omits conduct involving 'bad faith,' as such conduct infringes community standards of decency, fairness, or reasonableness.[26] It must be said, however, that the underlying bases between what the parties intended (or expected) and what community standards demanded may be quite different in operation, with no clear guarantees for their convergence.

5.2.1 What is the American Experience?

The American position is relevant in that Australian courts from the outset have referred to and seemed to favour the American experience.[27] In this regard, the

---

[24] Ibid.

[25] Ibid 669.

[26] Comment B to the Principles of European Contract Law also refers to 'community standards of decency, fairness and reasonableness.'.

[27] The American position on good faith was considered favourably in Priestley JA's judgment in the case of *Renard Constructions (ME) Pty Ltd v Minister of Public Works* (1992) 26 NSWLR 234;

following discussion concentrates on three leading theorists whose work has significantly influenced the good faith debate in the US. The discussion commences with Summers' 'excluder analysis,' followed by Burton's 'forgone opportunity analysis' and finally Farnsworth's 'gap filling analysis.' As a caveat in highlighting these theories, it must be made clear that they represent no more than attempts to find a workable standard or framework for the principle of good faith in contract law. These attempts have also been made in the context of American case law, which were decided on the basis of a mandatory general principle of good faith in contracts that are not present under Australian contract law. In line with the principal inquiry of this book, these theories shed light on how the question of good faith's standards may be tackled and the role it plays in commercial contracts.

5.2.1.1 The Excluder Analysis

The recognition of an obligation of good faith in the *UCC* and the *Restatement* has no doubt advanced the debate over this principle in American contract law. In the US, the question is no longer about the validity of the principle of good faith in contracts, as it now is in most common law countries. Rather, it is about how a workable standard or framework can be established for applying this duty in contracts.[28] Therefore, at the general level, there seems to be less hostility towards a general principle of good faith among American lawyers.[29] However, this general consensus appears to be sustainable as long as good faith means 'honesty in fact,' and beyond this basic understanding of the good faith principle, American lawyers have great difficulties in finding a workable standard for such an obligation in contract law.[30] As mentioned in chapter two and four, the basic element of good faith in contract law based upon the standard of honesty in commercial dealing does not seem to generate any difficulty under the common law in general. However, the principle of good faith in contract

Kiefel J also similarly acknowledged good faith obligation in civilian law jurisdictions and in the US: *Commonwealth Bank of Australia v Barker* [2014] HCA 32, [104]-[108].

[28] See, e.g. Farnsworth, 'Good Faith Performance', above n 24; Robert S Summers, 'Good Faith in General Contract Law and the Sales Provisions of the Uniform Commercial Code' (1968) 54 *Virginia Law Review* 195; Robert S Summers, 'The General Duty of Good Faith—Its Recognition and Conceptualization' (1982) 67 *Cornell Law Review* 810; Steven J Burton, 'Breach of Contract and The Common Law Duty to Perform in Good Faith' (1980) 94 *Harvard Law Review* 369; Steven J Burton, 'Good Faith in Articles 1 and 2 of the UCC: The Practice View' (1994) *William & Mary Law Review* 1533; Eric G Andersen, 'Good Faith in the Enforcement of Contracts' (1988) 73 *Iowa Law Review* 299; Dennis M Patterson, 'Wittgenstein and The Code: A Theory of Good Faith Performance and Enforcement under Article Nine' (1988) 137 *University of Pennsylvania Law Review* 335.

[29] E Allan Farnsworth, 'Good Faith in Contract Performance' in Jack Beatson and Daniel Friedmann (eds), *Good Faith and Fault in Contract Law* (Oxford University Press, 2001) 153, 169.

[30] Howard O Hunter, 'The Growing Uncertainty about Good Faith in American Contract Law' (2004) 20 *Journal Contract Law* 50, 51.

law goes beyond this basic element that should be recognised in any legal system.[31] Indeed, most of the current debates about good faith in contracts is mainly focused on whether contracting parties may be asked to act fairly and reasonably in a way that is clearly beyond the 'ordinary' requirement of honesty in contracts.

Summers' 1968 influential article, in which he attempted to articulate a workable standard, introduces the concept of good faith as an excluder 'which has no general meaning or meanings of its own, but which serves to exclude many heterogeneous forms of bad faith.'[32] Good faith is simply defined as a negative corollary of bad faith.[33] In anticipating critiques to his excluder analysis, Summers compiles a variety of recurring yet 'heterogeneous' forms of bad faith conduct,[34] which he has gathered from a comprehensive examination of the then-existing body of good faith cases. This list is not exhaustive.[35] Summers frames his analysis by outlining four broad categories of bad faith: 'bad faith in the negotiation and formation of contracts,[36] bad faith in performance,[37] bad faith in raising and resolving contract disputes[38] and bad faith in taking remedial action.'[39] Summers' starting point of good faith being devoid of meaning would not seem to be logical for lawyers unfamiliar with the principle of good faith. The very essence of the principle of good faith is that it should not be understood as a rule in contract law. For example, in *Clydesdale Bank plc v Black*,[40] Lord Coulsfield refused to lay down any precise requirements for the application of good faith under Scottish contract law. His Lordship accepted that this is how the principle works: 'To lay down any such detailed and prescribed requirements [for good faith] would, in any event, be difficult to reconcile with the normal approach of ... law to [the] questions of good faith.'[41]

Although this case was not concerned with the application of good faith in commercial contracts, Lord Coulsfield raised a very important point about how the principle of good faith works in contracts generally. It is clear from his Lordship's statement that good faith is not expected to behave like any other rules in contract law. The basic argument against the principle of good faith is simply based upon the difficulty, if not impossibility, of discerning the exact requirements it imposes on the contracting parties. If we accept that each party must act in accordance with good faith, what does this mean in terms of certain obligations or duties? Does this mean

[31] See Lord Bingham's judgement in *Interfoto Picture Library Ltd v Stiletto Visual Programmes Ltd* [1988] 1 All ER 348, 352. In Scotland, see *Smith v Bank of Scotland* (1997) SC (HL) 111, where the principle of good faith has been applied beyond the requirement of honesty in contracts.

[32] Summers, '"Good Faith" in General Contract Law', above n 28, 201.

[33] Ibid 200–201.

[34] Ibid 204.

[35] Ibid 203.

[36] Ibid 220–232.

[37] Ibid 232–243.

[38] Ibid 243–248.

[39] Ibid 248–252.

[40] (2002) SLT 764.

[41] Ibid 771.

that a contracting party in any contractual relationship must do A, B, C and D or not to satisfy the requirements of good faith? The answer is simply that we cannot lay down in advance any definite requirements that would enable contracting parties to know exactly how to act in good faith. This is why many common law lawyers find it extremely difficult to live with the principle of good faith.[42]

Although the excluder analysis may not satisfactorily provide a coherent meaning of good faith in contract law, the fact that good faith is an indefinable concept seems difficult to reject. At first sight, the excluder analysis might be understood as no more than an ad hoc approach towards fairness in contract law because it relieves courts from articulating a precise method that identifies circumstances for breach of good faith. In this regard, Bridge articulates a common sentiment pertaining to this approach against good faith obligation:

> Now, the drawback of such an approach is that it seems tantamount to saying that the good faith duty is breached whenever a judge decides that it has been breached. This hardly advances the cause of intellectual inquiry and it provides absolutely no guide to the disposition of future cases, except to the extent that they may be on all fours with a decided case.[43]

If this sentiment is accepted, good faith obligation would be redundant in modern contract law. However, if the historical role of the principle of good faith in the development of commercial law from Roman law to the emergence of modern contract theory was to be investigated, such an investigation would cast a different understanding of the application of good faith in contracts.[44] With respect, the obligation of good faith has a totally different role in contract law than any other rules. Good faith obligation is a bridge between new developments in commerce and society at large and the law in contracting relationships. It enables judges to develop existing rules to meet the need of new problems, which cannot be solved under existing rules.

---

[42] See Ewan McKendrick, 'Good Faith: A Matter of Principle?' in Angelo D M Forte (ed), *Good Faith in Contract and Property Law* (Hart Publishing, 1999) 39; Thomson, 'Good Faith Contracting: A Sceptical View', above n 11, 63.

[43] Bridge, 'Does Anglo-Canadian Contract Law Need', above n 3, 398; although American contract law believes in the relevancy of good faith principle, the excluder analysis has also been criticised by some American lawyers for being unsatisfactory in helping judges to articulate a coherent standard for the application of good faith in new problems, which cannot be solved by reference to previous cases. E.g. Dennis M Patterson rejected the excluder approach as the best statement of the meaning of good faith under the Code: 'The core excluder analysis logic is that courts cannot know in advance when conduct of a party amounts to bad faith unless identical conduct has been identified previously in that jurisdiction or by another court whose reasoning is regarded as persuasive. But how can courts reason about good faith when good faith cannot be identified outside the narrow designation provided by case law? How, in the absence of some forward looking logic of the concept of good faith, can that concept be employed unless the case under consideration is significantly similar to one in which the meaning of good faith has been established?': Patterson, 'Wittgensten and The Code', above n 28, 350. It should be noted, however, that Professor Summers' analysis has influenced the *Restatement of Contracts* (2nd) approach to the meaning of good faith.

[44] See the analysis of the historical role of the principle of good faith in the development of commercial contracts in Roman law and early English law in Chap. 2.

Table 5.1 Forms of bad faith conduct and Meaning of good faith

Forms of bad faith conduct	Meaning of good faith
1. Seller concealing a defect in what he is selling	Fully disclosing material facts
2. Builder wilfully failing to perform in full, though otherwise substantially full, though otherwise substantially performing	Substantially performing without knowingly deviating from specifications
3. Contractor openly abusing bargaining power to coerce an increase in the contract price	Refraining from abuse of bargaining power
4. Hiring a broker and then deliberately preventing him from consuming the deal	Acting cooperatively
5. Conscious lack of diligence in mitigating the other party's damages	Acting diligently
6. Arbitrarily and capriciously exercising a power to terminate a contract	Acting with some reasons
7. Adopting an overreaching interpretation of contract language	Interpreting contract language fairly
8. Harassing the other party for repeated assurance of performance	Accepting adequate assurances

That was how the Roman and medieval jurists dealt with the principle of good faith.[45] The excluder analysis itself does not stray far from the method in which medieval jurists dealt with the obligation of good faith.[46] This is because of the generality of the principle of good faith to all contracts. This generality makes any attempt to define good faith in contracts impossible. Definitions for such a principle in contract law tend to be either too abstract or applicable only to specific contexts. Summers offers the following (non-exhaustive) list (Table 5.1) as a representative example of this methodology for finding the meaning of good faith.[47]

In this respect, the focus is on developing a good faith obligation that is derived from Summers' categories of 'bad faith in performance' (in particular the subcategories of such performance). The subcategories of bad faith outlined by Summers include, 'evasion of the spirit of the deal, lack of diligence and slacking off, wilfully rendering only substantial performance, abuse of power to determine compliance and interfering with or failing to cooperate in the other party's performance.'[48] These

[45] See Schermaier, 'Bona Fides in Roman Contract Law', above n 5, 63; Gordley, 'Good Faith in Contract Law', above n 5, 93.

[46] In his study of the principle of good faith in contract law in the medieval, James Gordley concluded that: 'Perhaps the medieval experience suggests that we will always need an expression like "good faith" but we will never be able to define it. We should remain content with our list of *Fallgruppen* (groupings)': Gordley, 'Good Faith in Contract Law', above n 5, 93, 117.

[47] Robert S Summers, 'Good Faith in American Contract Law' in Reinhard Zimmermann and Simon Whittaker (eds), *Good Faith in European Contract Law* (Cambridge University Press, 2000) 127.

[48] Summers, '"Good Faith" in General Contract Law', above n 28; very similar words also appeared in the *Restatement* (Second) of Contracts, s 205.

subcategories would, therefore, enable judges to utilise their discretionary and equitable powers to identify a breach of good faith, even when the express terms of the contract may not support it. This effectively eliminates bad faith conduct manifesting as 'opportunistic behaviour, abuse of power and interfering with the other party's performance.'[49]

Summers is also adamant that good faith should not be treated as a legal rule but rather as a maxim, which 'cannot be reduced to a "vacuous" general definition.'[50] Many of Summers' contemporaries,[51] then and now, also support the view that a rule-based legal system is not desirable and 'not in accordance with reality.'[52] Summers further explains:

> In point of fact, our law recognises many kinds of non-legal rules as law. Why not similarly recognise the principle requiring contractual good faith? Furthermore, if we are to have doctrines which, among other things, perform safety valve functions, then isn't it inevitable that they will take rather general form? Of course, in their specific applications, they will generate rules.[53]

Summers contends that doctrines of equity, like good faith, act as crucial supplements to current legal rules. They not only serve as standalone bases for liability, but more significantly, they operate 'to limit and specify legal rules and contract terms.'[54] This is achieved by advancing 'the most fundamental policy objectives of any legal system,'[55] and in Summers' view, the obligation of good faith encapsulates the potential of the common law system: 'By invoking good faith ... it may be possible for a judge to do justice and do it according to law.'[56]

This understanding of the good faith principle in contract law may not satisfy those who still insist that accepting such a formula for the application of good faith would lead to uncertainty in the law. In a very strong criticism of the Official Comment (a) definition of s 205, Bridge said:

> This is as helpful as the definition of the elephant that tells us we will recognize it when we see it. With such a standard, individual decisions on good faith would appear to have very little predictive value in gauging the role of good faith in a different context. Moreover, good faith becomes vague to the point of meaninglessness, and quite possibly destructive in the hands of a court that does not know how to handle it but does not feel free to ignore it. Can it therefore be said that any good comes from introducing into contract law a standard of good faith?[57]

---

[49] Joel Iglesias, 'Comment Applying the Implied Covenant of Good Faith and Fair Dealing in United States Contract Law' (2004) 40 *Houston Law Review* 1423, 1451.

[50] Summers, 'The General Duty of Good Faith', above n 28, 821.

[51] E.g. Kennedy, above n 12, 1740–53; Ronald Dworkin, *Taking Rights Seriously* (Harvard University Press, 1977) 123–130.

[52] Summers, '"Good Faith" in General Contract Law', above n 28, 264–5.

[53] Ibid 265.

[54] Ibid 198.

[55] Ibid.

[56] Ibid.

[57] Bridge, 'Does Anglo-Canadian Contract Law Need', above n 3, 396–397.

This kind of criticism shows a degree of exaggeration among those who oppose the introduction of a good faith principle into contract law. First, it is not only the principle of good faith that cannot be defined with any degree of precision in contract law. There are several doctrines that are extremely difficult to define, but no attempts have been made to discredit them from contract law because of such difficulties. For example, the doctrine of undue influence, which the courts have never attempted to define with precision. As Lord Scarman said, 'There is no precisely defined law setting limits to the equitable jurisdiction of a court to relieve against undue influence. This is the world of doctrine, not of neat and tidy rules.'[58]

Second, Bridge's acceptance of the importance of protecting the justified expectations that arise in the contracting process indicates that his views on good faith are not entirely accurate. The principle of good faith has an ethical basis, to an extent; however, the principle is not purely based on abstract ethical ideals but also has relevance to business pragmatism. For example, the existence of a general principle of good faith under the *UNIDROIT Principles* demonstrates beyond any doubt the strong relationship between good faith and the reasonable or justified expectations of contracting parties in commercial contracts and that the requirements of good faith do not derive solely from abstract ethical ideals.[59] Third, the flexibility of the principle of good faith should not be taken as a weakness of its application in contractual relationships. Contracts are far from perfect, and the ability of contracting parties to protect their justified expectations through contractual terms is limited. The principle of good faith may provide an important instrument for contracting parties who cannot, for several reasons, fully protect their reasonable expectations through contractual terms. Under these circumstances, it is not unusual for contracting parties to rely on good faith.

Finally, though it may not satisfy those who want precise criteria for the application of good faith in contract law,[60] the excluder analysis offers an insight that may enable us to understand why it is so difficult to devise definite rules that prescribe exactly how contracting parties should act in accordance with good faith. In Australia, Priestly JA described good faith as having 'the great merit of being workable, without involving the use of fictions often resorted to by courts where the good faith obligation is not available and reflects what actually happens in decision making.'[61]

[58] *National Westminster Bank plc v Morgan* [1985] AC 686, 709.

[59] Steyn, 'The Role of Good Faith and Fair Dealing', above n 19, 131.

[60] Cf Philip Girard, 'Good Faith in Contract Performance: Principle or Placebo?' (1983) 5 *Supreme Court Law Review* 309.

[61] *Renard Constructions (ME) Pty Ltd v Minister of Public Works* (1992) 26 NSWLR 234, 266.

5.2.1.2 Burton Economic Approach: Foregone Opportunities

Despite the adoption of the excluder analysis into the *Restatement* and its acceptance by a considerable number of American courts,[62] American lawyers seem to be on the whole unimpressed by Summers' articulation of the principle of good faith in American law.[63] The position of American lawyers towards this question can generally be divided into two groups. The first group consists of those who do not think that the principle of good faith should have any role in commercial contracts beyond the requirement of honesty in commercial dealings, and any broad articulation of that principle in commercial law must, therefore, be rejected. Although this position does not initially reject the notion of good faith and fair dealing in commercial contracts, it gives the principle of good faith no role in measuring the conduct of commercial actors according to the prevailing standards of business decency and fair dealing. In other words, this view simply accepts the principle of good faith as an informing principle for many rules in contract law, rather than a workable principle in its own right. To some extent, this position is not far removed from the view expressed in other common law jurisdictions, even though there has been growing interest in the relevancy of good faith in contract law.[64]

The second group, which consists of those who believe in the importance of a good faith principle in commercial contracts, attempts to find a workable conceptualisation of that principle in commercial law.[65] The diversity among scholars in this group is not about whether or not the principle of good faith should be recognised in commercial contracts; there is no disagreement about the validity of good faith in commercial contracts in this school. However, there are differing views on the methods by which good faith should be employed by courts in commercial contracts.

Burton introduced a new approach in measuring good faith in contract performance.[66] His theory is based on several elements: first, questions of good faith in contract performance should be analysed from an economic perspective to articulate a workable standard of good faith in commercial contracts. This approach

---

[62] Some examples include *Carma Developers (Cal), Inc v Marathon Development California, Inc,* 826 P 2d 710, 727 (Cal, 1992); *Price v Wells Fargo Bank* 261 Cal Reporter 735, 741 (Ct App, 1989); *Occusafe, Inc v EG & G Rocky Flats, Inc,* 54 F 3d 618, 624 (10th Cir, 1995); *Fremont v E I DuPont DeNemours & Co,* 988 F Supp 870, 877 (Pa, 1997); see also Robert A Hillman, *The Richness of Contract Law. An Analysis and Critique of Contemporary Theories of Contract Law* (1997) 145 (a listing cases that have expressed support for the excluder analysis); Howard L Fink, 'The Splintering of the Implied Covenant of Good Faith and Fair Dealing in Illinois Courts' (1999) 30 *Loyola University of Chicago Law Journal* 247, 270.

[63] Patterson, 'Wittgensten and The Code', above n 28, 350; Clayton P Gillette, 'Limitations on the obligation of Good Faith' (1981) *Duke Law Journal* 619, 650; Girard, above n 60, 318.

[64] See Styles, 'Good Faith: A Principled Matter', above n 7, 172; Brownsword, 'Positive, Negative, Neutral', above n 12, 13.

[65] See commentary Farnsworth, 'Good Faith Performance', above n 22; Summers, '"Good Faith" in General Contract Law', above n 28; Summers, 'The General Duty of Good Faith', above n 28; Burton, 'Breach of Contract', above n 28; Burton 'Good Faith in Articles 1 and 2', above n 28; Andersen, above n 28; Patterson, 'Wittgenstein and The Code', above n 28.

[66] Burton, 'Breach of Contract', above n 28.

respects the autonomy of contracting parties because good faith would be based on the reasonable expectations of both parties to the contract. Second, the issue of good faith in contract performance arises when 'one party exercises discretion in performance and thereby controls the other party's anticipated benefit.'[67] Third, the economic approach to questions of good faith in contract performance, as Burton claims, moves the analysis from external factors of contracts, for example, business decency and community standard of fair dealing, to the expected cost of performance for the party who controls the performance of the contract. As Burton says:

> Bad faith performance occurs precisely when discretion is used to recapture opportunities forgone upon contracting—when the discretion-exercising party refuses to pay the expected cost of performance. Good faith performance, in turn, occurs when a party's discretion is exercised for any purpose within the reasonable contemplation of the parties at the time of formation—to capture opportunities that were preserved upon entering the contract, interpreted objectively. The good faith performance doctrine therefore directs attention to the opportunities forgone by a discretion-exercising party at formation, and to that party's reasons for exercising discretion during performance.[68]

Hence, good faith in contract performance occurs when contracting parties refrain from capturing future opportunities forgone at the formation of the contract. Under this approach, there are two inquiries that courts should carry out in deciding whether or not a party exercising discretion has acted in good faith. The first inquiry is an objective one, which is based on identifying forgone opportunities in accordance with 'the expectations of reasonable persons in the position of the dependent parties.'[69] There is also another subjective inquiry of the reasons behind exercising discretion in contract performance to recapture forgone opportunities: 'The question whether a party used its discretion in order to capture forgone opportunities is one of subjective intent.'[70] Burton's economic perspective analysis is that a bad faith breach is analytically similar to any simple breach of contract because both forms of breach involve a party's attempt to reclaim opportunities[71] forgone during the contracting process.[72] The fundamental premise of Burton's approach is that contracts frequently entail an imbalanced allocation of 'discretion in performance' among the contracting party to the point where a weaker party may need safeguards against the stronger party's designated discretion.[73]

---

[67] Ibid 369.

[68] Ibid 373.

[69] Ibid 391.

[70] Ibid 385–389: It has been suggested by Burton that this subjective inquiry into the reasons for exercising discretion in capturing forgone opportunities at the stage of performance is a key factor of the whole analysis: 'the fact that a discretion-exercising party causes the dependent party to lose some or all of its anticipated benefit from the contract thus is insufficient to establish a breach of contract by failing to perform in good faith. The cases suggest that the purpose of the discretion-exercising party is a key factor.'.

[71] They may be in the form of resources that either party have committed at the time of contracting for particular contracting uses in the arrangement.

[72] Burton, 'Breach of Contract', above n 28, 373–378.

[73] Ibid 380–384.

Finally, and most significantly, this approach to good faith in contract performance takes into account the importance of the reasonable expectations of contracting parties, which may not be covered by express terms in contracts. The introduction of good faith to commercial contracts enables courts to protect the justified expectations that arise in the contracting process.[74] Although parties to such contracts are acting at arm's length, the idea that a good faith principle should not be introduced between actors in commercial contracts is not convincing. Burton emphasised this point in his analysis of the American cases in which the Courts applied the principle of good faith:

> Good faith performance cases typically involve arm's length transactions, often between sophisticated businesspersons. The relative strength of the party exercising discretion typically arises from an agreement of the parties to confer control of a contract term on that party. The dependent party then is left to the good faith of the party in control.[75]

The good faith obligation addresses this issue by affording protection where its application in a given set of circumstances is reliant on the legitimacy of the exercise of that discretion.[76] What would be a legitimate or illegitimate use of discretion? This is answered by a critical evaluation of what Burton termed 'reasonable contemplation' argument as being too reliant on 'an amorphous totality of the circumstances at the time of [contract] formation.'[77] He disapproves the argument on the basis that this will have the potential that it could lead to an overly extensive and indefinite inquiry by the court to determine the parties' intentions and reasonable expectations.

Burton's formulation of the approach is to make it possible 'to identify with greater particularity the relevant expectations and motives that have been held to constitute bad faith.'[78] This presupposes that during the process of forming a contract, the contracting parties give up any opportunities to enter into other agreements. In this regard, bad faith conduct is the situation whereby the resulting opportunities have been forgone and the parties involved in the resulting contract should have been aware that they are barred from subsequently seizing those opportunities.[79] Burton proposes that this approach is preferable as it allows courts to conduct a less amorphous and more fact-specific inquiry when determining of whether a party has breached the implied duty of good faith in any given situation.[80]

Burton's analysis is far from being perfect, and his theory could not cover all situations of good faith in contracts. His claim that the 'forgone opportunities' analysis distances the principle of good faith from principles of fairness, morality, and policy

[74] See *North American and Continental Sales Inc v Bepi (Electronics) Ltd* 1982 SLT 47; *Thomson v Thomas Muir (Waste Management) Ltd* 1995 SLT 403; *Aitken v Standard Life Insurance* [2008] CSOH 162.

[75] Burton, 'Breach of Contract', above n 32, 385; cf John N Adam, 'The Economics of Good Faith in Contract Law' (1995) 8 *Journal of Contract Law* 126, 132–133.

[76] Burton, 'Breach of Contract', above n 28, 382–383.

[77] Ibid 387.

[78] Ibid.

[79] Ibid 388–389.

[80] Ibid 390–392.

is not entirely accurate.[81] Rightly or not, courts applying the principle of good faith in contractual disputes will still have to examine the conduct of contracting parties against existing standards of fairness and decency.[82] This is where the difficulty with the principle of good faith in contracts emerges.[83]

Nevertheless, Burton's analysis of the application of good faith in contract performance yields a coherent approach in limiting the unreasonable exercise of discretionary power in contracts. A contracting party who has bargained for discretion in contract performance must enjoy what he or she bargained for, the reasons for which were contemplated between the parties at the formation of the contract. The principle of good faith protects the reasonable expectations of a contracting party who confers to the other control over contract performance. In the absence of good faith requirements, a party who controls an aspect of contractual performance might easily abuse his or her power and deprive the other party of the benefit of the contract. Lücke suggests that the essence of Burton's approach is to curtail discretion in a way akin to Australian administrative law restricts the powers of the executive. This is particularly true when the discretion is used 'for the kinds of motives which the contract contemplates, and not for those which, by virtue of contractually created expectations … are reprehensible.'[84]

5.2.1.3 Farnsworth's Gap-Filler Approach to Good Faith

A conservative view of the principle of good faith is its application to contractual relationships as a 'gap-filler,' which enables courts to protect the reasonable expectations of contracting parties if their contract fails to uphold their expectations.[85]

---

[81] Steven J Burton, 'More on Good Faith Performance of a Contract: A Reply to Professor Summers' (1984) 69 *Iowa Law Review* 497, 499.

[82] E.g. under the Official Comment to art 1:201 of the *PECL* where it has been stated that the purpose of introducing a general principle of good faith in the *PECL* is to 'enforce community standards of decency, fairness and reasonableness in commercial transactions.' In the case of merchant, the *UCC* s 2–103(l)(b) provides that: 'Good faith in the case of a merchant means honesty in fact and the observance of reasonable commercial standards of fair dealing in the trade.'.

[83] In some situations, the reasonable expectations of contracting parties may not arise from the contract itself, but rather from the prevailing standards of fair dealing in the contracting parties' community. For instance, in *Smith v Bank of Scotland* 1997 SC 111, the expectation of cautioners for lenders to issue a warning is derived from what Banks themselves consider to be good practice in such circumstances in their *Banking Code*. The function of good faith is to introduce what is considered to be fair dealing in the community.

[84] Lücke, 'Good Faith and Contractual Performance', above n 1, 161.

[85] The implication of terms under the common law plays an important role in the absence of a general principle of good faith. See, e.g. *Scally v Southern Health and Social Services* [1991] 4 All ER 563; *Imperial Group Pension Trust Ltd v Imperial Tobacco L td* [1991] 2 All ER 597, 606. See also *North American and Continental Sales Inc v Bepi (Electronics) Ltd* 1982 SLT 47. Implied terms, however, are subject to strict tests that restrain the courts from invoking this doctrine in cases where the principle of good faith may yield a different result. See *The Moorcock* (1889) 14 PD 64; *Shirlaw v Southern Foundries (1926) Ltd* [1939] 2 KB 206, at 277; *M'Whirter v Longmuir* 1948 SLT 403. The relationship between the principle of good faith and implied terms is strongly

Farnsworth wrote an important article in 1963 about the principle of good faith under the *UCC*.[86] In his study, he distinguished between two standards of good faith: a subjective standard that is based on the *UCC* definition of good faith as 'honesty in fact in the conduct or transaction concerned,'[87] and an objective standard where the *UCC*'s art 2 defines good faith in terms of 'reasonable commercial standards of fair dealing.'[88] Predictably, Farnsworth sought to clear this confusion in the *UCC*'s conceptualisation of the duty of good faith. Good faith as 'honesty in fact' enfeebled the general provision of *UCC* 1-203.[89] As far as good faith in contract performance is concerned, the objective standard of good faith should be applied because the lack of dishonesty in contracts is not sufficient to satisfy the requirements of good faith in contract performance[90]: 'Here the inquiry goes to decency, fairness or reasonableness in performance or enforcement.'[91] In sustaining his argument for the relevancy of good faith in commercial contracts, Farnsworth attempted to link the Romans' experiences with the notion of good faith or bona fides in certain commercial contracts to the *UCC*'s general obligation of good faith. In his view.

> as to these commercially important contracts, 'good faith' was used in classical Roman law in the same sense in which it is used in the [*UCC*]'s general obligation of good faith—in the sense of good faith performance; and its significance was in implying terms in the agreement, just as it is under the [*UCC*].[92]

The analogy between good faith in modern contract law and its application in Roman law might easily be misunderstood. It can be argued that the strictness featured in Roman civil law necessitated the introduction of good faith in commercial contracts at that time and that modern contract law does not need such a principle for commercial contracts. However, this is not a correct reading of the relevancy of the Roman experiences to our concern of the principle of good faith in modern contracts. The point that Farnsworth wished to emphasise was that the good faith requirement is an indispensable part of a contract. Furthermore, it would have seemed that his emphasis on good faith in implying terms into contracts tends to restrain the application of good faith in contract law to the role of gap filler. However, an objective standard of good faith in contracts goes beyond this limited function in implying terms into contracts.

---

emphasised by Lord Steyn: 'In systems of law where there is a general duty of good faith in the performance of contracts the need to supplement the written contract by implied terms is less than in the English system. In our system, however, the implication of terms fulfils an important function in promoting the reasonable expectations of parties': Johan Steyn, 'Contract Law: Fulfilling the Reasonable Expectations of Honest Men' (1997) 113 *The Law Quarterly Review* 433, 441.

[86] Farnsworth, 'Good Faith Performance', above n 22.

[87] *UCC*, Sect. 5.1–5.201(19).

[88] *UCC*, Sect. 2–103(1)(b).

[89] Farnsworth, 'Good Faith Performance', above n 22, 674.

[90] Ibid 679: 'both common sense and tradition favour an objective standard of good faith performance; the Code does not prescribe an objective standard for its general obligation of good faith; but the courts can, by sound construction of the Code, arrive at an objective standard of good faith performance as to sales contracts by a merchant.'.

[91] Ibid 668.

[92] Ibid.

Although the introduction of good faith as another ground for implying terms would free that obligation from its initial restrictions under common law and help courts to protect the reasonable expectations of contracting parties, it is still difficult to pigeonhole the application of good faith in this area,[93] especially when one advocates for an objective standard of good faith. Good faith in contracts does not only involve what rights contracting parties have, but also the manner in which these rights can be enforced. Therefore, Farnsworth approaches good faith from an operational perspective as an implied term of cooperation from one contract party. This is to ensure that the other party is not denied their reasonable expectations.[94] In this respect, he is of the opinion that the role of good faith under the *UCC* does 'not go beyond those to which the traditional techniques of interpretation and gap filling were put in.'[95] In summary, the gap-filler approach to the obligation of good faith in contracts is an attempt to reconcile its application with the autonomy of contracting parties in commercial transactions[96] and to avoid intervention with parties' freedom in contracts.

Farnsworth's perspective appears analogous to the way good faith was developed under Australian common law as a duty to cooperate in enabling the other party to have the benefit of the contract.[97] Arguably, this analogy does not add anything meaningful to an understanding of good faith application in Australian law and would fuel arguments against its adoption. It would highlight what has already been suggested that Australian law has developed its own tools for achieving the same results that good faith obligation has done overseas.[98]

---

[93] Farnsworth admitted that the doctrine of good faith has several functions other than the implication of terms under American Courts: 'Courts have looked to all three of these views—Burton's, Summers', and mine—for support, often without recognizing a conflict among them, which is scarcely surprising, because in the context of performance the meaning of good faith may turn on which of its several functions is in issue. Sometimes good faith is the basis of a limitation on the exercise of discretion conferred on a party, as under Burton's view. Sometimes good faith is the basis for proscribing behaviour which violates basic standards of decency, as under Summers' view. Sometimes, it is merely the basis of implied term to fill a gap or deal with an omitted case': Farnsworth, 'Good Faith in Contract Performance', above n 29, 153, 163.

[94] Farnsworth, 'Good Faith Performance', above n 22, 673, 669; Farnsworth, 'Good Faith in Contract Performance', above n 29, 153, 156, 161.

[95] E Allan Farnsworth, *Contracts* (Little Brown & Co, 2nd ed, 1990); cited by Gummow J in *Service Station Association Ltd v Berg Bennett & Associates Pty Ltd* (1993) 117 ALR 393, 402.

[96] In *Kham & Nate's Shoes No 2 v First Bank* 908 F 2d 1351, Judge Frank Easterbrook said, 'When the contract is silent, principles of good faith, such as the *UCC*'s standard of honesty in fact, *UCC* s 1–201(19), and the reasonable expectations of the trade … fill the gap. They do not block use of terms that actually appear in the contract. … Any attempt to add an overlay of "just cause" … to the exercise of contractual privileges would reduce commercial certainty and breed costly litigation' (1357).

[97] This duty was discussed in *Butt v M'Donald* (1896) 7 QLJ 68 by Griffith CJ, 70–71: 'It is a general rule applicable to all contract that every party agrees, by implication, to do all such things that are necessary on his part to enable the other to have the benefit of the contract.'.

[98] Brownsword, 'Positive, Negative, Neutral', above n 4, 13, 15, 21; Geoffrey Kuehne, 'Implied Obligations of Good Faith and Reasonableness in the Performance of Contracts: Old Wine in New Bottles?' (2006) 33 *University of Western Australia Law Review* 63.

5.2.1.4 Shortcomings in the American Approach

One aspect of Summers' excluder analysis that remains unsatisfactory is that it 'provides no reason for characterising certain types of conduct as contrary to good faith.'[99] Both Summers and Lücke made similar observations on the Burton formulation, which should not be seen as an attempt to completely delineate the boundaries of good faith obligations.[100] The statutory adoption of good faith in the US has advantages in terms of its doctrinal legitimation. However, the shortcomings continue to include the lack of consensus on its scope and its limited operation under the *UCC*.

The subjective test under s 1-201(19) of the *UCC* requires that a party makes an honest judgement,[101] which presumably means an honest judgement in one's own interest. This alone may not be sufficient since honesty by one party is not necessarily reconcilable with fairness according to reasonable community standards. If a contract falls outside the ambit of the provision that imposes an objective test, and a dispute arises where a question of good faith calls to be answered, the courts would be constrained by the subjective test. Some of the provisions in the *UCC* refer only to general obligation of good faith without specifying the exact nature of the obligations.[102]

Farnsworth has suggested that, in some instances, the courts' own sense of fairness may be sufficient to guide it. However, the court may not always be in a situation where it is able to determine readily what would be equitable or what trade norms would be expected or reasonable. To facilitate a balanced test for good faith, an objective element should be added similar to s 205 of the *Restatement*. This would allow for evidence to be received in determining what the parties honestly thought and compare it with what is considered to be fair in the particular contractual setting. This would then bear the hallmark of a good faith regime along the lines of Brownsword's argument.[103]

5.2.1.5 Division Within the American Approach

Among academics and the judiciary, attempts have been made to provide meaning to the good faith obligation, which has seen widespread division and inconsistencies.

[99] Jeannie M Paterson, 'Good Faith in Commercial Contracts? A Franchising Case Study' (2001) 29(4) *Australian Business Law Review* 270, 277, which referred to Burton, 'More on Good Faith Performance', above n 81, 508–511.

[100] Summers, 'The General Duty of Good Faith', above n 28, 834; Lücke, 'Good Faith and Contractual Performance', above n 1, 155, 161.

[101] Lücke, 'Good Faith and Contractual Performance', above n 1, 163.

[102] E.g. *UCC* s 2–305(2) that governs open price items: there is no specific objective standard, but the term good faith is expressly mentioned so that the merchant's definition with its objective standard will apply where a merchant is involved.

[103] Brownsword, 'Positive, Negative, Neutral', above n 12, 33–34.

This can be aptly seen in the following quote by Hunter on the good faith obligation and its wider application[104]:

> Is the implied covenant a substantive term? If so, what is its content and how is that to be determined? Or is the concept simply a 'gap filler' to be used sparingly when the parties have left terms open or have used ambiguous language? Does it mean anything more than the absence of bad faith? What is the relationship between good faith and party autonomy?
>
> The answers to these various questions divide current American courts, roughly, into two camps. One might be called the 'neoformalist' camp in which party autonomy and the strict application of the language of an agreement are valued highly. The other might be called the 'contextualist' camp in which courts take a more active role in construing the concept of good faith to have an independent substantive content.[105]

Hunter noted that this judicial division in the US can be seen in Scalia J's decision in *Tymshare Inc v Covell*[106] where he stated that the concept of good faith honoured 'the reasonable expectations created by the autonomous expressions of the contracting parties.'[107] The good faith obligation, unfortunately, did not receive any clarification when the contextualist approach seized on the words 'reasonable expectations,' while the formalist approach,[108] predictably, seized on the words 'autonomous expressions of the contracting parties.' Formalists prioritise risk allocation from the beginning,[109] while contextualists consider how contractual rights are exercised in relation to the parties' specific relationship.[110] The ongoing divide between these two groups leads Hunter to surmise that the full extent of the concept of good faith remains unsettled.[111]

Since the good faith concept is yet to be clearly defined in the US,[112] its application has also suffered from unpredictability and inconsistency among the US States' Supreme Courts.[113] The good faith principle was described by the Illinois Supreme Court as a 'mystery' whose meaning is changeable depending on its contextual

---

[104] In an article referred to by Finn J: Paul Finn, 'Good Faith and Fair Dealing and "Boats against the Current"' (paper presented at the 2nd Biennial Conference on the Law of Obligations, Melbourne, 16 July 2004) 3.

[105] Hunter, 'The Growing Uncertainty', above n 30, 51.

[106] 727 F 2d 1145 (DC Cir 1984).

[107] *Tymshare Inc v Covell* 727 F 2d 1145 (DC Cir 1984), 1152.

[108] The decision most often associated with the neoformalist camp is *Kham & Nate's Shoes No 2, Inc v First Bank of Whitting* 908 F 2d 1351 (7th Cir 1990) as referred to by Hunter: Hunter, 'The Growing Uncertainty', above n 30, 52.

[109] As to the general rise of neoformalism, see John E Murray Jr, 'Contract Theories and Neoformalism' (2003) 71 *Fordham Law Review* 869.

[110] Hunter, 'The Growing Uncertainty', above n 30, 55.

[111] Ibid 56.

[112] Seth W Goren, 'Looking for Law in all the Wrong Places: Problems in Applying the Implied Covenant of Good Faith Performance' (2003) 37 *University of San Francisco Law Review* 257, 258, 267; William E Deitrick and Jeffrey C B Levine, 'Contractual Good Faith: Let the Contract, Not the Courts, Define the Bargain' (1997) 85 *Illinois Bar Journal* 120.

[113] Burton, 'Breach of Contract', above n 28, 370.

usage.[114] Farnsworth was also of the view that 'the doctrine ... has produced a tangled case law.'[115]

Due to these differing opinions, there is no doubt a schism exists in US jurisprudence when applying the good faith obligation. This has had a flow-on effect in Australia, whereby courts are divided on how to define the obligation. For example, Priestley JA (in *Renard*) simply reverted to Summers' excluder analysis and wholly avoided the definition of good faith, while Finn J in *South Sydney District Rugby League Football Club Ltd v News Ltd* implied that the obligation requires parties to adhere to the 'spirit of the bargain' and not undermine genuine contractual rights. Finn J's opinion has been preferred by the judiciary as it places a check on self-interest when it becomes unconscionable. However, Seddon and Ellinghaus argue that this approach blurs the lines between good faith and unconscionable conduct so as to confuse the concept further.[116] This issue will be discussed further under Part V below.

Mason outlined[117] three related aspects of good faith: (1) cooperation in achieving contractual objectives (loyalty to the promise),[118] (2) adherence to standards of honesty,[119] and (3) consideration of the parties' interest to reasonable standards. Barrett J highlighted that the latter two limbs are important to understand good faith.[120] These limbs exclude behaviour indicative of bad faith, which aligns with the excluder analysis. Despite general support for Mason's approach,[121] there is still

---

[114] The Illinois Supreme Court in *Watseka First International Bank v Ruda* 135 2d 140 (Ill, 1990), 145.

[115] Ian B Stewart, 'Good Faith in Contractual Performance and in Negotiation' (1998) *Australian Law Journal* 370, 376.

[116] See, e.g. Einstein J in *Aiton Australia Pty Ltd v Transfield Pty Ltd* (1999) 153 FLR 236, 263–265 adopting an approach similar to Stapleton: Jane Stapleton, 'Good Faith in Private Law' in Michael D A Freeman (ed), *Current Legal Problems* (Oxford University Press, 2000) vol 52, 1, 5–6; Nicholas C Seddon and Manfred Ellinghaus, *Cheshire and Fifoot's Law of Contract* (LexisNexis Butterworth, 8th Australian ed, 2002) 422.

[117] Anthony Mason, 'Contract and its Relationship with Equitable Standards and the Doctrine of Good Faith' (Paper presented at Cambridge Lectures, Cambridge, 8 July 2003).

[118] A duty of cooperation of the *Mackay v Dick* (1881) 6 App Cas 251 variety, as recently affirmed by the High Court in *Peters (WA) Ltd v Petersville* (2001) 75 ALJR 1385.

[119] A subjective requirement.

[120] *Overlook v Foxtel* (2002) Aust Contracts Rep 90–143 [64].

[121] For judicial citation of Mason's definition, see *Nauru Phosphate Royalties Trust (Receivers and Managers appointed) & Business Australia Capital Mortgage Pty Ltd v Nauru Phosphate Royalties Trust* [2008] NSWSC 916 at [43]; *J K Keir Pty Ltd v Priority Management Systems Pty Ltd* [2007] NSWSC 789 per Rein AJ at [27]; *Mangrove Mountain Quarries Pty Ltd v Barlow* [2007] NSWSC 492 at [27] per Windeyer J; *Vero Insurance New Zealand Ltd v Fleet Insurance & Risk Management Ltd* CIV 2007-404-001,438 (21 May 2007); *Bobux Marketing Ltd v Raynor Marketing Ltd* [2002] 1 NZLR 506; *Burger King Corporation v Hungry Jack's Pty Ltd* [2001] NSWCA 187; *Alcatel Australia Ltd v Scarcella* (1998) 44 NSWLR 349; *Hughes Aircraft Systems International v Airservices Australia* (1997) 146 ALR 1; *Renard Construction (ME) Pty Ltd v Minister of Public Works* (1992) 26 NSWLR 234. For academic citation, see Paul Finn, 'Good Faith and Fair Dealing: Australia' (2005) 11 *New Zealand Business Law Quarterly* 378, 381; Adam Wallwork, 'A Requirement of Good Faith in Construction Contracts?' (2004) 20 *Building and*

no uniform definition of good faith which has resulted in a scattered body of case law.[122]

5.3 Basis of Good Faith Obligation

The lack of a uniformly agreed definition (even in the US) poses a significant hurdle in establishing a basis for good faith obligation in Australia.[123] Is the underlying basis of the good faith obligation the reasonable expectations of the contractual parties or is it broadly based on a wider notion of community standards?

5.3.1 Reasonable Expectations or Community Standards

In Australian contract law, the implied obligation of good faith is assumed to reflect broad moral standards, such as fairness, loyalty, or cooperation, which are considered the ideal values of a contractual relationship.[124] Priestley JA endorsed this approach in *Renard* when he considered community expectations in discussing whether good faith was adhered to.[125]

Judicial support for this approach has waned over time with the prevailing trend of Australian court authority[126] preferring good faith obligation to be based on the reasonable expectations or legitimate interests of the contractual parties.[127] The reasonable expectations approach has the distinct advantage of allowing the courts to focus on a line of inquiry that directly relates to the contract and the circumstances in which the contracting parties are engaged in. This enables the court to evaluate, in a dispute, the parties' reasonable expectations of the contract's outcomes. On the other hand, the community standards approach would require the obligation of good faith

---

Construction Law 257; Elisabeth Peden, 'The Meaning of Contractual "Good Faith"' (2002) 22 *Australian Bar Review* 235; Pei Yee Woo, 'Rethinking a Principle Underlying Contract Law' (2002) 22 *Singapore Law Review* 132, 141.

[122] *Vodafone Pacific Ltd v Mobile Innovations Ltd* [2004] NSWCA 15 [192].

[123] The underlying basis of the good faith obligation will also be critical in the context of potential contractual exclusion of the implied obligation.

[124] Jeannie M Paterson, 'Limits on a Lender's Right to Repayment on Demand: Construction, Implication and Good Faith?' (1998) 26 *Australian Business Law Review* 258, 261.

[125] *Renard Construction (ME) Pty Ltd v Minister of Public Works* (1992) 26 NSWLR 234, 268.

[126] See, e.g. *Alcatel Australia Ltd v Scarcella* (1998) 44 NSWLR 349, 367; *Overlook v Foxtel* (2002) Aust Contracts Rep 90–143, [83]. In *Central Exchange Ltd v Anaconda Nickel Ltd* (2001) 24 WAR 382, Parker J referred to a 'reasonable standard of conduct having regard to the interest of both the plaintiff and the defendant' [39].

[127] There is also academic support for this approach given that it abdicates an approach to the implication of good faith based on 'some transcendent vision of fair dealing': Paterson, 'Limits on a Lender's Right', above n 131, 272.

to be gauged against an external standard beyond the contracting instrument. In a commercial contract, it may be possible to pinpoint the standard of conduct deemed appropriate in a homogenous business setting. However, it will become increasingly difficult in a broader business context since there may be various points of view about the type of conduct that would be considered contrary to good faith in contract performance. In addition, if the measure of the standard of good faith is that of the general community, the difficulties would be magnified as the viewpoints would be greatly varied and inconsistent. Such an application of good faith would justifiably open concerns about highly discretionary justice.[128]

This perspective is also observed in the US, where obligations of good faith, based on broad moral standards, have received less overt backing in court decisions.[129] In this sense, the conclusions of Barrett J in *Overlook v Foxtel* may serve as an instructive example:

> Foxtel did not act in a capricious way: on the contrary, its action was deliberate and reasoned and had both a rational basis and an objective explanation. Furthermore, the action was not purely selfish and destructive of the position of Overlook or such as to cause Overlook's rights to become nugatory, worthless or seriously undermined. ... Foxtel's actions involved no departure from standards of conduct which are honest, as well as being reasonable having regard to the parties' interest.[130]

Likewise, in the US, the Official Commentary on s 205 of the *Restatement* associates good faith with the legitimate expectations of the other party in the contract.[131] This approach have garnered support from various decisions in the US.[132]

5.3.2 Legitimate Interests

Finn was one of the first Australian commentators to associate an obligation of good faith with a positive obligation to consider the legitimate interests of the other contractual party.[133] In doing so, Finn recognised the power that one party might have over another in a contractual relationship:

> Relationships, whatever their type, inevitably give to one or both parties the de facto capacity to affect adversely the interests of the other. Expectations can be thwarted, obligations

---

[128] Jeannie M Paterson, 'The Standard of Good Faith Performance: Reasonable Expectations or Community Standards?' in Michael Bryan (ed), *Private Law in Theory and Practice* (Routledge-Cavendish, 1st ed, 2007) 153, 162–163.

[129] Jeannie M Paterson, 'Duty of Good Faith: Does it Have a Place in Contract Law?' (2000) 74 *Law Institute Journal* 47, 49.

[130] *Overlook v Foxtel* (2002) Aust Contracts Rep 90–143, [83].

[131] Although it is expressly acknowledged that the *Restatement* also invokes community standards.

[132] Relevant American authorities were cited by Paterson: Paterson, 'Limits on a Lender's Right', above n 124, 278.

[133] Paul Finn, 'The Fiduciary Principle' in Timothy G Youdan (ed), *Equity, Fiduciaries and Trusts* (Law Book Co, 1989) 4 as referred to by John W Carter and Michael P Furmston, 'Good Faith and Fairness in the Negotiation of Contracts: Part I' (1994) 8 *Journal of Contract Law* 1, 6.

> ignored, vulnerability exploited, legitimate interests disregarded, powers exercised harshly, and so on.[134]

Lubbe's views align with Finn's. Peden further defines good faith as considering the other party's interests without minimising their own interests and, in *Hospital Products Ltd v United States Surgical Corporation*, Mason J in endorsed the same view. He went on to expand on this idea extra-curially, noting:

> A contract may confer power on a contracting party in terms wider than are necessary for the protection of the legitimate interests of that party. In such a case, the courts will interpret the power as not extending to action proposed by the party in whom the power is vested when that action exceeds what is necessary for the protection of the party's legitimate interests.[135]

This approach has received express support where, for instance, Barratt J who opined that good faith involved 'a duty to recognise and to have due regard to the legitimate interests of both the parties in the enjoyment of the fruits of the contract as delineated by its terms.'[136] The direction taken for this perspective has also been followed in other common law jurisdictions. In the Supreme Court of Nova Scotia, Kelly J held that if a party acted in a way that would defeat the legitimate expectations of the other party in entering into a contract, without any reasonable justification, this would be a breach of the duty of good faith.[137] In Australia, the law also recognises the legitimate interests of the parties in the specific context of statutory unconscionability. For example, s 22 of the *Australian Consumer Law* (provided in the Second Schedule of the *Competition and Consumer Act 2010* (Cth)) acknowledges that conduct may not be unconscionable if a contract's conditions protect a supplier's legitimate interest.

For the purposes of this chapter, the distinction between reasonable expectations and legitimate interests is largely semantic and they are used interchangeably. The content of good faith obligations depends on the contract's context and the parties' reasonable expectations of the contract; however, this does not guarantee absolute clarity on the obligation's nature. This approach has obvious advantages and was aptly stated by Finn J as having:

> the virtue of conditioning the inquiry by reference to the actual circumstances of a given relationship: its nature, its terms, its contemplated purposes, the relative positions of the parties, the actual progress of the relationship, its business setting, the reasons for a decision or action taken, the consequences of the decision or action, and so on. Such is the material from which one will determine what, in the circumstance, one party is reasonably entitled to expect of the decision or action of the other. ... If the inquiry so raised is individualised, [and] it is neither amorphous nor unmanageable. Its focus ordinarily will be no more than

[134] Finn, 'Commerce', above n 16, 95.

[135] Mason, 'Contract, Good Faith and Equitable Standards', above n 20, 76.

[136] *Overlook v Foxtel* (2002) Aust Contracts Rep 90–143, [67]. Hasluck J adopted the same approach in *Automasters Australia Pty Ltd v Bruness Ptd Ltd* [2002] WASC 286, [388] and by Dodds-Stretton J in *Varangian v OFM Captial Ltd* [2003] VSC 444, [175]. Consistent with the need to have regard to the interests of both parties, in *Hoppers Crossing Club Ltd v Tattersalls Gaming Pty Ltd* [2005] VSC 114, Kaye J opined that the implied term of good faith 'would not operate so as to preclude the right of a party to act in pursuit of its own legitimate commercial interest' [25].

[137] *Gateway Realty Ltd v Arton Holdings Ltd (No 3)* (1991) 106 NSR (2d) 180, 197.

whether one party's conduct is consistent with (or faithful to) the relationship of the parties that is evidenced by their contract.[138]

5.3.3 *Obligation to Act Reasonably, Cooperatively, and Honestly*

Some members of the Australian judiciary have shown a propensity to align good faith with reasonableness.[139] The overlap of good faith obligation with reasonableness would allow greater effect to be given to the reasonable expectations of the contracting parties that would ultimately promote a culture of trust and cooperation as corollary notions in contractual relationships.[140] In this regard, good faith obligation inherently embraces these notions already and its outcome may conceivably enhance economic efficiency. From a commercial perspective, the law should promote cooperation between parties.[141] Without this cooperation, smooth business operations would not be possible, and the full benefit of a contract may not be realised by either party.[142]

An illustration was provided by *Australian Mutual Provident Society v 400 St Kilda Road*,[143] where the court did 'not perceive any difference between a rule that requires a lessor to act reasonably and a rule that requires a lessor to act in good faith in relation to a covenant against assigning without consent.'[144] A similar approach was seen in the judgement of Priestley JA in *Renard*, although Priestley JA noted that the two concepts, although separate and distinct, were nevertheless similar in application.[145] The same approach was also evident in the decision of the NSW Court of Appeal *Burger King Corporation v Hungry Jack's Pty Ltd* ('*Burger King*').[146] Consistent with this observation, the following also appeared in the judgement of *Hudson Resources Ltd v Australian Diatomite Mining Pty Ltd*:

> The ... decision of the New South Wales Court of Appeal in *Burger King Corporation v Hungry Jack's Pty Ltd* [2001] NSWCA 187 includes some particular focus upon the implied term of reasonableness, making the point that the Australian authorities make no distinction of substance between that term and the implied term of good faith. The close association of

[138] Finn, 'The Fiduciary Principle', above n 133, 10–11.

[139] As noted by Hasluck J in *Automasters Australia Pty Ltd v Bruness Pty Ltd* [2002] WASC 286, [388].

[140] Brownsword, 'Positive, Negative, Neutral', above n 12, 32.

[141] Cf Alessandro Arrighetti, Reinhard Bachmann and Simon Deakin, 'Contract Law, Social Norms and Inter-Firm Cooperation' (1977) 21 *Cambridge Journal of Economics* 171.

[142] Cf John Burrows, 'Contractual Co-operation and the Implied Term' (1968) 31 *Modern Law Review* 380.

[143] [1991] 2 VR 417.

[144] *Australian Mutual Provident Society v 400 St Kilda Road* [1991] 2 VR 417, 426.

[145] *Renard Constructions (ME) Pty Ltd v Minister of Public Works* (1992) 26 NSWLR 234, 265.

[146] [2001] NSWCA 187, [169–171]. Commonwealth Bank of Australia v Renstell Nominees Pty Ltd [2001] VSC 167, [47], provides a further example.

> ideas between the terms 'unreasonableness', 'lack of good faith' and 'unconscionability' is emphasised in *Burger King* at paragraphs 170 and 171 where the judgment of Priestley JA in *Renard Constructions (ME) Pty Ltd v Minister for Public Works* (1992) 26 NSWLR 234 at 263 and 265 is cited.[147]

Good faith is not breached if a party to a contract appears to have simply acted in a manner that could be objectively viewed as unreasonable. For example, bad faith cannot be established where a party exercises a right to terminate a contract, even if it negatively affects the innocent party's commercial objectives because good faith does not require a party to surrender its contractual rights or to restrict it from promoting its own 'legitimate interests.' If the good faith standard indeed required parties to act in a manner which is objectively reasonable in the context of the contract, it is expected that a further reasonableness caveat would be imposed. As this remains to be seen, it can be inferred that the good faith standard should not include an expectation for the parties to act in reasonable manner.

The conclusion is that acting reasonably is the same as acting in good faith.[148] This point was, indeed, made by Finkelstein J in *Garry Rogers* when his Honour observed that 'provided the party exercising the power acts reasonably in all the circumstances the duty to act fairly and in good faith will ordinarily be satisfied.'[149] However, acting unreasonably does not, in itself, equate to a breach of good faith, considering a party's right to consider its own interests: 'a party may have behaved in good faith, yet still have behaved unreasonably.'[150]

Peden noted that in other areas of contract (outside of good faith), such as in 'satisfactory finance' clauses, where the High Court has construed such provision as requiring honesty, it has not taken the further step of also requiring reasonable contractual behaviour.[151] It is hard, therefore, to disagree with the observation that the judicial equation of 'an obligation of reasonableness and one of good faith is misconceived,'[152] and in this respect, it seems 'the New South Wales Court of Appeal in *Burger King* is incorrect in assimilating good faith with objective reasonableness, as reasonableness sets too high a standard.'[153] While there may be some overlap in their content, 'unreasonableness' and 'lack of good faith' are distinct concepts and should not be used interchangeably.[154]

An important implication of Sir Anthony Mason's often cited conception of good faith that it includes cooperation, honesty, and reasonableness is that it does not

---

[147] *Hudson Resources Ltd v Australian Diatomite Mining Pty Ltd* [2002] NSWSC 314 [128] (Einstein J).

[148] *Lay v Alliswell Pty Ltd* (2002) V ConvR ¶54–651, [31].

[149] *Garry Rogers Motors Aust Pty Ltd v Subaru (Aust) Pty Ltd* (1999) ATPR ¶41–703, [37].

[150] Peden, *Good Faith in the Performance of Contracts*, above n 15, 164.

[151] Ibid 163 (citing *Meehan v Jones* (1982) 149 CLR 571).

[152] Peden, *Good Faith in the Performance of Contracts*, above n 15, 163.

[153] Ibid 184.

[154] An observation consistent with that of Hasluck J in *Automasters Australia Pty Ltd v Bruness Pty Ltd* [2002] WASC 286, [352].

preclude a party from acting in his or her self-interest.[155] Venning J's opinion in *Topline International Ltd v Cellular Improvements Ltd* confirms that the good faith obligation does not restrict parties to act only in the pursuance of all parties' common interests; they are able to advance their own commercial position. However, this does not mean that they can completely disregard the other parties' reasonable expectations, as is consistent with the neighbour principle. Based on this, the obligation of good faith would encompass: (a) the exercise of discretionary powers conferred by the contract to act reasonably and for the intended purpose, (b) the duty to cooperate in securing the objectives of the contract, and (c) the duty to avoid strategic conduct aimed at circumventing contractual obligations.[156]

The common law already requires a degree of cooperation between parties,[157] whereby the necessary acts are carried out to perform the contract.[158] The duty also requires that parties do not take steps to prevent the other party from fulfilling a condition of the contract. Where a party engages in this conduct, the contract is taken to be satisfied as it would be inequitable for the obstructing party to benefit from their uncooperative conduct.[159] The duty of cooperation is essentially a negative right that prohibits parties from interfering with each other's ability to fulfil the contract.[160] A more stringent interpretation might require positive acts from contracting parties, including that they do everything that is reasonably necessary to ensure that the contract is executed in line with their mutual intentions.

The duty to cooperate also serves as a check on the exercise of rights and powers, such as, the right to terminate a contract for non-performance of a contingent condition. If the condition remains unmet due to a breach by one of the contracting parties,

---

[155] Sir Anthony Mason suggested that good faith encompasses: (1) an obligation on the parties to co-operate in achieving the contractual objects (loyalty to the promise itself); (2) compliance with honest standards of conduct; and (3) compliance with standards of conduct which are reasonable having regard to the interests of the parties: Mason, 'Contract, Good Faith and Equitable Standards', above n 20, 69; Paul Finn, 'Good Faith and Fair Dealing: Australia' (2005) 11 *New Zealand Business Law Quarterly* 378, 381.

[156] John D McCamus, 'Abuse of Discretion, Failure to Cooperate, and Evasion of Duty: Unpacking the Common Law Duty of Good Faith Contractual Performance' [2004] 29 *The Advocates' Quarterly* 72; see also discussion in John W Carter and Elisabeth Peden, 'Good Faith in Australian Contract Law' (2003) 19 *Journal of Contract Law* 155; Kuehne, 'Implied Obligations of Good Faith', above n 98; Tyrone Carlin, 'Good Faith in Contractual Performance—Smoke Without Flame?' (2005) 4 *Journal of Law and Financial Management* 18; *Macquarie International Health Clinic Pty Ltd v Sydney South West Area Health Service* [2010] NSWCA 268.

[157] See *Concrete Pty Ltd v Parramatta Design & Developments Pty Ltd* (2006) 231 ALR 663, 704 (per Callinan J).

[158] Cf *Pierce Bell Sales Pty Ltd v Frazer* (1973) 130 CLR 575, 592 (per Gibbs J); *Concrete Pty Ltd v Parramatta Design and Developments Pty Ltd* (2006) 229 CLR 577, [14], [156]; *Secured Income Real Estate (Australia) Ltd v St Martins Investments Pty Ltd* (1979) 144 CLR 596, 607 (per Mason J); Samuel J Stoljar, 'Prevention and Cooperation in the Law of Contract' (1953) 31 *Canadian Bar Review* 231, 231–232.

[159] Cf *Peters (WA) Ltd v Petersville Ltd* (2001) 205 CLR 126, [36]; *Walker v Zurich Australian Insurance Ltd* [2001] QCA 296, [109]; *Ultimo Document Storage v Liquid Vision* [2003] NSWSC 1175; *Alstom Ltd v Yokogawa Australia Pty Ltd (No 7)* [2012] SASC 49, [574–575].

[160] *Shepherd v Felt and Textiles of Australia Ltd* (1931) 45 CLR 359, 378 (per Dixon J).

the party at fault loses the right to terminate the contract.[161] A lack of cooperation prevents the defaulting party from relying on the non-performance of the condition.[162] The principle to cooperate also applies to preclude the arbitrary, capricious, or unreasonable exercise of a right to terminate for breach.[163] In this regard, the duty to cooperate is often considered in connection with the duty to act in good faith and, as such, may not be necessary to distinguish between them.[164]

Considering the above, it is important to emphasise that the duty to cooperate necessitates only those actions that are essential to maintain the contract's benefit.[165] In other words, the cooperation required must be limited to what has been agreed upon in the contract and not based on any duty to safeguard the other contracting party's benefit.[166] Additionally, the scope of the duty to cooperate must also be affected by its commercial context in a particular contract.[167] In the case of *Australis Media Holdings Pty Ltd v Telstra Corporation Ltd*, the court made the remark that pay television was an 'emerging medium' in 'a highly competitive industry' in which the 'players were all corporate entities.'[168] In this regard, the degree of cooperation needed in a contract made between commercial parties, who are at arm's length and expected to act in their own interests, may be minimal.[169] In most commercial

---

161 *Quinn Villages Pty Ltd v Mulherin* [2006] QCA 433, [29–32].

162 This is analogous to the principle that precludes a party from relying on self-induced frustration: see *Plumor Pty Ltd v Handley* [1996] 41 NSWLR 30, 34–35.

163 See *Commonwealth of Australia v Amann Aviation Pty Ltd* (1991) 174 CLR 64, 74; *Renard Construction (ME) Pty Ltd v Minister of Public Works* (1992) 26 NSWLR 234; *Hughes Bros Pty Ltd v Trustees of the Roman Catholic Church for the Archdiocese of Sydney* (1993) 31 NSWLR 91; *Dickson Property Management Services Pty Ltd v Centro Property Management (Vic) Pty Ltd* (2000) 180 ALR 485; *Forklift Engineering Australia Pty Ltd v Powerlift (Nissan) Pty Ltd* [2000] VSC 443; *Bamco Villa Pty Ltd v Montedeen Pty Ltd* [2001] VSC 192.

164 In *Burger King Corporation v Hungry Jack's Pty Ltd* [2001] NSWCA 187, the court held that the factors that led it to conclude that the franchisor's termination was in bad faith also made it a breach of the duty to cooperate.

165 *Butt v M'Donald* (1896) 7 QLJ 68, 70–71.

166 *Australis Media Holdings Pty Ltd v Telstra Corporation Ltd* (1998) NSWLR 104, 124–125: 'there cannot be a duty to co-operate in bringing about something which the contract does not require to happen. … A contract may "contemplate" many benefits for the respective parties, but each can only call on the other to provide, or co-operate in the providing of, benefits promised by that party.'.

167 Cf in *Prophecy Mining No Liability v Kiwi Gold No Liability* (High Court, Auckland, CP 2264/88, 8 August 1990), at 14; (Court of Appeal, CA 30/91, 18 July 1991), Thomas J held that parties to a joint venture agreement were obliged to cooperate and assist each other in order to implement their joint enterprise as the contract is predicated on collaborative conduct between the parties; see also *Williams & Adams Ltd v Computer Systems Implementation Ltd* (High Court, Wellington, CP 215/92, 9 March 1995, Ellis J); *Devonport Borough Council v Robbins* [1979] 1 NZLR 1, 29; *Pacifica Shipping (1985) Ltd v Centreport Ltd* (High Court, Wellington, CP 230,100, 31 October 2000).

168 (1998) NSWLR 104, 117.

169 *Laurelmont Pty Ltd v Stockdale & Leggo (Queensland) Pty Ltd* [2001] QCA 212, [39]; *Central Exchange Ltd v Anaconda Nickel Ltd* [2002] WASCA 94, [66].

contexts, contracting parties will consider their own benefit in preference to that of the other, and as such the scope of cooperation is correspondingly limited.[170]

Contractual cooperation is well-established in common law and is not inherently ambiguous. Further, parallels can be made between the duty to cooperate and the duty to act in good faith and have been described by courts as equivalent principles in a bid to introduce good faith into the common law. Consequently, the duty to cooperate may be considered an element of good faith which includes the protection of the parties' reasonable expectations. Further, promoting contractual cooperation aligns with the four specific objectives of the duty of good faith, as identified by Thompson.[171]

The first objective is to prevent dishonesty, which may require that parties disclose material information during negotiations, implying that the rights and powers granted by the contract should be used for a proper purpose.[172] Honesty is regarded an essential norm in any commercial contract 'for the reduction of risk and the maximisation of efficient economic activity'.[173] It is, therefore, considered contentious within the context of good faith obligation whether the honesty element means only subjective honesty or whether it incorporates objective honesty. Some favour the former.[174] Subjective honesty implies honesty in the sense of a clear conscience or lack of a guilty mind.[175] In order for there to be a breach of good faith, the plaintiff would have to establish that the defendant intended to deceive the plaintiff or knowingly exercised a contractual discretion for an ulterior motive.[176]

The judiciary will be faced with the difficult task of determining the actual intentions of the contracting parties if good faith is to be characterised by honesty in the subjective sense. In the dissenting opinion of Bingham LJ in *Walford v Miles*, it was suggested that subjective intentions could be hard to decide, but no more difficult than certain other matters that regularly require judicial determination.[177] For example, judges may often be charged with making factual findings as to subjective intention

---

[170] Cf *Biotechnology Australia Pty Ltd v Pace* (1988) 15 NSWLR 130, 132–133 (per Kirby P); *GSA Group Pty Ltd v Siebe plc* (1993) 30 NSWLR 573, 579 (per Rogers CJ Comm D).

[171] Thomson, 'Good Faith in Contracting: A Sceptical View', above n 11, 66–70.

[172] Stapleton, 'Good Faith in Private Law', above n 116, 1, 9.

[173] James Allsop, 'Good Faith and Australian Contract Law: A practical Issue and a Question of Theory and Principle' (2011) 85 *Australian Law Journal* 341, 344.

[174] Peden, 'The Meaning of Contractual "Good Faith"', above n 121, 235: Peden suggests that subjective good faith means a lack of 'ill-will' and that the 'subjective sense of good faith would be appropriate in an imposed common law obligation of good faith in contracts'; cf Summers, '"Good Faith" in General Contract Law', above n 28.

[175] David McLauchlan, 'The Agreement to Negotiate in Good Faith: A Non-Justiciable Contract?' (2005) 11 *New Zealand Business Law Quarterly* 454, 462.

[176] *Interfoto Picture Library Ltd v Stiletto Visual Programmes Ltd* [1989] 1 QB 433, 439; *New Zealand Shipping Co Ltd v AM Satterthwaite & Co Ltd (The "Eurymedon")* [1975] AC 154, 167; *R (European Roma Rights Centre) v Immigration Officer, Prague Airport* [2005] 2 AC 1, [59–64] 50–53; Cf *Meehan v Jones* (1982) 149 CLR 571; *Stadhard v Lee* (1863) 122 ER 138, 141; *Carr v JA Berriman Pty Ltd* (1953) 89 CLR 527; *Godfrey Constructions Pty Ltd v Kanangra Park Pty Ltd* (1972) 128 CLR 529.

[177] [1992] 1 All ER 453.

in criminal proceedings. However, the view of Bingham LJ was not endorsed by the House of Lords.

In *Wellington City Council v Body Corporate 51,702* (‘*Wellington*’), the New Zealand (NZ) Court of Appeal went so far as to suggest that the determination of subjective good faith not only gives rises to an evidential difficulty but is so indeterminate as to not be capable of judicial consideration.[178] Arguably, the NZ Court of Appeal took the argument too far. Nonetheless, the perceived problems can be remedied by recognising that any reference to honesty when defining good faith should incorporate an objective element. In no part of commercial law is honesty determined by a purely subjective ‘Robin Hood’ standard.[179] Dishonesty in a civil liability sense is not the same as dishonesty in a criminal liability sense.[180] Thus, a person may be regarded as dishonest even if he or she does not contravene his or her own standard of honesty. Good faith obligation is not always to be measured by what a contracting party believes to be right or wrong.[181] Instead, honest good faith conduct must be gauged by that standard which the law deems appropriate to be observed between all contracting parties in their specific contractual dealings with one another.[182]

Guidance may, perhaps, be drawn from equity in determining an appropriate measure of honesty for good faith contractual conduct. In *Twinsectra Ltd v Yardley*,[183] the House of Lords considered the meaning of honesty in the context of liability for the assistance of a breach of trust. Such liability often arises in the circumstance of commercial and professional relationships.[184] The majority advocated a mixed subjective and objective test for dishonesty. In order to be found dishonest, the defendant would have to have breached the ordinary standards of reasonable and honest people but also he or she would have to appreciate that by those standards the conduct was dishonest.[185] Lord Millett (dissenting) omitted the last requirement. A defendant would not have to appreciate that he or she was acting dishonestly; it would

---

178 [2002] 3 NZLR 486, 495–496 (per Tipping J).

179 *Twinsectra Ltd v Yardley* [2002] 2 All ER 377, 384 (per Lord Hutton). See also McLauchlan, ‘The Agreement to Negotiate in Good Faith’ above n 175, 462.

180 *Royal Brunei Airlines Sdn Bhd v Tan* [1995] 3 All ER 97, 105 (per Lord Nicholls). Cf *R v Hayes* [2008] 2 NZLR 321 (for a discussion on dishonesty in a criminal liability context).

181 *First National Bank of Chicago v Trebein Co* (1898) 59 Ohio St 316, 324–325 (per Minshall J).

182 *United Group Rail Services Ltd v Rail Corporation (NSW)* (2009) 74 NSWLR 618; *Macquarie International Health Clinic Pty Ltd v Sydney South West Area Health Service* [2010] NSWCA 268.

183 [2002] 2 All ER 377.

184 See, e.g. *Royal Brunei Airlines Sdn Bhd v Tan* [1995] 3 All ER 97; *Grupo Torras SA v Al-Sabah (No 5)* [2001] Lloyd's Rep Bank 36; *US International Marketing Ltd v National Bank of NZ Ltd* [2004] 1 NZLR 589; *Equiticorp Industries Group Ltd (In Statutory Management) v The Crown (Judgment no 47)* [1998] 2 NZLR 481.

185 [2002] 2 All ER 377, 384 (per Lord Hutton). This test has also been utilised in criminal law in the context of obtaining property by deception. Thus, it has been observed that it ‘is no defence for a man to say,’ ‘I knew that what I was doing is generally regarded as dishonest; but I do not regard it as dishonest myself. Therefore, I am not guilty.’ What he is, however, entitled to say is, ‘I did not know that anybody would regard what I was doing as dishonest.’: *R V Ghosh* [1982] 2 All ER 689, 696 (per Lord Lane CJ).

be sufficient that he or she was.[186] His Lordship cogently justified his conclusion on the basis that civil liability is predicated on the conduct of the defendant rather than his or her state of mind.[187] Culpability results from unreasonable or negligent behaviour. Accordingly, neither an honest motive nor an innocent conscience can absolve a defendant who is objectively dishonest.

The test propounded by Lord Millett should be preferred in the context of honesty as a conceptualisation of good faith obligation.[188] The envisaged purpose of a good faith obligation is to protect the reasonable expectations of contracting parties. It would be anomalous if those reasonable expectations were subject to, or qualified by, the subjective viewpoints of a contracting counterparty. In keeping with traditional notions of civil liability, contractual good faith should be defined predominantly with regard to the objective nature of the impugned conduct and its effect on the rights of others. A requirement for the transgressor to act with a guilty state of mind should not enter into the equation.

Despite having determined that good faith may be characterised by objective honesty, it is recognised that a conceptualisation of good faith cannot be limited solely to honesty. For instance, a contractual power may be exercised in a capricious manner with an improper motive, but the transgressor may openly disclose that motives to the contacting counterparty. Although the defendant has not acted in an objectively dishonest manner per se, conceivably he or she has still acted in breach of good faith.

For example, in *The Atlantic Baron*[189] a firm of shipbuilders agreed to build a tanker for the plaintiff. Payment was to be made in five instalments. There was a currency decline after the first instalment was paid. In consequence, the shipbuilders demanded a ten per cent increase in the price. They threatened not to perform if the additional payment was not forthcoming. Both parties were well aware that

---

[186] [2002] 2 All ER 377, 408.

[187] Ibid 407 and 409; it seems anomalous that a dishonest state of mind is not necessary for liability for inducing a breach of contract, but such a state of mind is required for dishonest assistance, especially where equity is generally thought to impose more stringent requirements than the common law. See Rosy Thornton, 'Dishonest Assistance: Guilty Conduct or a Guilty Mind?' [2002] *Cambridge Law Journal* 524, 526.

[188] See Jessica Palmer, 'The Privy Council on Being (Dis)Honest About Dishonest Assistance' (2005) 24 *University of Queensland Law Journal* 539; the Privy Council in *US International Marketing Ltd v National Bank of NZ Ltd* [2004] 1 NZLR 589 favoured a more objective test by recognising that the subjective component is only relevant to assessing what objective standard of honesty is required. In determining the standard, the Court should consider the personal attributes of the defendant and his or her intelligence and experience. Cf *Barlow Clowes International Ltd (in liq) v Eurotrust International Ltd* [2006] 1 All ER 333. It is conceded that divorcing the state of mind of the defendant from the inquiry may produce severe outcomes in some instances. Take, e.g. 'a man who comes from a country where public transport is free. On his first day here, he travels on a bus. He gets off without paying. He never had any intention of paying. His mind is clearly honest; but his conduct, judged objectively by what he has done, is dishonest.': *R v Ghosh* [1982] 2 All ER 689, 696 (per Lord Lane CJ). Nonetheless, while the more stringent test for dishonesty may not be warranted in the criminal law, it is submitted that it is appropriate for the determination of civil liability.

[189] [1978] 3 All ER 1170.

the reason for the threat was a change in exchange rate. In fact, the plaintiff had made the shipbuilders aware that its business was also adversely affected by the currency devaluation. Mocatta J held that the threat amounted to economic duress.[190] At no time did the shipbuilders act dishonestly. The reason for the undue pressure was made clear. Nonetheless, the conduct displayed by the shipbuilders arguably contravened standards of good faith. The shipbuilders were endeavouring to recover opportunities forgone upon contracting. They sought to recapture the opportunity to include provision for currency alterations, which opportunity they had relinquished upon contracting by assuming the risks of currency fluctuations. The case clearly evidences that a definition of good faith based only on honesty is not sufficient. In some instances, a different, and, perhaps, more stringent measure of conduct is required.

A definition of good faith that requires an element of reasonableness may overcome the limitations of the honesty element. Certainly, reasonableness may impose a more stringent standard than honesty. A person who acts reasonably must be acting honestly; however, it is possible that a person acting honestly may be acting unreasonably.[191] Some believe that any concept of reasonableness within the meaning of good faith must be seen as limited to an element of honesty.[192] The scenario presented by *The Atlantic Baron* case shows that this should not necessarily be the case.

Second, good faith may ensure that a person keeps his or her word. Good faith may more readily require a promisor to be held to his or her word than existing contractual doctrine would allow. Good faith may, therefore, bear similarities to the notion of promissory estoppel.[193] The doctrine of estoppel is a paradigm example of the courts seeking to ensure good faith conduct. It protects against unfairness.[194] A promisor who seeks to renege on his or her word, leaving the promisee to suffer the detrimental consequences, fails to exercise good faith behaviour. Thus, promissory estoppel reinforces good faith by giving effect to the reasonable expectations of the parties.[195] Indeed, proponents of good faith suggest that the evolution of promissory

---

[190] Ibid 1174, 1184—relief, however, was not granted as the plaintiff had affirmed the contract by its conduct.

[191] It is arguable that reasonableness and fair dealings subsume the concept of honesty: Finn, 'Good Faith and Fair Dealing: Australia', above n 126, 380.

[192] See Carter and Peden, 'Good Faith in Australian Contract', above n 156.

[193] According to Richardson J in *Gillies v Keogh* [1989] 2 NZLR 327, there are three elements required to give rise to promissory estoppel. Firstly, an encouragement of a belief or expectation is needed. Secondly, there must be reliance on that belief or expectation. Thirdly, detriment must result from that reliance (346).

[194] See Justice Forrie Miller, 'Equitable Estoppel' in Christine French and Grant Hammond, *The Law of Obligations: 'Contract in Context'* (2007) 51.

[195] It has been argued that an estoppel is created where the promisee is entitled to expect good faith behaviour by the promisor. See Barbara Mescher, 'Promise Enforcement by Common Law or Equity?' (1990) 64 *Australian Law Journal Reports* 536, 543. See also Mason, 'Contract, Good Faith and Equitable Standards', above n 20, 90; Pei Yee Woo, 'Protecting Parties' Reasonable Expectations: A General Principle of Good Faith' (2001) 1 *Oxford University Commonwealth Law Journal* 195, 206.

estoppel evidences the inadequacy of classical contract law to meet the needs and expectations of contracting parties and the commercial community.[196]

Third, good faith may prevent a contracting party from, as a result of his or her behaviour, making the position of the other contracting party worse. For example, a good faith obligation may preclude a party to an agreement to negotiate from terminating negotiations for reasons that are capricious or arbitrary.[197] From an Australian common law perspective, this understanding must stem from the basis that good faith obligation can only apply where contract formation has already taken place and the obligation introduced as a principle of construction.[198] Good faith obligation cannot extend to regulate pre-contractual negotiations. Traditional reasoning would suggest that a distinction must be made between where there is an enforceable agreement and where there is no enforceable agreement. In the latter situation, instances of bad faith conduct may give rise to remedies in tort, equity and statute, but not in contract. The liability arises from an extra-contractual obligation.[199] Indeed, if a plaintiff complains that he or she believed that a contract would ensue and relied on that belief to his or her detriment, the claim is, in reality, one relating solely to detrimental reliance rather than expectation loss. The action would fall more naturally within a tortious action for deceit rather than a cause of action in contract law. The equitable doctrine of promissory estoppel may also provide a measure of protection in relation to pre-contractual promises and representations. The doctrine in Australia is not limited to dealings between parties who have prior contractual rights *inter se*.[200] Conceivably, s 18 of the *Australian Consumer Law* (*ACL*) might also be relied upon by a victim of misleading and deceptive conduct in pre-contractual bargaining. The most obvious way for Australian lawyers to frame pleadings that seek to impose liability for bad faith discontinuation of negotiations may be to allege misleading and deceptive behaviour under s 18 of the *ACL*.[201] This also does not mean that tort law

---

[196] Lord Steyn has contended that in 'the absence of a generalised duty of good faith the specific and concrete rules of estoppel are needed to deal with demonstrated problems of unfairness.': Johan Steyn, 'The Role of Good Faith and Fair Dealing in Contract Law: A Hair Shirt Philosophy?' in Johan Steyn, *Democracy Through Law: Selected Speeches and Judgment* (Routledge, 2004) 215.

[197] Edward Thomas, 'Good Faith in Contract: A Non-Sceptical Commentary' (2005) 11 *New Zealand Business Law Quarterly* 391, 393.

[198] The idea that a doctrine of good faith would encompass a pre-contractual duty to bargain in good faith whose breach may, at a minimum, justify an award of reliance damages seemingly compromises the dividing line between contractual and non-contractual obligations and generally considered to be axiomatic in Australian jurisprudence: See Friedrich Juenger, 'Listening to Law Professors Talk About Good Faith: Some Afterthoughts' (1995) 69 *Tulane Law Review* 1253, 1254.

[199] William Tetley, 'Good Faith in Contract: Particularly in the Contracts of Arbitration and Chartering' (2004) 35 *Journal of Maritime Law and Commerce* 561, 565. See also Nadia E Nedzel, 'A Comparative Study of Good Faith, Fair Dealing, and Precontractual Liability' (1997) 12 *Tulane European and Civil Law Forum* 97, 155.

[200] See *Waltons Stores (Interstate) Ltd v Maher* (1988) 164 CLR 387.

[201] John W Carter and Michael P Furmston, 'Good Faith and Fairness in the Negotiation of Contracts: Part II' (1995) 8 *Journal of Contract Law* 93, 99. The damages that might be awardable for a bad faith discontinuation of negotiations under the Australian Consumer Law may be limited. Conceivably damages might be claimed for wasted expenditure falling under the head of reliance

can serve as an adequate substitute for good faith in the negotiation of contracts. A somewhat restrictive approach has been adopted in tort jurisprudence in applying tort law by the courts, particularly in regard to overriding the freedom not to contract.[202] Indeed, there appears to be a general reluctance for the principles of tort law to interfere with the well-established rules of contract. Ordinarily, in this sense, there is no duty of care between business parties negotiating at arm's length.[203] As such, a wronged party in terminated negotiations would have no cause of action in contract on which to found a claim for a breach of good faith.

Finally, good faith may relieve contracting parties from absurd consequences that flow from their agreement. Like the doctrine of frustration, good faith might be utilised by the courts to construe a contract in a manner which produces a reasonable and substantively fair result. The doctrine of frustration is a principle of construction and can be modified by the express agreement of the parties. This can occur where the parties specifically provide for the frustrating event.[204] This analogy implies that contracting parties might also be free to expressly determine an obligation of good faith. Because construction is dependent on the nature of the contract and the surrounding circumstances, contracting parties could construe the duties of good faith by making their contracts sufficiently clear.[205]

5.4 Should Good Faith Be Equated to a Fiduciary Standard?

Carter and Stewart raised concerns about the possibility of good faith being equated to a fiduciary standard[206] and is undoubtedly an issue that requires clarification. It was not uncommon for Australian commercial plaintiffs to allege that the commercial relationship may be one governed by fiduciary standard, rather than one simply

loss. It is, however, contentious whether damages for loss of a chance to enter into a substantive contract could be sought as this may fall within the head of expectation loss which may not be contemplated by the Australian Consumer Law.

[202] See Paula Giliker, 'A Role for Tort in Pre-Contractual Negotiations? An Examination of English, French and Canadian Law' (2003) 52 *International Comparative Law Quarterly* 969.

[203] Basil S Markesinis and Simon F Deakin, *Tort Law* (Oxford University Press, 4th ed, 1999) 93; John Cartwright, *Misrepresentation, Mistake and Non-Disclosure* (2012) 282; See also *Martel Building Ltd v Canada* [2000] 2 SCR 860; *Banque Financière de la Cité SA v Westgate Insurance Co Ltd* [1989] 2 All ER 952; *Ontario Ltd v Cornell Engineering Co* (2001) 198 DLR (4th) 615; *Gross v Great-West Life Assurance Co* [2002] ABCA 37; *Prime Commercial Ltd v Wool Board Disestablishment Co Ltd* (Court of Appeal, CA 110/05, 18 October 2006), [39] per William Young P.

[204] Nicholas C Seddon and Manfred P Ellinghaus, *Cheshire and Fifoot's Law of Contract* (LexisNexis Butterworth, 9th Australian ed, 2008) 971.

[205] Elisabeth Peden, 'Incorporating Terms of Good Faith in Contract Law in Australia' (2001) 23 *Sydney Law Review* 222, 231.

[206] See, e.g. John W Carter and Andrew Stewart, 'Interpretation, Good Faith and the "True Meaning" of Contracts: the Royal Botanic Decision' (2002) 18 *Journal of Contract Law* 182, 194.

regulated by the terms of the contract, either express or implied. The motivation for a fiduciary plea was often the desire to obtain a gain-based remedy[207] rather than a loss-based remedy.[208] However, this 'great experiment'[209] was largely defused by the High Court. In *Breen v Williams*,[210] the High Court observed that a general fiduciary relationship will not arise on the basis of a contractual relationship. Due to this judicial approach, Australia has been kept relatively immune from 'an unprincipled penetration of the fiduciary principle into ordinary contractual dealings.'[211]

The fact that a fiduciary relationship per se will not commonly arise between parties in an arm's length commercial contract raises a further issue. Carlin has suggested that judicial reluctance to discover fiduciary relationships in these circumstances provides a context that militates against the implication of a term of good faith on the basis that the concepts of fiduciary obligations are closely intertwined.[212] In this sense, Carter and Stewart also observed this tendency, in Canada, to equate the standards imposed by the two obligations.[213] In part, this may be reflective of academic assertions that Canadian courts have deployed fiduciary law as 'an indirect method of enforcing a good faith standard in contractual relationships.'[214] Finn has also previously commented on this requirement of fair dealing in good faith obligation as being capable of being 'metamorphosed into a fiduciary duty.'[215]

While it is understandable that a plaintiff may wish to pursue a fiduciary claim,[216] is it correct to regard the concepts of good faith and fiduciary obligations as being closely intertwined? Although it is clear that the categories of fiduciary relationships are not close,[217] the central nature of a fiduciary relationship must be borne in mind:

> The critical feature ... is that the fiduciary undertakes or agrees to act for or on behalf of or in the interests of another person in the exercise of a power or discretion which will affect the interests of that other person in a legal or practical sense. The relationship between the parties is therefore one which gives the fiduciary a special opportunity to exercise the power

---

[207] This was the motivation for the plea in *Hospital Products Ltd v United States Surgical Corporation* (1984) 156 CLR 41.

[208] Alexander F H Loke, 'Fiduciary Duties and Implied Duties of Good Faith in Contractual Joint Ventures' [1999] *Journal of Business Law* 538, 539.

[209] Tyrone Carlin, 'The Rise (and Fall?) of Implied Duties of Good Faith in Contractual Performance in Australia' (2002) 25 *University of New South Wales Law Journal* 99, 101.

[210] (1996) 186 CLR 71.

[211] Paul Finn, 'Contract and the Fiduciary Principle' (1989) 12 *University of New South Wales Law Journal* 76, 82. Empirical analysis of decisions since *Breen v Williams* suggests that those seeking to impose fiduciary standards outside recognised categories will be disappointed: Carlin, 'The Rise (and Fall?), above n 209, 102.

[212] Carlin, 'The Rise (and Fall?), above n 209, 102.

[213] Carter and Stewart, 'Interpretation', above n 206, 194.

[214] These academic views are referred to by O'Byrne in O'Byrne, 'Contractual Performance', 70, 87.

[215] As referred to by Daniel Clough, 'Trends in the Law of Unconscionability' (1999) 18 *Australian Bar Review* 34, 52.

[216] For some of the practical and procedural advantages of a fiduciary claim refer to Loke, 'Fiduciary Duties', above n 208, 539–541.

[217] *Hospital Products Ltd v Untied States Surgical Corporation* (1984) 156 CLR 41.

> of discretion to the detriment of that other person who is accordingly vulnerable to abuse by the fiduciary of his position.[218]

As noted by Meagher, Heydon, and Leeming:

> The distinguishing characteristic of a fiduciary relationship is that its essence, or purpose, is to serve exclusively the interests of a person or group of persons; or, to put it negatively, it is a relationship in which the parties are not each free to pursue their separate interests.[219]

Despite concerns that the two concepts of good faith and fiduciary obligations may somehow be interwoven, it is clear from a number of Australian decisions concerning good faith that an allegation of self-interest (that would not be permissible in a fiduciary relationship) will not be sufficient, of itself, to sustain a claim based on breach of the good faith obligation. A clear example is provided by the NSW Court of Appeal in *Burger King Corporation v Hungry Jack's Pty Ltd* when it noted:

> That does not mean that Burger King is not entitled to have regard only to its own legitimate interests in exercising its discretion. However, it must not do so for a purpose extraneous to the contract—for example, by withholding financial or operational approval where there is no basis to do so, so as to thwart ... rights under the contract.[220]

The issue was directly addressed by Barratt J in *Overlook v Foxtel* when discussing the implied obligation of good faith:

> But no party is fixed with the duty to subordinate self-interest entirely which is the lot of the fiduciary. ... The duty is not to prefer the interests of the other contracting party. It is, rather, a duty to recognise and to have due regard to the legitimate interests of both the parties in the enjoyment of the fruits of the contract as delineated by its terms.[221]

As these quotations clearly indicate, contractual behaviour that would not be permissible in a fiduciary relationship will not necessarily infringe an implied obligation of good faith as the fiduciary standard is the highest protective responsibility that the law imposes on consensual relationships.[222] As succinctly noted by Loke, 'trust and confidence in the good faith performance of obligations is assumed different in quality from trust and confidence in the counter-party's subordination of self-interest to one's own.'[223]

This comment is consistent with the observation made by Finn that while a fiduciary duty denies the right to act in a self-interested manner, a good faith obligation simply qualifies (or curtails) the right to act in a self-interested manner[224] due to the need to have regard to the legitimate interests and reasonable expectations of

---

[218] Ibid 96–97 (Mason J).

[219] R P Meagher, J D Heydon and M J Lemming, *Meagher, Gummow and Lehane's Equity: Doctrines and Remedies* (LexisNexis Butterworths, 4th ed, 2002), 158.

[220] *Burger King Corporation v Hungry Jack's Pty Ltd* [2001] NSWCA 187, [185].

[221] *Overlook v Foxtel* (2002) Aust Contracts Rep 90–143, [67].

[222] Loke, 'Fiduciary Duties', above n 208, 542.

[223] Ibid 554.

[224] Finn, 'Contract and the Fiduciary Principle', above n 211, 82–83.

the other party. Finn's recognition of the more onerous duty of a fiduciary clearly discounts the possibility of the two obligations being intertwined. Similarly, Mason's observation is that the fiduciary principle is stronger than the good faith obligation in that it gives primacy to the interests of the party to whom the fiduciary obligation is owed.[225] Both these extrajudicial statements are consistent with the judicial observations (referred to above) that contractual parties are entitled to have regard to their separate commercial interests.

In essence, to equate good faith with a fiduciary standard is to make a fundamental mistake, both as to the incidence and the content of the two obligations. As noted, to invoke fiduciary duties is to seek the highest degree of protective responsibility.[226] This level of protective responsibility will be a rarity in commercial relationships in contrast to implied obligations of good faith, which will frequently arise. However, although far more frequent in their occurrence, the obligations arising due to an implied obligation of good faith are far less onerous than those owed in a fiduciary relation.[227]

5.5 Correlation Between Good Faith and Equitable and/or Statutory Unconscionability

Some academics seek to equate the notions of good faith and unconscionability[228] or, at the very least, seek to suggest that the standard of conduct which results in a breach of the implied duty of good faith is unconscionability.[229] These approaches are not without judicial support. It has been noted in *Renard* that Priestley JA made reference to the close association of ideas between the terms unreasonableness, lack of good faith, and unconscionability.[230] In *Alcatel Australia Ltd v Scarcella*, the NSW Court of Appeal seemed to equate unconscionability with a breach of the good faith obligation.[231] In a similar manner, in *Dickson Property Management Services Pty Ltd v Centro Property Management (Vic) Pty Ltd*, it was noted that the implied

---

[225] Mason, 'Contract, Good Faith and Equitable Standards', above n 20, 84.

[226] Loke, 'Fiduciary Duties', above n 208, 544.

[227] Consistent with the observation of Hollingworth J in *Esso Australia Resources Pty Ltd v Southern Pacific Petroleum NL* [2004] VSC 477, [126] that good faith imposes a narrower and less onerous standard than that required of fiduciaries.

[228] See, e.g. Stapleton, 'Good Faith in Private Law', above n 121, 1 and Eileen Webb, 'The Scope of the Implied Duty of Good Faith— Lessons from Commercial and Retail Lending Cases' (2001) 9 *Australian Property Law Journal* 1. Clough also argues that there is a trend to a general duty of good faith based upon a broad notion of unconscionability: Clough, 'Trends in the Law', above n 245. Cf Finn who describes the good faith standard as falling between the unconscionability standard and the fiduciary standard: Finn, 'The Fiduciary Principle', above n 140, 3–4 (referred to by Peter Heffey, Jeannie M Paterson and Andrew Robertson, *Principles of Contract Law* (2002) 262.

[229] Webb, 'The Scope of the Implied Duty of Good Faith', above n 228, 3.

[230] *Renard Constructions (ME) Pty Ltd v Minister of Public Works* (1992) 26 NSWLR 234, 265.

[231] *Alcatel Australia Ltd v Scarcella* (1998) 44 NSWLR 349, 369.

obligation of good faith may be breached if the actions were unreasonable, capricious, or unconscionable.[232] Hasluck J suggested that good faith was probably no more than a prohibition on acting unconscionably in *Automasters Australia Pty Ltd v Bruness Pty Ltd*.[233] By way of a final example, s 6 of the Franchising Code of Conduct[234] mandates all parties to a franchise agreement to act in good faith. The expert panel reporting to the Australian government in early 2010 on statutory unconscionable conduct reform and the franchising industry behaviours, stated, in this respect, that 'good faith … is intrinsically relevant to unconscionable conduct.'[235]

5.5.1 Different Meanings of the Term 'Unconscionability'

A difficulty with the term unconscionability is that it is not employed by either academics or the judiciary in a uniform manner.[236] Perhaps, influenced by statutory developments dealing with unconscionable conduct, it is not uncommon for academics to ascribe their own broad meanings to the term unconscionability. For example, one approach seeks to delineate the boundaries of good faith conduct by suggesting that contractual self-interest may be pursued to a point where it becomes unconscionable for certain specific reasons.[237]

By way of judicial example, Priestley JA in *Renard* opined that statutes proscribing unfair and unconscionable transactions could be used to bolster the development of

[232] *Dickson Property Management Services Pty Ltd v Centro Property Management (Vic) Pty Ltd* (2000) 180 ALR 485, 487.

[233] *Automasters Australia Pty Ltd v Bruness Pty Ltd* [2002] WASC 286, [372].

[234] *Competition and Consumer (Industry Codes—Franchising) Regulation 2014*, Schedule 1 Franchising Code of Conduct.

[235] Bryan Horrigan, David Lieberman and Ray Steinwall, *Strengthening Statutory Unconscionable Conduct and Franchising Code of Conduct* (2010) 85 http://archive.treasury.gov.au/documents/1744/PDF/unconscionable_conduct_report.pdf.

[236] In the context of the debate concerning discretionary remedialism, the word 'Unconscionable' has been described as so unspecific that it simply conceals private and intuitive evaluation: Peter Birks, 'Equity in the Modem Law: An Exercise in Taxonomy' (1996) 26 *University of Western Australia Law Review* 1, 16–17.

[237] Clough expressly gives unconscionability a much broader meaning than that traditionally ascribed in equity: Clough, 'Trends in the Law', above n 245, 53–54; see also *International Air Transport Association v Ansett Australia Holdings Ltd* [2008] HCA 3; F M Douglas, 'Modern Approaches to the Construction and Interpretation of Contracts' (2009) 32 *Australian Bar Review* 158.

a common law good faith obligation.[238] Clearly in this instance, the term unconscionability was not being used by Priestley JA[239] to indicate the specific equitable doctrine, but rather the broader generic meaning of unconscionability. This represents conduct that is regarded, in equity, as being against conscience, which provides the legal basis for equitable intervention in a variety of circumstances. It is suggested, with respect, that the use of the broader generic meaning of unconscionability has merely created unnecessary confusion in the good faith debate. This confusion largely disappears when the term unconscionability is used to refer to the specific equitable doctrine that is recognised in its own right. The statutory treatment of unconscionability is considered separately under Part V, C below.

5.5.2 The Equitable Doctrine of Unconscionability

The longstanding equitable doctrine of unconscionability was invigorated[240] by the High Court in *Commercial Bank of Australia v Amadio* (‘*Amadio*’).[241] As stated by Mason CJ, relief will be available where:

> a party makes unconscientious use of his superior position or bargaining power to the detriment of a party who suffers from some special disability or is placed in some special situation of disadvantage ... the will of the innocent party, even if independent and voluntary is the result of the disadvantageous position in which he is placed and of the other party unconscientiously taking advantage of that position.[242]

In these circumstances, ‘an onus is cast upon the stronger party to show the transaction was fair, just and reasonable.’[243] The equitable doctrine of unconscionability is intended to preclude advantage being taken of a person labouring under a disability such as, but not limited to, ‘poverty or need of any kind, sickness, age, sex, infirmity of body or mind, drunkenness, illiteracy or lack of education, lack of assistance or explanation where assistance or explanation is necessary.’[244]

---

[238] *Renard Constructions (ME) Pty Ltd v Minister of Public Works* (1992) 26 NSWLR 234, 268.

[239] Writing extra-judicially, Priestley JA clearly distinguished good faith and unconscionability: L J Priestley, ‘Contract—The Burgeoning Maelstrom’ (1988) 1 *Current Law Jornal* 15, 19–22, 28–29 (as referred to by Peden). See also Elisabeth Peden, ‘Contractual Good Faith: Can Australia Benefit from the American Experience?’ (2003) 15 *Bond Law Review* 175, 189.

[240] Anthony Mason, ‘Changing the Law in a Changing Society’ (1993) 67 *Australian Law Journal* 568, 571.

[241] *Commercial Bank of Australia v Amadio* (1983) 151 CLR 447.

[242] Ibid 461.

[243] Ibid 474 (Deane J).

[244] *Blomley v Ryan* (1956) 99 CLR 362, 405 (Fullagar J).

Unconscionability has also been extended and forms the underlying basis[245] for doctrines such as estoppel,[246] relief against forfeiture,[247] mistake[248] and rescission in cases of spousal guarantees.[249] These extensions suggested an open caption to the doctrine of unconscionability. In *Garcia v National Australia Bank Ltd*, the majority referred to Mason J's judgement in *Amadio*, where his Honour stated that it is 'impossible to describe definitely all the situations in which relief will be granted on the grounds of unconscionable conduct.'[250] The core understanding of unconscionability that unites the above doctrines is said to be extreme behaviour, especially where there is a clear disparity between the parties in terms of economic power, bargaining skill, or possession of information.[251] According to Finn's three tiered hierarchy of behaviour, the unconscionability standard is at the opposite end of the spectrum to the fiduciary standard and imposes lower standards of behaviour than the good faith standard.[252]

The limitations of the equitable doctrine were explicitly acknowledged by the High Court in *Louth v Diprose*:

> Although the concept of unconscionability has been expressed in fairly wide terms, the courts are exercising an equitable jurisdiction according to recognised principles. They are not armed with a general power to set aside bargains simply because, in the eyes of the judges, they appear to be unfair, harsh or unconscionable.[253]

Given this limitation, and the attendant requirement of a special (or serious) disadvantage, it is submitted that the specific equitable doctrine of unconscionability may be clearly distinguished from the common law implied obligation of good faith, as it may impact upon the performance and enforcement of commercial contracts.

---

[245] John W Carter and Andrew Stewart, 'Commerce and Conscience: The High Court's Developing View of Contract' (1993) 23 *Western Australian Law Review* 49, 65.

[246] *Walton Stores (Interstate) Ltd v Maher* (1988) 164 CLR 387.

[247] *Stern v McArthur* (1998) 165 CLR 489.

[248] *Taylor v Johnson* (1983) 151 CLR 422.

[249] The decision in *Garcia v National Australia Bank Ltd* confirmed the decision of *Yerkey v Jones* (1939) 63 CLR 649. The decision is a variant of the doctrine of undue influence and relates primarily to granting special protection in equity to women who guarantee their husband's debts by preventing the lender from recovering under the guarantee in cases where the wife did not understand the extent of the guarantee provided they received no benefit from the transaction. Kirby J, in dissent, noted that married women are not the only class of people who may need protection and it would be discriminatory to have a doctrine that only related to one class that might be in need. The majority stated that they were prepared to extend protection if the need is properly established, to other relationships such as de-facto or homosexual relationships. It may even extend to a husband who acts as surety for his wife. See generally Elizabeth Stone, 'Infants, Lunatics and Married Women: Equitable Protection in Garcia v National Australia Bank' (1999) 62 *The Modern Law Review* 604; Robyn Baxendale, 'Garcia v National Australia Bank Ltd: Ensuring Equity in Surety Transactions: A Legal Debt-End?' (1999) 21 *Sydney Law Review* 313.

[250] *Garcia v National Australia Bank Ltd* (1998) 155 ALR 614, 621.

[251] Carter and Stewart, 'Commerce and Conscience', above n 245, 65.

[252] Finn, 'The Fiduciary Principle', above n 133, 3.

[253] *Louth v Diprose* (1992) 175 CLR 621, 654 (Toohey J).

Despite the similarities between notions of good faith and unconscionability, it is submitted that there are fundamental differences between the law of unconscionable bargains and the contractual obligation of good faith. As exemplified by *Amadio*, the focus of the equitable doctrine of unconscionability is upon procedural or constitutional disability[254] arising at, or prior to, the time of contract formation as it impacts on whether a contract may be set aside.[255] Consistent with the observation that the equitable doctrine does not focus on substantive unconscionability,[256] the equitable doctrine fails to be considered in the formation of a contract rather than its termination.[257] *TriGlobal (Aust) Pty Ltd v Colonial Mutual Life Assurance Society Ltd*[258] demonstrated that the equitable doctrine of unconscionability will not generally have any application to the conduct of parties occurring after the formation of an ongoing contractual relationship.[259] This can be contrasted with a contractual obligation of good faith. As seen in chapter four, a common law obligation of good faith would not generally extend to the regulation of pre-contractual negotiations unless a contract comes into existence. Thus, the equitable jurisdiction is concerned with pre-contractual conduct, whereas a common law obligation of good faith would be concerned primarily with tempering the pursuit of self-interest following contract formation.

However, there has been attempts to allow a transaction to be set aside as unconscionable, even if the conscience of the stronger party is not affected strictly at the time of entering into the bargain. In *Gustav & Co Ltd v Macfield Ltd*,[260] the NZ Court of Appeal held that the date for assessing whether the stronger party had the requisite knowledge of the weaker party's qualifying disability was not necessarily the date that the conditional contract was executed. It could extend to the date on which the contract was confirmed by the weaker party. Notably, the stronger party

---

[254] Mistaken commercial judgment, without more, will not constitute a constitutional disability: *Australia Competition and Consumer Commission v Samton Holdings Pty Ltd* (2002) 189 ALR 76, [64–65].

[255] *Australia Competition and Consumer Commission v CG Berbatis Holdings Pty Ltd* (2003) 197 ALR 153, 165 (Gummow and Hayne JJ). See also Frank Zumbo, 'Unconscionability Within a Commercial Setting: An Australian Perspective' (1995) 3 *Trade Practices Law Journal* 183, 193. The non-application of the equitable doctrine post-contract formation has attracted criticism. See, e.g. John Swan, 'Party Autonomy and Judicial Intervention: The Impact of Fairness in Commercial Contracts' (1994) 7 *Journal of Contract Law* 1, 18; *Mackintosh v Johnson* [2013] VSCA 10; *Lee v Chai* [2013] QSC 136; *Kakavas v Crown Melbourne* (2013) 298 ALR 35; Warren Swain, 'The Unconscionable Dealing Doctrine: In Retreat?' (2014) 31 *Journal of Contract Law* 255.

[256] Anthony J Duggan, 'Is Equity Efficient?' (1997) 113 *Law Quarterly Review* 601, 612. In US jurisprudence, this distinction (between procedural and substantive unconscionability) is often referred to as the difference between 'bargaining naughtiness' and 'the inherent substantive unfairness of a disputed term': Ralph J Mooney, 'Hands Across the Water: The Continuing Convergence of American and Australian Contract Law' (2002) 23(1) *University ofNew South Wales Law Journal* 1, 28.

[257] Clough, 'Trends in the Law', above n 215, 38.

[258] (1992) ATPR ¶41–174.

[259] Clough, 'Trends in the Law', above n 215, 38.

[260] [2007] NZCA 205, [46] (per Arnold J).

had no discretion whether or not to accept the confirmation.[261] Notwithstanding, the Court suggested that it was sufficient that the stronger party might retain the benefit of the bargain unconscientiously, even if the bargain was not necessarily struck in unconscionable circumstances.[262] This decision could, perhaps, be seen as an example of judicial willingness for the doctrine of unconscionability to be extended to contractual performance and enforcement.

However, the observations of the NZ Court of Appeal were overruled on appeal to the NZ Supreme Court.[263] It was found that the relevant time for assessing knowledge of the qualifying disability is properly the time when the contract is made and not the time of confirmation. The Court rejected any possible policy grounds for keeping 'flexible' the equitable remedy to relieve against unconscionable bargains.[264] Arguably, a contractual obligation of good faith may have been a more suitable mechanism for the NZ Court of Appeal to regulate the conduct of the stronger party during the currency of the contract. It would have been unnecessary to compromise the traditional understanding of unconscionable bargain.

Another fundamental distinction between unconscionable bargains and the obligation of good faith is that the remedies would likely be distinct. An agreement deemed to have been made in unconscionable circumstances is voidable. The victim may affirm the contract, or it may be set aside, in which case the plaintiff is entitled to a declaration that it has been validly rescinded.[265] It follows that a deserving plaintiff can also use the doctrine as a valid defence to an action for specific performance. However, a victim cannot claim damages. Similarly, proprietary remedies such as a constructive trust are generally unavailable.[266] Thus, the equitable remedies available for unconscionable conduct do not cater for the regulation of a continuing contractual relationship.[267] On the other hand, the remedy for a plaintiff as a result of a breach of good faith must arise from the contract itself. Damages may be awarded, or the contract may be cancelled if the breach is sufficiently serious. The agreement will not however be set aside ab initio.

It is, therefore, suggested that the obligation of good faith and the law relating to unconscionable bargains is distinct. In this regard, the equivalence position does not hold. The law relating to the equitable jurisdiction to set aside an unconscionable bargain would remain largely unaffected, irrespective of the good faith situation. Prima facie, a contractual obligation of good faith would be unable to provide a remedy for the victim of an unconscionable bargain. Thus, there is no reason why the obligation of good faith and the law of unconscionable bargains could not coexist.

---

[261] [2007] NZCA 205, [49].

[262] Ibid [45–50]. The claim ultimately failed because it was found that the stronger party did not have the requisite knowledge of the qualifying disability either at the date of entering into the contract or at the date of confirmation.

[263] [2008] 2 NZLR 735.

[264] Ibid 745 (per Tipping J).

[265] See Clough, 'Trends in the Law', above n 215.

[266] See Ibid.

[267] See Ibid.

Notably, the same conclusions can be drawn in respect of the equitable doctrine of undue influence. While unconscionability and undue influence represent a conceptual form of good faith,[268] they apply in the context of contractual negotiation or, in some instances, contractual variation[269] and act to vitiate the agreement. In this respect, they are distinct from an obligation of good faith in contractual performance.

Further, even in the context of contract formation, the specific equitable doctrine of unconscionability is less likely to have application to parties in arm's length commercial transactions as the requisite special disability will be infrequently present and parties will often have professional assistance.[270] In *Overlook v Foxtel*, a claim based on the equitable doctrine was raised, amongst others, in a commercial context. The claim was quickly dismissed:

> It can be said at once that there is no scope for the operation of these principles in the present case of a contract negotiated at arm's length between corporations represented by commercial negotiators … each having the active and ongoing assistance of their respective lawyers. To the extent that a claim based on ordinary equitable notions of unconscionable dealing is seriously asserted by Overlook, it simply cannot be sustained in the particular commercial context.[271]

In contrast, the good faith obligation in contractual performance and enforcement will frequently be implied in contracts involving arm's length transactions, often between sophisticated businesspersons.[272] Unlike the equitable doctrine of unconscionability, there is scope for the operation of the implied obligation of good faith in contractual performance and enforcement regardless of the relative bargaining strengths of the parties to the commercial contract.

The international treatment of good faith has already been generally reviewed in chapter two. It is noteworthy in this chapter to briefly mention that in the *UNIDROIT Principles*, there are separate provisions dealing with the issue of unconscionability, apart from good faith duties. Cognisant of these international provisions, Finn has observed that the unconscionable dealings doctrine 'cannot be seen as a substitute for the good faith and fair dealing obligation itself.'[273] Similarly, in the US, where the *UCC* also has separate provisions addressing unconscionability,[274] Burton has noted that the obligation of good faith performance should be sharply distinguished from the doctrine of unconscionability.[275]

---

[268] Matthew D J Conaglen, 'Duress, Undue Influence, and Unconscionable Bargains: The Theoretical Mesh' (1999) 18 *New Zealand Universities Law Review* 509, 545.

[269] An unconscionable bargain may be found in respect of a contractual variation. See *Gustav & Co Ltd v Macfield Ltd* [2008] 2 NZLR 735, 741 (per Tipping J).

[270] Cf *Asia Pacific International Pty Ltd v Dalrymple* [2000] 2 Qd R 229; *Australia Competition and Consumer Commission v C G Berbatis Holdings Pty Ltd* (2003) 214 CLR 51.

[271] *Overlook v Foxtel* (2002) Aust Contracts Rep 90–143 [93].

[272] Burton, 'Breach of Contract', above n 28, 372, 383.

[273] Finn, 'Equity', above n 17, 419.

[274] *UCC* 2–302 (1) provides (in part): If the court as a matter of law finds the contract or any clause of the contract to have been unconscionable at the time it was made the court may refuse to enforce the contract.

[275] Burton, 'Breach of Contract', above n 28, 371.

In recent times, the understanding of unconscionable conduct has sought to be expanded. It has been suggested that a broad underlying principle of unconscionability is potentially becoming a common theme, if not a unifying principle, of the law of contract.[276] That contention, like proposals for a good faith doctrine, is met with concerns about self-interested competition and freedom of contract being sacrificed for altruism and vagueness.

Nonetheless, the courts at times seem to welcome the expansion of the unconscionability doctrine. In *Alcatel Australia Ltd v Scarcella*, Sheller JA suggested that a court may interpret a contract in such a manner that a contracting party may not be permitted to exercise a contractual power where it would be unconscionable to do so in the circumstances.[277] Similarly, in *Stern v McArthur*, a majority of the High Court of Australia held that although a contract for the sale of land had been lawfully rescinded in accordance with the agreement, the vendors had insisted on their strict legal rights in unconscionable circumstances.[278] The purchasers were entitled to relief against forfeiture and specific performance.

Seddon and Ellinghaus also observed that the courts have increasingly utilised unconscionability as an ultimate basis of liability in disputes between contracting parties.[279] It is further suggested that Australian contract endorses the view that a party may not assert a contractual right or deny a contractual obligation, if it would be unconscionable to do so.[280] This implies that the doctrine of unconscionability might be extended not only to the formation of a bargain but also to its performance and enforcement.

Finn has observed this development in Australia:

> [T]he revitalisation of the unconscionable dealings doctrine and the more general elaboration of an unconscionability principle have paralleled growing judicial preparedness to scrutinise the propriety of conduct in contract formation and performance.[281]

Inevitably, there would be an overlap in the application of an obligation of good faith and a doctrine of unconscionability if the latter could be applied to contractual performance. It has also been suggested that the developed equitable principle of unconscionability has occupied the position of an informing principle of good faith

---

[276] 'A compelling reason for adopting a general principle of unconscionability is the need to fill the gaps between existing islands of intervention. … Given the open recognition of a general principle of unconscionability, one would expect the courts to develop guidelines.': Stephen M Waddams, *The Law of Contracts* (Canada Law Books, 5th ed, 2005) 384–385.

[277] (1998) 44 NSWLR 349, 368.

[278] (1988) 81 ALR 463. See also *Legione v Hately* (1983) 46 ALR 1. A comprehensive discussion of the Australian position on relief against forfeiture on the grounds of unconscionability can be found in *Tanwar Enterprises Pty Ltd v Cauchi* (2003) 201 ALR 359.

[279] Seddon and Ellinghaus, *Cheshire and Fifoot's Law of Contract* (9th ed), above n 204, 6.

[280] Ibid 9.

[281] Finn, 'Contract and the Fiduciary Principle', above n 211, 82.

by default.[282] Accordingly, it is reasoned that a broad concept of unconscionability is a practical manifestation of some notion of a duty of good faith.[283]

It is certainly arguable that there are similarities in the meaning and application of good faith and unconscionability, particularly in light of the ongoing expansion of the latter. Whereas unconscionable dealing was previously thought of as conduct that shocked the conscience of the Court, there is now an inclination towards a less strict standard. This may embody synonyms such as unfairness, fair dealing, and good faith.[284] Similar to good faith, unconscionability is better described than defined.[285] Finn reasons that unconscionable conduct is conduct which is unfair to another where good faith can properly be expected by the other party.[286] A contracting party who acts in disregard of the reasonable expectations of his or her contracting counterparty may be said to have acted unconscionably. Stapleton has equated good faith and unconscionability on the basis that the 'principle of good faith restrains the deliberate pursuit of self-interest where this is judged unconscionable.'[287] She goes on to recognise that a contracting party will act unconscionably where he or she acts dishonestly, goes back on his or her word, or exploits a position of dominance over a vulnerable contracting counterparty.[288] The contended similarity between good faith and unconscionability is supported by the number of cases where the two principles have been concurrently pleaded in Australian cases.[289] Ultimately it may be that, at least in Australia, unconscionability could be perceived as a sufficient substitute for good faith, thereby negating the need for a separate doctrine. Harland asserts:

> [T]he increasing emphasis ... on unconscionable or unconscientious conduct as an element of other doctrines of the law of contract results in an emphasis on ideas of justice and fair dealing that may ultimately differ little from standards of good faith more familiar in many other legal systems.[290]

In this regard, the fact that unconscionable conduct tends to operate in a unifying manner does not suggest that courts can apply that feature as if it was an independent principle. Gummow and Hayne JJ state in *Australian Broadcasting Corporation v*

---

[282] Paula Baron, 'Resistance: A Consideration of the Opposition to a Duty of Good Faith in Australian Commercial Contracts' (2005) 11 *New Zealand Business Law Quarterly* 408, 420.

[283] See Clough, 'Trends in the Law', above n 215.

[284] Mason, 'Contract, Good Faith and Equitable Standards', above n 20, 90.

[285] *Antonovic v Volker* (1986) 7 NSWLR 151, 165 (per Mahoney JA).

[286] Paul Finn, 'Unconscionable Conduct' (1994) 8 *Journal of Contract Law* 37, 38.

[287] Stapleton, 'Good Faith in Private Law', above n 116, 1, 7; Agasha Mugasha, 'Good Faith Obligations in Commercial Contracts' (1999) 27 *International Business Lawyer* 355, 357.

[288] Stapleton, 'Good Faith in Private Law', above n 116, 1, 7–8.

[289] Baron, above n 312, 422; see *Garry Rogers Motors (Aust) Pty Ltd v Subaru (Aust) Pty Ltd* (1999) ATPR ¶41–703; *Alcatel Australia Ltd v Scarcella* (1988) 44 NSWLR 349; *Walker v ANZ Banking Group Ltd (No 2)* [2001] NSWSC 806.

[290] David Harland, 'Unconscionable and Unfair Contracts: An Australian Perspective' in Roger Brownsword, Norma J Hird and Geraint Howells (eds), *Good Faith in Contract: Concept and Context* (Dartmouth Publishing Co, 1999) 267.

Lenah Game Meats Pty Ltd that 'the notion of unconscionable behaviour does not operate wholly at large,'[291] unlike good faith obligation.

Having made this distinction, it is still necessary to consider separately the possible intersection between the broader statutory treatment of unconscionability and the common law implied obligation of good faith.

5.5.3 Statutory Unconscionability

One of the most well-known statutory provisions dealing with unconscionability[292] is s 22(1) of the *ACL*. The identical predecessor provision was s 51AC(1) of the *Trade Practices Act 1974* (Cth) (*TPA*), which was designed to be a legislative response to the findings of the 1997 *Reid Committee* report.[293] The *Reid Committee* report concluded that the effect of the predecessor s 51AA of the *TPA* (now s 20 of the *ACL*) did not adequately protect the small business sector in their dealings with big business[294] and a consequent recommendation that the protection against unconscionability be made available to consumers under s 51AB of the *TPA* (now s 21 of the *ACL*) as well as to small businesses.[295] In making this recommendation, the intention was to induce behavioural change on the part of big businesses towards smaller businesses and to provide unfairly treated small businesses with adequate means of redress.[296] Section 22(l) of the *ACL* provides:

> A person must not, in trade or commerce, in connection with: (a) the supply or possible supply of goods or services to a person (other than a listed public company); or (b) the

[291] (2001) 208 CLR 199, 245; See also *Australia Competition and Consumer Commission v C G Berbatis Holdings Pty Ltd* (2003) 214 CLR 51, 72; *Tanwar Enterprises Pty Ltd v Cauchi* (2003) 217 CLR 315, 326; *Clough Engineering Ltd v Oil and Natural Gas Corporation Ltd* (2008) 249 ALR 458, 492.

[292] There are many other statutory provisions, see, e.g. *Australian Securities and Investments Commission Act 2001* (Cth), s 12CC; *Retail Shop Leases Act 1994* (Qld), s 46B (l).

[293] House of Representatives Standing Committee on Industry, Parliament of Australia, *Science and Technology, Parliament of Australia, Finding a Balance: Towards Fair Trading in Australia* (Parliament of Australia, 1997).

[294] A narrow interpretation of Sect. 20 of the *Australian Consumer Law* (s 51AA of the *Trade Practices Act 1974* (Cth) was the former provision) caused problems for both franchisees and tenants alike in making complaints of unfair practices by franchisors and landlords. See, e.g. Robert Gardini, Report to Senator the Ron Chris Schacht, Minister for Small Business, Customs and Construction, Parliament of Australia, *Review of Franchising Code of Practise* (1995); Alan Wein, Report to The Hon Gary Gray AO MP, Minister for Small Business and The Hon Bernie Ripoll MP, Parliamentary Secretary for Small Business, *Review of Franchising Code of Conduct* (2013) https://www.treasury.gov.au/~/media/Treasury/Publications%20and%20Media/Publications/2013/Review%20of%20the%20Franchising%20Code%20of%20Conduct%20Report/downloads/pdf/ReviewoftheFranchisingCodeofConduct.ashx.

[295] House of Representatives Standing Committee on Industry, Parliament of Australia, above n 293, xv–xxix.

[296] Ibid.

acquisition or possible acquisition of goods or services from a person (other than a listed public company); or engage in conduct that is, in all the circumstances, unconscionable.

In determining if a supplier or acquirer has engaged in unconscionable conduct for the purposes of this section, the court is entitled to have regard to a non-exhaustive list of matters as specified in s 22(3). Given the breadth of this list of matters, it has been accepted that s 22 is not limited to the equitable doctrine of unconscionability of the *Amadio* type[297] and is wider than the concept of unconscionable conduct 'within the meaning of the unwritten law ... as regulated by s 51AA of the TPA [now section 20 of the ACL].'[298] The wording of the section is clearly intended to prohibit broadly unconscionable conduct in the range of transactions to which it is applicable.[299]

One of the listed matters that the court may have regarded to is the extent to which the supplier or acquirer acted in good faith.[300] There is no definition in the *ACL* or in the *Competition and Consumer Act 2010* (Cth) of the term good faith. Finn mentioned in his observation of s 51AC of the *TPA* (now s 22 of the *ACL*) that the good faith obligation has been thrust on us by stealth.[301] A key issue in the application of the provision will be whether the test of good faith obligation is subjective, objective, or possibly an amalgam of both. Unfortunately as a matter of statutory interpretation, as Corones observed, having regard to the other factors set out in ss 22(3) and (4) of the *ACL*, it is not possible to reach a conclusion on this issue.[302]

Finn suggested that the absence of the additional words, 'and fair dealing,' after the words 'good faith' may limit the operation of good faith in this particular statutory context to subjective considerations of honesty only, rather than the additional obligation of requiring conduct that may be considered objectively to be reasonable.[303] In the more general good faith context, Sir Anthony Mason has also drawn attention to the added significance of the words 'fair dealing.'[304] Peden also takes the view that the use of good faith in s 22 of the *ACL* could simply mean 'honesty' or a 'lack of ill will' as is the case in many other pieces of legislation.[305]

This is exemplified in a relatively notorious Australian franchise decision of *Australia Competition & Consumer Commission v Simply No-Knead (Franchising)*

---

297 See, e.g. *Auto masters Australia Pty Ltd v Bruness Pty Ltd* [2002] WASC 286, [361].

298 See, e.g. *Silver Fox Co Pty Ltd v Lenard's Pty Ltd* [2004] FCA 1225, [219]. Section 20 does not apply to conduct that is prohibited by Sect. 21 or Sect. 22 of the *Australian Consumer Law*.

299 *Automasters Australia Pty Ltd v Bruness Pty Ltd* [2002] WASC 286, [361].

300 Although there are twelve criteria listed, the Full Federal Court has made it clear that it distorts the proper operation of the section to search through the twelve criteria, find a criterion that seems apposite, and then make a conclusion of unconscionable conduct. In any given instance, some of the stipulated criteria may tell against a finding of unconscionable conduct. Further, the criteria do not limit the matters to which the court may have regard: *Australia Competition and Consumer Commission v Oceana Commercial Pty Ltd* [2004] FCAFC 174, [181].

301 Finn, 'Equity', above n 17, 421.

302 Stephen Corones, 'Does "Good Faith" in Sect. 51AC of the Trade Practices Act Deny Self-Interest?' (1999) 27 *Australian Business Law Review* 414, 415.

303 Finn, 'Equity', above n 17, 421.

304 Mason, 'Contract, Good Faith and Equitable Standards', above n 20, 76.

305 Peden, *Good Faith in Performance of Contracts*, above n 15, 169, 190.

Pty Ltd.[306] This case involved the franchise of a business for the making of bread and related products in the house. Unfortunately, relations between the franchisor and a number of its franchisees were poor, with the franchisees having various concerns about operational matters. On behalf of the franchisees, the Australia Competition and Consumer Commission alleged that the franchisor engaged in unconscionable conduct by refusing to deliver products to various franchisees. The franchisor had deleted the telephone numbers of certain franchisees without their knowledge or consent. It had also produced and distributed advertising and other material without the names of franchisees, competed for sales within the franchisees' territories and refused to provide disclosure documents despite written requests by franchisees. Sundberg J held that the accumulation of incidents disclosed an 'overwhelming case of unreasonable, unfair, bullying and thuggish behaviour'[307] in relation to each franchisee that constituted unconscionable conduct under s 22 of the *ACL*. Sundberg J further held that the conduct involved a demonstrated lack of good faith on the part of the franchisor.[308]

Unfortunately, the impugned conduct in question was so egregious that the decision adds little value in delineating the contours of the statutory standard and that good faith merely represents an indicator of statutory unconscionability.[309]

It should be mentioned that there are limitations to the operation and effectiveness of s 22 of the *ACL*. Apart from its express inapplicability to public companies, the statutory provision regulates unconscionable conduct essentially associated with the terms upon which goods or services are supplied or acquired. For this reason, it is at least arguable that s 22 of the *ACL* will have its greatest impact in relation to the issue of contract formation where it is clearly intended to apply.[310] Notwithstanding the apparent intention, it is submitted that there is generally less scope for the application of s 22 of the *ACL* in relation to contractual performance and the regulation of contractual rights occurring after the formation of the contract of supply or acquisition (as the case may be).[311] Consistent with this observation, it is relevant to note that in the context of the statutory unconscionability provisions of the *Retail Leases Act*

---

[306] *Australia Competition and Consumer Commission v Simply No-Knead (Franchising) Pty Ltd* (2000) 178 ALR 304.

[307] Ibid [51].

[308] Ibid [46].

[309] See *Australia Competition and Consumer Commission v Samton Holdings Pty Ltd* (2002) 189 ALR 76; *ASIC v National Exchange Pty Ltd* [2005] FCAFC 226; *Farah Constructions Pty Ltd v Say-Dee Pty Ltd* [2007] HCA 22.

[310] Peter van den Dungen, 'Good Faith, Unconscionable Conduct and Imaginary Community Standards: Sect. 51AC of the Trade Practices Act and the Insurance Industry' (1998) 10 *Insurance Law Journal* 1, 12.

[311] Of course, this will not preclude pleadings based on s 22 of the *Australian Consumer Law*. Pleadings based both on common law good faith and s 22 of the *Australian Consumer Law* failed in *Garry Rogers Motors (Aust) Pty Ltd v Subaru (Aust) Pty Ltd* (1999) ATPR ¶41–703 and *Overlook v Foxtel* (2002) Aust Contracts Rep 90–143. Cf *Automasters Australia Pty Ltd v Bruness Pty Ltd* [2002] WASC 286.

1994 (NSW), Barrett J has observed that the statutory examples are directed towards the formation of a lease.[312]

Despite these observations, there are instances where relief, founded on s 22 of the *ACL*, has been granted in relation to contractual conduct occurring after contract formation. For the purposes of this chapter, it is in this area of contractual performance and enforcement that the interplay between s 22 of the *ACL* and a common law claim based on breach of a good faith obligation needs to be considered. A decision that involved arguments based on an express good faith obligation and breach of s 22 of the *ACL* was *Automasters Australia Pty Ltd v Bruness Pty Ltd* ('*Automasters*').[313] As a rare example of where relief was considered available under both heads of claim, the significance of the decision warrants some examination.

Automasters Australia Pty Ltd (Automasters), as franchisor, alleged that Bruness Pty Ltd (Bruness), as franchisee, was in breach of a franchise agreement relating to the operation of an automotive service business. The alleged breaches were principally referable to an obligation to maintain the data entry system, which in time enabled the franchisor to ensure that the proper amount of royalties was being paid under the franchise agreement. Bruness maintained that problems with the data entry system were due to the quality of the computer system installed on behalf of Automasters and, in particular, the inability of the computer software to operate efficiently.[314]

Automasters purported to terminate the franchise agreement and sought damages and other relief. By way of counterclaim, Bruness sought, among other things, a declaration that the franchise had not been terminated, damages for breach of contract and damages under the *TPA* (now *ACL*). Bruness claimed that the conduct of Automasters was unconscionable under s 51AC of the *TPA* (now s 22 of the *ACL*) and also contravened clause 15.1 of their franchise agreement. Clause 15.1 obliged Automasters, as franchisor, to use its best endeavours to promote the performance and success of the franchise business and to deal with the franchisee in absolute good faith. It was not in dispute that effect could be given to an express contractual term concerning good faith even though the content of the express term may be a matter for individual determination.[315]

In particular, Bruness alleged that Automasters' actions were a manifestation of its determination to bring the franchise agreement to an end for reasons other than breaches of the contractual relationship. It was alleged that Automasters was not motivated by a desire to protect its legitimate interests but by malice and/or revenge[316] due to deterioration in the parties' relationship.[317]

---

[312] *Softplay v Perpetual* [2002] NSWSC 1059, [5] although Barrett J goes on to state that the statutory formulation is not explicitly confirmed by matters going to the granting and taking of a lease.

[313] *Automasters Australia Pty Ltd v Bruness Pty Ltd* [2002] WASC 286.

[314] Ibid [110].

[315] Ibid [140].

[316] Ibid [121].

[317] Ibid [122–123].

Bruness argued that Automasters leveraged the threat of termination to coerce Bruness into selling the franchise to Automasters at a significantly lower price than its actual market value.[318] Given the explicit provision regarding good faith in the franchise agreement, it was not necessary for Hasluck J to decide whether a good faith obligation should be implied. However, the court's findings are useful in defining the nature of the good faith obligation and the application of s 22 of the *ACL*. In assessing whether a party had acted in good faith, Hasluck J noted that the court may need to consider the party's motives.[319]

After reviewing all the circumstances, Hasluck J determined that the relevant officers of Automasters were seeking to terminate the franchise (similar to the case of *Australia Competition & Consumer Commission v Simply No-Knead (Franchising) Pty Ltd*). Their actions in issuing a default notice, in situations not anticipated by the quality assurance report, and amid significant doubt about the reliability of various data entry non-compliance lists, were deemed unreasonable and arbitrary.[320] Their disregard for the franchisee's legitimate interests constituted oppressive conduct[321] allowing Bruness to claim relief for breach of the express provision of good faith.

For reasons largely identical to those that led to a finding of a lack of good faith, Hasluck J described Automasters' conduct as unconscionable under s 22 of the *ACL*. The misconduct complained of was 'serious, unfair and oppressive and showed no regard for conscience.'[322] Hasluck J was not inclined to view this as a situation where the franchisor had merely exercised its contractual rights.[323] An observation was made regarding the interplay between contractual good faith and s 22 unconscionability:

> The notion of unconscionable conduct may not be co-extensive with conduct conforming to the requirement to act in good faith but conduct which is held to be unconscionable within the meaning of [section 22 of the *Australian Consumer Law*] will probably be sufficient to constitute a breach of an express term providing for absolute good faith between the parties.[324]

While this observation is correct, equating a lack of good faith with unconscionability—rather than vice versa—should be done with caution. *Automasters* is one of the few decisions where both lack of good faith and unconscionability were claimed where the Franchising Code of Conduct was breached. This is a markedly rare instance where both principles were invoked out of unreasonable conduct; however, it does not equate the two.

Unfortunately, there is limited progress in getting a definitive answer to the correlation (if any) between s 22 of the *ACL* and common law good faith. Commentators have argued that the reference to good faith under s 22 signifies a 'strong shift' away

[318] Ibid [385].

[319] Ibid [146], [148].

[320] Ibid [391].

[321] Ibid [393].

[322] Ibid [399].

[323] Ibid.

[324] Ibid [388].

from the equitable doctrine of unconscionability.[325] Kooy proposed that good faith under s 22 should serve as an interpretative principle to elucidate the meaning of the other factors specified in the provision.[326] This approach could help courts narrow the scope of the enquiry when considering the factors under s 22. However, further judicial interpretations are required to validate this suggestion. The High Court's decision in *Australian Securities and Investments Commission v Kobelt*,[327] which served as the catalyst for this argument, did not provide explicit guidance on how good faith should be applied. As pointed out by the Trade Practices Committee of the Business Law Section of the Law Council of Australia,[328] the development of precedent under s 22 will require some time due to the relative scarcity of judicial judgements.[329]

5.6 The Relevance of Other Statutory References to Good Faith

In addition to s 22 of the *ACL*, the term good faith appears in many other pieces of legislation.[330] As legislation often influences the evolution of the common law,[331] it is worth considering whether references to good faith in statute could inform the content and development of an equivalent common law obligation. In answer to this, Peden correctly concluded, after a survey of the relevant legislation,[332] that 'little can be gained from analogy with legislation in the context of contractual good faith, and that courts will need to concentrate on developing common law explanations.'[333]

---

[325] Ruth Kooy, 'Identifying Unconscionable Conduct Post-Kobelt: Is Good Faith the Key to Interpreting the Statutory Unconscionability Provisions in Australian Law?' (2021) 28(1) *Competition and Consumer Law Journal* 75; citing Liam Brown, 'The Impact of Sect. 51AC of the Trade Practices Act 1974 (Cth) on Commercial Certainty' (2004) 28(3) *Melbourne University Law Review* 589.

[326] Kooy, above n 325, 108.

[327] (2019) 267 CLR 1.

[328] Trade Practices Committee of the Business Law Section of the Law Council of Australia to the Senate Economic References Committee, *Inquiry into Whether the Trade Practices Act 1974* (Cth) *Adequately Protects Small Business From Anti-Competitive or Unfair Conduct* (2004) 30.

[329] A significant number of the cases brought by the *Australia Competition and Consumer Commission* under s 51AC of the *Trade Practices Act 1974* (Cth) (the predecessor to s 22 of the *Australian Consumer Law*) have been resolved by consent orders following agreement between the parties, undertakings or some other means of settlement.

[330] Good faith is referred to in at least 150 pieces of Commonwealth legislation: *Bropho v Human Rights and Equal Opportunity Commission* (2004) 204 ALR 761, [84] referred to in Bryan Horrigan, 'The Expansion of Fairness-Based Business Regulation: Unconscionability, Good Faith and the Law's Informed Conscience' (2004) 32 *Australian Business Law Review* 159, 187.

[331] *Esso Australia Resources Ltd v FCT* (1999) 201 CLR 49, [18–28]; *Brodie v Singleton Shire Council* (2001) 180 ALR 145, 184.

[332] And the multitudinous uses of 'good faith' within such legislation.

[333] Peden, *Good Faith in the Performance of Contracts*, above n 15, 185.

What is clear from what Peden has highlighted is that the strand of unconscionability jurisprudence is associated with the equitable requirement of special disadvantage as opposed to good faith obligation, which is concerned with unconscientious exercise of contractual rights. Furthermore, the potential to exclude the obligation of good faith obligation in contract does not equate to the possibility of excluding unconscionable conduct in the legislations dealing with it.[334] For this reason, it is not proposed that this discussion be carried any further.

5.7 Chapter Summary

This chapter has addressed the challenges associated in defining and applying good faith obligation in Australian law and questions the practicality of a universal doctrine. Clearly, defining good faith with reference to bad faith is unhelpful. It is better to establish good faith by considering the parties' actions in cooperation, honesty, and reasonableness, when ascertaining their reasonable expectations. However, the obligation's main issues lie in its ambiguity for the courts to determine the type and requisite degree of conduct required, as well as the class of contracts to which good faith can be implied. This is further complicated by the requirement for a court to assess each contractual relationship on a case-by-case basis.

The behaviour required of contracting parties can only be determined by general principles, judicial interpretation, and evolving case law. Currently, the obligation of good faith is shaped by court decisions that have been based on a set of unique fact scenarios, leading to a lack of uniformity for a universal application. Consistency might only be achieved from a substantial body of case law, or by a definitive High Court decision. Until then, the application of good faith in Australian contract law will remain uncertain.

The dilemma is that the relevance of good faith cannot be ignored in contract performance. The common law contains several doctrines (for example, implied terms) that might be invoked by courts to apply and sustain the notion of good faith in commercial contracts. However, this covert approach to the issue of good faith in contract performance does not provide a coherent and satisfactory approach through which to deal with this issue. The reasonable expectations of contracting parties in contract performance may not be wholly protected through the contract itself because, intuitively, contracting parties often do not form their contractual terms on the assumption that the other party may act in bad faith in performing his or her obligations.[335] The inherent principle of good faith in contract performance is to protect the reasonable expectations of contracting parties. This may be extremely difficult, if

---

334 Bryan Horrigan, 'New Directions in how Legislators, Courts and Legal Practitioners Approach Unconscionable Conduct and Good Faith' in John McKenna and Helen Jeffcoat (eds), *Queensland Legal Yearbook 2012* (Supreme Court Library Queensland, 2013) 179–180.

335 See Simon Deakin, Wilkinson, Frank, 'Contract Law and the Economics of Interorganizational Trust' in Christel Lane and Reinhard Bachmann (eds), *Trust Within and Between Organizations: Conceptual Issues and Empirical Applications* (Oxford University Press, 2002) 146.

not impossible, for them to protect at the formation stage of contract. The difficulties at the formation stage do not derive from the inequality of bargaining power between the contracting parties. Even in arm's length negotiations, contracting parties may not be able to produce a complete contract that deals with all contingencies at the performance stage. Good faith gives contracting parties a degree of assurance that neither party will act in a manner that will frustrate the other's reasonable or legitimate expectations from the contract. In this sense, good faith facilitates commercial transactions, and that is why the *UCC* and *UNIDROIT Principles* impose a general duty of good faith and fair dealing in contracts.[336]

In Australia, the doctrine of implied terms continues to play an important role in fulfilling this function in the absence of a general or defined duty of good faith. However, it is limited in dealing with the issues of good faith in contract performance. It is not surprising, therefore, to discover that courts have been asked to deal directly with the question of good faith in the performance of contracts. Australian courts have, perhaps, reached a degree of awareness that the question of good faith, whether in the enforcement or performance of contracts, should not be ignored.[337] In this regard, the time has come for Australian courts to start taking seriously a new approach by preferring and resorting to the principles of contractual interpretation and construction in order to construe the purpose and the objects that the contracting parties intended to secure rather than merely paying lip service to the method.[338] This allows for the starting point to be taken from what the contracting parties have agreed in considering the relevant questions of good faith in contract performance.[339] The principle of good faith does not protect what each party may have anticipated

[336] In the domain of international and transnational contracting, norms of good faith and fair dealing are becoming central elements of 'modern ... commercial law, as it was of the law merchant': Allsop, above n 173, 355.

[337] E.g. *Thiess Contractors v Placer (Granny Smith) Pty Ltd* (2000) 16 BCL 130; *Apple Communications v Optus Mobile* [2001] NSWSC 635; *Evans Deakin Pty Ltd v Sebel Furniture Ltd* [2003] FCA 171; *City of Sydney v Goldspar Australia Pty Ltd* [2006] FCA 472; *Australian Hotel Association (NSW) v TAB Ltd* [2006] NSWSC 293; *CGU Workers Compensation (NSW) Ltd v Carlos Garcia* [*2007*] NSWCA 193; *Jobern Pty Ltd v BreakFree Resorts (Victoria) Pty Ltd* [2007] FCA 1066; *Insight Oceania Pty Ltd v Philips Electronics Australia Ltd* [2008] NSWSC 710; *Tote Tasmania Pty Ltd v Garrott* [2008] TASSC 86; *Macquarie International Health Clinic Pty Ltd v Sydney South West Area Health Service* [2008] NSWSC 738; *Network Ltd v Speck* [2009] VSC 235; *United Group Rail Services Ltd v Rail Corporation of New South Wales* (2009) 74 NSWLR 618; *Driveforce Pty Ltd v Gunns Ltd (No 3)* [2010] TASSC 38; *Strzelecki Holdings Pty Ltd v Cable Sands Pty Ltd* [2010] WASCA 222.

[338] See *Pan Foods Co Importers & Distributors Pty Ltd v Australia and New Zealand Banking Group Ltd* (2000) 170 ALR 579, 584, [24]; *Elderslie Property Investments No 2 Pty Ltd v Dunn* [2008] QCA 158, [20–22]; *Bytan Pty Ltd v BB Australia Pty Ltd* (2012) 41 VR 46, 65 [96]; *Memery v Trilogy Funds Management Ltd* [2012] QCA 160, [14]; *North East Solution Pty Ltd v Masters Home Improvement Australia Pty Ltd* [2016] VSC 1, [32–35].

[339] *United Group Rail Services Ltd v Rail Corporation of New South Wales* (2009) 74 NSWLR 618, 639 [74]; *Macquarie International Health Clinic Pty Ltd v Sydney South West Area Health Service* [2010] NSWCA 268, [12]; *Commonwealth Bank of Australia v Barker* [2014] HCA 32; *Paciocco v Australia and New Zealand Banking Group Ltd* (2015) 321 ALR 584, 649–651 [287–293]; *North East Solution Pty Ltd v Masters Home Improvement Australia Pty Ltd* [2016] VSC 1, [56–62].

to benefit from the contract at the formation stage. There is a difference between the anticipated benefit of the contract and what each party may expect from the contract. Under a good faith regime, contracting parties still bear the risk of their failure to protect the benefit that they may anticipate from the contract. Any attempt to expand the application of good faith beyond the benefit of contracts, as proponents of the relational contract theory may suggest, could endanger the certainty of the law in commercial contracts.

The concept of good faith in Australian law is subject to many unresolved issues which require clarification by the High Court. However, the High Court would still face the challenge of creating a model that can provide a clear framework for handling claims relating to good faith obligation in commercial contracts.

In order to further explore the relevance of an obligation of good faith, the next chapter intends to examine whether insights may be offered from a law and economics perspective. The law aims for efficiency which is assessed by two standards: (1) by allocating resources to maximise collective wealth rather than individual gains; and (2) pareto efficiency which allocates resources to ensure one person is not benefited at the expense of another. Contact law is most efficient when it maximises individual transaction benefits while minimising costs. As efficiency determines whether a legal rule is desirable, the obligation of good faith would only be supported in Australia if it proves to be more efficient than the current state of contract law.

Part III

Chapter 6
An Economic and Practical Analysis of Good Faith Obligation

6.1 Introduction

Priestley JA's landmark judgement in *Renard Constructions*[1] held that in Australia there is an implied obligation of good faith in commercial contracts. This acceptance of the obligation of good faith, however, has remained controversial at best and certainly far from being universal in thoughts and application.[2] The current state of the law on good faith obligation in Australia has been described as being in a state of flux.[3] In line with this sentiment, the purpose of chapter six is to consider if good faith obligation can continue to be justified and validated in commercial contracts without degrading the concept of freedom of contract using an economic and practical analysis of the obligation.

This chapter examines whether insights may be offered from a law and economics perspective, and then considers a practical analysis of good faith provisions in contracts by investigating if the doctrinal obligation of good faith is aligned with

---

[1] *Renard Constructions (ME) Pty Ltd v Minister of Public Works* (1992) 26 NSWLR 234.

[2] Contrary judicial viewpoints have been expressed over years, for example in the following cases: *Saxby Bridge Mortgages Pty Ltd v Saxby Bridge Pty Ltd* [2000] NSWSC 433; *South Sydney District Rugby League Football Club Ltd v News Ltd* (2000) 177 ALR 611, 695; *NT Power Generation Pty Ltd v Power & Water Authority* (2001) 184 ALR 481; *Esso Australia Resources Pty Ltd v Southern Pacific Petroleum NL* [2005] VSCA 228; *Paciocco v Australia and New Zealand Banking Group Ltd* (2015) 321 ALR 584.

[3] Andrew Terry and Cary Di Lernia, 'Regulating the Franchise Relationship: Franchisor Opportunism, Commercial Morality and Good Faith' in Mika Tuunanen, Josef Windsperger, Gérard Cliquet and George Hendrikse (eds), *New Developments in the Theory of Networks: Franchising, Alliances and Cooperatives* (Springer, 2011) 179, 184; Kah Leng Ter, 'Good Faith in the Performance of Commercial Contract Revisited' (2014) 26 *Singapore Academy of Law Journal* 111, 113; Tyrone Carlin, 'Good Faith in Contractual Performance—Smoke without Flame' (2005) 4 *Journal of Law and Financial Management* 18; John W Carter and Elisabeth Peden, 'Good Faith in Australian Contract Law' (2003) *Commercial Law Quarterly* 15.

A. Wan and P. Guo, *Good Faith Obligation*, International and Comparative Law in the Asia Pacific, https://doi.org/10.1007/978-981-97-7035-9_6

commercial reality and whether their continued applicability or validity in practice can be supported.

One of the main issues with good faith obligation is that it makes much more sense when applied within a contracting context.[4] It is difficult to conceptualise good faith independently as its meaning cannot be specifically defined or applied in practice with sufficient precision.[5] The principle of good faith is often seen as a nebulous concept with undefined boundaries or parameters.[6] For instance, it is accepted that a good faith doctrine would limit the pursuit of self-interest to some degree, but the exact scope of this limitation remains unclear.[7] Further, the meaning of good faith varies depending on the contracting circumstance and the intent of the parties concerned.[8] Due to the fluid nature of good faith obligation and the fact that judicial discretion has not yielded a consistent approach,[9] it has become an impediment for its recognition as an overriding obligation and calls into question its continued presence and relevance within Australian contract law.

In chapters four and five, the relevance of good faith was considered by looking at the Australian and US judicial approaches. Both approaches consider the good faith obligation on the basis of a generalised standard of honesty, loyalty or cooperation.[10] The required conduct of the parties is wholly dependent on the circumstances of the case and, as good faith is fact-intensive, it is impossible to enunciate the principle without reference to a fact scenario. As the nature of a good faith inquiry is unique to

---

[4] Horst K Lücke, 'Good Faith and Contractual Performance' in Paul Finn (ed), *Essays on Contract* (Law Book Co, 1987) 160.

[5] Cf. *State v Robinson* (1893) 23 SW 1066, 1069; Lücke, 'Good Faith and Contractual Performance', above n 4, 160; Stephen M Waddams, 'Good Faith, Unconscionability and Reasonable Expectations' (1995) 9 *Journal of Contract Law* 55, 56–57; Klaus Peter Berger, *The Creeping Codification of the Lex Mercatoria* (1999) 5; *Macquarie International Health Clinic Pty Ltd v Sydney South West Area Health Service* [2010] NSWCA 268 (per Allsop P).

[6] Joseph M Thomson, 'Good Faith in Contracting: A Sceptical View' in Angelo D M Forte (ed), *Good Faith in Contract and Property Law* (Hart Publishing, 1999) 75.

[7] Roger Brownsword, 'Positive, Negative, Neutral: The Reception of Good Faith in English Contract Law' in Roger Brownsword, Norma J Hird and Geraint Howells (eds), *Good Faith in Contract: Concept and Context* (Dartmouth Publishing Co, 1999) 16.

[8] Michael Bridge, 'Does Anglo-Canadian Contract Law Need a Doctrine of Good Faith?' (1984) 9 *Canadian Business Law Journal* 385, 407.

[9] Leighton O'Brien, '"Good Faith: Practical Applications in Contract Law" in Contracts 2010: Optimising Contract Performance and Mitigating Risk' (Paper presented at the 10th Annual Conference Series, Sydney, 9–11 February 2010).

[10] It is also justified by a reflection of community sentiments or ideals about the desirable values in a contractual relationship: William D Duncan, 'The Implication of a Term of Good Faith in Commercial Leases' (2002) 9 *Australian Property Law Journal* 209, 216; Jeannie M Paterson, 'Limits on a Lender's Right to Repayment on Demand: Construction, Implication and Good Faith?' (1998) 26 *Australian Business Law Review* 258, 261; E Allan Farnsworth, 'Good Faith Performance and Commercial Reasonableness under the Uniform Commercial Code' (1963) 30 *Chicago Law Review* 666; Robert S Summers, 'The General Duty of Good Faith—Its Recognition and Conceptualization' (1982) 67 *Cornell Law Review* 810; Howard O Hunter, 'The Growing Uncertainty about Good Faith in American Contract Law' (2004) 20 *Journal Contract Law* 50.

each matter, it is important that the concept is still based on rational principles that a court can apply. The Court does not sit under a palm tree.[11]

Parties need clear guidance on the conduct required to fulfil their good faith obligations. Without such guidance, uncertainty becomes an ever constant presence for the commercial sector and, perhaps more concerning, lawyers would be unable to provide clear advice to contracting parties to ensure that they remain within the bounds of their good faith obligation.

Although chapter five dealt with the unresolved issues concerning the meaning and legal standards of good faith obligation, it did not deal with the practice of how good faith duties are expressed and formulated within a contractual transaction. This chapter, therefore, intends to cover this gap. Commercial contract negotiators and lawyers face a constant quagmire of cases and literature on good faith obligation in contract that still leaves questions about.

> whether to take the implied term path or the implicit and fundamental and underpinning approach which is favoured academically [and] if the former, will it be implied as a matter of fact or law and is it implied into all commercial contracts, or only a particular class, and then will it apply broadly (that is, at all times and in doing all things) or narrowly, such as in the exercise of discretions or exercise of significant powers such as termination?[12]

These considerations affect how commercial contracting parties approach good faith obligations in seeking to avoid uncertainty or unmanageable risks during negotiations and contract drafting. This includes reducing the likelihood of prolonged disputes, costs, and leverage from the other parties in case of disagreements, by ensuring the contract is explicit and unambiguous. The main issue for commercial parties is the significant uncertainty regarding when and how courts will imply good faith and what elements this will encompass. Additionally, there is also ambiguity regarding the extent in which contracting parties can mutually agree on the implication of good faith.

The cautious introduction of broader standards and value judgements such as fairness, reasonableness, and consideration of each other's interests into commercial dealings (beyond what the parties have explicitly accept or implicitly assume) underpins ongoing debates about good faith.[13] The support for good faith obligation often depends on the contractual circumstances[14] and the tactical approach as much as it is on legal principles. Even powerful commercial entities with expertly

---

[11] *Re J E Cade & Son Ltd* [1992] BCLC 213, 227 (per Warner J).

[12] O'Brien, 'Good Faith: Practical Applications in Contract Law', above n 9.

[13] Howard O Hunter, 'Good Faith and the Construction of Terms in Commercial Contracts: The American Perspective' (2009) 25 *Journal of Contract Law* 39, 39.

[14] Vanessa Sims, 'Good Faith in English Contract Law: Of Triggers and Concentric Circles' (2004) 1 *Ankara Law Review* 213, 216.

drafted contracts will invoke the implied terms of good faith when it is advantageous for them,[15] despite judicial indications of limited application for such terms.[16] The dilemma of good faith obligation in commercial contracts is well illustrated in Warren Grover QC's prescient advice to legal practitioners:

> Whether you characterise the question as one of 'good faith' or of the court believing that it has more wisdom than the parties to determine what is reasonable, the practitioner has a problem. With common sense and some sensitivity to his client's plight, a careful solicitor can normally rely on the enforceability of a properly drafted clause. The courts are not ready to read down freedom of contract explicitly if you can avoid the illegality and public policy arguments and your client does not have the status of [a] fiduciary. A clear clause will embarrass the judiciary into submission. ... It is my belief that 'good faith' normally remains within the contract and can be avoided by proper drafting. The worry is that 'good faith' may become another rule of public policy that operates outside the contract itself.[17]

This chapter employs a law and economics approach in understanding the relevance of good faith obligation. The main reason for using this method is to provide a basis to conceptualise the obligation practically.[18] As the issue of good faith obligation has yet to be clarified by the High Court, the economic analysis presented in this chapter provides insights into whether the obligation of good faith in contractual performance can be supported and justified commercially. The practical rationale behind the inclusion of good faith obligation by commercial parties is also considered by looking at the occurrence of specific good faith contracting provisions within a commercial contracting setting, which would provide a snapshot of the 'what' and the 'how' good faith obligation manifests. This would provide a useful practical perspective to appraise the applicability of good faith obligation and assess their utility in contractual undertakings.[19]

In this understanding, contract law becomes efficient where the benefit of individual transactions is maximised, and the corresponding associated costs minimised. It can provide a normative assessment in predicting the effect that changing legal rules or sanctions will have on the likely behaviour of contracting parties.[20] This

---

[15] See *Overlook v Foxtel* [2002] NSWSC 17; *Telstra Corporation Ltd v Optus Networks Pty Ltd* [2002] FCAFC 296; *Esso Australia Resources Pty Ltd v Southern Pacific Petroleum NL* [2005] VSCA 228; and *The Bell Group Ltd (In Liq) v Westpac Banking Corporation (No 9)* [2008] WASC 239 (on appeal *Westpac v Bell Group* [2012] WASCA 157).

[16] *Esso Australia Resources Pty Ltd v Southern Pacific Petroleum NL* [2005] VSCA 228, [4] (per Warren CJ).

[17] Warren Grover, 'A Solicitor Looks at Good Faith in Commercial Transactions', in Law Society of Upper Cananda, *Commercial Law: Recent Developments and Emerging Trends* (Richard De Boo Publishers, 1985) 106–107.

[18] See John N Adam, 'The Economics of Good Faith in Contract Law' (1995) 8 *Journal of Contract Law* 126; Arlen Duke, 'A Universal Duty of Good Faith: An Economic Perspective' (2007) 33 *Monash University Law Review* 182, 184.

[19] Muriel Fabre-Magnan, 'Duties of Disclosure and French Contract Law: Contribution to an Economic Analysis' in Jack Beatson and Daniel Friedmann (eds), *Good Faith and Fault in Contract Law* (Oxford Scholarship Online, 2001) 107.

[20] Michael Trebilcock, 'The Value and Limits of Law and Economics' in Megan Richardson and Gillian K Hadfield (eds), *The Second Wave of Law and Economics* (The Federation Press, 1999) 13.

approach aligns with Eisenberg's view that legal theories are significantly influenced by the relationship between doctrinal and social propositions. 'Social propositions' encompass all relevant considerations, including empirical and economic factors which lawmakers could consider.

The analysis that follows considers, first of all, the economic studies to see the effect good faith has on the likelihood that parties will cooperate throughout their contractual relationship. This is provided in Part II, which outlines a general account of the relevance of law and economics scholarship to good faith obligation. This section focuses on the need to deter opportunistic behaviour in contractual relationships being a key area. Issues concerning good faith obligations, in this regard, are commonly seen in two intrinsic phenomena of contracts, being incompleteness and sequential performance. A transactional cost analysis of good faith will also be considered, which should provide insights into what circumstance the obligation would benefit within contract law.

Part III considers the motivation of commercial parties and their legal advisors for the inclusion of good faith provisions in a specific contracting setting. This focuses on the contracting provisions itself and the strategies employed from a transactional perspective in arm's length commercial agreements. A case study approach is employed using Public Private Partnerships (PPPs) to represent an example of a type of arm's length commercial agreement that utilises good faith obligation in contractual performance and enforcement. This allows for an examination of the occurrence of specific good faith contracting provisions in PPPs to provide a snapshot of the 'what' and the 'how' good faith obligation manifests within a commercial contracting setting. Interview accounts are taken from legal practitioners and consultants, and contracting parties to provide a contextual representative background into whether the continued utility and validity of good faith obligation in practice can be supported.

6.2 Relevance of Law and Economics

The correlation between law and economics is that they complement one another in the allocation and control of resources.[21] In this regard, economics tend to dictate behaviour and the law controls behaviour by regulating conduct, providing incentives and imposing consequences for failure to adhere to those regulations.[22] As such, to achieve the aims and benefits of contract law, parties need to cooperate because economic reasoning suggests that contracting parties are self-interested.[23] This gives

[21] Frank Easterbrook, 'The Inevitability of Law and Economics' (1989) 1 *Legal Education Review* 1, 3.

[22] Thomas J Miceli, *The Economic Approach to Law* (Stanford University Press, 2nd ed, 2009) 1–2.

[23] Stewart Macaulay, 'Elegant Models, Empirical Pictures and the Complexities of Contract' (1977) 11 *Law & Society Review* 507, 509.

rise to suggestion that contracting parties' conduct may be predicated by norms and behavioural considerations.

In this respect, Macneil's essential contract theory sees contract as a social relationship as opposed to assumptions of well-defined structures containing rights and obligations.[24] His relational theory of exchange suggests that contracts vary on a spectrum from discrete, independent interactions to those that are highly relational. This continuum illustrates the importance of assessing the varying degrees of contractual relationships.

It is a consensus between contracting parties who adapt their agreement to changing circumstances—they are posited in a set of contract norms that govern such relationship as, '(i) role integrity; (ii) reciprocity; (iii) implementation of planning; (iv) effectuation of consent; (v) flexibility; (vi) contractual solidarity; (vii) the restitution, reliance and expectation interests; (viii) creation and restraints of power; (ix) propriety of means; and (x) harmonisation with the social matrix.'[25]

Discrete transactions can be characterised as a contractual event in contradistinction to a process. Rickett highlights that discrete contracts are impersonal and involve a straightforward exchange of value, like goods for money. The focus is on the event itself, where parties exchange values for their own economic benefit. Here, it is assumed parties can anticipate all risks beforehand, given they are presumed to have full knowledge of future possibilities and any legal rules which might impact the contractual relationship.

A key feature of the discrete transaction is that all contractual obligations are clearly defined when the contract is formed so that any third party might immediately understand the actions required to perform the contract. The contract norms or 'presentiation,'[26] as Macneil describes them, meant that a person effectively sees the effect of a future obligation on the present in order that it may be dealt with: '[t]he presentiation of a transaction involves restricting its expected future effects to those defined in the present, that is, at the inception of the transaction.'[27] Macneil criticises the classical contract system for focusing too much on enhancing presentiation and discreteness as they are overly simplistic and not reflective of the complex nature of contractual relationships.

Discrete transactions do not necessarily take place in the absence of social relations between the parties involved; of course, a contract is, in itself, a relationship. Therefore, wholly discrete transactions can only ever be considered in the abstract as almost all contracts require social relations. The presupposition of a market created by the discrete transactional system requires that any ongoing relationship between parties cease in the presence of any contractual dispute. Macneil suggests that discrete

---

[24] Ian R Macneil, 'Contracts: Adjustment of Long Term Economic Relations under Classical, Neoclassical and Relational Contract Law' (1978) 72 *Northwestern University Law Review* 854; Ian R Macneil, 'Relational Contract Theory: Challenges and Queries' (2000) 94 *Northwestern University Law Review* 877.

[25] Ian R Macneil, 'Values in Contract: Internal and External' (1983) 78 *Northwestern Law Review* 340, 347; Macneil, 'Relational Contract Theory: Challenges and Queries', above n 24.

[26] The contract norms referred to are the 10 relational norms identified by Macneil.

[27] Macneil, 'Contracts: Adjustment', above n 24, 863.

transactions can only have a limited role in economies and that these transactions bear similarities to the classical 'static' model of contract law, insofar as the discrete transaction may underpin this model. There is judicial recognition for this premise when Thomas J stated: 'Classical contract law is based on certain implicit paradigm cases, the most common of which is the contract for an identified commodity between two strangers operating in a perfect spot market.'[28]

The classical contract law model supports competition, encouraging contracting parties to pursue their own interests freely. This adversarial ethic is essential to laws governing discrete exchanges. However, the validity of this solely adversarial approach is unconvincing, and Macneil's relational contract theory becomes important in discussions about good faith, suggesting a need for more cooperative foundations.

In contrast, relational contracts typically manage ongoing relationships that develop over time and are not necessarily long-term contracts. Just as entirely discrete transactions are abstractions, a transaction cannot be entirely relational. Macneil states:

> The participant in a relation is a living human being with all its confusions, conflicts, and inconsistencies, interacting with one or more others of similar nature. Only if we could fully describe multi-variant human nature in its interactions with other multi-variant human nature could we even start thinking about what a 'purely relational transaction' might start to look like.[29]

This observation by Macneil concerning the width and breadth of the relational continuum supports the increasing popularity of various commercial arm's length contracts that carry relational underpinnings,[30] which include distributorships, agency relationships, joint ventures, franchise agreements,[31] and certain types of outsourcing/procurement and construction contracts such as PPPs. These types of commercial contracts are economically important. It is difficult in these types of contracts to optimally allocate all risks at the time of contracting due to their contractual longevity and with that comes a high possibility of unforeseen contingencies. Added to this is also the desire of the contracting parties wrestling to retain a degree of control.

---

[28] *Bobux Marketing Ltd v Raynor Marketing Ltd* [2002] 1 NZLR 506 [33].

[29] Ibid.

[30] Macneil observed that such contracts with relational elements are far more common than discreet exchanges: Ian R Macneil, 'Relational Contract: What We Do and Do Not Know' [1985] *Wisconsin Law Review* 483, 487.

[31] Charles J Goetz and Robert E Scott, 'Principles of Relational Contracts' (1981) 67 *Virginia Law Review* 1089, 1091; *Bobux Marketing Ltd v Raynor Marketing Ltd* [2002] 1 NZLR 506 [42].

6.2.1 Limitations of Law and Economics

There are, however, limitations in applying a strictly law and economic analysis in formulating and assessing legal principles. The basic economic principles often proceed from the rational actor model basis.[32] It is this approach that allows economic analysis to anticipate the beneficial effect of a legal rule on society:

> Too often legal policy makers (principally judges and legislatures) justify the rules that they adopt solely in terms of their underlying objective. The real value of a particular rule to society is not what the policy maker wished the rule to achieve, but rather what it actually achieves or what it can be expected to achieve, given our understanding of human affairs in general.[33]

This perspective makes an assumption that individuals have a defined set of preferences and will always act within a prescribed set of constraints to maximise the satisfactions of those preferences. It is arguable that such a model may be too simplistic in assessing how a person will act out in practice.[34] Nonetheless, the model is still reasonably reliable despite its simplistic assumptions.[35] The focus, after all, is on the merits of predictions rather than the merits of the assumptions.

Wealth maximisation and efficiency have been critiqued as too limited to be the goals of the law. This is because efficiency may not always align with ethical standards for decision-making in society. The Kaldor–Hicks efficiency criterion, which justifies an outcome as being economical where one person's gain supersedes the loss of another, is often criticised as being repugnant to justice and social policy. While economic efficiency is important, it should not be the only factor in evaluating the utility of a legal rule as it is unlikely that efficient outcomes will be produced in every instance. Yet, it is true that there is often an overlap between what is considered efficient by economists and what is deemed fair by lawyers.

6.2.2 Good Faith and Economics Framework

Despite the limitations indicated above, economic analysis is crucial to the good faith debate because legal rules can influence in contracting relationships. Therefore, the commercial community as a vested party makes this discussion all the more important. In *Austotel Pty Ltd v Franklin Selfserve Pty Ltd*, Kirby P recognised this fact in commercial dealings:

---

[32] Sir Ivor Richardson, 'Law and Economics—and Why New Zealand Needs It' (2002) 8 *New Zealand Business Law Quarterly* 151, 154.

[33] Kevin McGuinness, 'Law and Economics—A Reply to Sir Anthony Mason CJ Aust' (1994) 1 *Deakin Law Review* 117, 119.

[34] See Trebilcock, 'The Value and Limits of Law and Economics', above n 20.

[35] Richard A Posner, 'Some Uses and Abuses of Economics in Law' (1979) 46 *University of Chicago Law Review* 281, 303.

> [C]ourts should be careful to conserve relief so that they do not, in commercial matters, substitute lawyerly conscience for the hard-headed decisions of business people. ... The wellsprings of the conduct of commercial people are self-evidently important for the efficient operation of the economy. Their actions typically depend on self-interest and profit-making not conscience or fairness.[36]

Contract law is more suitable to economic analysis compared with other areas of law that solicit moral and social considerations, as these considerations are less compatible with economic analysis. As such, the obligation of good faith is ideal for applying economic principles.[37]

Notwithstanding, good faith doctrine has not garnered much attention from scholars in law and economics. There are reasons for this situation. The first is that good faith tends to be recognised incidentally in economics theory. This can be seen in studies comparing enforcement regimes in contractual provisions against performance indices of cooperation, fairness, adherence to contractual terms and reciprocity in contracting participants.[38] These studies consider the role contractual rules play in determining whether self-interested or reciprocally fair norms prevail within the contractual exchange relationship. It should also be noted that these academic works have come mainly from North America and Europe. This trend is due to the popularity of law and economic scholarship in these regions and their imposition of good faith obligations in contracts, unlike in Australia.

The other reason is that law and economic commentaries on good faith doctrine tend to be couched either in general terms where a general analysis is made on how to frame good faith efficiently within contract law or, alternatively, the analysis focuses on specific elements of contract law such as disclosure, unconscionability, mistake and frustration, which carries related notions of good faith obligation.[39]

---

[36] *Austotel Pty Ltd v Franklin Selfserve Pty Ltd* (1989) 16 NSWLR 582, 585–586.

[37] Similar comments have been made by Duke, above n 18, 202 and John Smillie, 'Certainty and Civil Obligations' (2000) 9 *Otago Law Review* 633, 639.

[38] Some major studies in this area include (1) Iris Bohnet, Bruno S Frey and Steffen Huck, 'More Order with Less Law: On Contract Enforcement, Trust and Crowding' (2001) 95 *American Political Science Review* 131; (2) Seggio G Lazzarini, Gary J Miller and Todd R Zenger, 'Order with Some Law: Complementarity Versus Substitution of Formal and Informal Arrangements' (2004) 20 *Journal of Law, Economics and Organization* 261; (3) Ernst Fehr and Armin Falk, 'Psychological Foundations of Incentives' (2002) 46 *European Economic Review* 687; (4) Ernst Fehr, Alexander Klein and Klaus Schmidt, 'Contracts, Fairness and Incentives' (Working Paper No 1215, CESifo, 2004); Robert E Scott, 'The Death of Contract Law' (2004) 54 *University of Toronto Law Journal* 369; (5) Bruno S Frey and Reto Jegen, 'Motivation Crowding Theory' (2001) 15(5) *Journal of Economic Surveys* 589; Chung-Cheng Lin and C C Yang, 'Fine Enough or Don't Fine at All' (2006) 59 *Journal of Economic Behavior and Organisation* 195.

[39] E.g. Richard A Posner and Andrew Rosenfield, 'Impossibility and Related Doctrines in Contract Law: An Economic Analysis' (1977) 6 *Journal of Legal Studies* 83; Kimberly Krawiec and Kathryn Zeiler, 'Common Law Disclosure Duties and the Sin of Omission: Testing the Meta-Theories' (2005) 91 *Virginia Law Review* 1795; Melvin A Eisenberg, 'Disclosure in Contract Law' (2003) 91 *California Law Review* 1645; Russell Korobkin, 'Bounded Rationality, Standard Form Contracts, and Unconscionability' (2003) 70 *University of Chicago Law Review* 1203; Megan Richardson, 'The Utilitarian-Economic Model of Contractual Obligation: Unconscionability at the Frontier' (1995) 20 *Melbourne University Law Review* 481; Andrew Kull, 'Mistake, Frustration and the

From this perspective, an economic analysis of an obligation of good faith can either be approached at a broad or general level to examine the obligation's efficiency implications, or it can focus on specific applications. This chapter aims to evaluate both perspectives. Initially, when contemplating the general approach, it will consider good faith as a preventive measure against opportunistic conduct.

6.2.3 *Deterring Opportunism*

In order to consider this economic view of good faith obligation that focuses on the need to deter opportunistic behaviour, two fundamental economic principles of contracts must be recognised. Firstly, contracts are intrinsically incomplete, and secondly, contracts necessitate sequential performance. And in this sense, opportunistic conduct can emanate from these phenomena.[40]

6.2.3.1 Contracts Are Incomplete

Ontologically speaking, all contracts are incomplete. It is often the result of both legal and actual limitations affecting the contracting parties.[41] The following is intended to provide a range of reasons why contracts may be incomplete. First, contractual incompleteness may be the result of ambiguity or vagueness in the words used for the contractual terms. This can be attributed to the inherent flaws and imperfections of language.[42]

Second, the contracting parties might have inadvertently overlooked a specific issue. This oversight may be due to the parties' neglect to account for a certain contingency, or it might have been completely unforeseen before the contract was entered into.

Third, contracting parties may choose not to include certain contingencies within their contract if the cost outweighs the benefit. Contingencies are often included where they are likely to occur, so less probable occurrences tend to be omitted. In this case, ambiguous language might be employed in the contract so as to finalise the contract while leaving interpretation of undefined terms to the courts if a situation that was not addressed in the contract eventuates.

Fourth, a contract may also be incomplete due to information asymmetry, where one party has information that could alter the agreement if disclosed. This concept

---

Windfall Principle of Contractual Remedies' (1991) 43 *Hastings Law Journal* 1; Alan O Sykes, 'The Doctrine of Commercial Impracticability in a Second-Best World' (1990) 19 *Journal of Legal Studies* 43.

[40] George M Cohen, 'The Negligence-Opportunism Tradeoff in Contract Law' (1992) 20 *Hofstra Law Review* 941, 953.

[41] Alan Schwartz, 'Legal Contract Theories and Incomplete Contracts' in Lars Werin and Hans Wijkander (eds), *Contract Economics* (Blackwell Publishing, 1992), 80.

[42] *River Wear Commissioners v Adamson* (1877) 2 App Cas 743, 763 (per Lord Blackburn).

suggests that contracts are often inherently incomplete, as parties may not be able to fully account for or disclose all relevant economic factors.

Fifth, contracting parties may intentionally prepare incomplete contracts where self-enforcement is more practical than legal enforcement. This is common when the parties' reputations are at stake, such as with government contracts, or in long-term agreements with repeated interactions between parties. In these cases, due to non-legal factors, the parties are more likely to cooperate in making adjustments to the terms of the contract once contingencies arise.

Hadfield observed that when a contractual relationship is embedded within an identifiable relationship, 'contractual obligations are often modified, supplemented or completely supplanted by the norms of the ongoing relations.'[43] This insight is consistent with the observation made by McHugh JA that.

> the majority of people in ongoing business relationships regulate their relationships in accordance with what they consider is fair and reasonable or commercially necessary at particular points of time rather than by reference to priori rights and duties arising under a contract. ... This is the case even where ... [it] is governed by a written contract.[44]

McHugh JA went on to say that it 'is therefore necessary to look at the whole relationship and not only at what was said and done when the relationship was first formed.'[45] This is well illustrated by Finn J:

> The more a contract provides the basis for an ongoing relationship (e.g. a franchise, a tenancy, an agency, an employment, a construction agreement, etc.) the greater is the likely capacities given one or both parties for opportunistic behaviour or for taking actions in or in consequence of the contract that adversely affect the interest of the other. These equally are the types of contract which often are poorly drafted or in which the prophesies of the parties' legal advisers as reflected in the contract's terms have the utility of tarot-card readings. Yet they are contracts in which the relationship of the parties and their expectations they reasonably come to entertain in consequence of their relationship can, and should, assume no little significance in regulating their conduct inter se.[46]

Contracts containing relational elements are characterised by mutual loyalty and interdependence, which guide the economic planning of the parties involved. This cooperative foundation supports joint ventures, in turn allowing the parties to exploit specific economies while both reaping the benefits.

As parties enter a contract with the expectation that working together will benefit both of them, neither party is likely to pursue purely self-serving interests as would be expected where a contract is governed by adversarial ethics. Parties are not expected to break the 'relational rules'[47]—'short-term self-interest sometimes needs to be

---

[43] Gillian K Hadfield, 'Problematic Relations: Franchising and the Law of Incomplete Contracts' (1990) 42 *Stanford Law Review* 927, 929.

[44] *Integrated Computer Services Pty Ltd v Digital Equipment Corporation (Australia) Pty Ltd* (1988) 5 BPR 11, 110–117.

[45] Nicholas C Seddon, 'Australian Contract Law: Maelstrom or Measured Mutation?' (1994) 7 *Journal of Contract Law* 93, 96.

[46] Paul Finn, 'Good Faith and Fair Dealing and "Boats against the Current"' (Paper presented at the 2nd Biennial Conference on the Law of Obligations, Melbourne, 16 July 2004) 6–7.

[47] Seddon, 'Australian Contract Law', above n 45, 96.

subordinated to long-term self-interest.'[48] This is consistent with the contract norms[49] that Macneil identified as being particularly important where there are relational elements in the contractual undertakings. This is succinctly captured by Feinman:

> Relational ... emphasizes the interdependence of individuals in social and economic relationships. Because its paradigmatic unit of inquiry is the extensive relation rather than the discrete transaction, [it] focuses on the necessity and desirability of trust, mutual responsibility and connection'.[50]

This aligns with Macneil's relational contract theory, which suggests that qualities such as honesty, trust, and flexibility are essential for the success of long-term business partnerships. Indeed, empirical research has consistently shown the importance of these values in commercial relationships. In this sense, contracting parties may prefer negotiation as the mechanism to ensure that their contract is efficient ex post and that the resulting benefit is shared in some manner between them by employing discretionary language in the contract like good faith obligation.[51]

It is apparent from the above that contractual incompleteness will inevitably feature in contractual undertakings. Notwithstanding, contracts can generally operate despite incompleteness as extra-legal mechanisms may be able to sufficiently resolve any issues that may arise during the life of the agreement. Australian contract law already uses elaborate and comprehensive rules of construction, such as implied terms, to fill contractual gaps and elucidate the intention of contracting parties. Courts may do this either by enhancing the existing contractual framework or by inferring terms, such as good faith, to uphold the agreement made by the parties involved and ensure contracts are complete and enforceable.

These measures are justified by economic principles. Rules of construction lower the initial costs of a contract by sparing parties from detailing every possible scenario and trusting that courts will incorporate certain provisions into a contract as a matter of law and convention. This in turn sees ex post transactions costs desirably reduced, which culminates in the maximisation of contractual surplus or benefits.

6.2.3.2 Sequential Contracting

In addition to being incomplete, contracts often require sequential performance; this is where one party performs the contract first. This may create transactional insecurity, whereby one party may not fulfil their obligations after the other has already performed their side of the bargain. It is common for this to occur in loan

---

48 Jay M Feinman, 'Relational Contract Theory in Context' (2000) 94 *Northwestern University Law Review* 737, 740.

49 Such as role integrity, preservation of the relation, harmonisation of relational conflict, propriety of means and supra contract norms: Macneil, 'Values in Contract', above n 38, 347.

50 Feinman, 'Relational Contract Theory', above n 48, 748.

51 Robert E Scott, 'The Law and Economics of Incomplete Contracts' (2006) 2 *Annual Review of Law and Social Science* 279, 292; Robert E Scott and George G Triantis, 'Anticipating Litigation in Contract Design' (2006) 115 *Yale Law Journal* 814.

agreements as the lender's advance can become a sunk cost, recoverable only if the borrower makes all relevant financial repayments. Sequential performance can shift a market from being competitive to a bilateral monopoly, potentially leading to exploitation by a party who might wish to take advantage of the monopoly.

Contracting parties are often aware of the risks associated with sequential performance and, thus, may include protective provisions in the contract. These may be security interests in the borrower's assets or instalment payments in construction contracts. Given contracts are manifestly incomplete and sequential contracts give rise to a higher incidence of opportunistic behaviour, good faith is crucial to minimise and deter this behaviour.

6.2.3.3 What is Opportunism?

It is difficult to settle on a universal definition for opportunism, much like the obligation of good faith.[52] Economists approach it by considering examples of opportunistic behaviour rather than a general conceptualisation. However, certain definitions have been advanced.

Opportunism in contract law involves exploiting another's vulnerability, which often stems from sequential contracts and the incompleteness of contracts which is intrinsic to their nature. However, this definition is too narrow for practical use as it does not specify the degree of exploitation required for behaviour to be determined as opportunistic.

Opportunism has also been defined as pursuing self-interest with guile. This introduces a subjective moral standard to the assessment of opportunistic behaviour. In this case, societal standards may be consulted given it is unclear what behaviour is considered as 'guile.' This, too, is not practical for use in contract law.

A third, more objective, approach suggests that opportunistic behaviour should be considered as conduct seeking to reallocate agreed-upon contractual benefits. Under this definition, a party's conduct is considered opportunistic when a party alters contractual performance to gain an advantage not previously provided by the contract, to the detriment of the other party. The application caters for both contractual benefits and contractual costs. If the opportunistic party tries to regain lost opportunities or avoid due costs. However, since parties cannot foresee all possibilities due to limited information and understanding, it is challenging to determine who should be entitled to the contractual surplus or which should bear the loss from unexpected events.

This was seen in *Mutual Life Assurance Co of New York v Tailored Woman Inc.* In this case, the defendant leased a retail space from the plaintiff with the rent payable being a share of the profits in the store. The defendant subsequently acquired another business in the same building with a fixed rent and redirected customers to the new business to reduce the profit-based rent. The plaintiff sued for additional rent, citing a breach of good faith. However, the court ruled that unforeseen profit loss does not impose new obligations, and the defendant did not violate its fair dealing obligation.

[52] Ibid 954.

The utility of the foregone opportunity approach in settling the case is debatable. Clearly, neither party could have anticipated that this possibility would have arisen at the time of entering the original lease. Dubroff acknowledges the constraints of the foregone opportunity approach when the parties have not anticipated the opportunity:

> Whether foregone opportunities were recaptured can be determined only by interpreting the contract. The foregone opportunities assessment is no more or less than a conclusion that follows a judgment that the contract has been breached or has not been breached. It provided no assistance in determining whether the contract has been breached.[53]

Despite its well-established role in contract economics, defining opportunism is quite challenging to do. However, three primary factors are acknowledged as prerequisites for post-contractual opportunistic behaviour. First, the opportunistic act occurs after the contract has been executed; second, the act exploits the other party's reliance on the contract; and third, the act takes advantage of the other party's failure to anticipate the conduct—either negligently or where it was irrational in the circumstances to plan for it. This implies that opportunistic actions can occur even when contractual terms are met, if they fall outside what was reasonably expected by the parties.

Shirking is another type of opportunistic behaviour which can occur in contractual relationships. Shirking is common in joint ventures and partnerships, where one party avoids contributing any real effort but still claims an equal share of profits. It is also often incited when an agreement is ambiguous as to the expected contributions of each party, leaving a shirking partner to do minimal work while still receiving an equal share of the gains afforded by the agreement. While this is not necessarily a breach of contract, shirking violates the reasonable expectations of the parties and, thus, undermines the implication of good faith.

The risks associated with shirking can sometimes be mitigated by non-legal means. For example, a partner may be deterred from shirking as it poses a risk to their reputation for future partnerships should their behaviour become public knowledge. The immediate benefits of opportunistic behaviour may not justify the long-term consequences.

This understanding is consistent with Macaulay's seminal study on non-contractual relations in business, as his findings provided empirical evidence of self-imposed rules of business behaviour being part of what he described as 'relatively non-contractual practices.'[54] The motivation behind these self-imposed business rules is the 'desire to continue successfully in business and to avoid conduct which might interfere with achieving that goal.'[55] Goldwasser and Ciro provide a useful summary of the findings of this aspect of Macaulay's research:

> Significant ongoing business relationships are regulated by the parties according to what is fair and reasonable, or commercially necessary, at particular points in time rather than by

[53] Harold Dubroff, 'The Implied Covenant of Good Faith in Contract Interpretation and Gap Filling: Reviving a Revered Relic' (2006) 80 *St John's Law Review* 559, 607.

[54] Stewart Macaulay, 'Non-Contractual Relations in Business: A Preliminary Study' (1963) 28 *American Sociological Review* 55, 62.

[55] Ibid 65.

> reference to rights and duties arising under a contract. Commercial players do not always insist on their legal rights and do not necessarily behave as short-term profit maximisers. Such relationships involve friendship, reputation, interdependence, morality and altruistic desires and one must view the whole relationship, rather than simply what was said and done at formation. Although trust can be misplaced, all involved must ultimately work to satisfy each other.[56]

In this sense, Macneil also similarly referred to the 'entangling strings of friendship, reputation, interdependence, morality and altruistic desires' as being relevant in the whole contractual relationship.[57] This also discredits the conventional assumption in contract law that people entered into contracts because it gave them 'bargaining endowments' to plan exchanges into the future and to allocate risks, costs and benefits in the transaction.[58] Beale and Dugdale's research suggests that excessive contractual planning can make a contract too rigid and, further, extensive negotiation may harm relationships. Contract law often serves as a residual form of security. Exhaustive contracts are generally only reserved for situations where there is no established trade practice. Operationally, reputation and cooperative concessions are key to maintaining and improving commercial relationships. Attempting to shelter behind contractual provisions too heavily can damage one's reputation, and unresolved disputes may inhibit future business.

Opportunism is a moral hazard, in that contracting parties who are more protected from risks may be averse to opportunistic acts than they would be if they were fully exposed to the risk. This often occurs in insurance contracts. If left unregulated, this conduct could lead to an unfair distribution of wealth between parties.

Holdout behaviour can also lead to opportunism. This is established where a party withholds consent or performance to gain additional benefits, exploiting the sequential nature of contract performance.

A clear example of holdout behaviour is seen in *Atlas Express Ltd v Kafco (Importers and Distributors) Ltd* ('*Atlas*'), whereby a plaintiff who is a national road carrier tried to increase the minimum amount payable for delivering cartons for the defendant, an importer and distributor of basket ware. The plaintiff knew the defendant was reliant on the plaintiff's services as there was no other carrier readily available. The defendant consented to pay the increased amount, however, the court subsequently held that the defendant's consent was made under economic duress. The plaintiff's behaviour was opportunistic given the defendant's vulnerability was leveraged to extract more money than initially agreed upon by the parties.

Further, the likelihood of an opportunistic threat of non-performance is tied to the victim's ability to recover damages and litigation costs. In *Atlas*, it is possible

---

[56] Vivian Goldwasser and Tony Ciro, 'Standards of Behaviour in Commercial Contracting' (2002) 30 *Australian Business Law Review* 369, 370.

[57] Ian R Macneil, 'A Primer of Contractual Planning' (1975) 48 *Southern California Law Review* 629, 633.

[58] Robert Cooter, Stephen Marks and Robert H Mnookin, 'Bargaining in the Shadow of the Law: A Testable Model of Strategic Behaviour' (1982) 11 *Journal of Legal Studies* 225; Robert H Mnookin and Lewis Kornhauser, 'Bargaining in Shadow of the Law: The Case of Divorce' (1978–1979) 88 *Yale Law Journal* 950.

the defendant might not have fully recovered its losses if it had sued for breach instead of paying more to the plaintiff. Hypothetically, if the defendant had not supplied its retailers on time, the potential damage to its reputation may not have been compensated in court. Such risks can make the victim more inclined to meet the opportunist's demands rather than seeking legal redress.

In some instances, contractual modifications may be justified and may not necessarily be considered opportunistic. This is primarily when circumstances change so as to warrant changes to the contractual agreement where the absence of such changes may cause a party to incur a loss. In this case, it may be more economical for the parties to modify the contract than to make a settlement payment for breach. An efficient post-modification contract can be achieved through a fair redistribution of expected benefits, assuming there is a surplus for renegotiation. This would allow the parties to efficiently perform the contract, while maintaining the contract's initial value and mitigating the risks associated with strict adherence to the original terms of the contract where they would no longer be conducive to performance.

The case of *Goebel v Linn* ('*Goebel*')[59] provides an example of efficient modification. The plaintiff had promised to provide the defendant brewer with all the ice they needed. This was contracted on a fixed price. It became apparent after a few months that the plaintiff would not be able to supply at the stipulated price. The plaintiff's ice production was severely limited (presumably due to extraordinary warm weather) and was facing commercial ruin due to increased cost. In response to this, the plaintiff raised the supply price for its customers which included the defendant. The defendant accepted the higher price, recognising that without ice, their entire stock would be at risk. The Supreme Court of Michigan held that the contractual variation was justified, stating that unforeseen circumstances made the original contract nugatory and, as such, the defendant had not agreed to the change under duress.

A less certain example, however, is found in the case of *Williams v Roffey Bros & Nicholls (Contractors) Ltd* ('*Williams*').[60] Here, the defendant, a builder, subcontracted carpentry work to the plaintiff as part of a refurbishment project for 27 flats. The plaintiff encountered financial difficulties because the contract price was too low and consequently risked breaching the contract unless additional payment was made. The defendant agreed to pay more, allowing the plaintiff to continue working for another two months. During this time, the plaintiff completed 8 out of the 27 flats, although the defendant only paid £1,500 out of the promised additional £10,300. The original contract was worth £20,000. The primary legal issue for the English Court of Appeal to decide was whether there was valid consideration for the defendant's promise to pay the additional amount. The Court held that the contractual modification in the additional payment was enforceable because the defendant benefited by avoiding a breach of their own head contract and the hassle of finding new carpenters. Glidewell LJ expressed the legal position as follows:

> (i) if A has entered into a contract with B to do work for, or to supply goods or services to, B in return for payment by B and (ii) at some stage before A has completely performed

---

[59] 47 Mich 489 (Mich, 1882).

[60] [1990] 1 All ER 512.

> his obligation under the contract B has reason to doubt whether A will, or will be able to, complete his side of his bargain and (iii) B thereupon promises A an additional payment in return for A's promise to perform his contractual obligations on time and (iv) as a result of his giving his promise B obtains in practice a benefit, or obviates a disbenefit, and (v) B's promise is not given as a result of economic duress or fraud on the part of A, then (vi) the benefit to B is capable of being consideration for B's promise, so that the promise will be legally binding.[61]

Although the principle enunciated by Glidewell LJ received judicial support in Australia,[62] law and economics is concerned less with the requirement of consideration as it is not always critical in respect to a contractual variation.[63] In *Atlas*, there was no sudden change in circumstances that would warrant a price increase, unlike in *Goebel* where the ex post modification was considered efficient. Issues arise where courts uphold modifications which potentially incentivise parties to threaten non-performance to benefit themselves, justifying it under false pretences. This behaviour is opportunistic as it creates a benefit for the party who has information of which the other party is unaware. *Williams* is a good example where an increase to the plaintiff's cost of performance was not evident, and it could continue to work without substantial payment from the defendant. As such, courts should be encouraged to decide on the evidence whether the requested contract modifications are due to a party's unprofitable circumstances to determine whether that party has made the request in good faith. However, this approach is limited by the court's difficulty to substantiate changes to a requesting party's circumstances that impact the cost of performance.

Allowing changes to contracts might also lead to lowballing, where a party may make an extremely low bid with the intention of renegotiating the price later. This is common in construction contracts, where the tenderer exploits the high social and economic costs for the invitor to replace them once an agreement is already in place. Parties engaging in this opportunistic behaviour are likely to be in economic turmoil and, potentially, facing insolvency. In *Pratt Contractors Ltd v Transit New Zealand* ('*Pratt*'), Lord Hoffman acknowledged suggestions of this behaviour by the plaintiff, whose bid—among eight tenderers—was the lowest by nearly $1,000,000:

---

[61] Ibid 521–522.

[62] The decision was accepted in *Musumeci v Winadell Pty Ltd* (1994) 34 NSWLR 723. Whether this acceptance of the principle in *Williams v Roffey Bros & Nicholls (Contractors) Ltd* will be adopted throughout Australia is yet to be definitively determined but it would seem very likely. *Musumeci v Winadell Pty Ltd* was assumed to be correct in *Conlan v Registrar of Titles* (2001) 24 WAR 299, 338; it was followed in *Mitchell v Pacific Dawn Pty Ltd* [2003] QSC 86, [37]; it was applied in *Vella v Ayshan* [2008] ANZ Conv R 8-013, [18]; and it was referred to with approval by Gummow and Hayne JJ in *DPP (Vic) v Le* (2007) 232 CLR 562, 577.

[63] *Anton Trawling Co Ltd v Smith* [2003] 2 NZLR 23, per Baragwanath J: The importance of consideration is as a valuable signal that the parties intend to be bound by their agreement, rather than an end in itself. Where the parties who have already made such intention clear by entering legal relations have acted upon an agreement to a variation, in the absence of policy reasons to the contrary they should be bound by their agreement.

> Pratt's reputation ... was not uncontroversial. It was thought by some to practise lowballing, that is to say, tendering a low price to obtain the contract in the expectation of being able to make a profit by aggressive claims for additional payments.[64]

This public tendering process creates a preliminary contract under which the invitor must treat all tenderers equally and in good faith. However, a lowball bid can make it difficult for the invitor to act in good faith, as it may be the best price on offer, but could end up leading to higher costs in the future when the tenderer attempts to renegotiate for a higher price.

Opportunistic lowballing might be mitigated by a surety bond, where a third party guarantees the successful bidder's performance. If the bidder defaults, both the bidder and the surety are accountable. The surety must demonstrate adequate assets to provide a bond. This is common practice in public tendering. However, as was seen in *Pratt*, the invitor's concerns about the potential for the bidder to recoup expenses through 'claimsmanship' were not relieved by the surety.

Contractual breaches do not always amount to opportunism whereby the parties' wealth is redistributed. If non-performance of the contract results in a better outcome than if it had been performed, the conduct is not opportunistic. This may be where the breaching party compensates the victim fully, with a guarantee that no loss is incurred and that the remaining contractual resources will be used to generate income. Further, breaches due to unforeseen circumstances that harm both parties do not constitute opportunism as wealth transfer is a necessary feature of opportunistic behaviour.

The economic implications of opportunistic conduct will now be examined in the light of the already discussed characteristics and examples of opportunistic conduct. Contract economists agree that such behaviour must be minimised to serve the values fundamental to contract law.

6.2.3.4 Why Should Opportunism Be Discouraged?

Opportunistic behaviour is designed to discourage actions that unfairly deprive a contracting party of their expected financial benefits arising out of a contract. It is not the opportunistic behaviour, itself, but the outcome of opportunistic behaviour in leading to a redistribution of wealth, that is inefficient. Individuals who are concerned about losing their contractual earnings may avoid entering into contracts altogether. Therefore, if the law does not address opportunistic actors, it could hinder relations that would otherwise be economically beneficial and increase wealth among parties through contracting.

Contracting parties who are concerned about potential opportunistic behaviour will also incur greater transaction costs. A person might write longer, detailed contracts or perform extensive background checks on another party as a preventative step. Other kinds of preventative conduct may also include requiring simultaneous performance or demanding a deposit. Such practices should be discouraged to keep transaction costs low and maximise the net gains from a contract.

---

[64] [2005] 2 NZLR 433, 438 (as per Lord Hoffmann).

6.2.3.5 Is Good Faith Obligation the Answer to Counter Opportunism?

Opportunism can be seen as a breach of good faith. Therefore, many commentators maintain that a good faith obligation may serve to prevent and punish opportunistic behaviour given the principles directly oppose one another.

A contractual obligation of good faith is economically beneficial to prevent opportunistic behaviour and safeguard the rights of the parties to a contract. Transaction costs would also be reduced as parties need not specify every conceivable opportunistic act in contract where they can rely on good faith.

The argument was made judicially in the US by Judge Posner in *Market Street Associates Ltd Partnership v Frey*:

> The concept of the duty of good faith ... is a stab at approximating the terms the parties would have negotiated had they foreseen the circumstances that have given rise to their dispute. The parties want to minimize the costs of performance. To the extent that a doctrine of good faith designed to do this by reducing defensive expenditures is a reasonable measure to this end, interpolating it into the contract advances the parties' joint goal. ... The office of the doctrine of good faith is to forbid the kinds of opportunistic behaviour that a mutually dependent, cooperative relationship might enable in the absence of [such a] rule.[65]

The main argument for the obligation of good faith in contracts is that contracts are inherently incomplete. If parties could foresee any and all future events and negotiate terms without any cost, there would be no need for a good faith obligation. However, as this is not possible, good faith may fill in the gaps created by incompleteness.

6.2.3.6 Opportunism, Good Faith, and Behavioural Economics

When evaluating the suitability of a good faith obligation to regulate opportunistic behaviour, it is important to consider behavioural economics as this will allow us to comprehend economic decision-making more effectively. Therefore, the impact of a good faith obligation should not be assessed only based on the expected conduct of a rational economic actor. It is also crucial to understand how people actually react to the law in practice. Contract economists should focus on these real-world responses to the obligation of good faith, rather than on ideal responses.

The ideal goal for courts is to establish a contract law system that encourages cooperative behaviour and discourages opportunistic actions, ultimately improving efficiency through comparative advantage.

While a traditional law and economics analysis generally assumes individuals are primarily self interested, behavioural studies show that some people value reciprocal fairness and may cooperate to reward or penalise certain behaviours. This reciprocal fairness is different from mere cooperative behaviour, as it includes a willingness to bear costs without expecting a benefit in return.

Consequently, individuals can be seen to have displayed a range of preferences. Empirical studies have tested which legal rules encourage ('crowd in') or discourage

---

[65] 941 F2d 588, 596 (1991, US App).

('crowd out') reciprocal and opportunistic behaviour. Bohnet, Frey, and Huck showed that minimal legal interference (Low Enforcement) fosters reciprocity in contracts.[66] The preference for reciprocity grows over time under Low Enforcement. Parties in contracts tend to be cautious, selecting non-opportunistic counterparts to avoid expropriation of contractual benefits. This selection might entail a thorough vetting process to increase the likelihood of dealing with an individual who is fair and not exploitative.

In contrast, a contract law system with moderate restrictions on freedom of contract (Medium Enforcement) diminishes reciprocity and promotes self-interested norms.[67] Theoretically, contracting is more appealing under Medium Enforcement compared to Low Enforcement due to the higher expected pay-off. However, institutional trust in contract laws replaces interpersonal trust.[68] The decision to act opportunistically is driven by the likelihood of court sanctions. Thus, legal intervention becomes the primary determinant of contractual behaviour, rather than intrinsic motivations. This results in a psychological shift, decreasing cooperative behaviour and increasing opportunistic dealings.[69]

In a legal environment that strictly regulates contracts (High Enforcement), opportunistic behaviour would likely be deterred. The increased risk of punishment makes the cost of breaching a contract high, which promotes adherence to the contract. Cooperation is enforced externally, regardless of whether individuals prefer to act fairly. Strong legal enforcement lowers the risk associated with contracts, creating an environment of trust that encourages contractual exchanges.

Bohnet, Frey, and Huck's experimental study therefore suggests that a Low or High Enforcement legal framework is preferable to Medium Enforcement as it promotes reciprocal and cooperative behaviour over opportunistic conduct. Whether Low or High Enforcement is more appropriate depends on transaction costs. A Low Enforcement system might lead to high transaction costs as parties spend more to verify each other's credibility from the outset, and fewer contracts might be made due to the difficulty in identifying opportunistic actors and the need for self-enforcing contract mechanisms. As such, a Low Enforcement system may prove challenging, inefficient and, ultimately, unrealistic. A High Enforcement system would be preferable, however, should a good faith obligation be established, costs incurred by litigation may be higher and predictability in contract law will likely suffer.

However, Duke has argued that a good faith obligation is a suitable method for implementing a High Enforcement system:

---

[66] Bohnet, Frey and Huck, 'More Order with Less Law', above n 38, 131, 132. The authors modelled an evolutionary game in which two contracting parties had the ability to produce a contractual surplus. Player One was required to decide whether to enter into a contract with Player Two but was unaware whether Player Two would perform. A total of 154 subjects participated. The game was repeated several times with varying payoff probabilities designed to reflect different contract law conditions, namely low, medium, or high enforcement regimes.

[67] Bohnet, Frey and Huck, 'More Order with Less Law', above n 38, 131, 132.

[68] Duke, above n 18, 190.

[69] Frey and Jegan, 'Motivation Crowding Theory', above n 38.

> Imposing an obligation to act in good faith is ... an effective way to ensure courts provide a performance-inducing high enforcement environment. Absent the implication of obligations of good faith, there is a chance that parties' reasonable expectations about how the other party will perform the contract will be disappointed if contractual parties are permitted to escape honouring their contractual obligations by resorting to the black letter of their agreements. As contracts are inevitably incomplete and static in nature, contractual doctrines that give unqualified effect to the express terms of the agreement will generate a medium enforcement regime.[70]

Duke's analysis suggests that a lack of a general good faith obligation in contract law may lead to inefficient enforcement. However, it is uncertain whether good faith would be effective in the Australian context. This is because it is likely that the current regime may produce similar outcomes to a regime founded on a good faith obligation. Despite this potential lack of change, behavioural economics theories strongly support good faith in promoting cooperative behaviour in contractual relationships.

The discussion above indicates that introducing a good faith obligation in Australia may prevent opportunistic behaviour and reduce transactional costs. Incomplete contracts and sequential performance often lead to this opportunism. It is important to consult behavioural economics in this analysis, as it helps to predict the obligation's likely potential impact. Empirical research suggests that good faith would encourage mutual cooperation while deterring opportunism. The following section aims to integrate these ideas within a transaction cost framework.

6.2.4 Transaction Cost Analysis

Generally, legal rules that lower transaction costs for contracting parties are favoured. To justify the introduction of a good faith obligation, it must be shown to reduce transaction costs. This requires a comparison of transaction costs in systems under which the obligation is present, and those under which it is not. Further to this, an assessment should be made of the potential for the obligation to provide clarity given the obligation is largely inconsistently applied.

6.2.4.1 Transaction Cost Factors

The transaction cost factors illustrated here are taken from the model formulated by Sepe who utilised equations to compare transaction costs, with and without good faith obligations.[71] Sepe's model considered two main factors that are incurred by contracting parties, which are made up of specification costs and the cost arising

---

[70] Ibid 197.

[71] Simone Sepe, 'Good Faith and Contract Interpretation: A Law and Economic Perspective' (2010) *Arizona Legal Studies Discussion Paper* No 10–28.

from incompleteness of contract.[72] These factors will also form the basis to assess a contracting environment with and without good faith obligation.

(a) Contracting Environment without Good Faith

In such an environment, the specification costs include the cost of drafting the contract and the time taken to do so. This is generally comprised of costs associated with discovering contingencies—the more detailed or comprehensive the contingencies, the greater the cost as it is linked with greater expertise in identifying and accommodating these contingencies, particularly when greater contractual specification is required in a contract.[73] Naturally, legal fees tend to increase with the number of contingencies included in a contract, as lawyers spend more time drafting the written document. It follows that an uninformed and inexperienced party might include additional contingencies in a contract as they see fit, making them incur higher legal costs than a knowledgeable party. This indicates that the marginal costs of contract specification can vary based on the contracting parties' experience.

Incomplete contracts result in opportunistic behaviour. For example, a party might exploit an ambiguous clause to redistribute the benefits of a contract from one party to another. The risk includes both the potential costs of each opportunistic act and the probability of such acts occurring. It also covers the costs of unforeseen contingencies that could make the contract inefficient. As more contingencies are specified, the risk and cost of opportunism decrease. Economic efficiency is achieved when the cost of detailing contingencies is equal to the marginal cost of an incomplete contract.

(b) Contracting Environment with Good Faith

Applying a similar analysis to a contractual regime with good faith, specification costs might not change as parties would still need to identify and provide for contingencies, aiming for an optimal balance between specificity and discretion.

However, the cost of contractual incompleteness would likely change under a good faith regime. Good faith endorses judicial intervention to prevent opportunistic actors from unfairly profiting at the expense of an innocent party, as it can regulate this kind of behaviour even when it is not explicitly stipulated in the contract.

This view may be too simplistic as good faith obligation lacks a precise definition and, further, it is not a complete and infallible replacement for detailed contract specification. This could be injurious where, for example, a contract states that one party is to profit from an unspecified contingency may breach good faith if they retain it at the expense of the other party. Additionally, the discretion conferred on courts by a good faith obligation may result in judicial interference with both specified and unspecified contingencies. There is also the possibility that the court may fail to find the 'correct answer.' This consideration does not automatically suggest that the obligation of good faith is inefficient, but only that any application of the obligation

[72] Ibid 31.

[73] Ibid 32.

must take into account the probability of court error.[74] The inherent uncertainty in defining and applying the good faith obligation suggests that its adoption could increase uncertainty regarding the entitlements of contracting parties. Consequently, the total transaction costs under a contract law system incorporating a good faith obligation might be higher than without such an obligation, even with the same number of specified contingencies.

Determining whether recognising a general duty of good faith is economically efficient is said to be challenging.[75] It is difficult to accurately measure the costs associated with administering a legal system that includes a good faith obligation.[76] Sepe's model allows for predictions on when the good faith obligation might be efficient or inefficient.[77] The good faith obligation is only transaction cost-efficient if courts are willing to redistribute contractual surplus. Inefficiency arises if courts are perceived as interfering with existing contractual rights. Therefore, the judiciary must be cautious of the negative economic consequences of rewriting contractual terms under the guise of good faith. Judicial decision tends to improve over time and with it the interpretation and application of good faith obligation becomes more efficient as the judiciary, legal advisors and contracting parties familiarise themselves with its scope.[78] Ultimately, the efficiency of the good faith obligation heavily relies on its predictability and the confidence contracting parties have in the judiciary's ability to reach correct outcomes. Behavioural economics becomes extremely relevant when dealing with the efficiency of a good faith obligation in contracting transactions.

6.2.4.2 Nature of Contracting Transactions

If court 'error' is perceived as less significant but more predictable, contracting parties may prefer to depend on the courts' interpretation of good faith to address any gaps in contractual specification. This would mean fewer contingencies need to be specified in a contract, reducing parties' legal costs.

As has been discussed, unsophisticated parties often face high costs when specifying contingencies. As they may not be able to afford the services of specialised

---

[74] Theoretically, a doctrine of good faith can be endorsed if 'the courts are able in all cases to determine the efficient outcome (taking into account the effect of any rule on *ex ante* incentives in future, similar contracts). … The reality of generalist courts, however, is that they possess only limited competence in any one area. Put simply, courts make mistakes about efficient outcomes. … [J]udicial competence is more or less limited because courts make errors more or less frequently in "observing" a contract variable or translating an observation into a conclusion about efficiency. In the incomplete contracting context, courts will display varying degrees of competence as they are more or less able to deduce efficient gap-filling terms.': Gillian K Hadfield, 'Judicial Competence and the Interpretation of Incomplete Contracts' (1994) 23 *Journal of Legal Studies* 159, 162.

[75] Summers, 'The General Duty of Good Faith', above n 10, 827.

[76] Ibid.

[77] Sepe, 'Good Faith and Contract Interpretation', above n 71, 51.

[78] See Ian Ayres and Robert Gertner, 'Filling Gaps in Incomplete Contracts: An Economic Theory of Default Rules' (1989) 99 *Yale Law Journal* 87.

advisers, like lawyers, to consult on negotiations, it may be more efficient for these parties to rely on the courts' good faith obligation ex post. This would reduce the costs involved in pre-contractual specification, but also inflates the risk borne out of the court making an error. However, as unsophisticated parties typically engage in simple transactions, court errors are likely to be minimal. Therefore, good faith is a more efficient approach where unsophisticated parties are contracting.

Unsophisticated individuals engaging in dealings with commercial parties are also likely to benefit from a good faith obligation. Due to the power imbalance between these parties, unsophisticated individuals will likely have little bargaining power in negotiations with commercial entities. The commercial party, being experienced, are likely to use a standard form contract with which an individual conforms with without negotiation.

Traditional economic theory suggests that standard form contracts are cost-effective and well-suited to unsophisticated actors. Provided some consumers scrutinise and 'shop around' for standard form contract clauses, their actions could pressure companies to adopt fair terms for all contracts of the kind. This results in an implied market approval that might eliminate the need for a good faith obligation to prevent exploitation of weaker parties.

As consumers are limited rationally, they often do not understand contract details or consider them in decisions. This can weaken the market pressures that ensure fair terms, requiring legislative or judicial intervention to curb opportunistic behaviour. These interventions are similar to those under a good faith obligation. Contract economists argue that courts should be able to challenge a standard form contract if a term is not clear to most consumers, removing the market's ability to check seller overreach.

Notably, applying a good faith obligation might lead to higher contract prices for unsophisticated parties. If these parties avoid relying on good faith obligation, they could potentially secure better contractual terms. Where compliance with an obligation of good faith is a compulsory standard in contracting, it may lead to a balance in the contract terms, whereby neither party is unfairly advantaged or disadvantaged.

However, the potential risks of not having a good faith obligation may be greater than the higher costs incurred by unsophisticated parties when contracting. A more informed commercial party may exploit opportunities that the less sophisticated party is unaware of. Even if the unsophisticated party possessed the bargaining power to account for contingencies, they might lack the resources to identify these contingencies. Therefore, it is logical for unsophisticated parties to depend on the protection provided by a good faith obligation. Sepe emphasises the point:

> [N]ot including good faith basically legitimates parties to behave opportunistically at the occurrence of unspecified contingencies. Then, due to the large number of contingencies that are unforeseeable for an unsophisticated party, [he or she] is better off by choosing good faith and accepting that [his or her] counterparty might still behave opportunistically

(anticipating the possibility of court error in the ex post enforcement of the contract) than, by excluding good faith, giving the counterparty 'the right' to do so.[79]

In situation where there is an imbalance in bargaining strength, the weaker party is likely to prefer an obligation of good faith. In these instances, it is more efficient for standard contracts governing low-value transactions to cover only generally plausible contingencies, as the cost of covering every possible eventuality would outweigh the benefits conferred to the party. Cost savings are high, and the likelihood of court error is low.

Unique, complex contracts involving large potential gains which are entered into by sophisticated commercial parties are, conversely, more susceptible to court error. This is because the terms are likely to be more meticulously designed as a consequence of using various trained professionals, with most foreseeable contingencies addressed, in comparison with unsophisticated contracting parties.

Further, specialised transactions will inevitably involve a vast number of contingencies which courts are likely to be unable to address adequately. Therefore, in more complex contracts, it is better to make express specifications as to contingencies. Clearly, this means that the difference between the specifications in a contract which is subject to a good faith obligation would not differ significantly from one that is not subject to the obligation.

These complex contracts often result in an imbalance of information between the parties involved and the judiciary. If these contracts lead to litigation, courts might struggle to determine the degree of good faith required due to a lack of relevant case law to draw on. Additionally, judges may not have the expertise to fully grasp specialised and technical contracts. As such, there is a significant probability of court error in these situations and parties are unlikely to benefit from the institution of a good faith obligation when making complex contracts. Therefore, parties involved should continue to independently determine their contractual rights and obligations, as good faith is likely to prove less efficient and effective. The principle of free contract could be undermined by mandated good faith obligations in these cases.

This discussion demonstrates that a general application of the good faith obligation in contract law may not always lead to lower transaction costs when compared to contracts without such an obligation. The suggested efficiency criterion indicates that experienced parties involved in distinctive contractual situations should define their rights and responsibilities themselves, rather than relying on courts to interpret how the obligation applies to their contract.

Consequently, imposing a mandatory good faith obligation in all contractual relationships within Australia may not be economically beneficial. Introducing such an obligation as a default could lead to parties (especially in cases where one is more sophisticated than the other) to contract out when it is more efficient for them to do so. A more effective approach may be to enforce good faith obligations in contracts that would benefit from improved economic efficiency. It would be particularly useful in contractual relationships where there lies a significant power imbalance. However, similar obligations are already partly enforced by existing legislation, like the *ACL*.

[79] Sepe, 'Good Faith and Contract Interpretation', above n 71, 46.

From a law and economics perspective, a universally applied good faith obligation would be inefficient for some contracts and, therefore, may not be ideal.

Be that as it may, current contracting practises and case law continue to point to a good faith obligation environment. Instead of fighting it, can good faith obligation possibly function as a governance device within commercial contractual provisions? The task in this respect is to consider if good faith obligation can serve and benefit commercial contracting parties. This is the basis to evaluate the value of good faith provisions in commercial contract in the next section.

6.3 Good Faith Obligation in Practice

The fact of the matter, in practice, is that contract practitioners who are faced with the unsatisfactory state of the law on good faith obligation tend to employ an array of drafting measures specifically to handle the effects of good faith provisions. The appropriate drafting approach taken is often informed by a range of considerations. The drafting approach is informed by several considerations, including negotiating power, preferences of the parties, industry norms, applicable legislation, and drafting practices of legal professionals.[80] As such, the way in which good faith obligation is employed practically is very much affected by the specific construction of the obligation in the contract.[81] This involves more than just adding or deleting terms under the current regime of implied good faith obligations.[82] Essentially, commercial parties are left at the mercy of how courts interpret and apply the relevant contract law's doctrines and principles to their contracts, unless parties take steps to optimise their control of how good faith obligation relates to them.[83]

---

[80] Cf. Alicia Hill, 'Good Faith—Enforcement in Australia' (2013) 11(3) *International Journal of Franchising Law* 1. http://www.mcw.com.au/Content/Attachment/Good%20faith%20-%20Enforcement%20in%20Australia.pdf; Bryan Horrigan, 'Good Faith from a Drafting and Pleadings Point of View' (Paper presented at the Commercial Court CPD Seminar, Melbourne, 4 June 2014); Bryan Horrigan, 'New Frontlines in Regulating Unconscionable, Unfair, and Bad Faith Business Conduct', *The Monash Law E-Briefing* (Melbourne), 2nd ed, 18 June 2014. http://themonashlaw-e-briefing.blogspot.com.au/2014/06/expert-legal-commentary-new-frontlines.html.

[81] This is also the position that is universally taken by all the legal practitioners interviewed.

[82] See *Vodafone Pacific Ltd v Mobile Innovations Ltd* [2004] NSWCA 15; *Macquarie International Health Clinic Pty Ltd v Sydney South West Area Health Service* [2010] NSWCA 268; *Alstom Ltd v Yokogawa Australia Pty Ltd (No 7)* [2012] SASC 49; *Cordon Investments Pty Ltd v Lesdor Properties Pty Ltd* [2012] NSWCA 184; The Hon Marilyn Warren, 'Good Faith: Where Are We At?' (2010) 34 *Melbourne University Law Review* 344; Justice James Allsop, 'Good Faith and Australian Contract Law: A Practical Issue and Question of Theory and Principle' (2011) 85 *Australian Law Journal* 341; The Hon Paul de Jersey, 'Good Faith in Contracts in Financial Services' (Paper presented at the 26th Annual Banking and Financial Services Law Association and Practice Conference, Queensland, 31 July 2009 – 1 August 2009).

[83] This was crystallised by Warren CJ in relation to good faith obligation: '[G]ood faith as a doctrine does not exist independently of the rules surrounding the construction and interpretation of contracts, or the rules of implication [and there] may be a merging of the two processes (interpretation and implication) in the arena of good faith': Warren, 'Good Faith: Where Are We At?', above n 82, 349.

This part of the chapter considers the approach and methodology employed that guide practical legal advice. The choice of using Public Private Partnerships (PPPs) as a case study is because it represents a type of arm's length commercial contract that utilises good faith obligation in contractual performance and enforcement. Specifically, a snapshot is taken of the occurrence of good faith contracting provisions to provide the 'what' and the 'how' good faith obligation manifests within a commercial contracting setting. Interviews have also been conducted with contracting participants for the purpose of obtaining a representative view of their understanding of good faith and whether it is practically beneficial.

6.3.1 Contracting Approach to Good Faith Obligation

The primary goal of a good faith obligation is to make contract law more attuned to the needs of commerce and the reasonable expectations of the contracting parties.[84] Lord Steyn, speaking extra-judicially, suggested that any legal doctrine should be evaluated based on its effectiveness in serving the intended legal obligation:

> It is right that academic lawyers, practitioners and judges should constantly consider whether rules of law under consideration serve the purpose which led to their formation. Or, putting it more simply, we must never lose sight of Lord Reid's observation in *Cartledge v E Jopling & Sons Ltd* that '[t]he common law ought never to produce a wholly unreasonable result.'[85]

In this respect, the reasonable expectations of the contracting parties must be kept at the forefront of this discussion and as a contractual objective, it must also be inherently protected in contract law:

> [I]f the prima facie solution to a problem runs counter to the reasonable expectations of honest men, this criterion sometimes requires a rigorous examination of the problem to ascertain whether the law does indeed compel demonstrable unfairness.[86]

In the context of the duty of good faith, the reasonable expectations approach requires considering what the contracting parties expect at the time of making the contract, which dictates how the contract will be performed.[87] This does not mean

---

[84] Edward Thomas, 'Good Faith in Contract: A Non-Sceptical Commentary' (2005) 11 *New Zealand Business Law Quarterly* 391, 393.

[85] Johan Steyn, 'The Role of Good Faith and Fair Dealing in Contract Law: A Hair Shirt Philosophy?' in Johan Steyn, *Democracy Through the Law: Selected Speeches and Judgments* (2004) 223; cf. Summers, 'The General Duty of Good Faith', above n 10, 818.

[86] *First Energy (UK) Ltd v Hungarian International Bank Ltd* [1993] Lloyd's Rep 194, 196.

[87] A number of theories on good faith are consistent with this approach: Burton, 'Breach of Contract', above n 117, 373, 391; Steven J Burton and Eric G Andersen, 'The World of a Contract' (1990) 75 *Iowa Law Review* 861; Frank H Easterbrook and Daniel R Fischel, 'Contract and Fiduciary Duty' (1993) 36 *Journal of Law and Economics* 425, 438; Muris, above n 118; *Market Street Associates Ltd Partnership v Frey* 941 F 2d 588, 595–596 (7th Cir, 1991); *Kham & Nate's Shoes No. 2 Inc v First Bank of Whiting* 908 F 2d 1351, 1357 (7th Cir, 1990); Jeannie M Paterson, 'The Standard of Good Faith: Reasonable Expectations or Community Standards?' in Michael Bryan (ed), *Private Law in Theory and Practice* (Routledge-Cavendish, 1st ed, 2007) 157.

the court will replicate the parties' reasonable expectations by implying good faith.[88] A 'reasonable expectation' is not necessarily an actual expectation.[89] The courts will consider both the contract terms and the surrounding circumstances to decide whether a term should be implied.[90] The surrounding circumstances shape the parties' expectations regarding how the contract will be performed. However, the reasonable expectations approach would still demand that the express terms be qualified on the basis of extrinsic factors. The community standards approach to good faith in Australia bases extrinsic factors on the standards of a 'judging community' rather than vague moral standards.[91] This approach may involve taking evidence from the relevant business or general community, which provides the sociological evidence required for those standards.[92] In essence, the obligation of good faith represents principles of mutual respect and cooperation, which is favoured in a contracting relationship.[93] This obligation serves to meet the reasonable expectations of the parties involved in the contract by requiring them to act in a way that is objectively reasonable, fostering cooperation and trust, and in the event that an unforeseen circumstances arising, not insist on contractual performance.[94] Thus, the concept of reasonable expectations plays a significant role in the distribution of contractual gains or losses.

6.3.1.1 A Practical Analysis

Keeping the above perspective at the forefront, the practical analysis in this part of the chapter considers Horrigan's four basic approaches (which overlap to a degree and are not necessarily distinct by themselves) to good faith obligation from a practical transactional viewpoint of drafting commercial agreements. Horrigan's approach was derived from existing case law on the application of good faith obligation in

---

[88] Cf. Catherine Mitchell, 'Leading a Life of its Own? The Roles of Reasonable Expectation in Contract Law' (2003) 23 *Oxford Journal of Legal Studies* 639, 642; Rick A Bigwood, *Exploitative Contracts* (Oxford University Press, 2003) 50–57; Elisabeth Peden, 'The Meaning of Contractual "Good Faith"' (2002) 22 *Australian Bar Review* 235.

[89] Cf. Glanville Williams, 'Language and the Law—I-V' (1945) 61 *The Law Quarterly Review* 384; Jeannie M Paterson, 'Terms Implied in Fact: The Basis for Implication' (1998) 13 *Journal of Contract Law* 103; Paterson, 'The Standard of Good Faith', above n 87, 153.

[90] Cf. *Codelfa Construction Pty Ltd v State Rail Authority of NSW* (1982) 149 CLR 337, 347–353; *Investors Compensation Scheme Ltd v West Bromwich Building Society* [1998] 1 WLR 896, 912–913; *Bank of Credit and Commerce International SA v Ali* [2001] 2 WLR 735, 739, 749.

[91] Barry J Reiter, 'Good Faith in Contracts' (1983) 17 *Valparaiso University Law Review* 705, 717; Steyn, 'The Role of Good Faith and Fair Dealing', above n 214, 222; Duncan Kennedy, 'Form and Substance in Private Law Adjudication' (1976) 89 *Harvard Law Review* 1685, 1721.

[92] E.g. in the US, the *Uniform Commercial Code*, s 2–103(1)(b) or the *Restatement (2d) Contracts*, s 205, comment (a); Cf. Farnsworth, 'Good Faith Performance', above n 10, 671–672; Reiter, above n 91, 706.

[93] Paterson, 'The Standard of Good Faith', above n 87, 158.

[94] *Co-operative Insurance Society Ltd v Argyll Stores Ltd* [1997] 3 All E R 297, 305 (per Lord Hoffmann).

contractual enforcement.[95] These four approaches are adopted in this chapter as a template for analysing the decision to include good faith obligation in commercial agreements.[96] They are (1) remaining silent on good faith in the contract; (2) expressly imposing a general and undefined obligation of good faith on all contracting parties; (3) expressly defining or confining obligations of good faith to particular contractual rights or provisions in the contract on some or all contracting parties; and (4) expressly excluding implications of good faith.[97]

6.3.1.2 A Study of Public Private Partnerships (PPPs)

The choice in considering PPPs as a study in this research is because PPPs, as a type of arm's length commercial contract, are generally not construed as relational contracts despite their long-term contracting arrangements, but rather operate predominantly on the basis of their discrete contracting characteristic.[98] Their long-term contracting arrangements inadvertently requires the contract to incorporate cooperative obligations, such as good faith, extensively.[99] It is this unique characteristic that makes this study relevant in understanding whether good faith obligation is beneficial in an arm's length contract.

PPPs are long-term contracting arrangements between public and private entities for the purpose of delivering public services or infrastructure. They may be defined as

[95] Bryan Horrigan, 'New Directions in how Legislators, Courts and Legal Practitioners Approach Unconscionable Conduct and Good Faith' in John McKenna and Helen Jeffcoat (eds), *Queensland Legal Yearbook 2012* (Supreme Court Library Queensland, 2013); cf. John W Carter and Elisabeth Peden, 'Good Faith in Australian Contract Law' (2003) 19 *Journal of Contract Law* 155, 155–156.

[96] Although Horrigan's template uses five basic approaches for transactional analysis of good faith, I have omitted the fifth approach as it involves considering the choice of legal jurisdiction as the basic setting governing good faith application and this discussion only considers domestic (Australian) commercial transactions: Horrigan, 'New Directions', above n 95, 171.

[97] Horrigan, 'New Directions', above n 95, 200.

[98] Cf. Macneil's characterisation of legally enforceable contracts suggests that they exist on a continuum (spectrum) ranging from highly discreet at one end to highly relational at the other. Discreet exchanges focus on maximising self-interests and contracting parties are guided strictly on agreed-upon exchanges. In relational exchange situations, contracting parties mutually seek to ensure the fulfilment of mutual interests and contractual outcomes: Ian R Macneil, 'Relational Contract Theory as Sociology: A Reply to Prof Lindenberg and de Vos' (1987) 143 *Journal of Institutional and Theoretical Economics* 272; Ian R Macneil, *The New Social Contract: An Inquiry into Modern Contractual Relations* (Yale University Press, 1980).

[99] Cf. Infrastructure Australia, *National Public Private Partnership Guidelines: Commercial Principles for Economic Infrastructure*, vol 7 (2011), http://www.infrastructureaustralia.gov.au/public_private/files/Vol_7_Commercial_Principles_Economic_Infrastructure_Feb_2011.pdf: Although the guidelines specified that implied good faith obligation would normally be excluded from PPP, it also provides that they may be expressly assumed by the contracting parties. The guidelines further recommend that good faith obligation should be assumed for all key risk events, negotiations, dispute resolutions, default events and notices. On an examination of 18 PPP contracts in Victoria, good faith obligations are extensively found in provisions that correspond to the guidelines provided by Infrastructure Australia.

cooperative ventures between public and private sector parties, aimed at expanding the opportunities for private sector involvement in areas that are traditionally confined to the preserve of the public sector (such as toll roads, prisons, hospitals and schools). PPPs are generally perceived as being more effective and efficient (greater 'value for money') than conventional public procurement processes.[100]

(a) PPPs' Contracting Arrangements

The key reason for the use of good faith obligation in PPPs is that the nature of the contracting arrangements aims to promote long-term intersectoral and organisational collaboration under conditions of imperfect information, at the same time maintaining the distinct autonomy of the contracting parties.[101] On average, PPPs tend to span a period of 30 years.[102] Both the public and private sector contracting parties agree on the degree of project risks that each are prepared to undertake based on projected assessment, which may not be adequately detailed or known, at the outset of the contractual negotiation and formulation.[103] The project risk may include specific financing arrangements and/or the granting of rights to collect payments from the eventual users of the project (e.g. road tolls).[104] In short, the features in a PPPs contracting arrangement includes, first, that the provider of the public infrastructure is the private sector; second, the contracting relationship is long term; third, both the public and private sector agree on the degree of risks sharing; fourth, the project is

---

[100] See Michael Spackman, 'Public–Private-Partnerships: Lessons from the British Approach' (2002) 26(3) *Economic Systems* 283; Paul Andon, 'Public Private Partnerships (PPPs): Current Accounting-Related Research and Future Research Opportunities' (Paper presented at the Fifth Asia Pacific Interdisciplinary Research in Accounting (APIRA) Conference, Auckland, 8–10 July 2007), http://www.mngt.waikato.ac.nz/ConferenceManager/report.asp?issue=5; National Public Private Partnership Policy and Guidelines. http://www.infrastructureaustralia.gov.au/public_private/ppp_policy_guidelines.aspx; HM Treasury, *PFI: Strengthening long-term partnerships* (2006). https://www2.unece.org/wiki/download/attachments/23758291/Treasury%20-%20PFI%20Strenghtening%20long%20term%20partnerships.pdf?api=v2; New South Wales Government, *Working with government: Guidelines for privately financed projects* (2006).http://www.treasury.nsw.gov.au/__data/assets/pdf_file/0009/3141/wwggui_1.pdf; Demi Chung, David A Hensher and John M Rose, 'Toward the Betterment of Risk Allocation: Investigating Risk Perceptions of Australian Stakeholder Groups to Public–Private Partnership Tollroad Projects' (2010) 30 *Research in Transportation Economics* 43.

[101] Cf. Gianni Lorenzoni and Charles Baden-Fuller, 'Creating a Strategic Center to Manage a Web of Partners' (1995) 37(3) *California Management Review* 146.

[102] Jon R Blöndal, 'Market-type Mechanisms and the Provision of Public Services' (2005) 5 (1) *OECD Journal on Budgeting* 79; Chung, Hensher and Rose, 'Toward the Betterment', above n 100, 44.

[103] Cf. Hans Van Ham and Joop Koppenjan, 'Building Public–Private Partnerships: Assessing and Managing Risks in Port Development' (2001) 4(1) *Public Management Review* 593; Jane Broadbent, Jas Gill and Richard Laughlin, 'Evaluating the Private Finance Initiative in the National Health Service in the UK' (2003) 16(3) *Accounting, Auditing and Accountability Journal* 422.

[104] Cf. Patricia Clarke Annez, 'Urban Infrastructure Finance from Private Operators: What Have We Learned from Recent Experience?' (Working Paper No 4045, World Bank Policy Research, 2006). https://openknowledge.worldbank.org/bitstream/handle/10986/9019/wps4045.pdf?sequence=1; Darrin Grimsey and Mervyn K Lewis, 'Accounting for Public Private Partnerships' (2002) 26(3/4) *Accounting Forum* 245.

sourced entirely through the private sector financing the project; and fifth, the public sector pays the private sector for the services it provides or allows the private sector to collect payments from the eventual users. As such, the contracting circumstance inevitably revolves around an 'ideology of trust.'[105]

Good faith provisions in PPPs serve a unique purpose of allowing contracting parties manoeuvrability within an adversarial form of contracting. This stems from the fact that PPPs' contracting exchanges are, by and large, configured as arms' length events.[106] The key difference with the traditional form of contracting is that the contracting arrangement in PPPs is founded on a relationship of considerable longevity having a deeper and more textured characteristic, as opposed to discrete one-off contractual episodes of limited duration in traditional contracts.[107] Despite the long-term underpinnings of PPPs' contracting arrangements, the relational qualities of the contracting context merely represents a means to an end, rather than an end in themselves.[108] The formal contracting provisions still represent a vital reference point and, where the contracting arrangements fail, the hard edges of the contract still exist and options such as litigation remain viable.[109]

All the 15 PPPs examined in this book contained either a right to resolve contractual disputes through an arbitration process only or the option to proceed with court litigation as well. However, dispute resolutions are generally formulated as a two-staged process.[110] This requires the contracting parties to engage in negotiations to resolve the dispute before proceeding to arbitration or court litigation (this may include a requirement to negotiate in good faith or it may not). If the dispute were to go to arbitration, would provisions requiring good faith obligation be dealt with in the same way as the courts? Although the arbitration proceeding rules prescribed by the Australian Centre for International Commercial Arbitration (ACICA Rules) lacked reference to good faith, it does not mean that the obligation will not be enforceable. There is a general expectations of good faith in arbitration[111] and that, as such, it is conceivable that an arbitral proceeding would not be burdened with the legal shackles existing in the application of good faith and be able to resolve the dispute

[105] Jan Mouritsen and Sof Thrane, 'Accounting, Network Complementarities and the Development of Inter-Organizational Relations' (2006) 31(3) *Accounting, Organizations and Society* 241, 243.

[106] Chung, Hensher and Rose, 'Toward the Betterment', above n 229, 47; this is also the view of all the interviewees.

[107] Douglas D Gransbery, Howard L Reynolds and Jack Boyd, 'Measuring Partnered Project Performance' (1999) 41(10) *Cost Engineering* 39; Cf. Julian Critchlow, *Making Partnering Work in the Construction Industry* (Chartridge Books, 1998).

[108] Gregory A Bigley and Jone L Pearce, 'Straining for Shared Meaning in Organization Science: Problems of Trust and Control' (1998) 23(3) *Academy of Management Review* 405.

[109] Karl N Llewellyn, 'What Price Contract? An Essay in Perspective' (1931) 40 *Yale Law Journal* 704.

[110] This is consistent in all the dispute resolution provisions of all the 15 PPPs considered in this discussion.

[111] For example, in the approved London Court of International Arbitration (LCIA) Rules of Article 14.5 and Article 32.1, there is an acknowledgement of good faith obligation in arbitration, binding not only the parties but also the LCIA Institution and Arbitral Tribunal.

in accordance with the construct of the contract and the expectation of the parties.[112] It is beyond the scope of this research to explore further this area of good faith and arbitration, except to indicate that it would not generally affect the assessment of good faith's viability and utility.

PPPs' contracting has also been argued to be a form of contractual arrangement that is influenced by three main considerations—bounded rationality, opportunistic behaviour and asset specificity.[113] These elements are fundamental to the economics of contracting in all arm's length transactions and are less prominent in purely relational contracts.[114] Bounded rationality dictates that uncertainty is present to the extent that contracting parties will not know of all of the options and alternatives open to them to anticipate future complexities and changes in a contractual transaction.[115] Due to the nature of PPPs, which are based on imperfect information, both transaction cost[116] and limited foresight make PPPs invariably 'incomplete.' Such incompleteness often requires the contracting parties to engage in gap-filling and, in this sense, good faith obligation has often operated to provide a framework in which to help mitigate contracting uncertainties, rather than a means to impose inflexible moral standards on commercial contracting parties.[117] Opportunistic behaviour may prevail in PPPs where the exchange (in some instances) is characterised by

---

[112] See *United Group Rail Services Ltd v Rail Corporation (NSW)* (2009) 74 NSWLR 618, *HSBC Institutional Trust Services (Singapore) Ltd (Trustee of Starhill Global Real Estate Investment Trust) v Toshin Development Singapore Pte Ltd* [2012] SGCA 48 and *Emirates Trading Agency LLC v Prime Mineral Exports Private Ltd* [2014] EWHC 2014 (Comm) on the enforceability of a duty of good faith as an express term in multi-tiered dispute resolution clauses involving arbitration; Duarte G Henriques, 'The Role of Good Faith in Arbitration: Are Arbitrators and Arbitral Institutions Bound to Act in Good Faith?' (2015) 33(3) *ASA Bulletin* 514.

[113] This argument on 'economics of contracting' is fundamental to inter-organisational forms of contracting, which was developed initially by Ronald Coase and built upon by Oliver Williamson: Ronald H Coase, 'The Nature of the Firm' (1937) 4(16) *Economica* 386; Oliver E Williamson, *Markets and Hierarchies: Analysis and Antitrust Implications* (1975); Oliver E Williamson, 'The Economics of Organization: The Transaction Cost Approach' (1981) 87(3) *American Journal of Sociology* 548; Oliver E Williamson, *The Economic Institutions of Capitalism: Firms, Markets, Relational Contracting* (Free Press, 1985); Oliver E Williamson, 'Comparative Economic Organization: The Analysis of Discrete Structural Alternatives' (1991) 36(2) *Administrative Science Quarterly* 269; cf. Oliver E Williamson, *The Mechanism of Governance* (Oxford University Press, 1996); Oliver E Williamson, 'Transaction Cost Economics and Business Administration' (2005) 21(1) *Scandinavian Journal of Management* 19.

[114] The key discussion on the economics of contracting is found in chapter five; Cf. Motiar M Rahman and Mohan M Kumaraswamy 'Joint Risk Management through Transactionally Efficient Relational Contracting' (2002) 20(1) *Construction Management and Economics* 45, 46; cf. Williamson, *The Mechanisms of Governance*, above n 113.

[115] Cf. Jane Broadbent, Jas Gill and Richard Laughlin, 'The Private Finance Initiative in the UK: Contracting in the Context of Infrastructure Investment and Control' (2003) 6(2) *International Public Management Journal* 622.

[116] Transaction costs are essentially the costs of using the market and include 'costs of negotiation and writing contingent contracts; costs of monitoring contractual performance; cost of enforcing contractual promises; and costs associated with breaches of contractual promises': Rahman and Kumaraswamy, above n 114, 46.

[117] Easterbrook and Fischel, 'Contract and Fiduciary Duty', above n 87, 427.

information asymmetries[118] with one party to the transaction possessing knowledge that the other contracting party does not, which may lead to 'calculated efforts to mislead, distort, disguise, obfuscate or otherwise confuse' the other.[119] In this scenario, the opportunist may be able to act outside of the reasonable expectations of the contracting parties or exploit the other contracting party's understanding of the contract.[120] The danger of opportunism is also markedly increased with asset specificity. This means that the degree in which the continuing viability of the contractual arrangement tends to be rigidly tied to the contractual transaction envisaged that, in turn, increases the bilateral dependence of the contracting parties involved.[121] The result of a high degree of asset specificity in PPPs contracts means a correspondingly high switching cost, which inevitably results in a form of 'asymmetric lock-in' between the public and private contracting parties.[122] Asymmetric lock-in can occur where one contracting party has committed to the majority of the specific investments and any shift in the balance of power can create opportunistic behaviour (or 'hold-up') in which the dependency of a contracting party can be exploited.[123]

Despite the above, the discrete functional operations of PPPs can still be promoted by using a range of 'elastic' contracting mechanisms and 'obligational market exchanges.'[124] Theoretically, the contracting mechanism includes using good faith

---

[118] One contracting party may possess information that if disclosed to the other would have resulted in a more complete or different agreement. Information may be asymmetric *ex ante*, that is, before the agreement is reached, but becomes symmetric ex post, that is, after the agreement is struck. This occurrence may often result in litigation based on misrepresentation or non-disclosure. The plaintiff claims that the bargain was tainted as a result of the inequality of correct information. Contracts can also be said to be incomplete 'if the parties would like to add contingent clauses but are prevented from doing so by the fact that the state of nature cannot be verified': Oliver Hart and John Moore, 'Foundations of Incomplete Contracts' (1999) 66 *Review of Economic Studies* 115, 134.

[119] Williamson, *The Economic Institution of Capitalism*, above n 113, 47–48.

[120] Ultimately, three key factors are recognised as conditions for post-contractual opportunistic conduct. First, the opportunist act takes place ex post. The concept does not relate to a pre-contractual monopoly. Second, the victim of the opportunistic conduct must place some value or reliance on the performance of the contract which the opportunist can appropriate or use to extract some other benefit. Finally, the victim must have omitted to plan for the opportunistic behaviour, either negligently or on the basis of bounded rationality. Muris, above n 118, 523–524.

[121] Williamson, 'Comparative Economic Organization', above n 113, 281; cf. Kieron Walsh, *Public Services and Market Mechanism: Competition, Contracting and the New Public Management*, (Palgrave Macmillan Publishing, 1995.

[122] Chris Lonsdale, 'Post-Contractual Lock-In and the UK Private Finance Initiative (PFI): The Cases of National Savings and Investments and the Lord Chancellor's Department' (2005) 83(1) *Public Administration*, 67, 72.

[123] Cf. Williamson, *The Economic Institution of Capitalism*, above n 242; Joseph Farrell and Carl Shapiro, 'Optimal Contracts with Lock-In' (1988) *The Hoover Institute Working Papers in Economics* E88-45.http://www.google.com.au/url?sa=t&rct=j&q=&esrc=s&source=web&cd=1&ved=0CB0QFjAA&url=http%3A%2F%2Fhoohila.stanford.edu%2Fworkingpapers%2FgetWorkingPaper.php%3Ffilename%3DE-88-45.pdf&ei=prN3VPziCOOaygP3ioDIBw&usg=AFQjCNEIv8i6V-In12QTZToYGHJvZkniag, .

[124] Williamson, 'Comparative Economic Organization', above n 113, 271.

obligations for specifically contracted provisions to cater for dispute resolution procedures, periodic competitive bidding or recontracting of specific contingencies, and also to cater for any public policy changes.[125] As such, the contracting emphasis becomes capable of facilitating interorganisational goal setting, planning and coordination.[126] Seemingly, this aspect of good faith's operation allows contracting parties to exercise control over its application, particularly in contractual phases that involve further negotiation or dispute resolution or rights of termination.[127] In fact, the official guidelines on commercial principles for PPPs provide drafting guidance along these lines.[128] Government contracting parties are expected to act as a moral exemplar in its commercial dealings and adhere to higher standards of conduct than is expected of private entities.[129] Good faith obligation fits this understanding.

(b) Occurrence of Good Faith Obligations in PPPs

The purpose of looking at the occurrence of good faith provisions in PPPs is to take a snapshot of the contracting environment. This is achieved by examining the number of provisions requiring good faith obligations and how contracting parties perceive its value in relation to the expectations and legal advice given, and whether they are consistent with the legal application of good faith obligations. Therefore, it is to explore whether good faith obligation promotes cooperative exchanges and reduces interparty opportunism, and if it validates good faith obligation as a contracting device without degrading the concept of freedom of contract. This should provide further illumination and operationalise the key research question on whether an obligation of good faith could be justified to serve commercial contracting parties better. In this

[125] Cf. Jason Scott Johnston, 'Default Rules/Mandatory Principles: A Game Theoretic Analysis of Good Faith and the Contract Modification Problem' (1993) 3 *Southern California Interdisciplinary Law Journal* 335.

[126] Cf. Henri Dekker, 'Control of Inter-Organizational Relationships: Evidence on Appropriation Concerns and Coordination Requirements' (2004) 29(1) *Accounting, Organizations and Society*, 27; Cyril Tomkins, 'Interdependencies, Trust and Information in Relationships, Alliances and Networks' (2001) 26(2) *Accounting, Organizations and Society*, 161; Peter Vincent-Jones, *The New Public Contracting: Regulation, Responsiveness, Relationality* (2006).

[127] As seen in the case of *Renard Constructions (ME) Pty Ltd v Minister of Public Works* (1992) 26 NSWLR 234, 267.

[128] Infrastructure Australia, *National Public Private Partnership Guidelines: Commercial Principles for Social Infrastructure*, vol 3 (2008) 1.6.1, 1.6.5. http://www.infrastructureaustralia.gov.au/public_private/files/National_PPP_Guidelines_Vol_3_Commercial_Principles_Social_Infrastructure_Dec_08.pdf. [All Australian, State and Territory Government agencies now apply the National Public Private Partnership Policy and Guidelines]; The procurement policies in Victoria also reflects some of the types of standards and behaviour that the legal requirements of good faith require (Eg, the Victorian Government Purchasing Board http://www.vgpb.vic.gov.au) that the government act with fairness, integrity and impartiality in its commercial dealings. Good faith also complements the standards adopted by the Victorian government in the conduct of litigation through the Model Litigant Guidelines—Stephen Lee, 'The State as Model Litigant' (Paper presented at Lunchtime Seminar Series, Victorian Government Solicitor's Office, 28 September 2006). www.vgso.vic.gov.au/.../The%20State%20as%20Model%20Litigant.pdf.

[129] Nicholas C Seddon, *Government Contracts: Federal, State and Local* (Federation Press, 4th ed, 2009) 7–10.

Table 6.1 Summary of case study process

Good faith provisions in Victoria's Public Private Partnerships contracts	
Aim	To identify how good faith obligations are structured in a contractual commercial setting like the PPPs. This would allow for insights to be discovered on whether good faith obligation can be validated as a governance device in contract law
Objectives	To investigate and explore the ways that contracting parties and their legal advisors utilise good faith obligations and the rationale behind the drafting and operationalising of these obligations
Procedures	Conduct a series of interviews with personnel involved who participated in the formulation of the PPPs and also legal practitioners and consultants involved in advising the contracting parties to identify their attitudes and understanding of the implications of good faith obligations in implementing or operationalising them in practice
Methods	• Semi-structured interviews • Document analysis of PPP

Table 6.2 Sources of evidence for case study

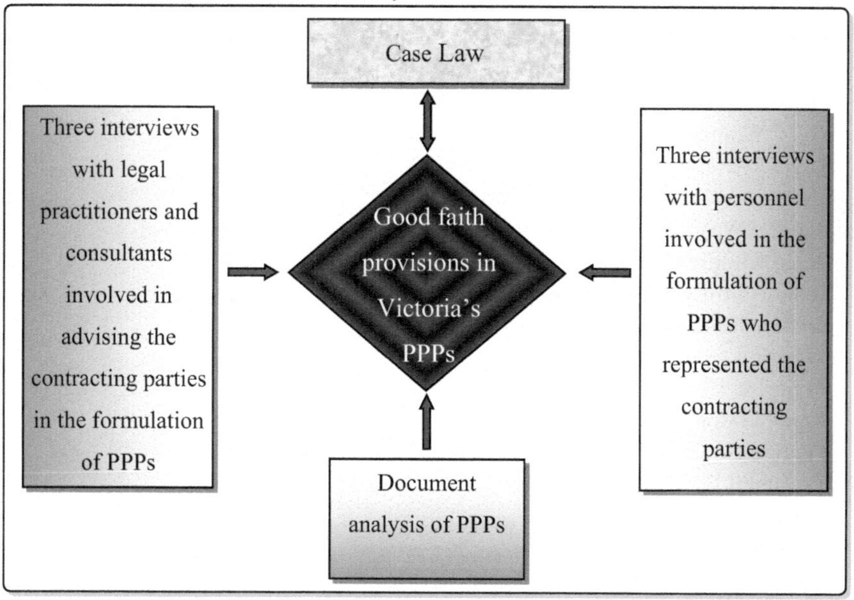

respect, the objectives in conducting the present study are summarised in Table 6.1 and the sources of evidence are shown in Table 6.2.

The present study explores the practical implication of good faith obligation in PPPs 'within its real-life context.'[130] It allows for the 'how' or 'why' questions to

[130] Colin Robson, *Real World Research* (Wiley, 2nd ed, 2002) 178.

be posed and also to discover any phenomenon in the particular contracting environment.[131] This is important to identify whether contracting parties view good faith obligations as relevant or beneficial in a commercial setting. It is also particularly useful in revealing the causal relationships between the contracting environment and the context in which it takes place.[132] In saying this, the intention here is not to suggest that any findings can be automatically generalised to a larger population. Rather, the present study looks at a typical circumstance in which good faith obligation operates.[133] It merely provides a form of representative snapshot in which to observe good faith obligation within a commercial contracting environment. As such, this approach is warranted 'when the internal validity of the study is more important than the generalisability of the results.'[134]

The sampling strategy in the present study identifies PPPs as the commercial setting for the study of good faith obligation. All 15 PPPs were made available through Victoria's Department of Treasury and Finance's website in which the contracting parties and the law firms (who prepared the PPPs) are identified. The pool of interview participants was sourced from this information. Altogether, six participants were interviewed from this pool, which were taken from the following PPPs projects:

- Southern Cross Station (Nov, 2002)
- Berwick Community Hospital (Nov, 2002)
- Victoria Correctional Facilities (Nov, 2003)
- Royal Women's Hospital (Apr, 2005)
- Royal Melbourne Showground (June, 2005)
- Melbourne Convention Centre (May 2006)
- Barwon Water (Aug, 2007)
- Royal Children's Hospital (Nov, 2007)
- Schools Project (Dec, 2008)
- BioSciences Research (Apr, 2009)
- Victoria Desalination (July, 2009)
- Peninsula Link (Jan, 2010)
- Ararat Prison (May, 2010)
- Victoria Comprehensive Cancer Centre (Dec, 2011).
- Ravenhall Prison (Sept, 2014).

[131] Robert K Yin, *Case Study Research: Designs and Methods* (SAGE Publications, 4th ed, 2009) 8–9; Martyn Denscombe, *The Good Research Guide for Small-Scale Social Research Projects* (McGraw-Hill Education, 1998) 31.

[132] David E Gray, *Doing Research in the Real World* (SAGE Publications, 2nd ed, 2009) 30.

[133] Yin, *Case Study Research*, above n 131, 48–49.

[134] Glenn B Voss and Zannie G Voss, 'Strategic Orientation and Firm Performance in an Artistic Environment' (2000) 64 *Journal of Marketing* 67, 78.

The research employed a purposive sampling approach in which personal judgement was used to select cases that would best meet the research questions and objectives.[135] The participants were selected based on their knowledge of the contracting provisions and their willingness to talk. As Schutt asserts about purposive sampling:

> Each sample element is selected for a purpose, usually because of the unique position of the sample elements. Purposive sampling may involve studying the entire population of some limited group ([for example] directors of shelters for homeless adults) or a subset of a population ([for example] mid-level managers with a reputation for efficiency). Or a purposive sample may be a 'key informant survey', which targets individuals who are particularly knowledgeable about the issues under investigation.[136]

The present study has, likewise, followed this strategy. The contracting parties' personnel involved in the formulation of the PPPs and legal advisers of major law firms were selected based on their knowledge and experience with good faith provisions. This allowed the analysis to consider the perception and input of the contract participants on the perceived value of good faith obligation in the PPPs and also allowed the approach and preference of legal advisers to be elicited in the light of the state of law on good faith obligations.[137]

(i) Research Methods

Crotty defines research methods as: '[t]he techniques or procedures used to gather and analyse data related to some research questions or hypothesises.'[138] Yin identifies six sources of evidence for case studies: documents, archival records, interviews, direct observation, participant observation, and physical artefacts.[139] Among these, a red boundary line can be seen drawn around the three methods used in the present research (Fig. 5.4), which were semi-structured interviews, case law (archival records), and document analysis of PPPs to distinguish them from other sources of evidence (Table 6.3).

(ii) Data Collection

Hammersley asserts that data collection is 'an account … [which] … represents accurately those features of the phenomena that it is intended to describe, explain

---

[135] Mark Saunders, Philip Lewis and Adrian Thornhill, *Research Methods for Business Students* (Financial Times Prentice Hill, 5th ed, 2009) 237.

[136] Russell K Schutt, *Investigating the Social World: The Process and Practice of Research* (SAGE Publications, 2006) 155.

[137] It has been generally conceded that any hold on the good faith doctrine in Australia is best seen as 'tentative' with the result that this aspect of the law is unresolved and still in a state of flux: cf. Bruno Zeller, 'Good Faith—Is It a Contractual Obligation?' (2003) 15 *Bond Law Review* 215; Carter and Peden, 'Good Faith in Australian Contract Law', above n 3; Elisabeth Peden, 'Good Faith in the Performance of Contract Law' (2004) *Law Society Journal* 64.

[138] Michael Crotty, *The Foundations of Social Research: Meaning and Perspective in The Research Process* (SAGE Publications, 1998) 3.

[139] Yin, *Case Study Research*, above n 131, 101.

Table 6.3 Research method

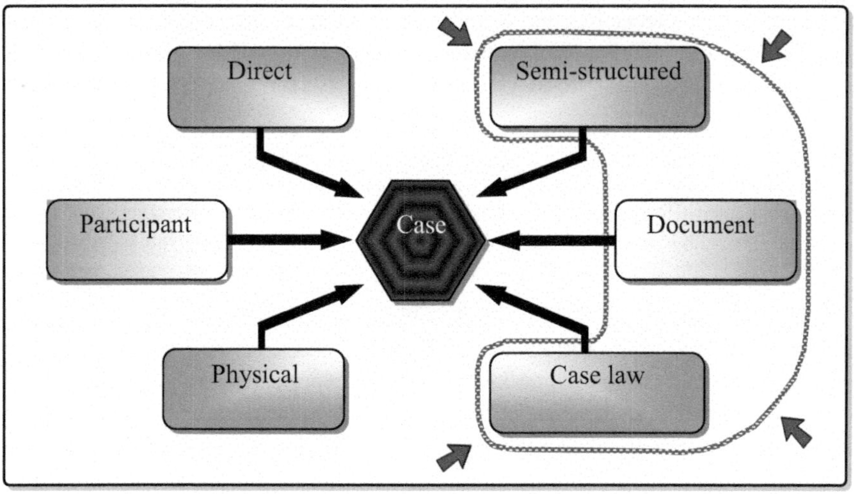

Adapted from Yin, Robert K., Case Study Research: Designs and Methods, 4th Edition, SAGE Publications, Thousand Oaks, 2009

or theorise.'[140] Therefore, assessment of data validity is concerned with two main issues: whether the instruments used for measurement are accurate and whether they are actually measuring what they want to measure.[141] Arksey, Knight, and Winter identified two different dimensions to the concept of validity, namely internal and external validity.[142]

Internal validity ensures that the research investigates what it claims to investigate, while external validity concerns the generalisability of findings to a wider population. Generalisation is defined as 'the assertions of enduring value that are context-free.'[143] This generalisation assesses the phenomenon based on the quality of the fieldwork, analysis, and interpretation, and how representative the sample is of the original population.[144] It is certainly possible to do this with a small-sized sample by studying

[140] Martyn Hammersley, 'Some Notes on the Terms "Validity" and "Reliability"' (1987) 13 (1) *British Educational Research Journal* (73–81) 79.

[141] Glyn Winter, 'A Comparative Discussion of the Notion of Validity in Qualitative and Quantitative Research' (2000) 4 (3) *The Qualitative Report*. http://www.nova.edu/ssss/QR/QR4-3/winter.html#hammersley; Jane Ritchie, Jane Lewis, Carol McNaughton Nicholls and Rachel Ormston, *Qualitative Research Practice: A Guide for Social Science Students and Researchers* (SAGE Publications, 2nd ed, 2014) 356.

[142] Hillary Arksey and Peter T Knight, *Interviewing for Social Scientists* (SAGE Publications, 1999) 49–56; Cf. Winter, 'A Comparative Discussion', above n 141.

[143] Yvonna S Lincoln and Egon G Guba, *Naturalistic Inquiry* (SAGE Publications, 1985) 110; Janet Ward Schofield, 'Increasing the Generalizability of Qualitative Research' in Martyn Hammersley (ed), *Social Research: Philosophy, Politics and Practices* (SAGE Publications, 2004) 206.

[144] Cf. Ritchie, Lewis, McNaughton Nicholls and Ormston, '*Qualitative Research Practice*', above n 141.

a typical case since it operates as a theory-guided study that seeks to explain or interpret a single historical episode, rather than generalise beyond the case itself.[145] Furthermore, employing multiple methods to investigate a single issue strengthens the research findings and enhances the validity of the data.[146]

In relation to the current research, the validity is gained with an analysis of the multiple sources of data available in the present study via semi-structured interviews, document analysis of PPPs and case law analysis. The basis of good faith derived from case law links and informs the design of the interview structure and also sets the perimeters of good faith obligation in the document analysis of the provisions in the PPPs.[147]

The reliability of data measures the extent to which research findings can be replicated using the same methods.[148] Marshall, Rossman, and Seale argue that absolute replication of qualitative studies is difficult, as they are a reflection of the time and situation realities of the specific study.[149] Rather to enhance reliability would involve reflexivity, which is 'showing the audience of research studies as much as possible of the procedures that have led to a particular set of conclusions.'[150]

Several measures have been taken to enhance the reliability of this research. All interviews were recorded using either a recording device or handwritten notes on-site, reducing bias that might occur if the researcher tried to remember the conversations later.[151] All questions were clearly worded and asked in a natural tone, with repetitions for clarity if misunderstandings arose. Interviewees were allowed to express their beliefs and thoughts freely without any intervention, avoiding bias in their responses.

---

145 Janet Ward Schofield, 'Increasing the Generalizability of Qualitative Research' in A Michael Huberman and Matthew B Miles, *The Qualitative Researcher's Companion* (2002) 171; Roger Gomm, Martyn Hammersley and Peter Foster, 'Case Study and Generalisation' in Roger Gomm, Martyn Hammersley and Peter Foster (eds), *Case Study Method: Key Issues, Key Texts* (SAGE Publications, 2000) 98; cf. John Gerring, 'Single-Outcome Studies: A Methodological Primer' (2006) 21 (5) *International Sociology*, 707–734; John Gerring, 'What is a Case Study and What Is It Good for?' (2004) 98 (2) *American Political Science Review*, 341–354.

146 Martyn Denscombe, *The Good Research Guide for Small-Scale Social Research Projects* (McGraw-Hill Education, 4th ed, 2010) 297–304.

147 Case law suggests that acting in good faith must always include the protection of the reasonable expectations of the contracting parties and that the parties will act honestly, reasonably and cooperatively (these will also form the basis for the key words analysis in the PPPs): Anthony Mason, 'Contract, Good Faith and Equitable Standards in Fair Dealing', (2000) 116 *Law Quarterly Review* 66, 72; *First Energy (UK) Ltd v Hungarian International Bank Ltd* [1993] 2 Lloyd's Rep 194; *HIH Casualty and General Insurance Ltd v Chase Manhattan Bank* [2003] 2 Lloyd's Rep 61, 68 [15]; *Yam Seng Pte Ltd v International Trade Corp Ltd* [2013] 1 All ER (Comm) 1321, 1351 [135] (per Leggatt J); *Bhasin v Hrynew* [2014] 3 SCR 494 at 514 [32], 518 [41].

148 Ritchie, Lewis, McNaughton Nicholls and Ormston, *Qualitative Research Practice*, above n 141, 355.

149 Cf. Catherine Marshall and Gretchen B Rossman, *Designing Qualitative Research* (SAGE Publications, 3rd ed, 1999); Clive Seale, *The Quality of Qualitative Research* (SAGE Publications, 1999); Gray, above n 132.

150 Seale, *The Quality of Qualitative Research*, above n 149, 158.

151 Gray, above n 132, 376–377.

(a) Semi-structured Interviews

Interviews are effective for gaining insights into how people experience, feel, and interpret the social world.[152] They are especially efficient when the research involves analysing people's understanding, motivations, and opinions, as in this study.[153]

The interview approach chosen was semi-structured for its flexibility.[154] In this type of interview, a set of questions were pre-established, which were aimed at obtaining more information about specific issues and, in the process, identify new issues that were not originally part of the interview. Semi-structured interviews allow for probing to be made of more detailed information by asking respondents for clarification, focusing on the meanings they ascribe to various events.[155] However, the interview's reliability can be influenced by the interviewee's awareness and emotional state, potentially distorting data if the interviewee is anxious or annoyed.[156] To avoid biased data, the interview was allowed to 'flow' freely.[157] A flexible and open-ended format is expected to elicit more genuine responses compared to a regulated, standard set of questions or surveys.[158] This does not mean the interviews lacked structure; a set of questions guided the discussion, ensuring that important topics were covered.[159]In spite of this, there was also flexibility to vary or ignore questions from the list based on the responses from the interviews and the flow of the conversation.[160]

In the interviews, a total of six people were involved who had either previously worked for or were currently advising the contracting parties directly in the formulation of the PPPs. Among these six personnel, one was a senior member of a contracting party's management group and two others held senior positions in contract management within the organisations of the contracting parties. The legal advisers and consultants were all at partner's level. The interviews took place in the offices of four of the personnel interviewed with the remainder over the telephone. All the interviews lasted at least 35 min. Three of the interviews were recorded with permission given by the participant and were subsequently transcribed into Microsoft Word. The tapes were subsequently replayed, and the transcripts amended, where necessary, in relation to inaccuracies with transcription and to clarify inaudible

---

[152] Natasha Mack et al., *Qualitative Research Methods: A Data Collector's Field Guide* (2005) 2–3. http://www.fhi360.org/sites/default/files/media/documents/Qualitative%20Research%20Methods%20-%20A%20Data%20Collector's%20Field%20Guide.pdf; Nigel King, 'Using interviews in qualitative research', in Catherine Cassell and Gillian Symon (eds), *Essential Guide to Qualitative Methods in Organizational Research* (SAGE Publications, 2004) 11.

[153] Daphne M Keats, *Interviewing: A Practical Guide for Students and Professionals* (UNSW Press, 2000) 72–73.

[154] Earl R Babbie, *The Basics of Social Research* (Cengage Learning, 6th ed, 2014) 324.

[155] Saunders, Lewis and Thornhill, *Research Methods for Business Students*, above n 135, 320.

[156] Michael Q Patton, *Qualitative Research and Evaluation Methods* (SAGE Publications, 3rd ed, 2002) 304.

[157] Tim May, *Social Research: Issues, Methods and Process* (Open University Press, 4th ed, 2011) 149.

[158] Uwe Flick, *An Introduction to Qualitative Research* (SAGE Publications, 4th ed, 2009) 150.

[159] Babbie, above n 154, 326.

[160] Saunders, Lewis and Thornhill, *Research Methods for Business Students*, above n 135, 320.

responses.[161] This process also allowed an additional opportunity to reflect on the content of each interview. Where interviewees chose not to have the interviews recorded, handwritten notes of the interviewees' responses were taken throughout the interview period. As soon as practical, after the interviews were concluded, reflective interview notes were made separately. The interviews were conducted from April 2014 to August 2014. All the interview participants requested anonymity (with the exception of identifying their reference group, either as legal practitioners, advisers, or consultants and contract personnel representing the contracting parties) and in this chapter the participants' responses are only referenced as P1 to P6.

The conduct of the interviews complied with Swinburne University of Technology's ethical guidelines. The research received ethical approval from Swinburne's Human Research Ethics Committee in line with the National Statement on Ethical Conduct in Human Research. This involved lodging an Application for Ethics Approval of a Research Protocol Form, along with a script of questions for the semi-structured interview with potential interviewees, the plain language Information Sheet to be presented to each interviewee prior to their interview, and the Interview Consent Form that each interviewee was required to sign before their interview. Interviewees were subsequently provided with a copy of the Interview Consent Form to retain for their records. Participants in the research were further informed that information provided was to be securely stored against access by persons other than the researcher for a period of five years.

In relation to the number of interviews required, Travers advises that researchers simply need 'enough data to explore and document a range of themes.'[162] It was considered that a representation from both the legal advisers and the contracting parties was sufficient for this research, with a range of perspectives taken from both an operational and a legal standpoint.

The themes for the interview were structured around the issues raised in the review of the case law relating to the development of good faith obligations that formed the basis of the research questions noted in chapter one. It was recognised that the schedule of interview questions may not necessarily be followed, in order to pursue fruitful lines of inquiry or elicit greater detail from interviewees.[163] The semi-structured interview, using the same questions and wording for each interviewee, is justified as it is an appropriate level of structure to ensure cross-interviews comparability.[164] Using semi-structured interviews allowed comparisons to be made between responses. The purpose of undertaking the interviews was to provide internal validation of the analysis completed on good faith obligations clauses in PPPs and the case law literature. Essentially, these interviews are intended to further explore the

---

[161] Cf. Lynne M MacLean, Mechthild Meyer and Alma Estable, 'Improving Accuracy of Transcripts in Qualitative Research' (2004) 14(1) *Qualitative Health Research*, 113–123.

[162] Max Travers, *Qualitative Research through Case Studies* (SAGE Publications, 2001) 37.

[163] King, 'Using interviews in qualitative research', above n 152.

[164] Cf. Alan Bryman and Emma Bell, *Business Research Methods* (Oxford University Press, 2nd ed, 2007).

determinants that affect the inclusion of good faith obligation clauses within the commercial setting of PPPs.

(b) Document Analysis of PPPs

A document is any substance that gives information about the investigated phenomenon and exists independently of the researcher's actions.[165] In the present study, the document analysis considered all the 15 PPPs made available through the Victorian Department of Treasury and Finance's website. Yin asserts that 'the most important use of documents is to corroborate and augment evidence.'[166] Corbetta identifies several advantages of document analysis: (a) it is a non-reactive technique, meaning the information is not subject to distortion, (b) it helps study the past, and (c) it is a cost-effective since the information has already been produced.[167] It is imperative that this analysis not only observe the subject through aspects of its social and contextual setting but may also reveal patterns that could be used to explain wider principles.[168] In addition, it is seen that there is no one reality, rather reality is based on the overall perceptions and experiences.[169] In this respect, the real-world contracting setting of the use of good faith provisions can be understood by studying the context in which they occur. The content analysis is aimed at the systematic organising and recording of the occurrence of good faith obligations data from the PPPs' contractual clauses using the keywords criteria established from the case law.[170] This allows valid inferences to be made of their use.[171]

(ii) Findings and Discussions

All the legal practitioners interviewed said that there is no 'one size fits all' approach when looking at good faith obligations in contracts. There is also consensus from the legal practitioners' interviews that the choice of whether to include good faith obligations as a contracting provision is informed by client input as well as commercial expedience. The ambiguous nature of good faith obligation makes such an approach pragmatic and would allow the contracting party to limit its effect. For the purpose of obtaining a framework to examine good faith obligation in action, Horrigan's transactional analysis was adopted in this analysis to observe the occurrence of good faith provisions in PPPs in the document analysis, as well as to provide a basis for

[165] It is normally produced for specific purposes other than those of the research but it can be used by the researcher for cognitive purposes; cf. Piergiorgio Corbetta, *Social Research: Theory, Methods and Techniques* (SAGE Publications, 2003) 287–309.

[166] Yin, *Case Study Research*, above n 131, 103.

[167] Corbetta, *Social Research*, above n 165, 287–288.

[168] Cf. Babbie, above n 154, 334–335.

[169] Cf. Robson, *Real World Research*, above n 130.

[170] Cf. Kimberley A Neuendorf, *The Content Analysis Guidebook* (SAGE Publications, 2002).

[171] Klaus Krippendorff, *Content Analysis: An Introduction to Its Methodology* (SAGE Publications, 2004) 18; cf. Daniel Riffe, Stephen Lacy and Frederick G Fico, *Analyzing Media Messages: Using Quantitative Content Analysis in Research* (1998) 24.

the interview structure.[172] As mentioned previously, the proceeding analysis uses the following headings from Horrigan to summarise the findings: (1) remaining silent on good faith in the contract; (2) expressly imposing a general and undefined obligation of good faith on all contracting parties; (3) expressly defining or confining obligations of good faith to particular contractual rights or provisions in the contract on some or all contracting parties; and (4) expressly excluding implications of good faith.[173]

Before reporting on the findings, it is relevant to indicate why Horrigan's first element regarding jurisdiction is not used in this analysis. It is, hereby, acknowledged that courts in different Australian jurisdictions have differing views on how good faith obligation is treated.[174] The contrasting judicial consideration is due to the different states jurisdictions' approach regarding good faith application, which has led to divergent views.[175] Such perception obviously has their legal limits as there is only one common law in Australia rather than a common law for each Australian state's jurisdiction.[176] In this regard, all the legal practitioners interviewed said that, in general, they do not approach the inclusion of good faith obligation in a contract differently from jurisdiction to jurisdiction, although it is relevant to have at the back of one's mind the understanding that some courts might be more willing to imply good faith obligations or to use such considerations in conditioning the exercise of contractual rights and discretions. Furthermore, the National PPP Policy and Guidelines (National Guidelines), which set out the processes that should be followed in the investment, procurement and delivery stages of PPPs that engender appropriate risk allocation and commercial principles, prescribe and expect all contracting parties to contract in good faith.[177] The National Guidelines do not mandate specific contracting provisions but provide standard guidelines regarding contracting terms for PPPs. The respective state and territorial governments are free to determine their

---

[172] Although Horrigan uses five basic approaches to consider his transactional analysis on good faith obligation, we have omitted from our analysis the choice of domestic legal jurisdiction (within Australia) as the National PPP Policy and Guidelines expects all contracting parties to contract in good faith, which acknowledges good faith's contracting role in PPP: Horrigan, 'New Directions', above n 95.

[173] Horrigan, 'New Directions', above n 95, 200.

[174] Allsop, above n 82, 354: choice of law issue also arises within Australia where perceived approach of courts in particular jurisdictions can influence how a particular contractual issue is tolerated; this has been acknowledged in chapter three.

[175] Justice Margaret Beazley, 'Terms: Good Faith in Contract' in *Australian Contract Law Commentary* (2013) [28–640]; cf. *Farah Construction Pty Ltd v Say-Dee Pty Ltd* [2007] 230 CLR 89 [151–152]; see also chapter three.

[176] Cf. Elisabeth Peden, *Good Faith in the Performance of Contracts* (LexisNexis Butterworths, 2003) 226; Andrew Stewart and John W Carter, 'The High Court and Contract Law in the New Millennium' (2003) 6 *Flinders Journal of Law Reform* 18; Bill Dixon, 'Can the Common Law Obligation of Good Faith be Contractually Excluded?' (2007) 35 *Australian Business Law Review* 110, 121; Warren, 'Good Faith: Where Are We At?', above n 82, 348; *Burger King Corporation v Hungry Jack's Pty Ltd* [2001] NSWCA 187, [159]; *Farah Construction Pty Ltd v Say-Dee Pty Ltd* [2007] 230 CLR 89.

[177] The National PPP Policy and Guidelines, Overview, Infrastructure Australia, 2008, 18; The National PPP Policy and Guidelines apply to all Australian state and territory government

own standard forms as long as they do not contradict the National Guidelines. It is for these reasons that state jurisdiction is not considered significant in the context of the enquiry here. In addition, since all PPPs in Australia conform to the National Guidelines, it is also unnecessary to justify why only Victorian PPPs were considered in this analysis.

Extracts from the participants' interview information are labelled P1 to P6 and denoted with this blue icon, P1 to P3 are legal practitioners and/or contract consultants, and P4 to P6 are contract personnel who represent the contracting parties.

(a) Remaining Silent on Good Faith Obligation

Partnership Victoria prescribes the following requirements in their PPPs: 'Government, as a contracting party, will be subject to any implied good faith obligations.'[178] It is, therefore, not surprising that all the Victorian PPPs investigated have remained silent on the express applicability of good faith obligation in the contract.

The main problem with this approach is that it leaves everything to the courts at a time when the contracting parties' relationships have broken down. There is already much uncertainty as to how an Australian court will apply the 'implied terms' approaches (that may be dependent on the court's jurisdiction). The implication of good faith obligation may only be advantageous from a contractual perspective to curtail opportunistic conduct as seen in these comments:

> Good faith sets a standard of dealing for the parties, like acting honestly, and relevant for it to be part of the contract (P5).

> It keeps the parties honest and prescribes a standard of dealing for the contract (P6).

(b) Imposing an Undefined Obligation of Good Faith

There was no definition of good faith in any of the PPPs even though good faith has been specified in particular contractual provisions such as financing options, access to work sites, termination and dispute resolutions. The interviews with the legal practitioners indicated that the preference is to have an expressed meaning for good faith in the contract as that would confine the interpretation of the obligation to the context of the contract although this is not the practice.

> Personally, I think it is important to express what good faith actually means for the contract in the light of the uncertainty regarding its actual scope but it is rarely seen apart from the standard contracts found in alliancing arrangements. It is expected that [good faith in]

---

agencies. It effectively replaces previously existing policy and guidelines in those jurisdictions affecting PPPs:http://infrastructureaustralia.gov.au/policy-publications/public-private-partnerships/national-ppp-policy-guidelines.aspx.

178 Partnership Victoria, *Annexure 1A—Commercial Principles for Social Infrastructure* (2009).http://www.dtf.vic.gov.au/files/b6329ae3-835d-4e13-bb60-a1dc00d32493/Victorian-Jurisdicational-Requirement-Annexure-1A.doc.

> PPPs take the same definition which is the duty to act cooperatively, reasonably, or honestly. (P1)

> [Good faith definition] is not commonly found in PPPs although having a definition of good faith in the contract could arguably confine the content of the obligation specifically with what the parties intended rather than leaving it to the court since the law on the application of good faith is still in a state of flux. (P3)

On the other hand, by not having a definition in the contract, it also allows the focus of interpreting the scope of good faith to be determined by the specific contractual context of the provision.

> What the duty incorporates is not unknown as such there is no practical need to have a separate definition. It may cloud the interpretation of the contract if a definition provided varies from established case law. (P2)

This is consistent with the NSW Court of Appeal decision in *Macquarie International Health Clinic Pty Ltd v Sydney South West Area Health Service.*[179] The NSW Court of Appeal held that good faith obligation that is confined to the specific contractual provision must be interpreted within the specific context of the provision and the overall intent of the contract as a whole, where possible.[180] In this regard, it would seem to suggest that it is possible to alternate between interpreting the contractual provision by confining good faith to particular contractual activities and leaving it at large to influence the construction of the whole contract.[181] This does not contribute to consistency of interpretation and may even increase uncertainty about how good faith obligation should apply. The number of separate contractual provisions in which good faith obligations are specified is illustrated in Table 6.4.

(c) Defining and Confining Good Faith's Contractual Operation

The specific clauses containing good faith obligation place these obligations upon specific contracting parties or accept them as mutual obligations. These good faith provisions generally capture the trilogy of honesty, cooperation, and reasonableness as the basis for good faith, which is in line with the judicial meaning given to good faith in Australia.[182] This is apart from other specific provisions in the contracts that individually require cooperation, reasonableness and honesty without a general good

---

[179] *Macquarie International Health Clinic Pty Ltd v Sydney South West Area Health Service* [2010] NSWCA 268.

[180] Ibid [144] and [155] per Hodgson JA (MacFarlan JA concurring).

[181] The High Court states that express good faith clause can successfully operate by requiring the contracting parties 'to act in good faith in all matters relating to the carrying out the works, derivation of rates and interpretation of this document': *Placer (Granny Smith) Pty Ltd v Thiess Contractors Pty Ltd* [2003] HCA 10.

[182] See *Renard Construction (ME) Pty Ltd v Minister of Public Works* (1992) 26 NSWLR 234, 268; *Alcatel Australia Ltd v Scarcella* (1998) 44 NSWLR 349, 367; *Overlook v Foxtel* (2002) Aust Contracts Rep 90–143, [83]. In *Central Exchange Ltd v Anaconda Nickel Ltd* (2001) 24 WAR 382; Paterson, 'Limits on a Lender's Right', above n 10; Paterson, 'The Standard of Good Faith', above n 87, 153; Nicholas C Seddon, Rick A Bigwood and Manfred P Ellinghaus, *Cheshire and Fifoot: Law of Contract* (LexisNexis Butterworth, 10th Australian ed, 2012) 465; Peden, *Good Faith in*

Table 6.4 Good faith provisions in PPPs

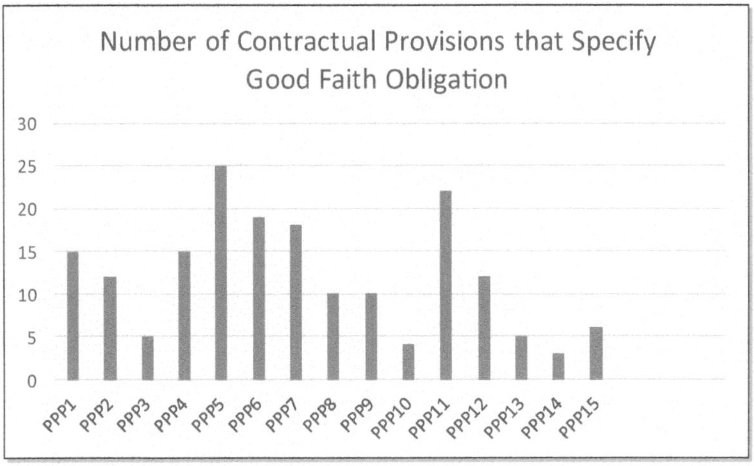

PPP1 Southern Cross Station (Nov, 2002)
PPP2 Berwick Community Hospital (Nov, 2002)
PPP3 Victoria Correctional Facilities (Nov, 2003)
PPP4 Royal Women's Hospital (Apr, 2005)
PPP5 Royal Melbourne Showground (June, 2005)
PPP6 Melbourne Convention Centre (May 2006)
PPP7 Barwon Water (Aug, 2007)
PPP8 Royal Children's Hospital (Nov, 2007)
PPP9 Schools Project (Dec, 2008)
PPP10 Bio Sciences Research (Apr, 2009)
PPP11 Victoria Desalination (July, 2009)
PPP12 Peninsula Link (Jan, 2010)
PPP13 Ararat Prison (May, 2010)
PPP14 Victoria Comprehensive Cancer Centre (Dec, 2011)
PPP15 Ravenhall Prison (Sept, 2014)

faith obligation. Interestingly, provisions requiring duties of cooperation, reasonableness and honesty together are not represented in the PPPs suggesting that good faith obligation already covered these expectations collectively.

These duties are part of good faith but the approach to good faith in PPPs is generally that it is not an overarching obligation but confined to specific provisions. (P3)

Good faith has always been understood to carry these duties [of cooperation, reasonableness and honesty]. (P4)

Good faith is associated with these duties [cooperation, reasonableness and honesty] although it is also common practice for these duties to be imposed individually in other clauses as well. (P2)

---

the Performance of Contracts, above n 176, 170; David McLauchlan, 'The Agreement to Negotiate in Good Faith: A Non-Justiciable Contract?' (2005) 11 *New Zealand Business Law Quarterly* 454; Peden, 'The Meaning of Contractual "Good Faith"', above n 88; Allsop, above n 82.

There is an average of two provisions in the PPPs that incorporate 'honesty' or 'cooperation' separately; although the use of 'reasonableness' alone is much more widespread in the contract. There is nothing surprising about that as contracting parties are expected to behave reasonably, which is the objective standard prescribed under contract law.

One observation where good faith obligation is included as a basis of cooperation, reasonableness and honesty is that it is non-exhaustive.[183] This allows room for the court to include other aspects of good faith, such as fairness, within the context of its use in the contractual provision.

> Good faith is relevant in PPPs as the nature and length of the contract provides an expectation that contracting parties behave or act cooperatively, honestly and fairly to one another. (P5)

Confining good faith's obligation specifically within the context of particular contractual provision allows the contracting parties to exercise more control over good faith's application.

> This is a better approach to handle good faith due to the current state of the law. (P1)

> I think good faith in the current state of the law should always be provided specifically to specific clauses as it provides the parties with greater control over what it affects. (P3)

This explains why good faith obligations are particularly prominent in contractual provisions that relate to negotiations, dispute resolution, and termination.

> The operation of good faith, for example, in situation where the contracting parties accept a mutual obligation of good faith which is confined to resolving dispute in a specific situation; the way in which good faith functions in this situation would not necessarily apply to other good faith obligations in the contract generally. The context determines how the obligation applies. If good faith does not appear in a provision, then it doesn't apply. It allows the parties to set the required expectations. (P2)

> Personally, it is a good approach as it allows for the selection of the sorts of provisions that good faith applies. It gives the parties control over the standards applicable in future performance for those provisions. (P3)

> By having good faith apply in specific contract provisions allow the parties to approach the contract positively on a 'best for contract' basis. (P5)

This approach suggests that it is feasible to isolate good faith obligation by using it specifically in one part of the contract and not allowing it in other parts of the contract that made no express mention of it.

---

[183] Cf. *Multiplex Constructions Pty Ltd v Abigroup Contractors Pty Ltd* [2005] QCA 61.

(d) Excluding the Implied Good Faith Obligation

Partnership Victoria includes the following requirement for all the project agreements (including PPPs) that it signs:

> Government, as a contracting party, will be subject to any implied good faith obligations that arise ... in commercial contracts. [P]roject agreement will specifically *disclaim* (emphasis added) that there is implied, whether from the concept of 'partnership', the PPP guidance materials or otherwise, any other general duties of good faith on the part of government towards the project or the project parties, unless expressly assumed by government under the project agreement.[184]

From the policy statements above, Partnership Victoria acknowledges that the implied obligation of good faith applies to its project agreements generally but, at the same time, confining it only to those provisions that have been expressly given to such obligation. Essentially this is a contradiction—it is either applicable generally or it is not. Of the PPPs surveyed, only 9 out of the 15 had a specific provision excluding the applicability of the implied term of good faith generally. This is consistent in the PPPs signed from 2007 onwards, with the exception of the Peninsula Link contract in 2014, and generally aligns with the policy statement of Partnership Victoria.

There is ample judicial and academic commentary to support that the implied term of good faith can be excluded or negated by appropriately drafted agreements.[185] Commercial contracting parties have considerable room to undertake modification or exclude any of the good faith obligation's perceived excesses as long as their inclusion does not make the contract uncertain or void for illegality or contrary to public policy.[186]

> All implied terms can be excluded and that's no different for good faith and it would not have any bearing on the enforcement of specific obligation of honesty, cooperation and reasonableness. (P3)

> Any general exclusion of good faith would not have a bearing on specific provisions in which good faith specifically applies. (P1)

O'Byrne summed this up as follows: '[P]roviding then that the 'opting out' clause in question is precise, specific, not antithetical to the entire purpose or intent of the

---

[184] Partnership Victoria.

[185] Refer to *Byrne v Australian Airlines Ltd* [1995] HCA 24; *GEC Marconi Systems Pty Ltd v BHP Information Technology Pty Ltd* [2003] FCA 50; *Vodafone Pacific Ltd v Mobile Innovations Ltd* [2004] NSWCA 15; Dixon, 'Can the Common Law Obligation of Good Faith', above n 175, 119–120; Nicholas C Seddon and Manfred P Ellinghaus, *Cheshire and Fifoot's Law of Contract* (9th Australian ed, 2008) [10.49]; de Jersey, 'Good Faith in Contracts in Financial Services', above n 211; Andrew Terry and Cary Di Lernia, 'Franchising and the Quest for the Holy Grain: Good Faith or Good Intentions?' (2009) 33 *Melbourne University Law Review* 542.

[186] Drafting limitations in the context of good faith are discussed in: Grover, 'Good Faith in Commercial Transactions', 106–107; Shannon K O'Byrne, 'Good Faith in Contractual Performance: Recent Developments' (1995) 74 *Canadian Bar Review* 70, 96; Paterson, 'Limits on a Lender's Right', above n 10, 280; Dixon, 'Can the Common Law Obligation of Good Faith', above n 175, 121.

remainder of the contract, and is not unconscionable or contrary to public policy, it ought to be enforceable.'[187]

Whether good faith obligation can be effectively excluded is still uncertain as resolution of its precise content and pervasiveness is still a moot point. Justice Douglas lends to this debate by tying together the criticism of the Carter-Peden view of implicit good faith[188] with its implications for the excludability of good faith:

> There is also an argument that 'good faith' is inherent in all common law contractual principles and that an attempt to imply an independent term requiring good faith is unnecessary. The authors who propound that theory argue that good faith is inherent in all aspects of contract law because good faith is the essence of contract. ... It is an interesting argument but not one that convinces me, partly because of the debate as to whether the law requires both honesty and reasonableness in performing obligations under a contract or merely honesty. If those authors are correct, however, then the argument against the ability to exclude such an obligation of good faith would be stronger.
>
> If, however, the obligation is one found to arise only in particular contracts or by implication from particular facts then there should be no reason in theory why such an implied implication might not be excluded just as fiduciary obligations that might otherwise arise may be excluded by agreement.[189]

There is high level judicial support for this view.[190] In the *Vodafone*'s case, there is authoritative confirmation that a 'negation of implied terms' clause can be used to exclude implied terms such as good faith, even where they are implied by law.[191] Justice Finkelstein's view that 'the duty of good faith is an incident (not an ad hoc implied term) of every commercial contract, *unless the duty is either excluded expressly or by necessary implication*'[192](emphasis added). Likewise, Justice Finn also viewed that, while the treatment of good faith in other jurisdictions might render it non-excludable simply by private agreement, 'as a matter of legal doctrine in this country it must be accepted that, *as an implied term, it is capable of being excluded by express or by inconsistent provision*'[193] (emphasis added).

---

[187] O'Byrne, 'Good Faith in Contractual Performance', above n 186, 96.

[188] See Carter and Peden, 'Good Faith in Australian Contract', above n 3.

[189] The Hon Justice James Douglas, 'Exploring the Recent Uncertainty Surrounding the Implied Duty of Good Faith in Australian Contract Law: The Duty to Act Reasonably—Its Existence, Ambit and Operation' (Paper present at the LexisNexis Contract Law Master Class, Sydney, 24 August 2006). http://www.CISG.law.pace.edu/CISG/biblio/douglas1.html.

[190] E.g. Sir Anthony Mason noted the fact that the judiciary has not embraced the Carter-Peden view of implicit good faith leaning instead towards the notion that good faith obligation carried the notion of reasonableness in commercial construction: Sir Anthony Mason, 'Opening Address for the 20th Anniversary of the Journal of Contract Law Conference' (2009) 25 *Journal of Contract Law* 1, 4–5.

[191] *Vodafone Pacific Ltd v Mobile Innovations Ltd* [2004] NSWCA 15, [184]-[185], [188], [198]-[200] per Giles JA (with Sheller JA and Ipp JA concurring).

[192] *Pacific Brands Sport & Leisure Pty Ltd v Underworks Pty Ltd* [2005] FCA 288, [64]; this was followed by Greenwood J in *Luce Optical v Budget Specs (Franchising) Pty Ltd* [2005] FCA 1486, [59].

[193] *GEC Marconi Systems Pty Ltd v BHP Information Technology Pty Ltd* [2003] FCA 50, [920].

6.4 Chapter Summary

This chapter has sought to identify whether good faith obligation may be justified and validated as a contracting device in commercial contract and how this might impact the good faith debate within Australia. Viewed under an economic lens, good faith obligations in contracts can prevent opportunistic behaviour which arises out of the inherent incompleteness of contracts and sequential performance.

Behavioural economics should be consulted when evaluating the suitability of a good faith doctrine to discourage opportunistic conduct. A good faith obligation should encourage cooperative conduct and reduce opportunism.

A good faith obligation is often perceived as a substitute for contractual specification, which in turn reduces transactional costs. However—as good faith lacks a clear definition—the introduction of a good faith obligation demands a trade-off on the savings made on specification costs and the cost of increased uncertainty in how the courts will interpret the good faith obligation. The economic model outlined in this chapter allows for predictions to be made as to when the obligation would be efficient, namely, in simple, low-value contracts. For idiosyncratic contracts, it may not be desirable to rely on a good faith obligation. As such, instead of a general application, it is arguable that good faith obligations should selectively apply to contracts where it would improve cost efficiency.

Stewart argues that contract law should evolve to mirror practical commercial practices, not just classical theories. This leads to Part III of this chapter, which analyses whether good faith clauses in contracts remain useful in practice. Legal scholarship benefits from such observations to better understand societal and economic functions, which consequently assists in refining legal tools to maintain alignment with commercial reality. This is consistent with Seddon's concept of measured mutation, which represents a broader movement towards substituting standards for the existing body of strict rules. Thus, the law will be predictable for business practitioners, resulting in better rates of compliance with the obligation as they will understand what is required of them. Eisenberg also shares the view that legal reasoning should be both logical and connected to real-life social contexts. Essentially, while commercial contract law aims to serve individual goals, these should be interpreted within the broader context of the commercial environment and the reasonable expectations arising out of it.

As can be seen, contract practitioners, faced with the unsatisfactory state of the law on good faith obligation in commercial contracting practice, have no alternative but to employ drafting strategies to handle the effects of good faith provisions. As far as drafting practices go, there is no 'one size fits all' solution on good faith obligation for commercial contracting parties as they are ultimately informed by their contractual context.[194] As such, the way in which good faith obligation applies in a contract is very much dictated by both the specific construction of the obligation

[194] Cf. Hill, above n 80; Horrigan, 'Good Faith from a Drafting and Pleadings Point of View', above n 80; Horrigan, 'New Frontlines', above n 80.

as well as the overall contractual provisions.[195] This essentially allows commercial parties to optimise their control of how good faith obligation relates to them rather than leaving it at the mercy of how courts interpret and apply the good faith obligation to their contracts.[196] Good faith obligation is clearly not redundant in practice as the evidence from the interviews among legal practitioners and contracting parties reveals the contrary, and the reason contracting manoeuvring is due to the consequence of having an unsettled definition of good faith.

Based on the discussion in this chapter, good faith obligation has both relevance and utility. The perception from the interviews is that good faith has the effect of curbing opportunistic conduct (whether real or imagined) and provides a flexible basis for future negotiations when contracting circumstances change.

This chapter concludes with two outcomes that add to the literature on good faith applications' perspectives. The first is that a settled definition of good faith is urgently required and cannot be put off any further and second, the economic benefits of having an overriding common law duty of good faith do not outweigh the benefits of imposing good faith obligation in those contractual relationships in which the dictates of efficiency require such obligations. Good faith obligation should not be applied to contractual scenarios where it is not justified in economic terms. The more popular piecemeal approach of applying good faith by the Australian judiciary is conceivably a better means of achieving economic efficiency rather than having an overriding obligation of contractual good faith.

[195] See *Vodafone Pacific Ltd v Mobile Innovations Ltd* [2004] NSWCA 15; *Macquarie International Health Clinic Pty Ltd v Sydney South West Area Health Service* [2010] NSWCA 268; *Alstom Ltd v Yokogawa Australia Pty Ltd (No 7)* [2012] SASC 49; *Cordon Investments Pty Ltd v Lesdor Properties Pty Ltd* [2012] NSWCA 184; Warren, 'Good Faith: Where Are We At?', above n 82; Justice Allsop, above n 82; de Jersey, 'Good Faith in Contracts in Financial Services', above n 82.

[196] This was crystallised by Warren CJ in relation to good faith obligation: '[G]ood faith as a doctrine does not exist independently of the rules surrounding the construction and interpretation of contracts, or the rules of implication [and there] may be a merging of the two processes (interpretation and implication) in the arena of good faith': Warren, 'Good Faith: Where Are We At?', above n 82, 349; *North East Solution Pty Ltd v Masters Home Improvement Australia Pty Ltd* [2016] VSC 1.

Chapter 7
Conclusion

7.1 Introduction

Good faith obligation as a commercial term has been linked to contract law since the times of the ancient Rome. Its roots in classical contract law have allowed the concept of good faith obligation to evolve through various legal frameworks, notably in canon law and civil law and, to a limited extent, in common law jurisdiction such as in the US. The majority of the developed legal systems around the world have, in one form or another, acknowledged a general principle of good faith in their respective contract law. However, this is not the case for Australia and most of the Anglo-Antipodean common law nations who have not yet acknowledged a comprehensive obligation of good faith in contracts. Despite this, the push for contract law harmonisation, driven by the impacts and influences of and the internationalisation of commercial transactions, undeniably necessitates a re-evaluation of this stance. As such, an appraisal of whether the obligation of good faith remains viable and relevant in Australian contractual relationships is a very significant issue.

Despite the growing awareness among legal commentators on the relevance of the good faith principle in modern commercial contracts, opponents of good faith continue to be preoccupied with the arguments concerning the element of certainty in commercial transactions,[1] while proponents of good faith also go too far with their

[1] E.g. in *Esso Australia Resources Pty Ltd v Southern Pacific Petroleum NL*, both Warren CJ and Osborn AJA described good faith obligation as a 'nebulous' standard that threatened commercial certainty ([2005] VSCA 228, [3]); *Walford v Miles* [1992] 2 WLR 174; Justice Rogers in *GSA Group Ltd v Siebe plc* (1993) 30 NSWLR 573, 579: 'courts should not be too eager to interfere in the commercial conduct of parties ... where ... the parties are wealthy, experienced, commercial entities able to attend to their own interests.'; Michael Bridge, 'Does Anglo-Canadian Law Need a Doctrine of Good Faith?' (1984) 9 *Canadian Business Law Journal* 385, 412; Gunther Teubner, 'Legal Irritants: Good Faith in British Law or How Unifying Law Ends Up in New Divergences' (1998) 61 *Modern Law Review* 11; James Davies, 'Why a Common Law Duty of Contractual Good Faith is Not Required' (2002) 8 *Canterbury Law Review* 529; Lord Justice Staughton, 'Good Faith and Fairness in Commercial Contract Law' (1994) 7 *Journal of Contract Law* 193, 194: 'businessmen

A. Wan and P. Guo, *Good Faith Obligation*, International and Comparative Law in the Asia Pacific, https://doi.org/10.1007/978-981-97-7035-9_7

implications and requirements upon contracting parties.[2] It is, perhaps, not surprising to find that 'the debate on the value of a principle of good faith in contracting has not been won by either side.'[3] This is one of the main contributory reasons for the current state of flux in the debate over the application of the principle of good faith in commercial contracts in Australia.

7.2 Review of the Research Paradigm

Despite the volume of case law in Australia on good faith obligation, it continues to be hailed as being one of the most important contractual issues in contract law.[4] The issue here is primarily concerned with consistency in application and whether good faith is even needed or relevant in the light of established doctrines under existing classical contract theory (such as fraud, misrepresentation, undue influence, or unconscionability), which already perform similar, but not identical, functions as the obligation of good faith.[5]

---

prefer certainty to justice, and like to know where they stand'; Maree Chetwin, 'Relational Contract Theory and the Good Faith Debate' (2003) 9 *New Zealand Business Law Quarterly* 211; Rick A Bigwood, 'Symposium Introduction: Confessions of a "Good Faith" Agnostic' (2005) 11 *New Zealand Business Law Quarterly* 371.

[2] See Roger Brownsword, 'Two Concepts of Good Faith' (1994) 7 *Journal of Contract Law* 197.

[3] Joseph M Thomson, 'Good Faith in Contracting: A Sceptical View' in Angelo D M Forte (ed), *Good Faith in Contract and Property Law* (Hart Publishing, 1999) 75.

[4] John W Carter and Andrew Stewart, 'Interpretation, Good Faith and the "True Meaning" of Contracts: The Royal Botanic Decision' (2002) 18 *Journal of Contract Law* 182, 190; Sir Thomas Bingham in the foreword to Reziya Harrison, *Good Faith in Sales* (Sweet & Maxwell, 1997) vi; Bill Dixon, 'Common Law Obligation of Good Faith in the Performance and Enforcement of Joint Ventures of a Non-Fiduciary Nature' in William D Duncan (ed), *Joint Ventures Law in Australia* (The Federation Press, 3rd ed, 2012) 108; Andrew Stewart, 'What's Wrong with the Australian Law of Contract?' (2012) 29 *Journal of Contract Law* 74, 85; *Commonwealth Bank of Australia v Barker* [2014] HCA 32, [107] (per Kiefel J); John W Carter et al., 'Terms Implied in Law: "Trust and Confidence" in the High Court of Australia' (2015) 32 *Journal of Contract Law* 203.

[5] Bridge, 'Does Anglo-Canadian Law Need', above n 1, 409; Johan Steyn, 'Contract Law: Fulfilling the Reasonable Expectations of Honest Me' (1997) 113 *Law Quarterly Review* 433, 441; Stephen M Waddams, 'Codification, Law Reform and Judicial Developments' (1996) 9 *Journal Contract Law* 192, 194; Stephen M Waddams, 'Good Faith, Unconscionability and Reasonable Expectations' (1995) 9 *Journal Contract Law* 55; Johan Steyn, 'The Role of Good Faith and Fair Dealing in Contract Law: A Hair-Shirt Philosophy?' [1991] *Denning Law Journal* 131, 133; Paul Finn, 'Commerce, The Common Law and Morality' (1989) 17 *Melbourne University Law Review* 87, 92–98; L J Priestley, 'Contract—The Burgeoning Maelstrom' (1988) 1 *Current Law Journal* 15; John R Peden, *The Law of Unjust Contracts* (Butterworths, 1982) 28; Harvey McGregor, *A Contract Code: Drawn Up on Behalf of the English Law Commission* (Sweet & Maxwell, 1994) 40: comments in relation to the Contract Code that good faith is 'implicit in the Moorcock rule'; Brownsword, 'Two Concepts of Good Faith', above n 2, 198; Michael Bridge, 'Good Faith in Commercial Contracts' in Roger Brownsword, Norma J Hird and Geraint Howells (eds), *Good Faith in Contract: Concept and Context* (Dartmouth Publishing Co,1999) 139; John W Carter and Elisabeth Peden, 'Good Faith in Australian Contract Law' (2003) 19 *Journal of Contract Law* 155.

This research exercise is approached as a diagnosis on whether good faith obligation should continue to command consideration in an adversarial contracting environment, like Australia, through an examination grounded in theory and commercial practice. Without this, it may not be possible to have a clear vision of the role of good faith in contract law.

In order to deal with this, the following research question was proposed:

Does an obligation of good faith (be it an overriding obligation or as an implied term or as a tool of construction) continue to be relevant and viable in arm's length commercial contract based on the reasonable expectations of the contracting parties?

This chapter concludes by summarising the outcomes considered for the research question, which were formulated in three parts as 'why,' 'what,' and 'how' questions. As a reminder, the three parts are as follows:

> Part 1: Why does good faith matter? Is the historical concept of good faith relevant to commerce? Can the obligation of good faith, as it is approached internationally, benefit Australian contract law?
>
> Part 2: What judicial approaches have been considered in applying good faith obligation? Is there a way forward in achieving judicial common ground?
>
> Part 3: How should good faith obligation be considered economically? Does it have a place in commercial contracting practice?

7.2.1 Part One

This is dealt with in Chaps. 2 and 3 and addressed the relevance of good faith by considering two main approaches. These were, first, how the historical concept of good faith relates to commercial contracts and second, the operation of good faith in other global jurisdictions as a comparative analysis and the effect of international treaties on good faith obligation in Australia. The comparative analysis takes its cue from Priestley JA's judgement in the *Renard Constructions*' case when he referred to US case law and foreign good faith obligations to favourably explain the role of good faith in Australia.[6]

The historical context of good faith obligation is well-established in ancient Roman law where the concept allowed Roman jurists to be kept abreast of contemporary developments of Roman commercial life at the time. The Roman experience with the doctrine of bona fides in commercial contracts provides a useful step in the process of discovering the relationship between good faith and commercial contracts. This discussion on good faith's historical background is intended to connect its roots with commercial contract and provide a fundamental basis in which to consider the relevance of good faith in current Australian commercial contracts. There is an important lesson to be learned from the Roman experience with the good faith principle, which is that static legal rules cannot answer all the issues that arise in commercial contracts. There must be a degree of flexibility in the law relating to commerce, which the obligation of good faith provides.

[6] *Renard Constructions (ME) Pty Ltd v Minister of Public Works* (1992) 26 NSWLR 234, 263.

For the second approach, the comparative discussion on the operation of good faith in other jurisdictions is not intended to be comprehensive but is limited to examining whether it would be appropriate for Australia to follow any of the approaches taken by the other foreign jurisdictions or develop its own theory within an Australian legal structure. It is concluded that the theories of good faith advanced in other jurisdictions are either foreign and not compatible to Australian law, or have too widely defined the scope of good faith for it to be effectively practical in an Australian business environment. For instance, the European good faith approaches have been developed for a codified system, which is fundamentally different from the Australian common law system. Their notion of good faith complements the provision of their Codes and cannot be realistically replicated in Australia. The French experience also indicates that the notion of good faith does not succeed where it has been defined too widely. In the US where good faith is accepted as an overarching principle in contract, there were great controversies surrounding its meaning, which has resulted in the failure to implement commercial norms for good faith application. The entangled theoretical legal debate in the American experience has yielded inconsistent and divisive outcomes.

The examination of good faith in Chinese contract law reveals a stark contrast to the Australian approach, offering valuable insights into alternative judicial strategies. Unlike Australia's struggle with the reception and content of good faith, China has embraced the principle as a cornerstone of its civil and contract law. This fundamental difference provides a compelling counterpoint to the Australian experience.

China's integration of good faith into its legal framework is both comprehensive and explicit. The *Civil Code* and judicial interpretations elevate good faith to a foundational status, applicable across all civil activities. This has resulted in a consistent application of good faith throughout the contractual lifecycle, from formation to post-contractual obligations.

However, the Chinese experience also highlights challenges that could inform Australian considerations. The broad and sometimes vague nature of good faith in Chinese law has led to some inconsistent judicial interpretations, echoing Australian concerns about the obligation's definition and scope. This highlights the importance of clear judicial guidance and standardisation in applying good faith obligations.

The Chinese courts' application of good faith in various contractual disputes provides valuable case studies that could shed light upon Australian jurisprudence. Cases such as *Beijing Longchang Weiye Trade Co Ltd v Beijing Urban Construction Heavy Industry Co Ltd*[7] illustrate how good faith can uphold contract voluntariness and honesty, addressing concerns about the obligation's practical implementation. Nevertheless, cultural and contextual factors influencing the interpretation of good faith in China highlight the need for careful consideration when drawing comparisons. The Australian legal system must develop its own understanding and application of good faith that aligns with its legal traditions and commercial practices.

---

[7] Second Intermediate People's Court of Beijing Municipality, People's Republic of China, Civil Final No 8676, 31 October 2017.

Finally, the Chinese experience suggests that explicit recognition of good faith, coupled with clear judicial guidelines, could benefit Australian contract law. However, this must be balanced against maintaining the integrity of existing legal doctrines and respect for party autonomy in commercial contracts.

An overriding notion of good faith, as practised in other jurisdictions, which requires contracting parties at arm's length to have regard to the interest of the other party is difficult to implement in Australia. Lord Justice Steyn, in *First Energy (UK) Ltd v Hungarian International Bank Ltd*, said:

> A theme that runs through [the] law of contract is that the reasonable expectations of honest men must be protected. It is not a rule or a principle of law. It is the objective which has been and still is the principal moulding force of our law of contract. … [I]f the prima facie solution to a problem runs counter to the reasonable expectations of honest men, this criterion sometimes requires a rigorous re-examination of the problem to ascertain whether the law does indeed compel demonstrable unfairness.[8]

It is this notion of good faith as being able to fulfil what the contracting parties reasonably expect that informs much of the current thinking about good faith. Commercial contracting parties assume a level of honesty and good faith from one another and they would not deal where such an assumption is absent.[9] This has been recognised by the judiciary as a general norm in commercial dealings.[10] Priestley JA in *Renard Constructions* considered that contract law should imply an obligation of reasonableness, in the sense of a duty of good faith and fair dealing. His Honour said that '[a]lthough this implication has not yet been [widely] accepted … there are many indications that the time may be fast approaching when the idea … will gain explicit recognition.'[11] His Honour's approach has been applied in subsequent Australian decisions,[12] although the approach remained without unanimity.[13] Notwithstanding, the question remains whether good faith is relevant in commercial contracts. The answer to that question is in the affirmative.

7.2.2 Part Two

One of the most significant impediments for good faith obligation in Australia is that its definition is unsettled. Priestly JA in *Renard Constructions* views good faith as

---

[8] [1993] 2 Lloyd's Rep 194, 196.

[9] This is taken from Lord Bingham's judgement in *HIH Casualty and General Insurance Ltd v Chase Manhattan Bank* [2003] 2 Lloyd's Rep 61, 68 [15].

[10] *Yam Seng Pte Ltd v International Trade Corp Ltd* [2013] 1 All ER (Comm) 1321, 1351 [135] (per Leggatt J); cf *Bhasin v Hrynew* [2014] 3 SCR 494, 514 [32], 518 [41].

[11] (1992) 26 NSWLR 234, 263–264, 268.

[12] See, e.g., *Macquarie International Health Clinic Pty Ltd v Sydney South West Area Health Service* [2010] NSWCA 268, [12]; *Burger King Corporation v Hungry Jack's Pty Ltd* (2001) 69 NSWLR 558, 566–567 [145]-[154]; *Alcatel Australia Ltd v Scarcella* (1998) 44 NSWLR 349, 369.

[13] See, e.g., *Service Station Association Ltd v Berg Bennett & Associates Pty Ltd* (1993) 45 FCR 84, 96–97; *Jobern Pty Ltd v BreakFree Resorts (Victoria) Pty Ltd* [2007] FCA 1066, [134]-[136].

a notion that is expressed as a standard,[14] which underpins specific legal doctrines that may apply in different situations.[15] The underlying basis is that contractual performance and enforcement in good faith accords with the reasonable expectations or legitimate interests of the contractual parties.[16] This, however, still does not answer what the obligation actually requires. Good faith obligation in Australian contract law is driven by two main issues: its reception and its contents.

The aim of the second part, which is addressed in Chaps. 4 and 5, is to consider the current legal landscape. This allows for good faith to be appraised of its long-term prospects as a legal obligation, and whether it is consistent with the protection of the reasonable expectations of the contracting parties.

In Australia, good faith has been promoted through implied terms. This approach of bringing good faith into Australian contract law has not been satisfactory as the legal methodology has not yielded a consistent application—is it a term implied in law or in fact?

If it is in law, it can only be implied as incidents of a certain class of contracts. The implied term in this category is presumed to be part of all contracts of that specific type of class, but it must also be a term that is necessary[17] and can be excluded by clear provision to that effect.[18] The rigidness of the test of necessity makes it impossible for the term to be implied in a comprehensive commercial contract. However, in the *Burger King Corporation v Hungry Jack's Pty Ltd* ('*Hungry Jack*') case[19] it was successfully argued that good faith and reasonableness were implied in law, notwithstanding the court's recognition that there was no relevant class of contract into which terms could be implied nor as terms identified as one which the 'nature of the contract itself implicitly requires.'[20] Implying good faith in law also presumes that the contracting parties intended the duty to exist in a particular type of contract independent of the contractual context in which the parties have entered into.

---

[14] (1992) 26 NSWLR 234, 268.

[15] Examples include cooperation in performance, acting reasonably and honestly and consistency of conduct amongst others; cf *Hughes Aircraft Systems International v Airservices Australia* (1997) 76 FCR 151, 192 (per Finn J); Waddams, 'Good Faith, Unconscionability and Reasonable Expectations', above n 5; *Bhasin v Hrynew* [2014] 3 SCR 494, 528 [64].

[16] Jeannie M Paterson, 'Limits on a Lender's Rights to Repayment on Demand: Construction, Implication and Good Faith' (1998) 26 *Australian Business Law Review* 258, 272; John W Carter and Michael P Furmston, 'Good Faith and Fairness in the Negotiation of Contracts: Part I' (1994) 8 *Journal of Contract Law* 1, 6; *Overlook Management BV v Foxtel Management Pty Ltd* (2002) Aust Contracts Rep 90–143, [83]; *Automasters Australia Pty Ltd v Bruness Pty Ltd* [2002] WASC 286, [388]; *Varangian Pty Ltd v OFM Capital Ltd* [2003] VSC 444, [175]; *Hoppers Crossing Club Ltd v Tattersalls Gaming Pty Ltd* [2005] VSC 114, [25]; *North East Solution Pty Ltd v Masters Home Improvement Australia Pty Ltd* [2016] VSC1.

[17] *Byrne v Australian Airlines Ltd* (1995) 185 CLR 410, 450 (McHugh & Gummow JJ); *Breen v Williams* (1996) 186 CLR 71.

[18] *Castlemaine Tooheys Ltd v Carlton & United Breweries* (1987) 10 NSWLR 468.

[19] [2001] NSWCA 187.

[20] *Burger King Corporation v Hungry Jack's Pty Ltd* [2001] NSWCA 187, [183]; cf Hooley, Richard, 'Controlling Contractual Discretion' [2013] 72(1) *Cambridge Law Journal* 65, 76.

If good faith is implied in fact, the uncompromising approach of the business efficacy requirement makes it difficult to imply a term where the contract would be effective without it,[21] or where it can operate in circumstances that allow the contracting parties to perform their obligations in their own interests,[22] or where the implication of the term is inconsistent with the overall terms of the contract.[23] The more detailed the contract, the less likely that it is a term that will be implied.[24] As such, it is, perhaps, not surprising that the preference has been the implication of good faith obligation through implication by law simply because of the 'difficulty of complying with the criteria for an implication in fact.'[25]

However, it has been proposed that the implication of good faith bears more resemblance to the implication of a term in fact, as the conduct required from the parties under a good faith duty is likely to vary based on the specific circumstances of the case.[26] This sensitivity to the contractual provisions, more than just focusing on clear words of exclusions, allows the contracting parties' reasonable expectations to be the central focus and allows judges to define the good faith duty according to the dictates of the facts.[27] This may explain the trend in case law which suggests that implication in fact rather than by law is the preferred approach because it represents a more pragmatic and useful method in dealing with an obligation of good faith under implied terms.[28]

Although doctrinal mechanisms (such as implied terms) are used to apply and sustain the notion of good faith in commercial contracts, the approach has been shown to be largely lacking in coherence and satisfaction. This is because the question of content is still unresolved. The obligation's content is critically important for

---

[21] For example, *South Sydney District Rugby League Football Club Ltd v News Ltd* (2000) 177 ALR 611.

[22] Elisabeth, *Good Faith in the Performance of Contracts* (LexisNexis Butterworths, 2003) 132.

[23] For example, *Saxby Bridge Mortgages Pty Ltd v Saxby Bridge Pty Ltd* [2000] NSWSC 433.

[24] See, e.g., *Codelfa Construction Pty Ltd v State Rail Authority of New South Wales* (1982) 149 CLR 337.

[25] *Central Exchange Ltd v Anaconda Nickel Ltd* [2002] WASCA 94, [52] (Steytler J).

[26] Jeannie M Paterson, 'Good Faith in Commercial Contracts? A Franchising Case Study' (2001) 29 *Australian Business Law Review* 270, 273.

[27] Cf Paul Finn, 'Good Faith and Fair Dealing: Australia' (Paper presented at the Commercial Good Faith Conference, Auckland, New Zealand, 2 September 2005): Finn considers the reasonable expectations approach as the greatest merit in unpacking the context of a contractual relationship.

[28] Examples of some of the cases that have adopted this position: *Esso Australia Resources Pty Ltd v Southern Pacific Petroleum NL* [2005] VSCA 228; *Council of the City of Sydney v Goldspar Australia Pty Ltd* [2006] FCA 472; *Australian Hotels Association (NSW) v TAB Ltd* [2006] NSWSC 293 (19 April 2006); *Meridian Retail Pty Ltd v Australian Unity Retail Network* [2006] VSC 223 (21 June 2006); *Maitland Main Collieries Pty Ltd v Xstrata Mt Owen Pty Ltd* [2006] NSWSC 1235 (23 November 2006); *Ingot Capital Investments v Macquarie Equity Capital Markets (No 6)* [2007] NSWSC 124 (30 March 2007); *Kellogg Brown & Root Pty Ltd v Australian Aerospace Ltd* [2007] VSC 200; *Insight Oceania Pty Ltd v Philips Electronics Australia Ltd* [2008] NSWSC 710; *Starlink International Group Pty Ltd v Coles Supermarket Australia Pty Ltd* [2011] NSWSC 1154; *Aquila Coal Pty Ltd v Bowen Central Coal Pty Ltd* [2011] QSC 264, [95]; *Oliver v Commonwealth Bank of Australia* [2011] FCA 1440; *Trans Petroleum (Australia) Pty Ltd v White Gum Petroleum Pty Ltd* [2012] WASCA 165, [152, 154]; *Beerens v Bluescope Distribution Pty Ltd* [2012] VSCA 209.

it concerns the role and application that good faith plays in contractual performance. The key is, undoubtedly, the definition of good faith. Unfortunately, attributing meaning and definitive content to good faith is difficult as it is capable of taking on new or expanded meaning depending on its contractual circumstance.[29] In other words, it is closely linked with the establishment or depiction of a standard, and as such, it is equivalent to the elements of cooperation, honesty and reasonableness, taking into account the reasonable expectations of the contracting parties.[30] The dilemma is that these contracting standards are fundamentally important to contract law and since good faith is associated with it, it is increasingly clear that it cannot be ignored in contract performance.[31]

The reasonable expectation of the contracting parties is a theme that runs through contract law[32] and it is also a theme of good faith obligation.[33] Courts achieved this by construing contracts in giving effects to what the parties have expressly agreed to and by ensuring that it is commercially workable. Anything less would be contrary to the principles of good faith, and Australian courts have always given effect in its judgements to commercially sensible outcomes.[34]

The approach of using contractual construction to bring good faith obligation into a contract should not be discounted for it allows the particular scope of terms to be determined based on its contractual context and particular fact situations.[35] This allows the use of construction as a legal methodology in which to determine the actual conclusion that a reasonable person would assume within the meaning and

---

[29] Horst K Lücke, 'Good Faith and Contractual Performance' in Paul Finn (ed), *Essays on Contract* (Law Book Co, 1987) 160.

[30] See analysis: Waddams, 'Good Faith, Unconscionability and Reasonable Expectations', above n 5.

[31] For example, *Thiess Contractors v Placer (Granny Smith) Pty Ltd* (2000) 16 BCL 130; *Apple Communications v Optus Mobile* [2001] NSWSC 635; *Evans Deakin Pty Ltd v Sebel Furniture Ltd* [2003] FCA 171; *City of Sydney v Goldspar Australia Pty Ltd* [2006] FCA 472; *Australian Hotel Association (NSW) v TAB Ltd* [2006] NSWSC 293; *CGU Workers* Compensation (NSW) Ltd v Carlos Garcia [*2007*] NSWCA 193; *Jobern Pty Ltd v BreakFree Resorts (Victoria) Pty Ltd* [2007] FCA 1066; *Insight Oceania Pty Ltd v Philips Electronics Australia Ltd* [2008] NSWSC 710; Tote *Tasmania Pty Ltd v Garrott* [2008] TASSC 86; *Macquarie International Health Clinic Pty Ltd v Sydney South West Area Health Service* [2008] NSWSC 738; *Network Ltd v Speck* [2009] VSC 235; *United Group Rail Services Ltd v Rail Corporation of New South Wales* (2009) 74 NSWLR 618; *Driveforce Pty Ltd v Gunns Ltd (No 3)* [2010] TASSC 38; *Strzelecki Holdings Pty Ltd v Cable Sands Pty Ltd* [2010] WASCA 222.

[32] *First Energy (UK) Ltd v Hungarian International Bank Ltd* [1993] 2 Lloyd's Rep 194, 196.

[33] Cf Steven J Burton, 'Breach of Contract and the Common Law Duty to Perform in Good Faith' (1980) 94 *Harvard Law Review* 369, 371.

[34] This has been a constant theme in High Court decisions: John W Carter, *The Constructions of Commercial Contracts* (Hart Publishing, 2013) ch 1; see, e.g., *Ringstad v Gollin & Co Pty Ltd* (1924) 35 CLR 303, 316 (per Starke J); *J Kitchen & Sons Pty Ltd v Stewart's Cash & Carry Stores* (1942) 66 CLR 116, 124–125 (per Latham CJ and McTiernan J); *Gollin & Co Ltd v Karenlee Nominees Pty Ltd* (1983) 153 CLR 455, 464; *Concut Pty Ltd v Worrell* (2000) 176 ALR 693, 708–709; *International Air Transport Association v Ansett Australia Holdings Ltd* [2008] HCA 3, [8] (per Gleeson CJ).

[35] Carter, *The Constructions of Commercial Contracts*, above n 34, §4–22.

context of the expressed words in the contract.[36] In this regard, the impact on the contracting parties' autonomy is reduced as long as the application of good faith is grounded on this default position.[37] Hence, it is argued that the obligation of good faith would be more effectively applied in a consistent manner if it were introduced as a rule of construction, rather than as an implied term. By and large, the obligation of good faith does not align well with either approach to implied term. However, the constructivist approach aligns more closely with the idea of a universally applicable rule and could be offered as a real alternative to implied terms. Critically, the existing law would remain unaffected.

In this respect, the time has come for Australian courts to seriously consider this approach of applying good faith using contractual interpretation and construction in order to construe the intentions of the contracting parties rather than merely paying lip service to the method.[38] This allows for the starting point to be taken from what the contracting parties have agreed in considering the relevant questions of good faith in contract performance.[39]

The reasonable expectations of contracting parties in contract performance may not be wholly protected through the contract itself because, intuitively, contracting parties often do not form their contractual terms on the assumption that the other party may act in bad faith in performing his or her contracted obligations.[40] The inherent principle of good faith in contract performance is to protect the reasonable expectations of contracting parties. This may be extremely difficult, if not impossible, for them to protect at the formation stage of the contract. The difficulties at the formation stage are not necessarily derived from the inequality of bargaining power between the parties. Even in arm's length negotiations, contracting parties may not be able to produce a complete contract that deals with all contingencies at the performance stage. The principle of good faith does not protect what each party

---

[36] See *Toll (FGCT) Pty Ltd v Alphapharm Pty Ltd* (2004) 219 CLR 165, 179; cf *Attorney General of Belize v Belize Telecom Ltd* [2009] 1 WLR 1988, 1994 (per Lord Hoffmann); Wayne Courtney and John W Carter, 'Implied Terms: What is the Role of Construction?' (2014) 31 *Journal of Contract Law* 151.

[37] Roger Brownsword, 'Positive, Negative, Neutral: The Reception of Good Faith in English Contract Law' in Roger Brownsword, Norma J Hird and Geraint Howells (eds), *Good Faith in Contract: Concept and Context* (Dartmouth Publishing Co, 1999) 37.

[38] See *Pan Foods Co Importers & Distributors Pty Ltd v Australia and New Zealand Banking Group Ltd* (2000) 170 ALR 579, 584, [24]; *Elderslie Property Investments No 2 Pty Ltd v Dunn* [2008] QCA 158, [20]-[22]; *Bytan Pty Ltd v BB Australia Pty Ltd* (2012) 41 VR 46, 65 [96]; *Memery v Trilogy Funds Management Ltd* [2012] QCA 160, [14]; *North East Solution Pty Ltd v Masters Home Improvement Australia Pty Ltd* [2016] VSC 1, [32]-[35].

[39] *United Group Rail Services Ltd v Rail Corporation of New South Wales* (2009) 74 NSWLR 618, 639 [74]; *Macquarie International Health Clinic Pty Ltd v Sydney South West Area Health Service* [2010] NSWCA 268, [12]; *Commonwealth Bank of Australia v Barker* [2014] HCA 32; *Paciocco v Australia and New Zealand Banking Group Ltd* (2015) 321 ALR 584, 649–651 [287]-[293]; *North East Solution Pty Ltd v Masters Home Improvement Australia Pty Ltd* [2016] VSC 1, [56]-[62].

[40] See Simon Deakin, Wilkinson, Frank 'Contract Law and the Economics of Interorganizational Trust' in Christel Lane and Reihard Bachmann (eds), *Trust Within and between Organizations: Conceptual Issues and Empirical Applications* (Oxford University Press, 2002) 146.

may have anticipated to benefit from the contract at the formation stage. There is a difference between the anticipated benefit of the contract and what each party may expect from the contract. Under a good faith regime, contracting parties still bear the risk of their failure to protect the benefit they may anticipate from the contract. Any attempt to expand the application of good faith beyond the benefit of contracts would endanger the certainty of the law in commercial contracts. Good faith obligation, however, gives contracting parties a degree of assurance that neither party will act in a manner that will frustrate the other's reasonable or legitimate expectations from the contract. In this sense, good faith facilitates commercial transactions, and that is why international treaties such as the *UNIDROIT Principles* impose a general duty of good faith and fair dealing in contracts, which, incidentally, is applicable under Australian law.[41] Ultimately, the issue of good faith still needs to be clarified definitively by the High Court.

7.2.3 Part Three

This third part considers the relevance of good faith obligation by examining its effect and usage from an economic perspective and a practical analysis of commercial contractual behaviour. Part three is dealt with in Chap. 6 and intended to investigate if the doctrinal principles of good faith are aligned with commercial reality and whether the continued validity of good faith obligation in practice can be supported.

From an economic perspective, good faith is primarily seen as a tool to prevent opportunistic conduct. The term opportunism is often used by scholars in the area of contractual economics, but defining universally is challenging. The emergence of opportunistic behaviour is largely due to the incomplete nature of contracts and their sequential execution. The field behavioural economics is also considered when assessing if good faith could effectively counteract opportunism. To be relevant, good faith should encourage cooperative behaviour and deter opportunistic dealings.

The obligation of good faith is often seen as an alternative to contractual specification, leading to savings in transactional cost. However, the ambiguity surrounding the content or definition of good faith cannot be overlooked. This presents a balance between the cost savings from contractual specifications and the cost associated with increased uncertainty due to a reliance on good faith obligation. The economic analysis chapter provides for predictors on when good faith could be efficient. The analysis indicates that good faith does not always enhance economic efficiency. The challenges in applying good faith to contracts were highlighted in the analysis of specific applications of the duty. The findings suggest that a universal rule of good faith disclosure is not desirable. It is questionable whether negotiating parties will

---

[41] In the domain of international and transnational contracting, norms of good faith and fair dealing are becoming central elements of 'modern … commercial law, as it was of the law merchant': James Allsop, 'Good Faith and Australian Contract Law: A practical issue and a question of theory and principle' (2011) 85 *Australian Law Journal* 341, 355.

place enough trust in their counterparts to achieve significant transaction cost savings. Similar challengers were observed in judicial attempts to apply good faith to open quantity contracts, often leading to inefficient redistribution of contractual risk. In such cases, the obligation of good faith is not a suitable replacement for contractual specification by the parties. Its applications to the transaction costs model confirms that the efficiency criterion of good faith is unlikely to be met. Therefore, a comprehensive obligation of good faith may not be the best way to maximise efficiency. It could be argued that good faith should only be imposed in contractual relationships where efficiency demands it. Good faith should not be applied to contractual situations where it is not economically justified. The current piecemeal approach in Australia may be a more effective way to achieve economic efficiency than a comprehensive requirement of good faith application.

The second aspect of the chapter considered a practical analysis of good faith in a commercial contractual setting. The purpose of the practical analysis is to evaluate if good faith obligation in contracts actually serve and benefit commercial contracting parties. This is relevant as current contracting practice and case law continue to point to a good faith contracting environment, notwithstanding the uncertainty surrounding its application. In this respect, legal or contract practitioners often approach good faith obligation by employing drafting measures specifically to handle the uncertain effects of good faith on contracting parties.[42] As such, the choice and combination of measures in the contracting provisions are driven by factors such as the negotiating power and preferences of the contracting parties, which in turn dictates the specific construction of the obligation in the contract.[43]

From the analysis, all the legal practitioners interviewed said that there is no 'one size fits all' approach in approaching good faith obligations in contracts. The contracting parties indicated that legal advice affects the decision whether good faith provisions are included in the contract or not. They are, however, not adverse to it and are generally comfortable with having the obligation included in the contract. There is general consensus from the interviews that the inclusion and formulation of good faith provisions are informed by commercial expedience for particular types of commercial transaction. The ambiguous nature of good faith obligation makes such an approach pragmatic and would allow the contracting party to impose limits on its effect where desired. Is good faith useful or relevant for the contracting

---

[42] This was crystallised by Warren CJ in relation to good faith obligation: '[G]ood faith as a doctrine does not exist independently of the rules surrounding the construction and interpretation of contracts, or the rules of implication [and there] may be a merging of the two processes (interpretation and implication) in the arena of good faith': The Hon Marilyn Warren, 'Good Faith: Where Are We At?' (2010) 34 *Melbourne University Law Review* 344, 349.

[43] Cf Alicia Hill, 'Good Faith—Enforcement in Australia' (2013) 11(3) *International Journal of Franchising Law* 1 < http://www.mcw.com.au/Content/Attachment/Good%20faith%20-%20Enforcement%20in%20Australia.pdf > ; Bryan Horrigan, 'Good Faith from a Drafting and Pleadings Point of View' (Paper presented at the Commercial Court CPD Seminar, Melbourne, 4 June 2014); Bryan Horrigan, 'New Frontlines in Regulating Unconscionable, Unfair, and Bad Faith Business Conduct', *The Monash Law E-Briefing* (Melbourne), 2nd ed, 18 June 2014. < http://themonashlaw-e-briefing.blogspot.com.au/2014/06/expert-legal-commentary-new-frontlines.html > ; this is also the position that is universally taken by all the legal practitioners interviewed.

parties? The answer from the analysis is in the affirmative and the perception is that having good faith obligation in the contract curbs opportunistic conduct and allows contracting parties some negotiating flexibility when contracting circumstances changed. Whether this is a reality is unclear from the interviews. What is more definite is that contracting parties still regard the overall contracting provisions they have committed to as the final arbiter of their contracting relationship.

7.3 Research Significance, Benefits, and Implications

As this book concludes, it is important to reflect on its significance, benefits, and implications.

7.3.1 Significance

The main significance of this research is that the issue regarding the place of good faith obligation in Australian contract law has continued for more than two decades since the *Renard Construction*'s case and yet the reality is that there has been little progress in obtaining a settled position. There remains no High Court decision deciding the application and definition of good faith, and the closest it went was in the case of *Royal Botanic Gardens and Domain Trust v South Sydney City Council*. However, Kirby J held that: 'Whilst the issues respecting the existence and scope of a 'good faith' doctrine are important, this is an inappropriate occasion to consider them.'[44] Previous research has generally focused on either doctrinal debates or the limited development of the doctrine in case law. Perhaps, this highlights the limitations of a single category approach to comprehend good faith, which overlooks the scope and impact of the concept. Consequently, this has led to more hesitations in its application. It has certainly substantiated Carter and Stewart's description of good faith obligation in contractual performance and enforcement as the most important unresolved issue in Australian contract law.[45] Notwithstanding, the current judicial trend is still in favour of having a good faith contracting environment. Should the next step, perhaps, be to leave it with the legislature as in Israel or in the US with the *UCC*?[46]

[44] (2002) 186 ALR 289, 312.

[45] Carter and Stewart, 'Interpretation', above n 4, 190.

[46] For example, see Nili Cohen, 'The Effect of the Duty of Good Faith on a Previously Common Law System: The Experience of Israeli Law' in Roger Brownsword, Norma J Hird and Geraint Howells (eds), *Good Faith in Contract: Concept and Context* (Dartmouth Publishing Co, 1999) 189–212.

Finn J noted that the possibility of a uniform Australian legislative response to the issue of good faith obligation would not appear likely.[47] This leaves the judiciary to grapple with the issue, where recent trends suggest an increasing number of commercial disputes pleading good faith.[48] There is also a new wave of case law and judicial commentaries on good faith obligation in other common law jurisdictions that may offer possible outcomes that could potentially translate to Australian contractual conditions.[49] The common thread connecting these outside offerings is that good faith remains a relevant organising obligation for commercial contracts and that it is possible to achieve certainty in application as long as the court focuses its ambit on the factual setting of the contract and context of the dispute, while still maintaining the basic notion of freedom of contract.[50] For these reasons, this research on good faith's continued relevance and viability commercially is valid and continues to be significant in Australia.

7.3.2 Benefit

Good faith does play a useful role in contractual relationships. It is intended to fill the lacuna when existing rules fail to outlaw bad faith conduct. But how do you operationalise it? The approach suggested in this book is for the obligation to be incorporated into contract law by way of a rule of construction. At present, the approach using implied terms has its own drawbacks. Moreover, contracting parties are still at liberty to exclude it and it is also improbable that it would apply to conduct prior to the contract. A claim for a good faith breach would also need to be specifically pleaded. A potential way forward could be a legislative approach over a judicial one

[47] Paul Finn, 'Good Faith and Fair Dealing and "Boats against the current"' (Paper presented at the 2nd Biennial Conference on the Law of Obligations, Melbourne, 16 July 2004) 11.

[48] Examples of recent decisions include *Commonwealth Bank of Australia v Barker* [2014] HCA 32; *Paciocco v Australia and New Zealand Banking Group Ltd* (2015) 321 ALR 584; *Mineralogy v Sino Iron Pty Ltd (No 6)* [2015] FCA 825; *North East Solution Pty Ltd v Masters Home Improvement Australia Pty Ltd* [2016] VSC 1.

[49] Examples of cases from the UK: *Bristol Groundschool v Intelligent Data Capture* [2014] EWHC 2145; *TSG Building Services v South Anglia Housing* [2013] EWHC 1151; *Emirates Trading Agency LLC v Prime Mineral Exports Private Ltd* [2014] EWHC 2014 (Comm); *Acer Investment Management v Mansion Group* [2014] EWHC 3011; *Greenclose Ltd v National Westminster Bank* [2014] EWHC 1156; *Myers v Kestrel Acquisitions* [2015] EWHC 916; *MSC Mediterranean Shipping Co v Cottonex Anstalt* [2015] EWHC 283; *Portsmouth City Council v Ensign Highways Ltd* [2015] EWHC 1969; *Braganza v BP Shipping Ltd* [2015] UKSC 17; Canadian: *Bhasin v Hrynew* [2014] SCC 71; Singapore: *Ng Giap Hon v Westcomb Securities Pte Ltd* [2009] 3 SLR(R) 518; *HSBC Institutional Trust Services (Singapore) Ltd (Trustee of Starhill Global Real Estate Investment Trust) v Toshin Development Singapore Pte Ltd* [2012] SGCA 48.

[50] See Canadian Supreme Court decision in *Bhasin v Hrynew* [2014] SCC 71, [64], [65], [70]; *MSC Mediterranean Shipping Co v Cottonex Anstalt* [2015] EWHC 283, [97].

for good faith obligation to have a broad impact; however, this approach appears unlikely due to the lack of a universally accepted definition of good faith.[51]

It must be noted in the introductory first chapter that any final determination of this research is necessarily a balancing exercise. The competing arguments have been weighed up. It can be concluded at this juncture that if there is no rethink or fine tuning of current approaches (the preference for using implied terms in good faith application) then good faith obligation would continue to yield inconsistent application in Australia. While good faith may encompass duties of cooperation, honesty and reasonable behaviour, pinpointing the specific conduct required in each case to meet the standard of good faith can be inherently uncertain. If the High Court were to openly endorse the view prevalent in the lower courts—that the fundamental basis of the good faith obligation is reasonable expectations, rather than community standards or the like—it would signify the adoption of a doctrinal approach in line with a generally acknowledged legal trend, if not the perpetuation of a long-established theme. Similar to the idea of 'doing the right thing',[52] a good faith obligation explicitly grounded on reasonable expectations could be more easily comprehended by commercial parties[53] and align with the economic evidence of commercial contractual behaviour. Seen in this light, commercial contract law would still primarily focus on achieving individual objectives, but these objectives would be 'understood largely in terms of the context out of which they arise' and the reasonable expectations fostered by that commercial context.[54] Therefore, this research benefits from integrating legal analysis with economic and empirical methodologies to examine good faith obligation in a broader context and contributing to its commercial understanding. It also aids in the ongoing evolution of the common law and equitable rules governing contractual transactions.

---

[51] See Australian Government, Business Law Branch Attorney-General's Department, *Improving Australia's Law and Justice Framework: A Discussion Paper Exploring The Scope for Reforming Australian Contract Law* (2012) http://observgo.uquebec.ca/observgo/fichiers/85195_DAEPI.pdf.

[52] Nicholas C Seddon, 'Australian Contract Law: Maelstrom or Measured Mutation?' (1994) 7 *Journal of Contract Law* 93, 94.

[53] Seddon notes that where a legal standard is based on common experience and reasonable expectations it is not difficult to know what to do: Seddon, 'Australian Contract Law', above n 52, 104, 110.

[54] Jay M Feinman, 'Relational Contract Theory in Context' (2000) 94 *Northwestern University Law Review* 737, 739.

7.3.3 *Implications*

7.3.3.1 Practical

Bridge states that any person who supports the principle of good faith in contracts must answer these questions honestly: 'why do we need to introduce … good faith? and what do we want it to do?'.[55]

It is impossible to answer these questions definitively or conclusively. This is not because good faith is not suitable as a fundamental principle in contract law but because good faith operates within a flexible contextual framework. To demand that good faith obligation operates within some defined perimeters of limits and specific circumstances would be futile and unworkable.[56] This, unfortunately, is often the normal approach taken in good faith in contracts. The obligation of good faith does not work in a way that could generate in advance certain requirements that all contracting parties should follow, whether at the formation or performance stage of the contracting process. This research acknowledges this aspect of good faith but, more importantly, it examines whether good faith can command a valid principle in contract law. Good faith is not validated as a contractual principle simply on the basis of the international treaties affecting Australia (like the *UNIDROIT Principles* and the *CISG*) or on the fact that other established jurisdictions have good faith taking a central role in commercial contracting arrangements (such as the *UCC*).[57]

Internationally, these contractual instruments clearly demonstrate the importance and value of good faith in contracts and have shown that a strong and valid relationship exists in commercial contracts. In this respect, the utility of the good faith principle practically in commercial contracts stems from its recognition of the parties' right to act in self-interest. Thus, good faith in commercial contracts is capable of operating within a doctrinal domain that is sensitive to the freedom of contract. This is reflective of the applicable standards concerning good faith obligation in commercial undertakings.[58]

7.3.3.2 Future Research Directions

The obligation of good faith holds potential for further development. For instance, good faith could play a significant role in mainstream areas such as agreements

---

[55] Bridge, 'Good Faith in Commercial Contracts', above n 1, 141.

[56] As Lord Coulsfield said: 'To lay down any such detailed and prescribed requirements would, in any event, be difficult to reconcile with the normal approach … to questions of good faith.': *Clydesdale Bank plc v Black* [2002] SLT 764, 771(E).

[57] See Chap. 2.

[58] Allsop, above n 41; Finn, Paul, 'Internationalisation or Isolation: The Australian Cul de Sac? The Case of Contract Law' (Paper presented at the 20th Anniversary Symposium, The Internationalisation of Law: Legislating, Decision-Making, Practice and Education, Bond University, Gold Coast, 26–27 June 2009); Commonwealth Attorney-General's Department, *Review of Australian Contract Law* (2012).

to negotiate, process contracts, regulation of contractual discretions, contractual amendments or variations and even in differentiating between liquidated damages and penalty clauses.[59] A comparative study of good faith with Islamic law could provide an intriguing insight into the operation of the obligation. In Islamic law, good faith is deemed considered a core principle and frequently acts as a behavioural etiquette throughout the contracting process.[60] Consequently, there is room for additional research to identify those sectors of contract law where the application of good faith could be suitably placed in the future.

7.4 Chapter Summary

For the moment, it is clear that the 'piecemeal' approach to contract law is preferred to a general overriding obligation of good faith. In saying this, it is also felt that the time has come to recognise that where parties have agreed to contract on good faith that it is recognised explicitly rather than seeking a different principle to apply to their contracts. By doing this, Australian commercial law will be given a new option and flexibility that will make our contracting environment more appealing in the global marketplace. Thus, it is concluded that there is value and validity in having a good faith obligation in arm's length commercial contracts but the way in which the incorporation of the obligation takes in contract law must continue to be the focus of legal developments for a consistent application of the obligation.

[59] See, e.g., John W Carter and Elisabeth Peden, 'A Good Faith Perspective on Liquidated Damages' (2007) 23 *Journal of Contract Law* 157; Lindsey Alford and Eden Bird, 'Tendering for Government Business: Process Contracts, Good Faith, Fair Dealing and Probity' (2011) 85 *Australian Law Journal* 678; Zoe Ollerenshaw, 'Managing Change in Uncertain Times: Relational View of Good Faith' in Larry A DiMatteo, Qi Zhou, Severine Saintier and Keith Rowley (eds), *Commercial Contract Law: Transatlantic Perspectives* (2013) 201; Richard Hooley, 'Controlling Contractual Discretion' [2013] 72(1) *Cambridge Law Journal* 65.

[60] See Nurhidayah Binti Abdullah, *'Good Faith and Fair Dealing in Hire Purchase Contract in Malaysia' (2007) 15(2) Journal Syariah 99.*

Bibliography

I Articles, Books, and Reports

Abdullah, Nurhidayah Binti, *'Good Faith and Fair Dealing in Hire Purchase Contract in Malaysia' (2007) 15(2) Journal Syariah 99*

Abyad, Imad D, 'Commercial Reasonableness in Karl Llewellyn's Uniform Commercial Code Jurisprudence' (1997) 83 *Virginia Law Review* 429

Adam, John N, 'The Economics of Good Faith in Contract Law' (1995) 8 *Journal of Contract Law* 126

Alford, Lindsey and Eden Bird, 'Tendering for Government Business: Process Contracts, Good Faith, Fair Dealing and Probity' (2011) 85 *Australian Law Journal* 678

Allen, David E and Mary E Hiscock, *Law of Contract in Australia* (CCH Australia, 2nd ed, 1992)

Allsop, James, 'Good Faith and Australian Contract Law: A Practical Issue and a Question of Theory and Principle' (2011) 85 *Australian Law Journal* 341

American Law Institute, *Restatement (Second) of Contracts* (1981) <http://www.lexinter.net/LOTWVers4/restatement_(second)_of_contracts.htm>

Ames, James B, 'Parol Contracts Prior to Assumpsit' (1895) 8 *Harvard Law Review* 252

Andersen, Camilla B, *Reasonable time in Article 39(1) of the CISG—Is Article 39(1) Truly a Uniform Provision?* (1998) <http://www.cisg.law.pace.edu/cisg/biblio/andersen.html>

Andersen, Eric G, 'Good Faith in the Enforcement of Contracts' (1988) 73 *Iowa Law Review* 299

Aristotle, *Nicomachean Ethics*, Book IV, 1 (trans Ross, W D) <http://classics.mit.edu/Aristotle/nicomachaen.4.iv.html>

Aristotle, *Nicomachean Ethics*, Book V, 2 (trans Ross, W D) <http://classics.mit.edu/Aristotle/nicomachaen.5.v.html>

Arksey, Hillary and Knight Peter T, *Interviewing for Social Scientists* (SAGE Publications, 1999)

Arrighetti, Alessandro, Reinhard Bachmann and Simon Deakin, 'Contract Law, Social Norms and Inter-Firm Cooperation' (1977) 21 *Cambridge Journal of Economics* 171

Atias, Christian, *French Civil Law* (trans Levasseur, Alain A) (2002)

Atiyah, Patrick S, *Consideration in Contracts: A Fundamental Restatement* (Australian National University Press, 1971)

Atiyah, Patrick S, *The Rise and Fall of Freedom of Contract* (Clarendon Press, 1985)

Atiyah, Patrick S, *Essays on Contract* (Clarendon Press, 1986)

Atiyah, Patrick S and Stephen A Smith, *Atiyah's Introduction to the Law of Contract* (Clarendon Press, 6th ed, 2005)

Australian Audit Office, *Developing and Managing Contracts: Getting the Right Outcome, Paying the Right Price* (2007)

A. Wan and P. Guo, *Good Faith Obligation*, International and Comparative Law in the Asia Pacific, https://doi.org/10.1007/978-981-97-7035-9

Ayres, Ian and Robert Gertner, 'Filling Gaps in Incomplete Contracts: An Economic Theory of Default Rules', (1989) 99 *Yale Law Journal* 87

Babbie, Earl R, *The Basics of Social Research* (Cengage Learning, 3rd ed, 2005)

Babbie, Earl R, *The Basics of Social Research* (Cengage Learning, 14th ed, 2015)

Baird, Douglas G, Robert H Gertner and Randal C Picker, *Game Theory and the Law* (Harvard University Press, 1988)

Baker, John, *An Introduction to English Legal History* (LexisNexis Butterworths, 4th ed, 2005)

Ball, S N, 'Work Carried Out in Pursuance of Letters of Intent—Contract or Restitution?' (1983) 99 *Law Quarterly Review* 572

Barbour, Willard T, 'The History of Contract in Early English Equity' in Vinogradoff, Paul (ed), *Oxford Studies in Social and Legal History* (Clarendon Press, 1914) vol IV

Barnett, Randy E, 'Conflicting Visions: A Critique of Ian Macneil's Relational Theory of Contract' (1992) 78 *Virginia Law Review* 1175

Baron, Adrian, '"Good Faith" and Construction Contracts—From Small Acorns Large Oaks Grow' (2002) 22 *Australia Bar Review* 54

Baron, Paula, 'Resistance: A Consideration of the Opposition to a Duty of Good Faith in Australian Commercial Contracts' (2005) 11 *New Zealand Business Law Quarterly* 408

Barr, Nicholas, *Economics of the Welfare State* (Oxford University Press, 5th ed, 2012)

Baxendale, Robyn, 'Garcia v National Australia Bank Ltd: Ensuring Equity in Surety Transactions: A Legal Debt-End?' (1999) 21 *Sydney Law Review* 313

Beale, Hugh and Tony Dugdale, 'Contracting Between Businessmen: Planning and the Use of Contractual Remedies' (1975) 2 *British Journal of Law and Society* 45

Beatson, Jack and Daniel Friedman, 'From Classical to Modern Contract Law' in Jack Beatson and Daniel Friedman (eds), *Good Faith and Fault in Contract Law* (Oxford University Press, 2001)

Beazley, Margaret Justice, 'Terms: Good Faith in Contract' in *Australian Contract Law Commentary* (2013)

Bederman, David J, *International Law in Antiquity* (Cambridge University Press, 2007)

Bellah, Robert N (ed), *Emile Durkheim on Morality and Society* (The University of Chicago Press, 1973)

Belobaba, Edward P, 'Good Faith in Canadian Contract Law' in Law Society of Upper Canada, *Commercial Law: Recent Developments and Emerging Trends* (Richard De Boo Publishers, 1985)

Bennett, Howard H, 'Utmost Good Faith, Materiality and Inducement' (1996) 112 *Law Quarterly Review* 405

Bennett, Howard H, 'Mapping the Doctrine of Utmost Good Faith in Insurance Contract Law' (1999) *Lloyd's Maritime and Commercial Law Quarterly* 165

Berger, Adolf, *Encyclopedic Dictionary of Roman Law* (American Philosophical Society, 1991) vol 43 Part 2

Berger, Klaus Peter, 'The *Lex Mercatoria* Doctrine and the UNIDROIT Principles of International Commercial Contracts' (1997) 28 *Law and Policy in International Business* 943

Berger, Klaus Peter, *The Creeping Codification of the Lex Mercatoria* (Kluwer Law International, 1999)

Bigley, Gregory A and Jone L Pearce, 'Straining for Shared Meaning in Organization Science: Problems of Trust and Control' (1998) 23(3) *Academy of Management Review* 405

Bigwood, Rick A, 'Conscience and Liberal Conception of Contract: Observing Basic Distinctions Part II' (2000) 16 *Journal of Contract Law* 191

Bigwood, Rick A, *Exploitative Contracts* (Oxford University Press, 2003)

Bigwood, Rick A, 'Symposium Introduction: Confessions of a "Good Faith" Agnostic' (2005) 11 *New Zealand Business Law Quarterly* 371

Birds, John, *Birds' Modern Insurance Law* (Sweet & Maxwell, 9th ed, 2013)

Birks, Peter, 'Equity in the Modem Law: An Exercise in Taxonomy' (1996) 26 *University of Western Australia Law Review* 1

Blöndal, Jon R, 'Market-type Mechanisms and the Provision of Public Services' (2005) 5 (1) *OECD Journal on Budgeting* 79

Boge, Christopher J F, 'Does the Trade Practices Act Impose a Duty to Negotiate in Good Faith? Part I' (1998) 6 (1) *Trade Practices Law Journal* 4

Boge, Christopher J F, 'Does the Trade Practices Act Impose a Duty to Negotiate in Good Faith? Part II' (1998) 6 (2) *Trade Practices Law Journal* 68

Bohnet, Iris, Bruno S Frey and Steffen Huck, 'More Order with Less Law: On Contract Enforcement, Trust and Crowding' (1995) 95 *American Political Science Review* 131

Bonell, Michael J, 'Article 7: Interpretation of the CISG' in Bonell, Michael J and Bianca, Massimo C, *Commentary on the International Sales Law: The 1980 Vienna Sales Convention* (1987)

Bonell, Michael J, 'The UNIDROIT Principles of International Commercial Contracts: Why? What? How?' (1995) *Tulane Law Review* 1121

Bonell, Michael J (ed), *The UNIDROIT Principles in Practice: Case law and Bibliography on the Principles of Commercial Contracts* (2nd ed, 2006)

Bozeman, Adda B, *Politics and Culture in International History: From the Ancient Near East to the Opening of the Modern Age* (2nd ed, 2010)

Bradgate, Robert, 'Unreasonable Standard Terms' (1997) 60 *Modern Law Review* 582

Brennan, Gerard, 'Opening Address' (1990) 3 *Journal of Contract Law* 85

Bridge, Michael, 'Does Anglo-Canadian Contract Law Need a Doctrine of Good Faith?' (1984) 9 *Canadian Business Law Journal* 385

Bridge, Michael, 'Good Faith in Commercial Contracts' in Roger Brownsword, Norma J Hird and Geraint Howells (eds), *Good Faith in Contract: Concept and Context* (Dartmouth Publishing Co, 1999)

Bridge, Michael, 'Doubting Good Faith' (2005) 11 *New Zealand Business Law Quarterly* 426

Broadbent, Jane, Gill, Jas and Laughlin, Richard, 'The Private Finance Initiative in the UK: Contracting in the Context of Infrastructure Investment and Control' (2003) 6(2) *International Public Management Journal* 622

Broadbent, Jane, Jas Gill and Richard Laughlin, 'Evaluating the Private Finance Initiative in the National Health Service in the UK' (2003) 16(3) *Accounting, Auditing and Accountability Journal* 422

Brown, Ian, 'The Contract to Negotiate: The Thing Writ in Water?' [1982] *Journal of Business Law* 353

Brown, Liam, 'The Impact of Section 51AC of the *Trade Practices Act 1974* (Cth) on Commercial Certainty' (2004) 28(3) *Melbourne University Law Review* 589

Brownsword, Roger, Norma J Hird and Geraint Howells, 'Good Faith in Contract: Concept and Context' in Roger Brownsword, Norma J Hird and Geraint Howells (eds), *Good Faith in Contract: Concept and Context* (Dartmouth Publishing Co, 1999)

Brownsword, Roger, 'Two Concepts of Good Faith' (1994) 7 *Journal of Contract Law* 197

Brownsword, Roger, 'Positive, Negative, Neutral: The Reception of Good Faith in English Contract Law' in Roger Brownsworth, Norma J Hird, and Geraint Howells (eds), *Good Faith in Contract: Concept and Context* (Dartmouth Publishing Co, 1999)

Bryan, Michael and Manfred P Ellinghaus, 'Fault Lines in the Law of Obligations: *Roxborough v Rothmans of Paul Mall Australia Ltd*' (2000) 22 *Sydney Law Review* 636

Bryman, Alan and Emma Bell, *Business Research Methods* (Oxford University Press, 2nd ed, 2007)

Buckland, William W, '*Culpa* and *Bona Fides* in the *Actio Ex Emptio*' (1932) 48 *Law Quarterly Review* 217

Buckland, William W and Peter Stein, *A Text-Book of Roman Law: From Augustus to Justinian* (Cambridge University Press, 3rd ed, 2007)

Buckland, William W, *Equity in Roman Law: Lectures Delivered in the University of London, at the Request of the Faculty of Laws (1911)* (2009)

Burrows, John, 'Contractual Co-operation and the Implied Term' (1968) 31 *Modern Law Review* 380

Burton, Steven J and Eric G Andersen, 'The World of a Contract' (1990) 75 *Iowa Law Review* 861

Burton, Steven J and Eric G Andersen, *Contractual Good Faith:* Formation, Performance, Breach, Enforcement (Little, Brown & Co, 1995)

Burton, Steven J, 'Breach of Contract and the Common Law Duty to Perform in Good Faith' (1980) 94 *Harvard Law Review* 369

Burton, Steven J, 'Good Faith Performance of a Contract within Article 2 of the Uniform Commercial Code' (1981) 67 *Iowa Law Review* 1

Burton, Steven J, 'More on Good Faith Performance of a Contract: A Reply to Professor Summers' (1984) 69 *Iowa Law Review* 497

Burton, Steven J, 'Good Faith in Articles 1 and 2 of the UCC: The Practice View' (1994) *William & Mary Law Review* 1533

Calveras, Aleix, Juan-Jose Ganuza and Esther Hauk , 'Wild Bids. Gambling for Resurrection in Procurement Contracts' (2004) 26 *Journal of Regulatory Economics* 41

Capuano, Angelo, 'Not Keeping the Faith: A Critique of Good Faith in Contract Law in Australia and the United States' (2005) 17(1) *Bond Law Review* 29

Carlin, Tyrone, 'The Rise (and Fall?) of Implied Duties of Good Faith in Contractual Performance in Australia' (2002) 25 *University of New South Wales Law Journal* 99

Carlin, Tyrone, 'Good Faith in Contractual Performance—Smoke Without Flame?' (2005) 4 *Journal of Law and Financial Management* 18

Carlin, Tyrone and Louise Chau, 'Good Faith—Time to Put the Genie Back in the Bottle', (2009) 3(2) *Journal of Law and Financial Management* 22

Carter, John W, 'Problems in Enforcement—Part 1' (1992) 5 *Journal of Contract Law* 199

Carter, John W, 'The Renegotiation of Contracts' (1998) 13 *Journal of Contract Law* 185

Carter, John W, *Contract Law in Australia* (LexisNexis Butterworths, 6th ed, 2012)

Carter, John W, *The Constructions of Commercial Contracts* (Hart Publishing, 2013)

Carter, John W, 'Context and Literalism in Construction' (2014) 31(1) *Journal of Contract Law* 100

Carter, John W et al, 'Terms Implied in Law: 'Trust and Confidence' in the High Court of Australia' (2015) 32 *Journal of Contract Law* 203

Carter, John W and Andrew Stewart, 'Commerce and Conscience: The High Court's Developing View of Contract' (1993) 23 *Western Australian Law Review* 49

Carter, John W and Andrew Stewart, 'Interpretation, Good Faith and the "True Meaning" of Contracts: The Royal Botanic Decision' (2002) 18 *Journal of Contract Law* 182

Carter, John W and Michael P Furmston, 'Good Faith and Fairness in the Negotiation of Contracts: Part 1' (1994) 8 *Journal of Contract Law* 1

Carter, John W and Michael P Furmston, 'Good Faith and Fairness in the Negotiation of Contracts: Part II' (1995) 8 *Journal of Contract Law* 93

Carter, John W and Elisabeth Peden, 'Good Faith in Australian Contract Law' (2003) Commercial Law Quarterly 15

Carter, John W and Elisabeth Peden, 'Good Faith in Australian Contract Law' (2003) 19 *Journal of Contract Law* 155

Carter, John W and Elisabeth Peden, 'A Good Faith Perspective on Liquidated Damages' (2007) 23 *Journal of Contract Law* 157

Cartwright, John, *Misrepresentation, Mistake and Non-Disclosure* (Sweet & Maxwell, 2012)

Chen, Nianbing, 'On the Principle of Good Faith - An Analysis from the Perspective of Norms' [2003] (06) Science of Law (Journal of Northwest University of Political Science and Law) 59

Chetwin, Maree, 'Relational Contract Theory and the Good Faith Debate' (2003) 9 *New Zealand Business Law Quarterly* 211

China University of Political Science and Law (ed), Speech on the General Principles of the Civil Law of the People's Republic of China (China University of Political Science and Law Press, 1986)

Chung, Demi, David A Hensher and John M Rose, 'Toward the Betterment of Risk Allocation: Investigating Risk Perceptions of Australian Stakeholder Groups to Public-Private Partnership Toll road Projects' (2010) 30 *Research in Transportation Economics* 43

Cicero, Marcus Tullius, *De officiis*, Book 1 (Miller, Walter trans, 1913) <http://www.constitution.org/rom/de_officiis.htm#book1>

Cicero, Marcus Tullius, *De officiis*, Book 3 (Miller, Walter trans, 1913) <http://www.constitution.org/rom/de_officiis.htm#book3>

Clarke, Philip and Julie Clarke, *Contract Law: Commentaries, Cases and Perspectives* (Kenyon House Press, 2nd ed, 2012)

Clough, Daniel, 'Trends in the Law of Unconscionability' (1999) 18 *Australian Bar Review* 34

Coase, Ronald H, 'The Nature of the Firm' (1937) 4(16) *Economica* 386

Cohen, George M, 'The Negligence-Opportunism Tradeoff in Contract Law' (1992) 20 *Hofstra Law Review* 941

Cohen, George M, 'The Fault that Lies within Our Contract Law' (2009) 107 *Michigan Law Review* 1446

Cohen, Nili, 'The Effect of the Duty of Good Faith on a Previously Common Law System: The Experience of Israeli Law' in Roger Brownsword, Norma Hird and Geraint Howells (eds), *Good Faith in Contract: Concept and Context* (Dartmouth Publishing Co, 1999)

Cohen, Nili, 'Pre-contractual Duties: Two Freedoms and the Contract to Negotiate' in Jack Beatson and Daniel Friedmann (eds), *Good Faith and Fault in Contract Law* (Dartmouth Publishing Co, 2001)

Cole, Terence R H, 'Law – All in Good Faith' (1994) *Building & Construction Law Journal* 18

Collins, Hugh, 'Good Faith in European Contract Law' (1994) 14 *Oxford Journal of Legal Studies* 229

Collins, Hugh, 'The Sanctimony of Contract' in Rawlings, Richard (ed), *Law, Society and Economy, Centenary Essays for the London School of Economics and Political Science 1895–1995* (Clarendon Press, 1997)

Conaglen, Matthew D J, 'Duress, Undue Influence, and Unconscionable Bargains: The Theoretical Mesh' (1999) 18 *New Zealand Universities Law Review* 509

Cooter, Robert, Stephen Marks and Robert H Mnookin, 'Bargaining in the Shadow of the Law: A Testable Model of Strategic Behaviour' (1982) 11 *Journal of Legal Studies* 225

Corbetta, Piergiorgio, *Social Research: Theory, Methods and Techniques* (SAGE Publications, 2003)

Corones, Stephen, 'Does 'Good Faith' in section 51AC of the Trade Practices Act Deny Self-Interest?' (1999) 27 *Australian Business Law Review* 414

Corones, Stephen, 'Implied Good Faith and Unconscionability in Franchises: Moving towards Relational Contract Theory' (2000) 28 *Australian Business Law Review* 462

Courtney, Wayne and John W Carter, 'Implied Terms: What is the Role of Construction?' (2014) 31 *Journal of Contract Law* 151

Critchlow, Julian, *Making Partnering Work in the Construction Industry* (Chartridge Books, 1998)

Crotty, Michael, *The Foundations of Social Research: Meaning and Perspective in The Research Process* (SAGE Publications, 1998)

Cui, Jianyuan, *Analysis of New Contract Law Theory and Cases* (Jilin University Press, 1999)

Cumerbatch, Jeff, 'In Freedom's Cause: The Contract to Negotiate' (1992) 12 *Oxford Journal of Legal Studies* 586

Dalhuisen, Jan H, *Dalhuisen on Transnational and Comparative Commercial, Financial and Trade Law*, vol 1 (Hart Publishing, 4th ed, 2010)

Dalhuisen, Jan H, *Dalhuisen on Transnational, Comparative, Commercial, Financial and Trade Law*, vol 2 (Hart Publishing, 5th ed, 2013)

Dannermann, Gerhard, *An Introduction to German Civil and Commercial Law* (The British Institute of International and Comparative Law, 1993)

David, Rene, *French Law, Its Structure, Sources and Methodology* (trans Kindred, Michael) (Louisiana State University Press, 1972)

Davies, James, 'Why a Common Law Duty of Contractual Good Faith is Not Required' (2002) 8 *Canterbury Law Review* 529

Davies, Kevin E, 'The Demand for Immutable Contracts: Another Look at the Law and Economics of Contract Modifications' (2006) 81 *New York University Law Review* 487

Dawson, John P, 'Unconscionable Coercion: The German Version' (1976) 89 *Harvard Law Review* 1041

Deakin, Simon and Frank Wilkinson, 'Contract Law and the Economics of Interorganizational Trust' in Christel Lane and Reinhard Bachmann (eds), *Trust Within and Between Organizations: Conceptual Issues and Empirical Applications* (Oxford University Press, 2002)

Dean, Meryll, 'Unfair Contract Terms: The European Approach' (1993) 56 *Modern Law Review* 581

De Cruz, Peter, *Comparative Law in a Changing World* (Cavendish Publishing, 3rd ed, 2006)

Deitrick, William E and Jeffrey C B Levine, 'Contractual Good Faith: Let the Contract, Not the Courts, Define the Bargain' (1997) 85 *Illinois Bar Journal* 120

Dekker, Henri, 'Control of Inter-Organizational Relationships: Evidence on Appropriation Concerns and Coordination Requirements' (2004) 29(1) *Accounting, Organizations and Society*, 27

Delaume, Georges R, 'The Myth of the Lex Mercatoria and State Contracts' in Thomas E Carbonneau (ed), *Lex Mercatoria and Arbitration: A Discussion of the New Law Merchant* (Juris Publishing, 1998)

Denscombe, Martyn, *The Good Research Guide for Small-Scale Social Research Projects* (McGraw-Hill Education, 1998)

Denscombe, Martyn, *The Good Research Guide for Small-Scale Social Research Projects* (McGraw-Hill Education, 4th ed, 2010)

DiMatteo, Larry A, "Rule of Law' in China: The Confrontation of Formal Law with Cultural Norms' (2018) 51 *Cornell International Law Journal* 391

DiMatteo, Larry A and Lei Chen (eds), *Chinese Contract Law: Civil and Common Law Perspectives* (University Press, 2018)

Dixon, Bill, 'Common Law Obligations of Good Faith in Australian Commercial Contracts—a Relational Recipe' (2005) 33 *Australian Business Law Review* 87

Dixon, Bill, 'Can the Common Law Obligation of Good Faith Be Contractually Excluded?' (2007) 35 *Australian Business Law Review* 110

Dixon, Bill, 'What is the Content of the Common Law Obligation of Good Faith in Commercial Leases?' (2007) 14 *Australian Property Law Journal* 113

Dixon, Bill, 'Common Law Obligations of Good Faith in the Performance and Enforcement of Joint Ventures of a Non-Fiduciary Nature' in William D Duncan (ed), *Joint Ventures Law in Australia* (The Federation Press, 3rd ed, 2012)

Dobbins, Teri J, 'Losing Faith: Extracting the Implied Covenant of Good Faith from (Some) Contracts' (2005) 84 *Oregon Law Review*, 227

Donnenberg, Vicki, 'Judicial Review of Arbitral Awards Under the Commercial Arbitration Acts' (2008) 30 *Australian Bar Review* 177

Dorsey, Roscoe, 'Roman Sources of Some English Principles of Equity and Common Law Rules' (1938) 8 *American Law School Review* 1233

Douglas, F M, 'Modern Approaches to the Construction and Interpretation of Contracts' (2009) 32 *Australian Bar Review* 158

Dubroff, Harold, 'The Implied Covenant of Good Faith in Contract Interpretation and Gap Filling: Reviving a Revered Relic' (2006) 80 *St John's Law Review* 559

Duffy, Peter 'Unfair Contract Terms and the Draft EC Directive' (1993) *Journal of Business Law* 67

Dugdale, Anthony M and Nigel V Lowe, 'Contracts to Contract and Contracts to Negotiate' (1976) *Journal of Business Law* 28

Duggan, Anthony J, 'Is Equity Efficient?' (1997) 113 *Law Quarterly Review* 601

Duke, Arlen, 'A Universal Duty of Good Faith: An Economic Perspective' (2007) 33 *Monash University Law Review* 182

Duncan, William D, 'The Implication of a Term of Good Faith in Commercial Leases' (2002) 9 *Australian Property Law Journal* 209

Dungen, Peter van den, 'Good Faith, Unconscionable Conduct and Imaginary Community Standards: Section 51AC of the Trade Practices Act and the Insurance Industry' (1998) 10 *Insurance Law Journal* 1

Dworkin, Ronald, *Taking Rights Seriously* (Harvard University Press, 1977)

Dyson, Robert W, *Natural Law and Political Realism in the History of Political Thought: From the Sophists to Machiavelli*, vol 1 (Peter Lang, 2005)

Easterbrook, Frank, 'The Inevitability of Law and Economics' (1989) 1 *Legal Education Review* 1

Easterbrook, Frank H and Daniel R Fischel, 'Contract and Fiduciary Duty' (1993) 36 *Journal of Law and Economics* 425

Ebke, Werner F and Matthew W Finkin, *Introduction to German Law* (Kluwer Law International, 1996)

Ebke, Werner F and Bettina M Steinhauer, 'The Doctrine of Good Faith in German Contract Law' in Jack Beatson and Daniel Friedmann (eds), *Good Faith and Fault in Contract Law* (Oxford University Press, 2001)

Eisenberg, Melvin A, 'Why There is No Law of Relational Contracts' (2000) 94 *Northwestern University Law Review* 805

Eisenberg, Melvin A, 'The Emergence of Dynamic Contract Law' (2001) 2 *Theoretical Inquiries in Law* 1

Eisenberg, Melvin A, 'The Theory of Contracts' in Peter Benson (ed), *The Theory of Contract Law: New Essays* (Cambridge University Press, 2001)

Eisenberg, Melvin A, 'Disclosure in Contract Law' (2003) 91 *California Law Review* 1645

Elias, Dame Sian, 'Opening Address to the 10th Annual Journal of Contract Law Conference' (2000) 6 *New Zealand Business Law Quarterly* 79

Enonchong, Nelson, *Duress, Undue Influence and Unconscionable Dealing* (Sweet & Maxwell, 2nd ed, 2012)

Fabre-Magnan, Muriel, 'Duties of Disclosure and French Contract Law: Contribution to an Economic Analysis' in Jack Beatson and Daniel Friedmann (eds), *Good Faith and Fault in Contract Law* (Oxford University Press, 2001)

Farnsworth, E Allan, 'Good Faith Performance and Reasonableness under the Uniform Commercial Code' (1963) 30 *University of Chicago Law Review* 666

Farnsworth, E Allan, '"Meaning" in the Law of Contract' (1967) 76 *Yale Law Journal* 939

Farnsworth, E Allan, 'The Past of Promise: An Historical Introduction to Contract' (1969) 69 *Columbia Law Review* 576

Farnsworth, E Allan, 'Precontractual Liability and Preliminary Agreements: Fair Dealing and Failed Negotiations' (1987) *Columbia Law Review* 217

Farnsworth, E Allan, *Contracts* (Little Brown & Co, 2nd ed, 1990)

Farnsworth, E Allan, 'Duties of Good Faith & Fair Dealing under the UNIDROIT Principles, Relevant International Conventions, and National Laws' (1994) 3 *Tulane Journal of International and Comparative Law* 47

Farnsworth, E Allan, 'The Eason—Weinmann Colloquium on International and Comparative Law: Duties of Good Faith and Fair Dealing under the UNIDROIT Principles, Relevant International Conventions and National Laws' (1995) 3 *Tulane Journal of International and Comparative Law* 54

Farnsworth, E Allan, 'Good Faith in Contract Performance' in Jack Beatson and Daniel Friedmann (eds), *Good Faith and Fault in Contract Law* (Oxford University Press, 2001)

Farnsworth, E Allan, 'Ten Questions About Good Faith and Fair Dealing in United States Contract Law' [2002] *AMPLA Yearbook* 1

Farrell, Joseph and Carl Shapiro, 'Optimal Contracts with Lock-In' (1988) *The Hoover Institution Working Papers in Economics* E88-45. <http://www.google.com/au/url?sa=t&rct=j&q=&esrc=s&source=web&cd=1&ved=0CB0QFjAA&url=http%3A%2F%2Fhoohila.stanford.edu%2Fworkingpapers%2FgetWorkingPaper.php%3Ffilename%3DE-88-45.pdf&ei=prN3VPziCOOaygP3ioDIBw&usg=AFQjCNEIv8i6V-In12QTZToYGHJvZkniag>

Fauvarque-Cosson, Bénédicte and Denis Mazeaud (eds), *European Contract Law Materials for a Common Frame of Reference: Terminology, Guiding Principles, Model Rules* (European Law Publishers, 2008)
Fehr, Ernst and Armin Falk, 'Psychological Foundations of Incentives' (2002) 46 *European Economic Review* 687
Fehr, Ernst and Klaus Schmidt, 'A Theory of Fairness, Competition and Cooperation' (1999) 114 *Quarterly Journal of Economics* 817
Fehr, Ernst and Simon Gächter, 'Fairness and Retaliation: The Economic of Reciprocity' (2000) 14(3) *Journal of Economic Perspectives* 159
Fehr, Ernst, Simon Gächter and Georg Kirchsteiger, 'Reciprocity as a Contract Enforcement Device: Experimental Evidence' (1997) 65 *Econometrica* 833
Feinman, Jay M, 'Relational Contract Theory in Context' (2000) 94 *Northwestern University Law Review* 737
Ferrari, Franco, 'Uniform Interpretation of the 1980 Uniform Sales Law' (1994) 24 *Georgia Journal of International and Comparative Law* 183
Fielder, Hayden, 'Good Faith vs Absolute and Unfettered Discretion in Commercial Contracts' (2021) 50 *Australian Bar Review* 324
Fink, Howard L, 'The Splintering of the Implied Covenant of Good Faith and Fair Dealing in Illinois Courts' (1999) 30 *Loyola University of Chicago Law Journal* 247
Finn, Paul, *Fiduciary Obligations* (Law Book Company, 1977)
Finn, Paul, 'Commerce, the Common Law and Morality' (1989) 17 *Melbourne University Law Review* 87
Finn, Paul, 'Contract and the Fiduciary Principle' (1989) 12 *University of New South Wales Law Journal* 76
Finn, Paul, 'The Fiduciary Principle' in Timothy G Youdan (ed), *Equity, Fiduciaries and Trusts* (Law Book Co, 1989)
Finn, Paul, 'Unconscionable Conduct' (1994) 8 *Journal of Contract Law* 37
Finn, Paul, 'Equity and Commercial Contracts: A Comment' (2001) *AMPLA Yearbook* 414
Finn, Paul, 'Good Faith and Fair Dealing: Australia' (2005) 11 *New Zealand Business Law Quarterly* 378
Fischel, Daniel, 'The Economics of Lender Liability' (1989) 99 *Yale Law Journal* 131
Fleming, John G, 'Insurer's Breach of Good Faith—A New Tort?' (1992) 108 *Law Quarterly Review* 357
Flick, Uwe, *An Introduction to Qualitative Research* (SAGE Publications, 4th ed, 2009)
Forte, Angelo D M, 'The United Nations Convention on Contracts for the International Sale of Goods: Reason and Unreason in the United Kingdom' (1997) 26 *Baltimore Law Review* 51
Forte, Angelo D M, 'Good Faith and Utmost Good Faith' in Angelo D M Forte (ed), *Good Faith in Contract and Property Law* (Hart Publishing, 1999)
French, Christine and Grant Hammond, *The Law of Obligations: 'Contract in Context'* (2007)
Frey, Bruno S and Reto Jegen, 'Motivation Crowding Theory' (2001) 15(5) *Journal of Economic Surveys* 589
Gardini, Robert, Report to Senator the Ron Chris Schacht, Minister for Small Business, Customs and Construction, Parliament of Australia, *Review of Franchising Code of Practise* (1995)
Garello, Pierre, 'The Breach of Contract in French Law: Between Safety of Expectations and Efficiency' (2002) 22 *International Review of Law and Economics* 407
Garro, Alejandro M, 'The Gap-Filling Role of the UNIDROIT Principles in International Sales Law: Some Comments on the Interplay between the Principles and The CISG' (1995) *Tulane Law Review* 1149
Gauthier, David, *Morals by Agreement* (Clarendon Press, 1986)
Gava, John and Peter Kincaid, 'Contract and Conventionalism: Professional Attitudes to Changes in Contract Law in Australia' (1996) 10 *Journal of Contract Law* 141
Gerring, John, 'Single-Outcome Studies: A Methodological Primer' (2006) 21 (5) *International Sociology* 707

Gerring, John, 'What is a Case Study and What Is It Good for?' (2004) 98 (2) *American Political Science Review* 341
Gillette, Clayton P, 'Limitations on the Obligation of Good Faith' (1981) *Duke Law Journal* 619
Giliker, Paula, 'A Role for Tort in Pre-Contractual Negotiations? An Examination of English, French and Canadian Law' (2003) 52 *International Comparative Law Quarterly* 969
Girard, Philip, 'Good Faith in Contract Performance: Principle or Placebo?' (1983) 5 *Supreme Court Law Review* 309
Gleeson, Anthony Murray, 'Individualised Justice—The Holy Grail' (1995) 69 *Australian Law Journal* 421
Goez, Charles J and Robert E Scott, 'Principles of Relational Contracts' (1981) 67 *Virginia Law Review* 1089
Goldberg, Victor P, 'Institutional Change and the Quasi-Invisible Hand' (1974) 17(2) *Journal of Law and Economics* 461
Goldwasser, Vivian and Tony Ciro, 'Standards of Behaviour in Commercial Contracting' (2002) 30 *Australian Business Law Review* 369
Gomm, Roger, Martyn Hammersley and Peter Foster, 'Case Study and Generalisation' in Roger Gomm, Martyn Hammersley and Peter Foster (eds), *Case Study Method: Key Issues, Key Texts* (SAGE Publications, 2000)
Gooley, John, Peter Radan and Illija Vickovich, *Principles of Contract Law* (2013)
Gordley, James, *The Philosophical Origins of Modern Contract Doctrine* (Oxford University Press, 1993)
Gordley, James, 'Good Faith in Contract Law in the Medieval *Ius Commune*' in Reinhard Zimmermann and Simon Whittaker (eds), *Good Faith in European Contract Law* (Cambridge University Press, 2000)
Gordon, Marcel, 'Discreet Digression: The Recent Evolution of the Implied Duty of Good Faith' (2007) 19 *Bond Law Review* 26
Goren, Seth W, 'Looking for Law in all the Wrong Places: Problems in Applying the Implied Covenant of Good Faith Performance' (2003) 37 *University of San Francisco Law Review* 257
Gransbery, Douglas D, Howard L Reynolds and Jack Boyd, 'Measuring Partnered Project Performance' (1999) 41(10) *Cost Engineering* 39
Gray, Anthony, 'Developments in Good Faith in Canada, Great Britain and Australia' (2015) 55(3) *Canadian Business Law Journal* XX
Gray, Anthony, 'Good Faith in Australian Contract Law after Barker' (2015) 43 *Australian Business Law Review* 358
Gray, David E, *Doing Research in the Real World* (SAGE Publications, 2nd ed, 2009)
Grimsey, Darrin and Mervyn K Lewis, 'Accounting for Public Private Partnerships' (2002) 26(3/4) *Accounting Forum* 245
Grover, Warren, 'A Solicitor Looks at Good Faith in Commercial Transactions', in Law Society of Upper Canada, *Commercial Law: Recent Developments and Emerging Trends* (Richard De Boo Publishers, 1985)
Grubb, Andrew and Michael Furmston, *The Law of Contract* (LexisNexis Butterworths, 1999)
Guo, Peng, *Good Faith in Long-Term Relational Supply Contracts in the Context of Hardship from a Comparative Perspective* (Springer, 2022)
Guo, Peng, Shu Zhang, and Lixuan Li, 'CISG and Chinese Contract Law Reform in the New Chinese Civil Code: Impacts, Interactions and Implications' (2021) 37(3) *Journal of Contract Law* 192
Hadfield, Gillian K, 'Problematic Relations: Franchising and the Law of Incomplete Contracts' (1990) 42 *Stanford Law Review* 927
Hadfield, Gillian K, 'Judicial Competence and the Interpretation of Incomplete Contracts' (1994) 23 *Journal of Legal Studies* 159
Hammersley, Martyn, 'Some Notes on the Terms "Validity" and "Reliability"' (1987) 13 (1) *British Educational Research Journal*, (73–81) 79
Han, Shiyuan, 'Codified Contract Law: New Progress, New Problems and Countermeasures' [2021] (06) *Research on Rule of Law*

Harland, David, 'Unconscionable and Unfair Contracts: An Australian Perspective' in Roger Brownsword, Norma Hird and Geraint Howells (eds), *Good Faith in Contract: Concept and Context* (Dartmouth Publishing Co, 1999)

Harrison, Reziya, *Good Faith in Sales* (Sweet & Maxwell, 1997)

Hart, Oliver and John Moore, 'Foundations of Incomplete Contracts' (1999) 66 *Review of Economic Studies* 115

Hartkamp, Arthur S, 'The Concept of Good Faith in the UNIDROIT Principles for International Commercial Contracts' (1994) 3 *Tulane Journal of International and Comparative Law* 65

Hayek, F A, *Law, Legislation and Liberty* (Routledge, 1982)

Hayward, Jack E S, '*The Official Social Philosophy of the French Third Republic: Leon Bourgeois and Solidarism*' (1961) 6(1) *International Review of Social History 19*

Heffey, Peter, Jeannie M Paterson and Andrew Robertson, *Principles of Contract Law* (2002)

Helmholz, Richard H, 'Assumpsit and *Fidei Laesio*' (1975) 91 *Law Quarterly Review* 406

Helmholz, Richard H, *Roman Canon Law in Reformation England* (2004)

Henchliffe, Scott, 'Insurance Claims: Fraud and the Duty of Utmost Good Faith' (1997) 8 *Insurance Law Journal* 210

Henriques, Duarte G, 'The Role of Good Faith in Arbitration: Are Arbitrators and Arbitral Institutions Bound to Act in Good Faith?' (2015) 33(3) *ASA Bulletin* 514

Hesselink, Martijn W, 'The Concept of Good Faith' in Arthur S Hartkamp et al (eds), *Towards a European Civil Code* (Wolters Kluwer, 4th ed, 2010)

Hibbert, Stephen and Emma Moloney, 'Good Faith in Commercial and Construction Contracts' (1993) 9 *Building and Construction Law* 183

Hill, Alicia, 'Good Faith: Enforcement in Australia' (2013) 11(3) *International Journal of Franchising Law* 1 <http://www.mcw.com.au/Content/Attachment/Good%20faith%20-%20Enforcement%20in%20Australia.pdf>

Hillman, Robert A, *The Richness of Contract Law. An Analysis and Critique of Contemporary Theories of Contract Law* (1997)

Holdsworth, Sir William, *A History of English Law*, vol 2 (Sweet & Maxwell, 1972)

Holdsworth, Sir William, *A History of English Law*, vol 5 (Sweet & Maxwell, 1972)

Holmes, Eric M, 'A Contextual Study of Commercial Good Faith Disclosure in Contract Formation' (1978) 39 *University of Pittsburgh Law Review* 381

Holmes, Oliver W, 'Early English Equity' (1885) II *Law Quarterly Review* 162

Hooley, Richard, 'Controlling Contractual Discretion' [2013] 72(1) *Cambridge Law Journal* 65

Horrigan, Bryan, 'The Expansion of Fairness-Based Business Regulation: Unconscionability, Good Faith and the Law's Informed Conscience' (2004) 32 *Australian Business Law Review* 159

Horrigan, Bryan, 'New Directions in how Legislators, Courts and Legal Practitioners Approach Unconscionable Conduct and Good Faith' in John McKenna and Helen Jeffcoat (eds), *Queensland Legal Yearbook 2012* (Supreme Court Library Queensland, 2013)

Horrigan, Bryan, David Lieberman and Ray Steinwall, *Strengthening Statutory Unconscionable Conduct and Franchising Code of Conduct* (2010) <http://archive.treasury.gov.au/documents/1744/PDF/unconscionable_conduct_report.pdf>

Houh, Emily, The Doctrine of Good Faith in Contract Law: A (Nearly) Empty Vessel? (2005) *Utah Law Review* 1

Hunter, Howard O, 'Commentary on "the Renegotiation of Contracts"' (1988) 13 *Journal of Contract Law* 205

Hunter, Howard O, 'The Growing Uncertainty about Good Faith in American Contract Law' (2004) 20 *Journal of Contract Law* 50

Hunter, Howard O, 'Good Faith and the Construction of Terms in Commercial Contracts: The American Perspective' (2009) 25 *Journal of Contract Law* 39

Hutchison, Dale, 'Good Faith in the South African Law of Contract' in Roger Brownsword, Norma Hird and Geraint Howells (eds), *Good Faith in Contract: Concept and Context* (Dartmouth Publishing Co, 1999)

Hutchinson, Terry C and Kylie Burns, 'The Impact of "Empirical Facts" on Legal Scholarship and Legal Research Training' (2009) 43(2) *The Law Teacher*, 153 <http://eprints.qut.edu.au/30075/1/c30075.pdf>

Ibbetson, David J, *A Historical Introduction to the Law of Obligations* (Oxford University Press, 2001)

Iglesias, Joel, 'Comment Applying the Implied Covenant of Good Faith and Fair Dealing in United States Contract Law' (2004) 40 *Houston Law Review* 1423

Jiang, Ping, *A Detailed Explanation of Contract Law* (China University of Political Science and Law Press, 1999)

Jiao, Fumin, 'Good Faith Principle Perfecting Chinese Contract Law' [2002] (04) *Hebei Law Science* 35

Johns, Francis, 'Building Contracts—Good Faith—Quantum Meruit Claim' (1992) 5(3) *Journal of Contract Law* 269

Johnson Jr, Alex M, 'Correctly Interpreting Long-Term Leases Pursuant to Modem Contract Law: Towards a Theory of Relational Leases' (1988) 74 *Virginia Law Review* 751

Johnston, Jason Scott, 'Default Rules/Mandatory Principles: A Game Theoretic Analysis of Good Faith and the Contract Modification Problem' (1993) 3 *Southern California Interdisciplinary Law Journal* 335

Johnston, Jason Scott, 'The Return of Bargain: An Economic Theory of How Standard-Form Contracts Enable Cooperative Negotiation Between Businesses and Consumers' (2005) 104 *Michigan Law Review* 857

Jolls, Christine, 'Contracts as Bilateral Commitments: A New Perspective on Contract Modifications' (1997) 26 *Journal of Legal Studies* 203

Jolls, Christine, Cass Sunstein and Richard Thaler, 'A Behavioural Approach to Law and Economics' (1998) 50 *Stanford Law Review* 1471

Juenger, Friedrich, 'Listening to Law Professors Talk About Good Faith: Some Afterthoughts' (1995) 69 *Tulane Law Review* 1253

Kamp, Allen R, 'Uptown Act: A History of the Uniform Commercial Code: 1940–49' (1998) 51 *Santa Monica University Law Review* 275

Kaplow, Louis, 'Rules Versus Standards: An Economic Analysis' (1992) 42 *Duke Law Journal* 557

Kaser, Max, *Roman Private Law* (Butterworths, 2nd ed, 1968)

Keats, Daphne M, *Interviewing: A Practical Guide for Students and Professionals* (UNSW Press, 2000)

Kennedy, Duncan, 'Form and Substance in Private Law Adjudication' (1976) 89 *Harvard Law Review* 1685

Kessler, Friedrich and Edith Fine, 'Culpa in Contrahendo, Bargaining in Good Faith and Freedom of Contract: A Comparative Study' (1964) 77 *Harvard Law Review* 401

King, Nigel, 'Using Interviews in Qualitative Research', in Catherine Cassell and Gillian Symon (eds), *Essential Guide to Qualitative Methods in Organizational Research* (SAGE Publications, 2004)

Klein, Benjamin, 'Why Hold-Ups Occur: The Self-Enforcing Range of Contractual Relationships' (1991) 34 *Economic Inquiry* 444

Klein, Benjamin, Robert G Crawford and Armen A Alchian, 'Vertical Integration, Appropriate Rents, and the Competitive Contracting Process' (1978) 21 *Journal of Law and Economics* 297

Klein, John, 'Good Faith in International Transactions' (1993) 15 *Loyola of Los Angeles Law Review* 115

Knapp, Charles, 'Enforcing the Contract to Bargain' (1969) 44 *New York University Law Review* 673

Koneru, Phanesh, 'The International Interpretation of the UN Convention on Contracts for the International Sale of Goods: An Approach Based on General Principles' (1997) 6 *Melbourne Journal of International Law* 120

Koneru, Phanesh, 'The International Interpretation of the UN Convention on the International Sale of Goods: An Approached Based on General Principles' (1997) *Minnesota Journal of Global Trade* 105 <http://www.cisg.law.pace.edu/cisg/biblio/koneru.html>

Kooy, Ruth, 'Identifying Unconscionable Conduct Post-*Kobelt*: Is Good Faith the Key to Interpreting the Statutory Unconscionability Provisions in Australian Law?' (2021) 28 *Competition & Consumer Law Journal* 75

Korobkin, Russell, 'Bounded Rationality, Standard Form Contracts, and Unconscionability' (2003) 70 *University of Chicago Law Review* 1203

Kostritsky, Juliet P, 'Bargaining with Uncertainty, Moral Hazard, and Sunk Cost: A Default Rule for Precontractual Negotiations' (1993) 44 *Hastings Law Journal* 623

Kötz, Hein, 'Towards a Europe Civil Code' in Peter Cane and Jane Stapleton (eds), *The Law of Obligations: Essays in Celebration of John Fleming* (Clarendon Press, 1998)

Krawiec, Kimberly and Kathryn Zeiler, 'Common Law Disclosure Duties and the Sin of Omission: Testing the Meta-Theories' (2005) 91 *Virginia Law Review* 1795

Krippendorff, Klaus, *Content Analysis: An Introduction to Its Methodology* (SAGE Publications, 2004)

Kronman, Anthony T and Richard A Posner, 'Introduction: Economic Theory and Contract Law' in Anthony T Kronman and Richard A Posner (eds), *The Economics of Contract Law* (Little Brown, 1979)

Kronman, Anthony T, 'Contract Law and the State of Nature' (1985) 1 *Journal of Law, Economics and Organization* 5

Kuehne, Geoffrey 'Implied Obligations of Good Faith and Reasonableness in the Performance of Contracts: Old Wine in New Bottles' (2006) 33 *University of Western Australia Law Review* 63

Kull, Andrew, 'Mistake, Frustration and the Windfall Principle of Contractual Remedies' (1991) 43 *Hastings Law Journal* 1

Kunkel, Wolfgang, *An Introduction to Roman Legal and Constitutional History* (Oxford University Press, 2nd ed, 1973)

Lando, Ole and Hugh Beale (eds), The *Principles of European Contract Law, Parts I and II* (Kluwer Law International, 1999)

Lazzarini, Seggio G, Gary J Miller and Todd R Zenger, 'Order with Some Law: Complementarity Versus Substitution of Formal and Informal Arrangements' (2004) 20 *Journal of Law, Economics and Organization* 261

Lee, Robert W, *The Elements of Roman Law* (Sweet & Maxwell, 4th ed, 1986)

Lee, Robert G, 'The UN Convention on Contracts for the International Sale of Goods: OK for the UK?' (1993) *Journal of Business Law* 131

Lees, Matthew, 'Contract, Conscience, Communitarian Conspiracies and Confucius: Normativism Through the Looking Glass of Relational Contract Theory' (2001) 25 *Melbourne University Law Review* 82

Leonhard, Chunlin, 'A Legal Chameleon: An Examination of the Doctrine of Good Faith in Chinese and American Contract Law' (2009) 25 *Connecticut Journal of International Law* 305

Lewis, Carole, "The Demise of the *exceptio doli* is there Another Route to Contractual Equity?" (1990) 107 *The South African Law Journal* 26

Li, Xie, 'On the Typology of the Principle of Good Faith Again: With Reference to the Traditional Thought of Abstract Concept' [2013] (05) *Journal of Southwest University of Political Science and Law* 68

Liang, Huixing, 'The Principle of Good Faith and Gap Filling' (1994) 91(2) *Chinese Journal of Law* 22

Liang, Huixing, 'Uniform Contract Law: Successes and Shortcomings' [1999] (03) *China Legal Science*

Liew, Colin, 'A Leap of Good Faith in Singapore Contract Law' (2012) *Singapore Journal of Legal Studies* 416

Lin, Chung-Cheng and CC Yang, 'Fine Enough or Don't Fine at All' (2006) 59 *Journal of Economic Behavior and Organisation* 195

Lincoln, Yvonna S and Egon G Guba, *Naturalistic Inquiry* (SAGE Publications, 1985)
Ling, Bing, *Contract Law in China* (Sweet & Maxwell Asia, 2002)
Ling, Bing, 'The New Contract Law in the Chinese Civil Code' (2020) 8(3) *The Chinese Journal of Comparative Law* 558
Litvinoff, Saul, 'Good Faith', (1997) 71 *Tulane Law Review* 1645
Liu, Chuntian, 'Regarding Intellectual Property as the First Property Rights Is a Discovery in Civil Law' [2015] (10) *Intellectual Property* 3
Llewellyn, Karl N, 'What Price Contract? An Essay in Perspective' (1931) 40 *Yale Law Journal* 704
Llewellyn, Karl N, 'Why a Commercial Code?' (1953) 22 *Tennessee Law Review* 779
Llewellyn, Karl N, *State of New York Law Revision Commission Report: Hearing on the Uniform Commercial Code* (1954)
Loke, Alexander F H, 'Fiduciary Duties and Implied Duties of Good Faith in Contractual Joint Ventures' [1999] *Journal of Business Law* 538
Lonsdale, Chris, 'Post-Contractual Lock-In and the UK Private Finance Initiative (PFI): The Cases of National Savings and Investments and the Lord Chancellor's Department' (2005) 83(1) *Public Administration*, 67
Lorenzoni, Gianni and Charles Baden-Fuller, 'Creating a Strategic Center to Manage a Web of Partners' (1995) 37(3) *California Management Review* 146
Lou, Jianbo and Yan Liu, 'The Limitation of the Principle of Freedom of Contract and Its Relationship with the Principle of Good Faith' [1995] (06) *Peking University Law Journal* 35
Loughlan, Patricia, 'The Historical Role of Equitable Jurisdiction' in Patrick Parkinson (ed), *The Principles of Equity* (Law Book Co, 2nd ed, 2003)
Lubbe, Gerhard, 'Bona Fides, *Billikheid en die Openbare Belang in die Suid-Afrkaanse Kontraktereg* (1990) 1 *Stellenbosch Law Review* 7
Lücke, Horst K, 'Ad Hoc Implications in Written Contracts' (1973–76) 5 *Adelaide Law Review* 32
Lücke, Horst K, 'Good Faith and Contractual Performance' in Paul Finn (ed), *Essays on Contract* (Law Book Co, 1987)
Luo, Peixin, 'Good Governance Relies on Good Law: A Discussion on Social Credit Legislation' [2016] (12) *Law Science* 104
Macaulay, Stewart, 'An Empirical View of Contract' (1985) *Wisconsin Law Review* 465
Macaulay, Stewart, 'Non-Contractual Relations in Business: A Preliminary Study' (1963) 28 *American Sociological Review* 55
Macaulay, Stewart, 'Elegant Models, Empirical Pictures and the Complexities of Contract' (1977) 11 *Law & Society Review* 507
MacCormick, Neil, *Legal Reasoning and Legal Theory* (Oxford Scholarship Online, 2003)
Mack, Natasha et al, *Qualitative Research Methods: A Data Collector's Field Guide* (2005) <http://www.fhi360.org/sites/default/files/media/documents/Qualitative%20Research%20Methods%20-%20A%20Data%20Collector's%20Field%20Guide.pdf>
MacLean, Lynne M, Mechthild Meyer and Alma Estable, 'Improving Accuracy of Transcripts in Qualitative Research', (2004) 14(1) *Qualitative Health Research* 113
Macneil, Ian R, 'The Many Futures of Contract' (1974) 47 *Southern California Law Review* 691
Macneil, Ian R, 'A Primer of Contractual Planning' (1975) 48 *Southern California Law Review* 629
Macneil, Ian R, 'Contracts: Adjustments of Long-Term Economic Relations under Classical, Neo-Classical and Relational Contract Law' (1978) 72 *Northwestern University Law Review* 854
Macneil, Ian R, *The New Social Contract: An Inquiry into Modern Contractual Relations* (Yale University Press, 1980)
Macneil, Ian R, 'Values in Contract: Internal and External' (1983) 78 *Northwestern Law Review* 340
Macneil, Ian R, 'Relational Contract: What We Do and Do Not Know' [1985] *Wisconsin Law Review* 483

Macneil, Ian R, 'Relational Contract Theory as Sociology: A Reply to Prof Lindenberg and de Vos' (1987) 143 *Journal of Institutional & Theoretical Economics* 272

Macneil, Ian R, 'Relational Contract Theory: Challenges and Queries' (2000) 94 *Northwestern University Law Review* 877

Maggs, Gregory E, 'Karl Llewellyn's Fading Imprint on the Jurisprudence of the Uniform Commercial Code' (2000) 71 *University of Colorado Law Review* 541

Manukka, Jori, "Harmonisation of Contract Law: In Search of a Solution to the Good Faith Problem' (2005) 48 *Scandinavian Studies in Law* 229

Markesinis, Basil S and Simon F Deakin, *Tort Law* (Oxford University Press, 4th ed, 1999)

Marshall, Catherine and Gretchen B Rossman, *Designing Qualitative Research* (SAGE Publications, 3rd ed, 1999)

Marsh, Peter D V, *Comparative Contract Law: England, France, Germany* (Gower, 1994)

Mason, Anthony, 'Changing the Law in a Changing Society' (1993) 67 *Australian Law Journal* 568

Mason, Anthony, 'Contract, Good Faith and Equitable Standards in Fair Dealing' (2000) 116 *Law Quarterly Review* 66

Mason, Sir Anthony, 'Foreword' (1989) 12 *University of New South Wales Law Journal* 1

Mason, Sir Anthony, 'Opening Address for the 20th Anniversary of the Journal of Contract Law Conference' (2009) 25 *Journal of Contract Law* 1

May, Tim, *Social Research: Issues, Methods and Process* (Open University Press, 4th ed, 2011)

McCamus, John D, 'Abuse of Discretion, Failure to Cooperate, and Evasion of Duty: Unpacking the Common Law Duty of Good Faith Contractual Performance' [2004] 29 *The Advocates' Quarterly* 72

McDougall, Robert, 'The Implied Duty of Good Faith in Australian Contract Law' (2006) 108 *Australian Construction Law Newsletter* 28

McDougall, Robert, *The Implied Duty of Good Faith in Australian Contract Law* (2006) <http://www.austlii.edu.au/au/journals/NSWJSchol/2006/2.pdf>

McGregor, Harvey, *A Contract Code: Drawn Up on Behalf of the English Law Commission* (Sweet & Maxwell, 1994)

McGuinness, Kevin, 'Law and Economics—A Reply to Sir Anthony Mason CJ Aust' (1994) 1 *Deakin Law Review* 117

McInnis, J Arthur, 'Frustration an Force Majeure in Building Contracts' in Ewan McKendrick (ed), *Force Majeure and Frustration of Contracts* (Informa Law from Routledge, 2nd ed, 2013)

McKendrick, Ewan, 'Good Faith: A Matter of Principle?' in Angelo D M Forte (ed), *Good Faith in Contract and Property Law* (Hart Publishing, 1999)

McKendrick, Ewan, *Contract Law: Text, Cases and Materials* (Oxford University Press, 6th ed, 2014)

McLauchlan, David, 'The Agreement to Negotiate in Good Faith: A Non-Justiciable Contract?' (2005) 11 *New Zealand Business Law Quarterly* 454

McLauchlan, David and Matthew Lees, 'Construction Controversy' (2011) 28 *Journal of Contract Law* 101

McLean, Janet and Toni Ashton, 'Quasi-Markets and Pseudo-Contracts in the New Zealand Public Health System' (2001) 10(1) *Otago Law Review* 17

McMeel, Gerard, *The Construction of Contracts* (Oxford University Press, 2nd ed, 2011)

Meagher, R P, J D Heydon and M J Lemming, *Meagher, Gummow and Lehane's Equity: Doctrines and Remedies* (LexisNexis Butterworths, 4th ed, 2002)

Meng, Qinguo, 'The Historical Progress of the Civil Judicial Interpretations - The Commentary on the Highlights of the Judicial Interpretations of the General Principles of the Contracts of the Civil Code by the Supreme People's Court' (2024) 39(02) *Journal of Shanghai University of Political Science and Law (The Rule of Law Forum)* 42

Menkel-Meadow, Carrie, 'Introduction: What Will We Do When Adjudication Ends? A Brief Intellectual History of ADR' (1997) 44 *UCLA Law Review* 1613

Mescher, Barbara, 'Promise Enforcement by Common Law or Equity?' (1990) 64 *Australian Law Journal Reports* 536

Miceli, Thomas J, *The Economic Approach to Law* (Stanford University Press, 2nd ed, 2009)

Milgrom, Paul R, Douglas C North and Barry R Weingast, 'The Role of Institutions in the Revival of Trade: The Law Merchant, Private Judges, and the Champagne Fairs' in Daniel B Klein (ed), *Reputation: Studies in the Voluntary Elicitation of Good Conduct* (University of Michigan Press, 1997)

Mitchell, Catherine, 'Leading a Life of its Own? The Roles of Reasonable Expectation in Contract Law' (2003) 23 *Oxford Journal of Legal Studies* 639

Mitchell, Sara M and Emilia J Powell, *Domestic Law Goes Global: Legal Traditions and International Courts* (Cambridge University Press, 2011)

Mnookin, Robert H and Lewis Kornhauser, 'Bargaining in Shadow of the Law: The Case of Divorce' (1978–1979) 88 *Yale Law Journal* 950

Moens, Gabriel and Peter Gillies, *International Trade and Business: Law, Policy and Ethics* (Routledge-Cavendish, 2000)

Mooney, Ralph J, 'Hands across the Water: The Continuing Convergence of American and Australian Contract Law' (2000) 23(1) *University of New South Wales Law Journal* 1

Mouritsen, Jan and Sof Thrane, 'Accounting, Network Complementarities and the Development of Inter-Organizational Relations' (2006) 31(3) *Accounting, Organizations and Society* 241

Mousourakis, George, *The Historical and Institutional Context of Roman Law* (Routledge Publishing, 2003)

Mousourakis, George, *A Legal History of Rome* (Taylor & Francis, 2007)

Mugasha, Agasha, 'Good Faith Obligations in Commercial Contracts' (1999) 27 *International Business Lawyer* 355

Munro, Howard, 'The Good Faith Controversy in Australian Contract Law: A Survey of the Spectrum of Academic Legal Opinion' (2009) *The University of Queensland Law Journal* 167

Muris, Timothy, 'Opportunistic Behaviour and the Law of Contracts' (1981) 65 *Minnesota Law Review* 521

Murray Jr, John E, 'Contract Theories and Neoformalism' (2003) 71 *Fordham Law Review* 869

Musy, Alberto M, 'The Good Faith Principle in Contract Law and the Precontractual Duty to Disclose: Comparative Analysis of New Differences in Legal Cultures' (2001) 1(1) *Global Jurist* 1535

Nassar, Nagla, *Sanctity of Contracts Revisited: A Study in the Legal Theory and Practice of Long-Term International Commercial Transactions* (Kluwer Law International, 1995)

National Public Works Council (Australia), *General Conditions of Contract* (3rd ed, 1987)

Nedzel, Nadia E, 'A Comparative Study of Good Faith, Fair Dealing, and Precontractual Liability' (1997) 12 *Tulane European and Civil Law Forum* 97

Nehf, James, 'Bad Faith Breach of Contract in Consumer Transactions' in Roger Brownsword, Norma J Hird and Geraint Howells (eds), *Good Faith in Contract: Concept and Context* (Dartmouth Publishing Co, 1999)

Neuendorf, Kimberley A, *The Content Analysis Guidebook* (SAGE Publications, 2002)

Nicholas, Barry, *An Introduction to Roman Law* (Oxford University Press, 1976)

Nicholas, Barry, *The French Law of Contract* (Clarendon Press, 2nd ed, 1992)

O'Byrne, Shannon K, 'Good Faith in Contractual Performance: Recent Developments' (1995) 74 *Canadian Bar Review* 70

O'Byrne, Shannon K, 'The Implied Term of Good Faith and Fair Dealing: Recent Developments' (2007) 86 *The Canadian Bar Review* 193

O'Connor, Jack, 'The Enforceability of Agreements to Negotiate in Good Faith' (2010) 29(2) *University of Tasmania Law Review* 177

O'Connor, John F, *Good Faith in English Law* (Dartmouth Publishing, 1990)

O'Connor, John F, *Good Faith in International Law* (Dartmouth Publishing, 1991)

Ollerenshaw, Zoe, 'Managing Change in Uncertain Times: Relational View of Good Faith' in Larry A DiMatteo, Qi Zhou, Severine Saintier and Keith Rowley (eds), *Commercial Contract Law: Transatlantic Perspectives* (2013)

Palmer, Jessica, 'The Privy Council on Being (Dis)Honest About Dishonest Assistance' (2005) 24 *University of Queensland Law Journal* 539

Park, Semin, *The Duty of Disclosure in Insurance Contract Law* (Dartmouth Publishing, 1997)

Paterson, Jeannie M, 'The Contract to Negotiate' (1996) 10 *Journal of Contract Law* 120

Paterson, Jeannie M, 'The Contract to Negotiate in Good Faith: Recognition and Enforcement' (1996) 10 *Journal of Contract Law* 120

Paterson, Jeannie M, 'Limits on a Lender's Right to Repayment on Demand: Construction, Implication and Good Faith?' (1998) 26 *Australian Business Law Review* 258

Paterson, Jeannie M, 'Terms Implied in Fact: The Basis for Implication' (1998) 13 *Journal of Contract Law* 103

Paterson, Jeannie M, 'Duty of Good Faith: Does it Have a Place in Contract Law?' (2000) 74 *Law Institute Journal* 47

Paterson, Jeannie M, 'Good Faith in Commercial Contracts: A Franchising Case Study?' (2001) 29 *Australian Business Law Review* 270

Paterson, Jeannie M, 'The Standard of Good Faith: Reasonable Expectations or Community Standards?' in Michael Bryan (ed), *Private Law in Theory and Practice* (Routledge-Cavendish, 1st ed, 2007)

Paterson, Jeannie M, 'Implied Fetters on the Exercise of Discretionary Contractual Powers' (2009) 35(1) *Monash University Law Review* 45

Patterson, Dennis M, 'Wittgensten and the Code: A Theory of Good Faith Performance and Enforcement Under Article Nine' (1988) 137 *University of Pennsylvania Law Review* 335

Patton, Michael Q, *Qualitative Research and Evaluation Methods* (SAGE Publications, 3rd ed, 2002)

Paulus, Christopher G, 'Legis actio', in Cancik, Hubert et al (eds), *Brill's New Pauly: Encyclopaedia of the Ancient World* (2006) <http://referenceworks.Brillonline.com/entries/brill-s-new-pauly/legis-actio-e700130>

Peden, Elisabeth, 'Incorporating Terms of Good Faith in Contract Law in Australia' (2001) 23 *Sydney Law Review* 222

Peden, Elisabeth, 'The Meaning of Contractual "Good Faith"' (2002) 22 *Australian Bar Review* 235

Peden, Elisabeth, *Good Faith in the Performance of Contracts* (LexisNexis Butterworths, 2003)

Peden, Elisabeth, 'Contractual Good Faith: Can Australia Benefit from the American Experience?' (2003) 15 *Bond Law Review* 175

Peden, Elisabeth, 'Good Faith in the Performance of Contract Law' (2004) *Law Society Journal* 64

Peden, Elisabeth, '"Implicit Good Faith"—or Do We Still Need an Implied Term of Good Faith?' (2009) 25 *Journal of Contract Law* 50

Peden, Elisabeth, 'Penalties after *Paciocco* – the Enigma of 'Legitimate Interests'?' (2019) 35 *Journal of Contract Law* 263

Peden, John R, *The Law of Unjust Contracts* (Butterworths, 1982)

Perillo, Joseph M, 'UNIDROIT Principles of International Commercial Contracts: The Black Letter and a Review' (1994) 63 *Fordham Law Review* 281

Pollock, Frederick, 'Contracts in Early English Law' (1893) 6 *Harvard Law Review* 389

Pollock, Sir Frederick and Frederick Maitland, *The History of English Law Before the Time of Edward I* (Liberty Fund, New ed, 2010)

Posner, Richard A and Andrew Rosenfield, 'Impossibility and Related Doctrines in Contract Law: An Economic Analysis' (1977) 6 *Journal of Legal Studies* 83

Posner, Richard A, 'Some Uses and Abuses of Economics in Law' (1979) 46 *University of Chicago Law Review* 281

Posner, Richard A, *Economic Analysis of Law* (Aspen Publishers, 8th ed, 2011)

Powell, Raphael, 'Good Faith in Contracts' (1956) 9 *Current Legal Problems* 16

Powers, Paul J, 'Defining the Undefinable: Good Faith and the United Nations Convention on the Contracts for the International Sale of Goods' (1999) 18 *Journal of Law and Commerce* 333
Priestley L J, 'Contract—The Burgeoning Maelstrom' (1988) 1 *Current Law Journal* 15
Priestley L J, 'A Guide to a Comparison of Australian and United States Contract Law' (1989) 12 *University of New South Wales Law Journal* 4
Pringsheim, Fritz, 'The Inner Relationship Between English and Roman Law' (1933) 5 *Cambridge Law Journal* 347
Quick, Roger, 'Queensland ECI Contract' (2007) 24(1) *International Construction Law Review* 3
Rabinow, Paul, French Modern: Norms and Forms of the Social Environment (University of Chicago Press, 1995)
Rahman, Motiar M and Mohan M Kumaraswamy, 'Joint Risk Management through Transactionally Efficient Relational Contracting' (2002) 20(1) *Construction Management and Economics* 45
Rein, Nigel G, 'Utmost Good Faith in Marine Insurance' (1999) 10 *Insurance Law Journal* 145
Reiter, Barry J, 'Good Faith in Contracts' (1983) 17 *Valparaiso University Law Review* 705
Richardson, Megan, 'The Utilitarian-Economic Model of Contractual Obligation: Unconscionability at the Frontier' (1995) 20 *Melbourne University Law Review* 481
Richardson, Ivor, 'Law and Economics — and Why New Zealand Needs It' (2002) 8 *New Zealand Business Law Quarterly* 151
Rickett, Charles, 'Some Reflections on Open-Textured Commercial Contracting' (2001) *AMPLA Yearbook* 374
Riffe, Daniel, Stephen Lacy and Frederick G Fico, *Analyzing Media Messages: Using Quantitative Content Analysis in Research* (Routledge, 3rd ed, 2014)
Ritchie, Jane, Jane Lewis, Carol McNaughton Nichollsand Rachel Ormston, *Qualitative Research Practice: A Guide for Social Science Students and Researchers* (SAGE Publications, 2nd ed, 2014)
Robertson, Andrew, Arlen Duke and Jeannie Peterson, *Principles of Contract Law* (Thomson Reuters, 4th ed, 2011)
Robertson, Donald, 'The International Harmonisation of Australian Contract Law' (2012) 29 *Journal of Contract Law* 1
Robson, Colin, *Real World Research* (Wiley, 2nd ed, 2002)
Rokkan, Aksel I, Jan B Heideand Kenneth H Wathne, 'Specific Investments in Marketing Relationships: Expropriation and Bonding Effects' (2003) 40 *Journal of Marketing Research* 210
Rosett, Arthur, 'Critical Reflections on the United Nations Convention on Contracts for the International Sale of Goods' (1984) 45 *Ohio State Law Journal* 290
Saunders, Mark, Philip Lewis and Adrian Thornhill, *Research Methods for Business Students* (Financial Times Prentice Hill, 5th ed, 2009)
Schermaier, Martin Josef, 'Bona Fides in Roman Contract Law' in Reinhard Zimmermann and Simon Whittaker (eds), *Good Faith in European Contract Law* (Cambridge University Press, 2000)
Schlechtriem, Peter and Ingeborg Schwenzer(eds), *Commentary on the UN Convention on the International Sale of Goods (CISG)* (Oxford University Press, 2nd ed, 2005)
Schmitz, Amy, 'Confronting ADR Agreements' Contract / No Contract Conundrum with Good Faith' (2006) 56 *DePaul Law Review* 55
Schofield, Janet Ward, 'Increasing the Generalizability of Qualitative Research' in A Michael Huberman and Matthew B Miles, *The Qualitative Researcher's Companion* (SAGE Publications, 2002)
Schofield, Janet Ward, 'Increasing the Generalizability of Qualitative Research' in Martyn Hammersley (ed), *Social Research: Philosophy, Politics and Practices* (SAGE Publications, 2004)
Schutt, Russell K, *Investigating the Social World: The Process and Practice of Research* (SAGE Publications, 2006)

Schwartz, Alan, 'Legal Contract Theories and Incomplete Contracts' in Lars Werin and Hans Wijkander (eds), *Contract Economics* (Blackwell Publishing, 1992)

Schwartz, Alan, 'Incomplete Contracts' in Newman, Peter (ed), *The New Palgrave Dictionary of Economics and Law* (Macmillan, 1998) vol 2

Schwartz, Alan and Robert E Scott, 'Precontractual Liability and Preliminary Agreements' (1997) 20 *Harvard Law Review* 661

Scott, Robert E, 'Conflict and Co-operation in Long Term Contracts' (1987) 75 *California Law Review* 2005

Scott, Robert E, 'A Theory of Self-Enforcing Indefinite Agreements' (2003) 103 *Columbia Law Review* 1641

Scott, Robert E, 'The Death of Contract Law' (2004) 54 *University of Toronto Law Journal* 369

Scott, Robert E, 'The Law and Economics of Incomplete Contracts' (2006) 2 *Annual Review of Law and Social Science* 279

Scott, Robert E and George G Triantis, 'Anticipating Litigation in Contract Design' (2006) 115 *Yale Law Journal* 814

Seale, Clive, *The Quality of Qualitative Research* (SAGE Publications, 1999)

Seddon, Nicholas C, 'Australian Contract Law: Maelstrom or Measured Mutation?' (1994) 7 *Journal of Contract Law* 93

Seddon, Nicholas C, Government Contracts: Federal, State and Local (Federation Press, 4th ed, 2009)

Seddon, Nicholas C and Manfred P Ellinghaus, *Cheshire and Fifoot's Law of Contract* (LexisNexis Butterworths, 8th Australian ed, 2002)

Seddon, Nicholas C and Manfred P Ellinghaus, *Cheshire and Fifoot's Law of Contract* (LexisNexis Butterworths, 9th Australian ed, 2008)

Seddon, Nicholas C, Rick A Bigwood and Manfred P Ellinghaus, *Cheshire and Fifoot: Law of Contract* (LexisNexis Butterworths, 10th Australian ed, 2012)

Sepe, Simone, 'Good Faith and Contract Interpretation: A Law and Economic Perspective' (2010) *Arizona Legal Studies Discussion Paper* No 10–28

Shell, G Richard, 'Opportunism and Trust in the Negotiation of Commercial Contracts: Toward a New Cause of Action' (1991) 44 *Vanderbilt Law Review* 221

Sherman, Charles, *Roman Law in the Modern World* (Baker, Voorhis & Company, 1937)

Sim, Disa, 'The Scope and Application of Good Faith in the Vienna Convention on Contracts for the International Sale of Goods' in Michael Maggi (ed), *Review of the Convention on Contracts for the International Sale of Goods (CISG) 2002–2003* (Kluwer Law International, 2004)

Simpson, A W Brian, *A History of the Common Law of Contract: The Rise of the Action of Assumpsit* (Clarendon Press, 1996)

Sims, Vanessa, 'Good Faith in English Contract Law: Of Triggers and Concentric Circles' (2004) 1 *Ankara Law Review* 213

Skeggs, Chris, 'Project Partnering in the International Construction Industry' (2004) 20(4) *International Construction Law Review* 456

Skinner, Quentin, *Visions of Politics* (Cambridge University Press, 2002)

Smillie, John, 'Certainty and Civil Obligations' (2000) 9 *Otago Law Review* 633

Smith, Thomas B, *A Short Commentary on the Law of Scotland* (W Green & Sons, 1962)

Snyderman, Mark, 'What's so Good about Good Faith? The Good Faith Performance Obligation in Commercial Lending' (1988) 55 *University of Chicago Law Review* 1335

Sohm, Rudolph, James Ledlie, Gruber Crawford and Erwin Bernhard, *The Institutes: A Textbook of the History and System of Roman Private Law* (Clarendon Press, 2009)

Spackman, Michael, 'Public-Private-Partnerships: Lessons from the British Approach' (2002) 26(3) *Economic Systems* 283

Stapleton, Jane, 'Duty of Care and Economic Loss: A Wider Agenda' (1991) 107 *The Law Quarterly Review* 249

Stapleton, Jane, 'Good Faith in Private Law' (1999) 52 *Current Legal Problems* 1

Stapleton, Jane, 'Good Faith in Private Law' in Michael D A Freeman (ed), *Current Legal Problems* (Oxford University Press, 2000) vol 52
Staughton, Lord Justice, 'Good Faith and Fairness in Commercial Contract Law' (1994) 7 *Journal of Contract Law* 193
Stein, Peter, *Fault in the Formation of Contract in Roman Law and Scots Law* (Oliver and Boyd, 1957)
Stein, Peter, *Roman Law in European History* (Cambridge University Press, 1999)
Stewart, Andrew and John W Carter, 'The High Court and Contract Law in the New Millennium' (2003) 6 *Flinders Journal of Law Reform* 18
Stewart, Andrew and Leanne McClurg, 'Playing Your Cards Right: Obligations of Disclosure in Commercial Negotiations' [2007] *Australian Mining and Petroleum Law Association Yearbook* 36
Stewart, Andrew, 'What's Wrong with the Australian Contract Law?' (2012) 29 *Journal of Contract Law* 74
Stewart, Ian B, 'Good Faith in Contractual Performance and in Negotiation' (1998) *Australian Law Journal* 370
Steyn, Johan, 'Contract Law: Fulfilling the Reasonable Expectations of Honest Men' (1997) 113 *Law Quarterly Review* 433
Steyn, Johan, 'The Role of Good Faith and Fair Dealing in Contract Law: A Hair Shirt Philosophy?' in Johan Steyn, *Democracy Through the Law: Selected Speeches and Judgments* (Routledge, 2004)
Steyn, The Hon Mr Justice, 'The Role of Good Faith and Fair Dealing in Contract Law: A Hair-Shirt Philosophy?' [1991] *Denning Law Journal* 131
Stoljar, Samuel J, 'Prevention and Cooperation in the Law of Contract' (1953) 31 *Canadian Bar Review* 231
Stone, Elizabeth, 'Infants, Lunatics and Married Women: Equitable Protection in Garcia v National Australia Bank' (1999) 62 *The Modern Law Review* 604
Styles, Scott C, 'Good Faith: A Principled Matter' in Angelo D M Forte (ed), *Good Faith in Contract and Property Law* (Hart Publishing, 1999)
Sun, Meng, 'Probe into the Rules of Contracts Interpretation' [2013] (10) *Citizen and Law* 22
Summers, Robert S, '"Good Faith" in General Contract Law and Sales Provisions of the Uniform Commercial Code' (1968) 54 *Virginia Law Review* 195
Summers, Robert S, 'The General Duty of Good Faith—Its Recognition and Conceptualization' (1982) 67 *Cornell Law Review* 810
Summers, Robert S, 'Good Faith in American Contract Law' in Reinhard Zimmermann and Simon Whittaker (eds), *Good Faith in European Contract Law* (Cambridge University Press, 2000)
Summers, Robert S, 'The Conceptualisation of Good Faith in American Contract Law: A General Account' in Reinhard Zimmermann and Simon Whittaker (eds), *Good Faith in European Contract Law* (Cambridge University Press, 2000)
Sutton, Kenneth, *Insurance Law in Australia* (Law Book Company, 2nd ed, 1991)
Swain, Warren, 'The Unconscionable Dealing Doctrine: In Retreat?' (2014) 31 *Journal of Contract Law* 255
Swan, John, 'Party Autonomy and Judicial Intervention: The Impact of Fairness in Commercial Contracts' (1994) 7 *Journal of Contract Law* 1
Sykes, Alan O, 'The Doctrine of Commercial Impracticability in a Second-Best World' (1990) 19 *Journal of Legal Studies* 43
Taylor, Veronica L, 'Contracts with the Lot: Franchisees, Good Faith and Contract Regulations (1997) *New Zealand Law Review* 459
Ter, Kah Leng, 'Good Faith in the Performance of Commercial Contracts Revisited' (2014) 26 *Singapore Academy of Law Journal* 111
Terre, François, Philippe Simler and Yves Laquette, *Droit Civil: Les Obligations* (6th ed, 1996)
Terry, Andrew and Cary Di Lernia, 'Franchising and the Quest for the Holy Grain: Good Faith or Good Intentions?' (2009) 33 *Melbourne University Law Review* 542

Terry, Andrew and Cary Di Lernia, 'Regulating the Franchise Relationship: Franchisor Opportunism, Commercial Morality and Good Faith' in Mika Tuunanen, Josef Windsperger, *Gérard Cliquet and George Hendrikse (eds), New Developments in the Theory ofNetworks: Franchising, Alliances and Cooperatives* (Springer, 2011)

Tetley, William 'Good Faith in Contract: Particularly in the Contracts of Arbitration and Chartering' (2004) 35 *Journal of Maritime Law and Commerce* 561

Teubner, Gunther, 'Legal Irritants: Good Faith in British Law or How Unifying Law Ends Up in New Divergences' (1998) 61 *Modern Law Review* 11

Thensted, Charles, 'Litigation and Less: The Negotiation Alternative' (1984) 59 *Tulane Law Review* 76

Thomas, Edward, 'Good Faith in Contract: A Non-Sceptical Commentary' (2005) 11 *New Zealand Business Law Quarterly* 391

Thomson, Joseph M, 'Good Faith in Contracting: A Sceptical View' in Angelo D M Forte (ed), *Good Faith in Contract and Property Law* (Hart Publishing, 1999)

Thornton, Rosy, 'Dishonest Assistance: Guilty Conduct or a Guilty Mind?' [2002] *Cambridge Law Journal* 524

Tian, Ye, 'The Amendment and Judicial Application of Contract Interpretation Rules in Civil Code' [2020] (09) *Academic Journal of Zhongzhou* 55

Tomkins, Cyril, 'Interdependencies, Trust and Information in Relationships, Alliances and Networks' (2001) 26(2) *Accounting, Organizations and Society*, 161

Tong, Rou (ed), *A Brief Introduction to the General Principles of the Civil Law of the People's Republic of China* (China University of Political Science and Law Press, 1987)

Travers, Max, *Qualitative Research through Case Studies* (SAGE Publications, 2001)

Trebilcock, Michael, 'The Value and Limits of Law and Economics' in Megan Richardson and Gillian K Hadfield (eds), *The Second Wave of Law and Economics* (Federation Press, 1999)

Van den Berg, Matton and Peter Kamminga, "Optimising Contracting for Alliances in Infrastructure Projects' (2006) 23(1) *International Construction Law Review* 4

Van Ham, Hans and Joop Koppenjan, 'Building Public-Private Partnerships: Assessing and Managing Risks in Port Development' (2001) 4(1) *Public Management Review* 593

Van Houtte, Hans, 'The UNIDROIT Principles of International Commercial Contracts' (1996) *International Trade and Business Law Annual* 1

Vigneau, Christophe, 'The Obligation of Good Faith in France' (2010) 32 *Comparative Labor Law and Policy Journal* 593

Vincent-Jones, Peter, *The New Public Contracting: Regulation, Responsiveness, Relationality* (Oxford University Press, 2006)

Viscasillas, Maria, 'UNIDROIT Principles of International Commercial Contracts: Sphere of Application and General Provisions' (1996) 13 *Arizona Journal of International and Comparative Law* 381

Voss, Glenn B and Zannie G Voss, 'Strategic Orientation and Firm Performance in an Artistic Environment', (2000) 64 *Journal of Marketing* 67

Waddams, Stephen M, 'Good Faith, Unconscionability and Reasonable Expectations' (1995) 9 *Journal of Contract Law* 55

Waddams, Stephen M, 'Codification, Law Reform and Judicial Developments' (1996) 9 *Journal Contract Law* 192

Waddams, Stephen M, *The Law of Contracts* (Canada Law Books, 5th ed, 2005)

Wallwork, Adam, 'A Requirement of Good Faith in Construction Contracts?' (2004) 20 *Building and Construction Law* 257

Walsh, Kieron, *Public Services and Market Mechanism: Competition, Contracting and the New Public Management* (Palgrave Macmillan Publishing, 1995)

Wan, Alex, *Corporations and Contract Law* (Thomson Reuters, 3rd ed, 2022)

Wan, Alex and Guo, Peng, *Contract Law (Nutshell Series)* (Thomson Reuters, 8th ed, 2024)

Wang, Liming, *Studies on Contract Law* (China Renmin University Press, 2002)

Wang, Liming and Chuanxi Xu, 'Fundamental Principles of China's Contract Law' (1999) 13(1) *Columbia Journal of Asian Law* 1

Wang, Xu, 'Fundamental Principles of China's Contract Law' (1999) 13 *Columbia Journal of Asian Law* 1

Warren, The Hon Marilyn, 'Good Faith: Where Are We At?' (2010) 34 *Melbourne University Law Review* 344

Watts, Peter, *Bowstead and Reynolds on Agency* (Sweet & Maxwell, 19th ed, 2012)

Webb, Eileen, 'The Scope of the Implied Duty of Good Faith—Lessons from Commercial and Retail Leasing Cases' (2001) 9 *Australian Property Law Journal* 1

Weigand, Troy A, 'The Duty of Good Faith and Fair Dealing in Commercial Contracts in Massachusetts' (2004) 88 *Massachusetts Law Review* 174

Wein, Alan, Report to The Hon Gary Gray AO MP, Minister for Small Business and The Hon Bernie Ripoll MP, Parliamentary Secretary for Small Business, *Review of Franchising Code of Conduct* (April, 2013) <https://www.treasury.gov.au/~/media/Treasury/Publications%20and%20Media/Publications/2013/Review%20of%20the%20Franchising%20Code%20of%20Conduct%20Report/downloads/pdf/ReviewoftheFranchisingCodeofConduct.ashx>

Whitman, James Q, 'Commercial Law and the American Volk: A Note on Llewellyn's German Sources for the Uniform Commercial Code' (1987) 97 *Yale Law Journal* 156

Whittaker, Simon and Reinhard Zimmermann, 'Coming to Terms with Good Faith' in Reinhard Zimmermann and Simon Whittaker (eds), *Good Faith in European Contract Law* (Cambridge University Press, 2000)

Whittaker, Simon and Reinhard Zimmermann, 'Good Faith in European Contract Law: Surveying the Legal Landscape' in Reinhard Zimmermann and Simon Whittaker (eds), *Good Faith in European Contract Law* (Cambridge University Press, 2000)

Wieacker, Franz, 'The Importance of Roman Law for Western Civilization and Western Legal Thought' (1981) 4(2) *Boston College International and Comparative Law Review* 257

Wieacker, Franz, 'Foundations of European Legal Culture' (1990) 28 *American Journal of Comparative Law* 1

Willett, Chris, 'Good Faith in Consumer Contracts: Rule, Policy and Principle' in Angelo D M Forte (ed), *Good Faith in Contract and Property Law* (Hart Publishing, 1999)

Williams, Glanville 'Language and the Law—I-V' (1945) 61 *The Law Quarterly Review* 384

Williamson, Oliver E, *Markets and Hierarchies: Analysis and Antitrust Implications* (The Free Press, 1975)

Williamson, Oliver E, 'The Economics of Organization: The Transaction Cost Approach' (1981) 87(3) *American Journal of Sociology* 548

Williamson, Oliver E, *The Economic Institutions of Capitalism: Firms, Markets, Relational Contracting* (The Free Press, 1985)

Williamson, Oliver E, 'Comparative Economic Organization: The Analysis of Discrete Structural Alternatives' (1991) 36(2) *Administrative Science Quarterly* 269

Williamson, Oliver E, *The Mechanism of Governance* (Oxford University Press, 1996)

Williamson, Oliver E, 'Transaction Cost Economics and Business Administration' (2005) 21(1) *Scandinavian Journal of Management* 19

Willmott, Lindy, Sharon Christensen and Desmond Butler, *Contract Law* (Oxford University Press, 2nd ed, 2005)

Willmott, Lindy, Sharon Christensen and Desmond Butler, *Contract Law* (Oxford University Press, 4th ed, 2013)

Winship, P, 'Commentary on Professor Kastely's Rhetorical Analysis' (1988) 3 *Northwestern Journal of International Law and Business* 631

Winter, Glyn, 'A Comparative Discussion of the Notion of Validity in Qualitative and Quantitative Research' (2000) 4 (3) *The Qualitative Report* <http://www.nova.edu/ssss/QR/QR4-3/winter.html#hammersley>

Woo, Pei Yee, 'Protecting Parties' Reasonable Expectations: A General Principle of Good Faith' (2001) 1 *Oxford University Commonwealth Law Journal* 195

Woo, Pei Yee, "Rethinking a Principle Underlying Contract Law" (2002) 22 *Singapore Law Review* 132

Xie, Hongfei, 'Legislative Technology and Institutional Arrangement of Contract General of Civil Code' [2017] (06) *Henan Social Sciences* 28

Xu, Guodong, *The Interpretation of the Basic Principles of Civil Law - Centered on the Legal Analysis of the Principle of Good Faith* (China University of Political Science and Law Press, 2001)

Yang, Lixin, '40 Years of Chinese Civil Law: From Quasi-Codification to Codification' [2023] (12) *Chinese Rule of Law* 14

Yang, Lixin, 'Significant Progress of The Interpretation of the General Principles of Chapter of Contract of Civil Code in the Perfection of the Rule of Contract' [2024] (04) *Journal of Law Application* 24

Yin, Robert K, *Case Study Research: Designs and Methods* (SAGE Publications, 4th ed, 2009)

Zeller, Bruno, 'The UN Convention on Contracts for the International Sale of Goods (CISG)—A Leap Forward Towards Unified International Sales Laws' (2000) 12 *Pace International Law Review* 79

Zeller, Bruno, 'Good Faith—The Scarlet Pimpernel of the CISG' [2000] 7 *International Trade and Business Law Annual* 2 <http://www.cisg.law.pace.edu/cisg/biblio/zeller2.html>

Zeller, Bruno, 'Determining the Contractual Intent of Parties under the CISG and Common Law—A Comparative Analysis' (2002) 4 *European Journal of Law Reform* 629 <http://www.cisg.law.pace.edu/cisg/biblio/zeller8.html>

Zeller, Bruno, 'Good Faith—Is It a Contractual Obligation?' (2003) 15 *Bond Law Review* 215

Zhang, Dejiang, *Report on the Work of the Standing Committee of the National People's Congress* (the Fifth Session of the Twelfth National People's Congress, 3 March 2017)

Zhang, Mo, *Chinese Contract Law - Theory & Practice* (Brill, 2nd ed, 2020)

Zhang, Xiaoyang, *Chinese Civil Law for Business* (Open University of Hong Kong Press, 1st ed, 2013)

Zheng, Qiang, *A Study on the Principle of Good Faith in Contract Law: A Legal Interpretation of the Empire Provision* (Law Press (China), 2000)

Zhong, Jianhua and Guanghua Yu, 'China's Uniform Contract Law: Progress and Problems' (1999) 17 *UCLA Pacific Basin Law Journal* 1

Zhou, Hailin, 'Interpretation Path Based on the Structure of the Civil Code' [2022] (03) *Journal of CUPL* 76

Zhu, Guangxin, 'Codification of Civil Law: Unified Recodification of Civil Special Law' [2017] (6) *Journal of Comparative Law* 169

Zimmermann, Reinhard, *The Law of Obligations: Roman Foundations of the Civilian Tradition* (1996)

Zimmermann, Reinhard, *Roman Law, Contemporary Law, European Law: The Civilian Tradition Today* (2001)

Zumbo, Frank, 'Unconscionability Within a Commercial Setting: An Australian Perspective (1995) 3 *Trade Practices Law Journal* 183

II Case Law

A Finance Company v Shanghai B Bank - Tortious Liability Dispute, High People's Court of Shanghai Municipality, People's Republic of China, Civil Final No 962, 27 October 2022

A Property Management Co v B Bank Qingdao Branch & C Commercial Co - Service Contract Dispute, Supreme People's Court, Civil Retrial No 223, 28 June 2023

ACMI (IO) Pty Ltd v Aquila Steel Pty Ltd [2009] QSC 139

ACN 074 971 109 Pty Ltd v National Mutual Life Association of Australasia Ltd [2013] VSCA 241

Acer Investment Management v Mansion Group [2014] EWHC 3011

Advance Fitness v Bondi Diggers [1999] NSWSC 264
Aitken v Standard Life Insurance [2008] CSOH 162
Aiton Australia Pty Ltd v Transfield Pty Ltd (1999) 153 FLR 236
Aiton Australia Pty Ltd v Transfield Pty Ltd [1999] NSWSC 996
Aiton Australia Pty Ltd v Transfield Pty Ltd (2000) 16 BCL 70
Alcatel Australia Ltd v Scarcella (1998) 44 NSWLR 349
Alstom Ltd v Yokogawa Australia Pty Ltd (No 7) [2012] SASC 49
AMC Commercial Cleaning (NSW) Pty Ltd v Coade [2011] NSWSC 932
Androvitsaneas v Members First Broker Network Pty Ltd [2013] VSCA 212
Anhui Rice Industry Co Ltd v Anhui Agricultural Science and Technology Co Ltd - Dispute over Infringement of the Right to New Plant Varieties, Supreme People's Court, Intellectual Property Civil Final No 605, 5 December 2023
Antonovic v Volker (1986) 7 NSWLR 151
Anton Trawling Co Ltd v Smith [2003] 2 NZLR 23
Apple Communications v Optus Mobile [2001] NSWSC 635
Aquila Coal Pty Ltd v Bowen Central Coal Pty Ltd [2011] QSC 264
Archibald Barr Motor Company Ltd v ATECO Automotive New Zealand Ltd (High Court, Auckland, CIV 2007–404–5797, 26 October 2007)
Arhanghelschi v Ussher (2013) ACSR 86
Armstrong v Victoria (No 2) (1957) 99 CLR 28
Asia Pacific International Pty Ltd v Dalrymple [2000] 2 Qd R 229
Asia Pacific Resources Pty Ltd v Forestry Tasmania (Unreported, Tasmanian Supreme Court (Full Court), 4 September 1997)
Asia Television Ltd v Yau's Entertainment Pty Ltd (2000) 48 IPR 283
ASIC v National Exchange Pty Ltd [2005] FCAFC 226
Atlas Express Ltd v Kafco (Importers and Distributors) Ltd [1989] 1 All ER 641
Attorney General of Belize v Belize Telecom Ltd [2009] 1 WLR 1998
Attorney General of Hong Kong v Humphreys Estate (Queen's Gardens) Ltd [1987] AC 114
Aurizon Network Pty Ltd v Glencore Coal Queensland Pty Ltd (2019) 1 QR 392
Australia Competition and Consumer Commission v C G Berbatis Holdings Pty Ltd (2003) 214 CLR 51
Australia Competition and Consumer Commission v Oceana Commercial Pty Ltd [2004] FCAFC 174
Australia Competition and Consumer Commission v Samton Holdings Pty Ltd (2002) 189 ALR 76
Australia Competition and Consumer Commission v Simply No-Knead (Franchising) Pty Ltd (2000) 178 ALR 304
Australian Broadcasting Corp v Lenah Game Meats Pty Ltd (2001) 208 CLR 199
Australian Co-operative Foods Ltd v Norco Co-operative Ltd (1999) 46 NSWLR 267
Australian Hotels Association (NSW) v TAB Ltd [2006] NSWSC 293
Australian Mutual Provident Society v 400 St Kilda Road [1991] 2 VR 417
Australis Media Holdings Pty Ltd v Telstra Corporation Ltd (1998) 43 NSWLR 104
Australian Securities and Investments Commission v Kobelt (2019) 267 CLR 1
Austotel Pty Ltd v Franklins Selfserve Pty Ltd (1989) 16 NSWLR 582
Automasters Australia Pty Ltd v Bruness Pty Ltd [2002] WASC 286
Baglehole v Walters (1811) 3 Camp 154; 170 ER 1338
Bagot v Stevens Scanlan & Co [1964] 3 All ER 577
Baltimore & Ohio Railroad Co v Brydon 3A 306, (Md, 1886)
Baldwin v Icon Energy Ltd [2015] QSC 12
Bamco Villa Pty Ltd v Montedeen Pty Ltd [2001] VSC 192
Bank of Credit and Commerce International SA v Ali [2001] 2 WLR 735
Banque Financière de la Cité SA (formerly Banque Keyser Ullmann SA) v Westgate Insurance Co (formerly Hodge General & Mercantile Co Ltd) [1990] 2 All ER 947
Banque Financière de la Cité SA v Westgate Insurance Co Ltd [1989] 2 All ER 952

Banque Keyser Ullmann SA v Skandia (UK) Insurance Co Ltd [1987] 2 All ER 923
Barlow Clowes International Ltd (in liq) v Eurotrust International Ltd [2006] 1 All ER 333
Beerens v Bluescope Distribution Pty Ltd [2012] VSCA 209
Beijing Longchang Weiye Trade Co Ltd v Beijing Urban Construction Heavy Industry Co Ltd - Appeal on Contract Dispute, Second Intermediate People's Court of Beijing Municipality, People's Republic of China, Civil Final No 8676, 31 October 2017
Benjamin Developments Ltd v Robert Jones (Pacific) Ltd [1994] 3 NZLR 189
Bensons Property Pty Ltd v Key Infrastructure Australia Pty Ltd [2021] VSCA 69
Bhasin v Hrynew [2014] SCC 71
Bhasin v Hrynew [2014] 3 SCR 494
Biotechnology Australia Pty Ltd v Pace (1988) 15 NSWLR 130
Biscayne Partners Pty Ltd v Valance Corporation Pty Ltd [2003] NSWSC 874
Blackler v Felpure Pty Ltd [1999] NSWSC 958
Blackpool & Fylde Aero Club Ltd v Blackpool Borough Council [1990] 1 WLR 1195
Blomley v Ryan (1956) 99 CLR 362
Boat Park Ltd v Hutchinson [1999] 2 NZLR 74
Bobux Marketing Ltd v Raynor Marketing Ltd [2002] 1 NZLR 506
Booker Industries Pty Ltd *v Wilson Parking* (Qld) Pty Ltd (1982) 149 CLR 600
Bournemouth and Boscombe Athletic Football Club v Manchester United Football Club (The Times, 22 May 1980)
BP Refinery (Westernport) Pty Ltd v Shire of Hastings (1977) 180 CLR 266
Braganza v BP Shipping Ltd [2015] UKSC 17
Breen v Williams (1996) 186 CLR 71
Bristol Groundschool v Intelligent Data Capture [2014] EWHC 2145
Brodie v Singleton Shire Council (2001) 180 ALR 145
Bropho v Human Rights and Equal Opportunity Commission (2004) 204 ALR 761
Brown v Superior Court 2 12 P 2d 878 (Cal, 1949)
Bundanoon Sandstone Pty Ltd v Cenric Group Pty Ltd [2019] NSWCA 87
Burger King Corporation v Hungry Jack's Pty Ltd [2001] NSWCA 187
Burger King Corporation v Hungry Jack's Pty Ltd (2001) 69 NSWLR 558
Burns v MAN Automotive (Aust) Pty Ltd (1986) 161 CLR 653
Butt v M'Donald (1896) 7 QLJ 68
Byrne v Australian Airlines Ltd (1995) 185 CLR 410
Byrne v Australian Airlines Ltd [1995] HCA 24
Byrnes v Kendle (2011) 243 CLR 253
Bytan Pty Ltd v BB Australia Pty Ltd (2012) 41 VR 46
Bytan Pty Ltd v BB Australia Pty Ltd [2012] VSCA 233
Cable & Wireless plc v IBM (UK) Ltd [2002] EWHC (Comm) 2059
Carma Developers (Cal), Inc v Marathon Development California, Inc, 826 P 2d 710 (Cal, 1992)
Carr v Brisbane City Council [1956] St R Qd 402
Carr v J A Berriman Pty Ltd (1953) 89 CLR 527
Carter v Boehm (1766) 3 Burr 1905
Carter v Boehm (1766) 97 ER 1162
Cartledge v E Jopling & Sons Ltd [1963] 1 All ER 341
Castlemaine Tooheys Ltd v Carlton & United Breweries (1987) 10 NSWLR 468
Central Exchange Ltd v Anaconda Nickel Ltd (2001) 24 WAR 382
Central Exchange Ltd v Anaconda Nickel Ltd [2002] WASCA 94
CGU Workers Compensation (NSW) Ltd v Carlos Garcia (2007) 69 NSWLR 680
CGU Workers Compensation (NSW) Ltd v Carlos Garcia [*2007*] NSWCA 193
Chan v Ng (2008) HC, Auckland CIV 2007–404–6226
Channel Home Centers v Grossman 755 F 2d 291 (3rd Cir, 1986)
Chaplin v Hicks [1911] 2 KB 786
Chartbrook Ltd v Persimmon Homes Ltd [2009] 1 AC 1101

Chengdu Hexin Zhiyuan Real Estate Consulting Co Ltd v Sichuan Nanbu Jinli Real Estate Development Co Ltd - Appeal on the Agency Contract Dispute, Supreme People's Court, Civil First Branch Final No 226, 29 June 2016
Chillingworth v Esche [1924] 1 Ch 97
Christopher John De Pasquale v The Australian Chess Federation Inc (AO 1325) [2000] ACTSC 94
City of Sydney v Goldspar Australia Pty Ltd [2006] FCA 472
Clough Engineering Ltd v Oil and Natural Gas Corporation Ltd (2008) 249 ALR 458
Clydesdale Bank plc v Black [2002] SLT 764
CME Cooperative Maritime Etaploise SACV v Bos Fishproducts Urk BV (1997) HA-ZA 95–640
Coal Cliff Collieries Pty Ltd v Sijehama Pty Ltd (1991) 24 NSWLR 1
Codelfa Construction Pty Ltd v State Rail Authority of New South Wales (1982) 41 ALR 367
Codelfa Construction Pty Ltd v State Rail Authority of New South Wales (1982) 149 CLR 337
Comandate Marine Corporation v Pan Australia Shipping Pty Ltd (2006) 157 FCR 45
Commercial Bank of Australia v Amadio (1983) 151 CLR 447
Commonwealth Bank of Australia v Barker [2014] HCA 32
Commonwealth Bank of Australia v Renstell Nominees Pty Ltd [2001] VSC 167
Commonwealth Bank of Australia v Spira [2002] NSWSC 905
Commonwealth Development Bank of Australia Pty Ltd v Cassegrain [2002] NSWSC 965
Commonwealth of Australia v Amann Aviation Pty Ltd (1991) 174 CLR 64
Computer Services Pty Ltd v Digital Equipment Corporation (Australia) Pty Ltd (1988) 5 BPR 11
Comunale v Traders & General Insurance Co 328 P 2d 198 (Cal, 1958)
Concrete Pty Ltd v Parramatta Design & Developments Pty Ltd (2006) 231 ALR 663
Concrete Pty Ltd v Parramatta Design and Developments Pty Ltd (2006) 229 CLR 577
Concut Pty Ltd v Worrell (2000) 176 ALR 693
Con Kallergis Pty Ltd v Calshonie Pty Ltd (1998) 14 BCL 201
Conlan v Registrar of Titles (2001) 24 WAR 299
Co-operative Insurance Society Ltd v Argyll Stores Ltd [1997] 3 All ER 297
Cordon Investments Pty Ltd v Lesdor Properties Pty Ltd [2012] NSWCA 184
Council of the City of Sydney v Goldspar Australia Pty Ltd [2006] FCA 472
Courtney & Fairbarn Ltd v Tolaini Brothers (Hotels) Ltd [1975] 1 All ER 716
Courtney & Fairbairn Ltd v Tolani Brothers (Hotels) Ltd [1975] 1 WLR 297
CTN Cash and Carry Ltd v Gallagher Ltd [1994] 4 All ER 714
Cubic Transportation Systems, Inc v State of New South Wales [2002] NSWSC 656
D & G Cars Ltd v Essex Police Authority [2015] EWHC 226
Dalcon Constructions Pty Ltd v State Housing Commission (1998) 14 BCLC 477
Dalian Azimut Yacht Co Ltd v Gu & Li - Retrial of the culpa in contrahendo dispute, Supreme People's Court, Civil Complaint No 299, 9 April 2022
Dalton v Education Testing Service 87 NY 2d 384 (NY, 1995)
Davis Contractors Ltd v Fareham UDC [1956] 2 All ER 145
Devonport Borough Council v Robbins [1979] 1 NZLR 1
Dickson Property Management Services Pty Ltd v Centro Property Management (Vic) Pty Ltd (2000) 180 ALR 485
Director-General of Fair Trading v First National Bank Plc [2002] 1 Lloyd's Rep 489
Dockpride Pty Ltd v Subiaco Redevelopment Authority [2005] WASC 211
Doll v Noble 22 NE 406 (NY, 1889)
Donoghue v Stevenson [1932] AC 562
Dovey v Bank of New Zealand [2000] 3 NZLR 641
DPP (Vic) v Le (2007) 232 CLR 562
Driveforce Pty Ltd v Gunns Ltd (No 3) [2010] TASSC 38
Duquesne Light Co v Westinghouse Electric Co, 66 F3d 604 (US App, 1995)
Dymocks Franchise Systems (NSW) Pty Ltd v Bilgola Enterprises Ltd (1999) 8 TCLR 612
Dymocks Franchise Systems (NSW) Pty Ltd v Todd [2004] 1 NZLR 289

Easts Van Villages Pty Ltd v Minister Administering the National Parks and Wildlife Act [2001] NSWSC 559
Edensor Nominees Pty Ltd v Anaconda Nickel Ltd [2001] VSC 502
EFT Commercial Ltd v Security Change (1992) SC 414
Elderslie Property Investments No 2 Pty Ltd v Dunn [2008] QCA 158
Elfic Ltd v Macks [2000] QSC 18
Eline Realty Co v Foeman 252 SW 2d 15 (KY, 1952)
Elizabeth Bay Developments Pty Ltd v Boral Building Services Pty Ltd (1995) 36 NSWLR 709
Emirates Trading Agency LLC v Prime Mineral Exports Private Ltd [2014] EWHC 2014 (Comm)
Equitable Life Assurance Society v Hyman [2002] 1 AC 408
Equiticorp Industries Group Ltd (In Statutory Management) v The Crown (Judgment No 47) [1998] 2 NZLR 481
Esso Australia Resources Ltd v FCT (1999) 201 CLR 49
Esso Australia Resources Ltd v Plowman (1995) 183 CLR 10
Esso Australia Resources Pty Ltd v Southern Pacific Petroleum NL [2004] VSC 477
Esso Australia Resources Pty Ltd v Southern Pacific Petroleum NL [2005] VSCA 228
Evans Deakin Pty Ltd v Sebel Furniture Ltd [2003] FCA 171
Farah Construction Pty Ltd v Say-Dee Pty Ltd [2007] 230 CLR 89
Farah Constructions Pty Ltd v Say-Dee Pty Ltd [2007] HCA 22
Far Horizons Pty Ltd v McDonald's Australia Ltd [2000] VSC 310
First Energy (UK) Ltd v Hungarian International Bank Ltd [1993] Lloyd's Rep 194
First National Bank of Chicago v Trebein Company (1898) 59 Ohio St 316
Fitzgerald v FJ Leonhardt Pty Ltd (1997) 189 CLR 215
Fonderie Officine Meccaniche Tacconi SpA v Heinrich Wagner Sinto Maschinenfabrik GmbH (HWS) ECJ, September 17 2002 <http://curia.europa.eu/jcms/jcms/j_6/>
Forklift Engineering Australia Pty Ltd v Powerlift (Nissan) Pty Ltd [2000] VSC 443
Fremont v E I DuPont DeNemours & Co, 988 F Supp 870 (Pa, 1997)
Garcia v National Australia Bank Ltd (1998) 155 ALR 614
Garry Rogers Motors (Aust) Pty Ltd v Subaru (Aust) Pty Ltd (1999) ATPR ¶41–703
Garry Rogers Motors (Aust) Pty Ltd v Subaru (Aust) Pty Ltd [1999] FCA 903
Gateway Realty Ltd v Arton Holdings Ltd (No 3) (1991) 106 NSR (2d) 180
GEC Marconi Systems Pty Ltd v BHP Information Technology Pty Ltd (2003) 128 FCR 1; [2003] FCA 50
Genet v President of Delaware & H Canal Co 32 NE 1078 (NY, 1893)
George Mitchell (Chesterhall) Ltd v Finney Lock Seeds Ltd [1983] 2 AC 803; [1983] 2 All ER 737 (House of Lords)
George W Crouch v Max L Gutmann, 134 NY 45 (NY, 1892)
Gibbons Holdings Ltd v Wholesale Distributors Ltd [2008] 1 NZLR 277
Gibson v Parkes District Hospital (1991) 26 NSWLR 9
Gillies v Keogh [1989] 2 NZLR 327
Godfrey Constructions Pty Ltd v Kanangra Park Pty Ltd (1972) 128 CLR 529
Goebel v Linn 47 Mich 489 (Mich, 1882)
Golden Sands Pty Ltd v Davegale Pty Ltd [2003] VSC 458
Gollin & Co Ltd v Karenlee Nominees Pty Ltd (1983) 153 CLR 455
Governors of the Peabody Donation Fund v Sir Lindsay Parkinson & Co Ltd [1984] 3 All ER 529
Greater London Council v Conolly [1971] 2 QB 100
Greenclose Ltd v National Westminster Bank [2014] EWHC 1156
Greenhill v Federal Insurance Co (1927) 1 KB 65
Gross v Great-West Life Assurance Co [2002] ABCA 37
Grupo Torras SA v Al-Sabah (No 5) [2001] Lloyd's Rep Bank 36
GSA Group Ltd v Siebe plc (1993) 30 NSWLR 573
Guangdong Zhende Pharmaceutical Co Ltd v Hunan Hengsheng Pharmaceutical Co Ltd - Appeal on the Deposit Contract Dispute, Supreme People's Court, Civil Retrial No 115, 29 June 2016

Guo Ziyan v Cai Fuying - Claim raised by the Third Party on the Enforcement of Judgment of the Debt Dispute, Supreme People's Court, Civil First Branch Final No 200, 15 November 2014
GuoHua Life Insurance Co Ltd v He & Wang, Second Intermediate People's Court of Beijing Municipality, People's Republic of China, Civil Final No 7960, 3 September 2020
Gullett v Gardner (1948) 22 ALJ 151
Gustav & Co Ltd v Macfield Ltd [2008] 2 NZLR 735
Harmer v Cornelius [1843–1860] All ER 624
Hart v MacDonald (1910) 10 CLR 417
Heavy Plant Leasing Pty Ltd (in liq) v McConnell Dowell Constructors (Aust) Pty Ltd (No 2) [2022] NSWSC 1775
Hewlett Packard Pty Ltd v Subasic [2021] ACTCA 3
HIH Casualty and General Insurance Ltd v Chase Manhattan Bank [2003] 2 Lloyd's Rep 61
Hillas & Co Ltd v Arcos Ltd [1932] All ER 494
Hillas & Co Ltd v Arcos Ltd (1932) 147 LT 503
Hoppers Crossing Club Ltd v Tattersalls Gaming Pty Ltd [2005] VSC 114
Hospital Products Ltd v United States Surgical Corporation (1984) 156 CLR 41
Howtek v Relisys 958 F Supp 46 (DNH 1997)
Howtrac Rentals Pty Ltd v Thiess Contractors (NZ) Ltd [2000] VSC 415
HSBC Institutional Trust Services (Singapore) Ltd (Trustee of Starhill Global Real Estate Investment Trust) v Toshin Development Singapore Pte Ltd [2012] SGCA 48
Huaihua Fuda Property Development v Huaihua Kailedi Hotel, Supreme People's Court, Civil Retrial No 399, 9 September 2015
Hubei Jinhua Industry Co Ltd v Wuhan Haoyu Real Estate Consulting Co Ltd - Retrial of the Commercial Estate Sale Agency Dispute, Civil Retrial No 143, 30 April 2014
Hudson Resources Ltd v Australian Diatomite Mining Pty Ltd [2002] NSWSC 314
Hughes Aircraft Systems International v Airservices Australia (1997) 146 ALR 1
Hughes Aircraft Systems International v Airservices Australia (1997) 76 FCR 151
Hughes Bros Pty Ltd v Trustees of the Roman Catholic Church for the Archdiocese of Sydney, unreported, NSWSC, 21 September 1989
Hughes Bros Pty Ltd v Trustees of the Roman Catholic Church for the Archdiocese of Sydney (1993) 31 NSWLR 91
Hunan Huaihua Highway Bridge Construction Corporation v Hunan Tanheng Expressway Development Co Ltd - Appeal on the Debt Contract Dispute, Supreme People's Court, Civil Final No 504, 22 December 2017
Hunan Province No 3 Construction Engineering Co Ltd v Xiangxi Autonomous City Xinhui Real Estate Development Co Ltd - Retrial on the Construction Engineering Project Contract Dispute, Supreme People's Court, Civil Retrial No 1472, 30 June 2017
Hunter Business Finance v Australian Commercial and Equipment Finance [2003] NSWSC 122
Huyton SA v Peter Cremer GmbH & Co [1999] 1 Lloyd's Rep 620
Hyundai Engineering & Construction Co Ltd v Vigour Ltd [2005] 3 HKLRD 723
Imperial Group Pension Trust Ltd v Imperial Tobacco L td [1991] 2 All ER 597
Inglis v John Buttery & Co (1878) 3 App Cas 552
Ingmar GB Ltd v Eaton Leonard Technologies Inc [2001] 1 CMLR 9 <http://curia.europa.eu/jcms/jcms/j_6/>
Ingot Capital Investments v Macquarie Equity Capital Markets (No 6) [2007] NSWSC 124 (30 March 2007)
Insight Oceania Pty Ltd v Philips Electronics Australia Ltd [2008] NSWSC 710
Insurance Corporation of the Channel Islands Ltd v The Royal Hotel Ltd [1998] Lloyd's Rep IR 151
Integrated Computer Services Pty Ltd v Digital Equipment Corporation (Australia) Pty Ltd (1988) 5 BPR 11
Interfoto Picture Library Ltd v Stiletto Visual Programmes Ltd [1988] 1 All ER 348
Interfoto Picture Library Ltd v Stiletto Visual Programmes Ltd [1989] QB 433

International Air Transport Association v Ansett Australia Holdings Ltd [2008] HCA 3
Investors Compensation Scheme Ltd v West Bromwich Building Society [1998] 1 All ER 98
Investors Compensation Scheme Ltd v West Bromwich Building Society [1998] 1 WLR 896
Italy v Germany (1995) 7 U 1720/94 <http://cisgw3.law.pace.edu/cases/950208g1.html>
J E Cade & Son Ltd [1992] BCLC 213
J K Keir Pty Ltd v Priority Management Systems Pty Ltd [2007] NSWSC 789
J Kitchen & Sons Pty Ltd v Stewart's Cash & Carry Stores (1942) 66 CLR 116
Jiangsu Suzhong Construction Group Co Ltd v Xinjiang Shuiqingmuhua Property Investment Co Ltd - Appeal on the Construction and Engineering Contract Dispute, Supreme People's Court, Civil Final No 733, 28 June 2017
Jireh International Pty Ltd t/a Gloria Jean's Coffee v Western Exports Services Inc [2011] NSWCA 137
Jobern Pty Ltd v BreakFree Resorts (Victoria) Pty Ltd [2007] FCA 1066
Kakavas v Crown Melbourne (2013) 298 ALR 35
K & S Freighters Pty Ltd v Linfox Transport (Aust) Pty Ltd [1999] FCA 1325
Kellogg Brown & Root Pty Ltd v Australian Aerospace Ltd [2007] VSC 200
Kelly v New Zealand Insurance Co Ltd [1996] 130 FLR 97
Kevin A Copeland v Baskin Robbins USA 96 Cal App 4th 2d 1251 (2002)
Kham & Nate's Shoes No 2, Inc v First Bank of Whitting 908 F 2d 1351 (7th Cir, 1990)
Kinetic Construction Ltd v Regional District of Comox-Strathcona (2004) BCCA 485 (British Columbia Court of Appeal)
Kirk La Shelle Co v Paul Armstrong Co 188 NE 163 (NY, 1933)
Klienwort Benson Ltd v Malaysian Mining Corporation Berhad [1988] 1 WLR 799
Laing O'Rourke (BMC) Pty Ltd v Transport Infrastructure Development Corporation [2007] NSWSC 723
Laurelmont Pty Ltd v Stockdale & Leggo (Queensland) Pty Ltd [2001] QCA 212
Lay v Alliswell Pty Ltd (2002) V ConvR ¶54–651
Lee v Chai [2013] QSC 136
Legione v Hately (1983) 46 ALR 1
Le Walays v Melsamby Year Books 1 & 2 Edward II (vol 17, 1903)
Li Jinfang & Ors v Hainan Tianjing Farm Co Ltd & Ors - Appeal on the Joint Venture and Cooperation on Development of Property Contract Dispute, Supreme People's Court, Civil Final No 517, 23 January 2017
Lin Shuni v Cai Fuying - Claim raised by the Third Party on the Enforcement of Judgment of the Debt Dispute, Supreme People's Court, Civil First Branch Final No 201, 14 November 2014
Lister v Romford Ice [1957] AC 555
Liverpool City Council v Irwin [1977] AC 239
LMI Australasia Pty Ltd v Baulderstone Hornibrook Pty Ltd [2001] NSWSC 886
Lou Xibiao v Yili Xinlei Residential Property Construction Co Ltd - Retrial of the Sale Contract Dispute, Supreme People's Court, Civil Retrial No 1057, 28 September 2014
Loudenback Fertilizer Co v Tennessee Phosphate Co 121 F 298 (6th Cir, 1903)
Louth v Diprose (1992) 175 CLR 621
L Schuler A G v Wickman Machine Tool Sales Ltd [1974] AC 235
Lu'an City Huayu Property Development Co Ltd v Zhang Yu - Appeal on the Debt Transfer Dispute, Supreme People's Court, Civil First Branch Final No 144, 20 December 2013
Luce Optical v Budget Specs (Franchising) Pty Ltd [2005] FCA 1486
Lyttelton Times Co Ltd v Warners Ltd [1907] AC 476
Mackay v Dick (1881) 6 App Cas 251
Mackay v Scottish Airways Ltd (1948) SC 254
Mackintosh v Johnson [2013] VSCA 10
MacLean v Arklow Investments Ltd [1998] 3 NZLR 680
Macquarie International Health Clinic Pty Ltd v Sydney South West Area Health Service [2008] NSWSC 738

Macquarie International Health Clinic Pty Ltd v Sydney South West Area Health Service [2010] NSWCA 268
Maggbury Pty Ltd v Hafele Australia Pty Ltd (2001) 210 CLR 181
Maitland Main Collieries Pty Ltd v Xstrata Mt Owen Pty Ltd [2006] NSWSC 1235 (23 November 2006)
Mallozzi v Carapelli SpA [1975] 1 Lloyd's Rep 229
Mallozzi v Carapelli SpA [1976] 1 Lloyd's Rep 407
Mangrove Mountain Quarries Pty Ltd v Barlow [2007] NSWSC 492
Mannai Investment Co Ltd v Eagle Star Life Assurance Co Ltd [1997] 3 All ER 352
March Construction Ltd v Christchurch City Council (1995) 5 NZBLC 103
Market Street Associates Ltd Partnership v Frey 941 F 2d 588 (7th Cir, 1991)
Martel Building Ltd v Canada [2000] 2 SCR 860
Masters v Cameron (1954) 91 CLR 353
Matzen v Horwitz 228 P 2d 841 (Cal Ct App 1951)
Meehan v Jones (1982) 149 CLR 571
Mellish v Motteux (1792) Peake 156; 170 ER 113
Memery v Trilogy Funds Management Ltd [2012] QCA 160
Meridian Retail Pty Ltd v Australian Unity Retail Network [2006] VSC 223 (21 June 2006)
Mid Essex Hospital Services NHS Trust v Compass Group UK and Ireland Ltd (T/A Medirest) [2013] EWCA Civ 200
Mineralogy v Sino Iron Pty Ltd (No 6) [2015] FCA 825
Minister of Public Works v Renard Constructions (ME) Pty Ltd (1992) 26 NSWLR 234
Minshull v Minshull (1737) 1 Atk 411
Mirvac (WA) Pty Ltd v Binningup Nominees Pty Ltd [2020] WASC 28
Mitchell v Pacific Dawn Pty Ltd [2003] QSC 86
MJB Enterprises Ltd v Defence Construction (1951) Ltd (1999) 44 CLR (2d) 163 (Supreme Court of Canada)
Mona Oil Equipment and Supply Company Ltd v Rhodesia Railways Ltd (1949–1950) 83 Lloyd's Rep 178
Money v Ven-Lu-Ree Ltd [1989] 3 NZLR 129
Mount Joy Farms Ltd v Kiwi South Island Co-operative Dairies Ltd (Court of Appeal, CA 297/00, 6 December 2001)
MSC Mediterranean Shipping Co v Cottonex Anstalt [2015] EWHC 283
Multiplex Constructions Pty Ltd v Abigroup Contractors Pty Ltd [2005] QCA 61
Musumeci v Winadell Pty Ltd (1994) 34 NSWLR 723
Mutual Life Assurance Co of New York v Tailored Woman Inc 309 NY 248 (NY, 1953)
M'Whirter v Longmuir 1948 SLT 403
Myers v Kestrel Acquisitions [2015] EWHC 916
Nanjing Baoqing Yinlou Chain Development Co Ltd, Jiangsu Chuangyu Industry and Trade Co Ltd & Nanjing Baoqing Yinlou Jewellery Co Ltd - Retrial of Franchise Contract Dispute, High People's Court of Jiangsu Province, People's Republic of China, Intellectual Property Civil Final No 0154, 30 July 2014
National Transport Co-operative Society Ltd v The Attorney General of Jamaica [2009] UKPC 48
National Westminster Bank plc v Morgan [1985] AC 686
National Westminster Bank plc v Rabobank Nederland [2007] EWHC 1056 (Comm)
Nauru Phosphate Royalties Trust (Receivers and Managers appointed) & Business Australia Capital Mortgage Pty Ltd v Nauru Phosphate Royalties Trust [2008] NSWSC 916
Network Ltd v Speck [2009] VSC 235
News Ltd v Australian Rugby Football League Ltd (1996) 135 ALR 33
New York Central Ironworks Co v United States Radiator Co 66 NE 967 (1903)
New Zealand Shipping Co Ltd v AM Satterthwaite & Co Ltd (The "Eurymedon") [1975] AC 154
Ng Giap Hon v Westcomb Securities Pte Ltd [2009] 3 SLR(R) 518

Ning v Zhongrong - Partnership Agreement Dispute Civil Application for Retrial Review, Supreme People's Court, Civil Final Complaint No 994, 14 December 2022
Nissho Iwai Petroleum Co Inc v Cargill International SA (1993) 1 Lloyd's Rep 80
Nordern v Blueport Enterprises Ltd [1996] 3 NZLR 450
North American and Continental Sales Inc v Bepi (Electronics) Ltd 1982 SLT 47
North East Solution Pty Ltd v Masters Home Improvement Australia Pty Ltd [2016] VSC 1
NT Power Generation Pty Ltd v Power and Water Authority (2001) 184 ALR 481
Occusafe, Inc v E G & G Rocky Flats, Inc, 54 F 3d 618, 624 (10th Cir, 1995)
Oliver v Commonwealth Bank of Australia [2011] FCA 1440
Ontario Ltd v Cornell Engineering Co (2001) 198 DLR (4th) 615
O'Neill v Phillips [1999] 2 All ER 961
Overlook Management BV v Foxtel Management Pty Ltd (2002) Aust Contracts Rep 90–143
Overlook Management BV v Foxtel Management Pty Ltd [2002] NSWSC 17
Pacifica Shipping (1985) Ltd v Centreport Ltd (High Court, Wellington, CP 230100, 31 October 2000
Pacific Brands Pty Ltd v Underworks Pty Ltd [2005] FCA 288
Pacific Brands Sports & Leisure Pty Ltd v Underworks Pty Ltd [2005] FCA 288
Paciocco v Australia and New Zealand Banking Group Ltd (2015) 321 ALR 584; [2015] FCAFC 50
Pan Foods Co Importers & Distributors Pty Ltd v Australia and New Zealand Banking Group Ltd (2000) 170 ALR 579
Pan Shouxiang v Anhui Si County Rural Commercial Bank Co - Appeal on the Deposit Contract Dispute, Supreme People's Court, Civil First Branch Final No 238, 27 November 2014
Peters (WA) Ltd v Petersville Ltd (2001) 205 CLR 126
Peters (WA) Ltd v Petersville (2001) 75 ALJR 1385
Pierce Bell Sales Pty Ltd v Frazer (1973) 130 CLR 575
Pioneer Shipping Ltd v BTP Tioxide Ltd,The Nema [1981] 2 All ER 1030
Placer (Granny Smith) Pty Ltd v Thiess Contractors Pty Ltd [2003] HCA 10
Playcorp Pty Ltd v Taiyo Kogyo Ltd[2003] VSC 108
Plumor Pty Ltd v Handley [1996] 41 NSWLR 30
Portsmouth City Council v Ensign Highways Ltd [2015] EWHC 1969
Pratt Contractors Ltd v Transit New Zealand [2002] 2 NZLR 313
Prenn v Simmonds [1971] 1 WLR 1381
Presmist Pty Ltd v Turner Corporation Pty Ltd (1992) 30 NSWLR 478
Price v Wells Fargo Bank 261 Cal Reporter 735 (Ct App, 1989)
Prime Commercial Ltd v Wool Board Disestablishment Co Ltd (Court of Appeal, CA 110/05, 18 October 2006)
Printing and Numerical Registering Co v Sampson (1875) 19 Eq 462
Printing & Numerical Registering Co v Sampson (1875) LR 19 Eq 462
Progress & Properties (Straithfield) Pty Ltd v Crumblin (1984) 3 BPR 9496
Prophecy Mining No Liability v Kiwi Gold No Liability (High Court, Auckland, CP 2264/88, 8 August 1990)
Pyne Gould Guinness Ltd v Montgomery Watson (NZ) Ltd [2001] NZAR 789
Qingdao Wanhe Thermal Power Co Ltd v Qingdao Houhai Thermal Power Co Ltd & Anor - Appeal on the Contract Dispute, Supreme People's Court, Civil Second Branch No 364, 7 July 2016
Qinhuangdao Qiuran Property Development Co Ltd v Geshan Construction Group Co Ltd, Supreme People's Court, Civil Retrial No 2023, 23 August 2021
Queensland Electricity Generating Board v New Hope Collieries Pty Ltd [1989] 1 Lloyd's Rep 205
Quinn Villages Pty Ltd v Mulherin [2006] QCA 433
Radley Corp Ltd v Suncorp Metway Ltd [2001] VSC 272
R & D Construction Group Ltd v Hallam Land Management Ltd **[2009] CSOH 128**
Renard Constructions (ME) Pty Ltd v Minister of Public Works (1992) 26 NSWLR 234
R (European Roma Rights Centre) v Immigration Officer, Prague Airport [2005] 2 AC 1

Ridgway v Wharton (1857) 10 ER 1287
Ringrow Pty Ltd v BP Australia Pty Ltd (2005) 224 CLR 656
Ringstad v Gollin & Co Pty Ltd (1924) 35 CLR 303
River Wear Commissioners v Adamson (1877) 2 App Cas 743
Roxborough v Rothmans of Pall Mall Australia Pty Ltd (2001) 185 ALR 335
Royal Botanic Gardens and Domain Trust v South Sydney City Council (2002) 186 ALR 289
Royal Brunei Airlines Sdn Bhd v Tan [1995] 3 All ER 97
RPR Maintenance Pty Ltd v Marmax Investments Pty Ltd [2014] FCA 409
R v Ghosh [1982] 2 All ER 689
R v Hayes [2008] 2 NZLR 321
Sacher Investments Pty Ltd v Forma Stereo Consultants Pty Ltd [1976] 1 NSWLR 5
Saxby Bridge Mortgages Pty Ltd v Saxby Bridge Pty Ltd [2000] NSWSC 433
Scanlan v 2–4 McCabe Pty Ltd [2023] WASCA 135
Secured Income Real Estate (Australia) Ltd v St Martins Investments Pty Ltd (1979) 144 CLR 596
Service Station Association Ltd v Berg Bennett & Associates Pty Ltd (1993) 117 ALR 393
Service Station Association Ltd v Berg Bennett & Associates Pty Ltd (1993) 45 FCR 84
Scally v Southern Health and Social Services [1991] 4 All ER 563
Scally v Southern Health and Social Services Board [1992] 1 AC 294
Scruttons Ltd v Midland Silicones Ltd [1962] AC 446
SGS (NZ) Ltd v Quirke Export Ltd [1988] 1 NZLR 52
Shadbolt v The King (1909) 28 NZLR 1026
Shanghai Biotech Co Ltd v Zhuhai Co Ltd & Zhuhai International Holding Co Ltd - Retrial Review, Supreme People's Court, Civil Complaint No 1690, 30 March 2021
Shann v Dunk [1996] USCA2 372
Shepherd v Felt and Textiles of Australia Ltd (1931) 45 CLR 359
Shijiazhuang Zexin Amino Acid Co Ltd & Anor v Beijing Junde Tongchuang Biotechnology Co Ltd, Intellectual Property Civil Final No 621, 18 December 2021
Shirlaw v Southern Foundries (1926) Ltd [1939] 2 KB 206
Shann v Dunk [1996] USCA2 372
Shore v Wilson (1842) 8 ER 450
Shorrlong Pty Ltd v Northern Territory Housing Commission [1999] NTSC 140
Silver Fox Company Pty Ltd v Lenard's Pty Ltd [2004] FCA 1225
Simonius Vischer & Co Holt & Thompson [1979] 2 NSWLR 322
Smith v Bank of Scotland (1997) SC (HL) 111
Socimer International Bank Ltd (in liq) v Standard Bank London Ltd (No 2) [2008] EWCA (Civ Div) 116
Socimer International Bank Ltd v Standard Bank Ltd [2008] 1 Lloyd's Rep 558
Softplay v Perpetual [2002] NSWSC 1059
South Sydney District Rugby League Football Club Ltd v News Ltd (2000) 177 ALR 611
Specialist Diagnostic Services Pty Ltd (formerly Symbion Pathology Pty Ltd) v Healthscope Pty Ltd [2012] VSCA 175
Stadhard v Lee (1863) 122 ER 138
Starlink International Group Pty Ltd v Coles Supermarket Australia Pty Ltd [2011] NSWSC 1154
State of New South Wales v Banabelle Electrical Pty Ltd (2002) 54 NSWLR 503
State Rail Authority of NSW v Heath Outdoor Pty Ltd (1986) 7 NSWLR 170
State v Robinson (1893) 23 SW 1066
Stern v McArthur (1998) 165 CLR 489
Stewart Gill Ltd v Horation Myer Ltd [1992] QB 600, [1992] 2 All ER 257 (Court of Appeal)
St George Soccer Football Association Inc v Soccer NSW Ltd [2005] NSWSC1288
Strzelecki Holdings Pty Ltd v Cable Sands Pty Ltd [2010] WASCA 222
Sundararajah v Teachers Federal Health Ltd [2009] NSWSC 1443
Tan v Chang & Chang - Disputes over Land Management Rights, Liaocheng Intermediate People's Court of Shandong Province, People's Republic of China, Civil Final No 3926, 28 March 202

Tangshan Xindaihe Real Estate Development Co Ltd v Tangshan Kangtai Construction & Engineering Co Ltd - Retrial of the Contract of the Transfer of the Land Use Right, Supreme People's Court, Civil Retrial No 35, 26 November 2015
Tanwar Enterprises Pty Ltd v Cauchi (2003) 201 ALR 359
Tanwar Enterprises Pty Ltd v Cauchi (2003) 217 CLR 315
Taylor v Johnson (1983) 151 CLR 422
Telstra Corporation Ltd v Optus Networks Pty Ltd [2002] FCAFC 296
The Atlantic Baron [1978] All ER 1170
The Antaios [1984] 3 All ER 229
The Bell Group Ltd (in liq) v Westpac Banking Corporation (No 9) [2008] WASC 239
The Fina Samco [1995] 2 Lloyd's Rep 344
The Moorcock (1889) 14 PD 64
The Tropwind [1982] 1 Lloyd's Rep 232
Thiess Contractors Pty Ltd v Placer (Granny Smith) Pty Ltd (2000) 16 BCL 130
Thomas v Fleury 26 NY 26 (NY, 1862)
Thomas v Thomas (1842) 2 QB 851
Thomson v Thomas Muir (Waste Management) Ltd 1995 SLT 403
Thorby v Goldberg (1964) 112 CLR 597
Toll (FGCT) Pty Ltd v Alphapharm Pty Ltd (2004) 219 CLR 165
Trollope & Colls Ltd v North West Metropolitan Regional Hospital Board [1973] 1 WLR 601
Topline International Ltd v Cellular Improvements Ltd CP 144-SW02 (17 March 2003)
Tote Tasmania Pty Ltd v Garrott [2008] TASSC 86
Trans Petroleum (Australia) Pty Ltd v White Gum Petroleum Pty Ltd [2012] WASCA 165
Trawl Industries of Australia v Effem Foods Pty Ltd (1992) 27 NSWLR 326
Trentham (G Percy) Ltd v Archital Luxfer Ltd [1993] 1 Lloyd's Rep 25
TriGlobal (Aust) Pty Ltd v Colonial Mutual Life Assurance Society Ltd (1992) ATPR ¶41–174
TSG Building Services v South Anglia Housing [2013] EWHC 1151
Twinsectra Ltd v Yardley [2002] 2 All ER 377
Tymshare Inc v Covell 727 F 2d 1145 (DC Cir, 1984)
Ultimo Document Storage v Liquid Vision [2003] NSWSC 1175
Ultraframe (UK) Ltd v Tailored Roofing Systems Ltd [2004] EWCA (Civ Div) 585
United Group Rail Services Ltd v Rail Corporation (NSW) (2009) 74 NSWLR 618
United Group Rail Services Ltd v Rail Corporation of New South Wales [2009] NSWCA 177
Uproar Co v National Broad Co 81 F 2d 373 (1st Cir 1936)
US International Marketing Ltd v National Bank of NZ Ltd [2004] 1 NZLR 589
Varangian v OFM Captial Ltd [2003] VSC 444
Vella v Ayshan [2008] ANZ Conv R 8–013
Vero Insurance New Zealand Ltd v Fleet Insurance & Risk Management Ltd CIV 2007–404–001438 (21 May 2007)
Victoria University of Technology v Wilson [2004] VSC 33
Vodafone Pacific Ltd v Mobile Innovations Ltd [2004] NSWCA 15
Walford v Miles [1992] 2 AC 128
Walford v Miles [1992] 2 WLR 174
Walker v ANZ Banking Group Ltd (No 2) (2001) 39 ACSR 557
Walker v ANZ Banking Group Ltd (No 2) [2001] NSWSC 806
Walker v Zurich Australian Insurance Ltd [2001] QCA 296
Walton Mountain Ltd v Apple New Zealand Ltd (2004) 5 NZCPR 241
Walton Stores (Interstate) Ltd v Maher (1988) 164 CLR 387
Wang Shuijing v Cai Fuying - Claim Raised by the Third Party on the Enforcement of Judgment of the Debt Dispute, Supreme People's Court, Civil First Branch Final No 166, 14 November 2014
Wang Suiping v Wang Yongqin & Anor, Guangzhou Intermediate People's Court of Guangdon Province, People's Republic of China, Civil Final No 18160, 7 November 2022
Watseka First International Bank v Ruda 135 2d 140 (Ill, 1990)

Weifang Shengda Real Estate Development Co Ltd v Wang Gen Zhao - Retrial on the Residential Property Pre-sale Contract Dispute, Supreme People's Court, Civil Retrial No 3103, 28 February 2017
Wenzel v Australian Stock Exchange Ltd [2002] FCAFC 400
Westfield Management Ltd v AMP Capital Property Nominees Ltd (2012) 293 ALR 241
Westpac v Bell Group [2012] WASCA 157
Whitlock v Brew (1968) 118 CLR 445
Whitson Trustee v *Neilson and Company* (1828) 6 S 579
William Cory & Son Ltd v London Corporation [1951] 2 KB 476
Williams & Adams Ltd v Computer Systems Implementation Ltd (High Court, Wellington, CP 215/92, 9 March 1995)
Williams v Roffey Bros & Nicholls (Contractors) Ltd [1990] 1 All ER 512
WMC Resources Ltd v Leighton Contractors Pty Ltd (1999) 20 WAR 489
Wood v Lucy, Lady Duff Gordon 222 NY 88; 118 NE 214 (NY 1917)
Woolworths Ltd v Kelly (1991) 22 NSWLR 189
Xinjiang Eagle Property Development Co Ltd v Nantong Fourth Construction Group Co Ltd, Supreme People's Court, Civil Final No 133, 30 November 2017
Xinjiang Huacheng Anju Real Estate Development Co Ltd v China Railway Construction Bridge Engineering Bureau Group Co Ltd, Supreme People's Court, Civil Final No 347, 30 April 2019
Yam Seng Pte Ltd v International Trade Corporation Ltd [2013] 1 All ER (Comm) 1321; [2013] EWHC 111
Yinchuan Xinhua Commercial Group Co Ltd v Ningxia Great World Industrial Co Ltd - Retrial of the Property Lease Contract Dispute, Supreme People's Court, Civil Retrial No 116, 28 September 2020
Yerkey v Jones (1939) 63 CLR 649
Yoshimoto v Canterbury Golf International Ltd [2001] 1 NZLR 523
You Co Ltd v Zhong International Trading Co Ltd - Appeal on Contract Dispute, High People's Court of Beijing Municipality, People's Republic of China, Civil Final No 726, 2 February 2023
Zeng v Wuhan A Fitness Management Co Ltd – Case of Service Contract Dispute, Wuhan Qiaokou District People's Court of Hubei Province, People's Republic of China, Civil First No 109, 15 December 2021
Zhongning County Rural Credit Cooperation Association v Xing Xuehua - Retrial on the Auction Contract Dispute, Supreme People's Court, Civil Retrial No 1077, 16 May 2015
Zhongyi Huahai Import & Export Co Ltd v Fugu County Miaogoumen Village Hongsheng Colliery & Ors - Appeal on the Contract Dispute, Supreme People's Court, Civil Second Branch Final No 129, July 2015
Zibo Gaoqing County Luhu Sub-district Dazhuang Village Committee of Shandong Province v Zibo Huixin Transport Co Ltd - Dispute Over the Land Least Contract, Zibo Intermediate People's Court of Shandong Province, People's Republic of China, Civil Final No 880, 28 March 2023
Ziyun Miao and Buyi Autonomous County People's Government of Guizhou Province v Guizhou Ziyun Shunxing Property Co Ltd - Appeal on Contract Dispute, Supreme People's Court, Civil Final No 440, 7 November 2016
Zurich Australia Insurance Ltd v St Andrew's War Memorial Hospital [1998] QSC 209
Zurich Insurance (Singapore) Pte Ltd v B-Gold Interior Design & Construction Pte Ltd [2008] 3 SLR(R) 1029

III Legislation

Australian Consumer Law (prescribed as Schedule 2 of *Competition and Consumer Act 2010* (Cth))
Australian Securities and Investments Commission Act 2001 (Cth)

Commercial Agents (Council Directive) Regulations 1993
Competition and Consumer Act 2010 (Cth)
Competion and Consumer Legislation Amendment Act 2011 (Cth)
Competition and Consumer (Industry Codes—Franchising) Regulation 2014
Consumer Protection (Distance Selling) Regulations 2000
Contracts Review Act 1980 (NSW)
Conventions on the International Sale of Goods
Credit Act 1984 (NSW)
French Civil Code
German Civil Code
Hire Purchase Act 1960 (NSW)
Industrial Arbitration Act 1959 (NSW)
Insurance Contracts Act 1984 (Cth)
Judicature Act 1873
LCIA Arbitration Rules 2014
Marine Insurance Act 1906
Moneylenders and Infants Loan Act 1905 (NSW)
Restatement (2d) Contracts
Retail Shop Leases Act 1994 (Qld)
The Principles of European Contract Law
The UNIDROIT Principles of International Commercial Contracts
Trade Practices Act 1974 (Cth)
Unfair Contract Terms Act 1977
Unfair Terms in Consumer Contracts Regulations 1999
Uniform Commercial Code (US)
Usury Bills of Lading and Written Memoranda Act 1902 (NSW)
《中华人民共和国合同法》[Contract Law of the People's Republic of China] (People's Republic of China) National People's Congress, Order No 15, 15 March 1999
《中华人民共和国技术合同法》[Law of the People's Republic of China on Technology Contracts] (People's Republic of China) Standing Committee of the National People's Congress, Order No 53, 23 June 1987
《中华人民共和国民法典》[Civil Code of the People's Republic of China] (People's Republic of China) National People's Congress, Order No 45, 28 May 2020
《中华人民共和国民法总则》[General Provisions of the Civil Law of the People's Republic of China] (People's Republic of China) National People's Congress, Order No 66, 15 March 2017
《中华人民共和国民法通则》[General Principles of the Civil Law of the People's Republic of China] (People's Republic of China) National People's Congress, Order No 37, 4 December 1986
《中华人民共和国涉外经济合同法》[Law of the People's Republic of China on Economic Contracts Involving Foreign Interest] (People's Republic of China) Standing Committee of the National People's Congress, Order No 22, 21 March 1985
《中华人民共和国种子法》[Seed Law of the People's Republic of China] (People's Republic of China) Standing Committee of the National People's Congress, Order No 34, 8 July 2000
《中华人民共和国经济合同法》[Economic Contract Law of the People's Republic of China] (People's Republic of China) National People's Congress, Order No 12, 13 December 1981

IV Other Sources

Andon, Paul, 'Public Private Partnerships (PPPs): Current Accounting-Related Research and Future Research Opportunities' (Paper presented at the Fifth Asia Pacific Interdisciplinary Research in

Accounting (APIRA) Conference, Auckland, 8–10 July 2007) <http://www.mngt.waikato.ac.nz/ConferenceManager/report.asp?issue=5>

Annez, Patricia Clarke, 'Urban Infrastructure Finance from Private Operators: What Have We Learned from Recent Experience?' (Working Paper No 4045, World Bank Policy Research, 2006) <https://openknowledge.worldbank.org/bitstream/handle/10986/9019/wps4045.pdf?sequence=1>

Australian Government, Business Law Branch Attorney-General's Department, *Improving Australia's Law and Justice Framework: A Discussion Paper Exploring The Scope for Reforming Australian Contract Law* (2012)

<http://observgo.uquebec.ca/observgo/fichiers/85195_DAEPI.pdf>

Carter, John W, 'Good Faith in Contract: Why Australian Law is Incoherent?' (Research Paper No 14/38, Sydney Law School, 2014)

Commonwealth Attorney-General's Department, *Review of Australian Contract Law* (2012)

de Jersey, The Hon Paul, 'Good Faith in Contracts in Financial Service' (Paper presented at the 26th Annual Banking and Financial Services Law Association and Practice Conference, Queensland, 31 July-1 August 2009)

Douglas, The Hon Justice James, 'Exploring the Recent Uncertainty Surrounding the Implied Duty of Good Faith in Australian Contract Law: The Duty to Act Reasonably—Its Existence, Ambit and Operation' (Paper presented at the LexisNexis Contract Law Master Class, Sydney, 24 August 2006) <http://www.cisg.law.pace.edu/cisg/biblio/douglas1.html>

Farnsworth, E Allan, 'The Concept of Good Faith in American Law' (Paper presented at Centro di studi e ricerche di diritto comparator e straniero, Saggi, Conferenze e Seminari 10, Rome, April 1993) <http://www.cisg.law.pace.edu/cisg/biblio/farnsworth3.html>

Fehr, Ernst, Alexander Klein and Klaus Schmidt, 'Contracts, Fairness and Incentives' (Working Paper No 1215, CESifo, 2004)

Finn, Paul, '"Good Faith, Unconscionability and Fiduciary Duties" in Energy Law '90: Changing Energy Markets—the Legal Consequences' (Paper presented at the 9th Advanced Seminar on Petroleum, Mineral, and Energy Resources Law Proceedings, London, 22–27 April 1990)

Finn, Paul, 'Good Faith and Fair Dealing and "Boats against the Current"' (Paper presented at the Second Biennial Conference on the Law of Obligations, Melbourne, 16 July 2004)

Finn, Paul, 'Good Faith and Fair Dealing: Australia' (Paper presented at the Commercial Good Faith Conference, Auckland, New Zealand, 2 September 2005)

Finn, Paul, 'Internationalisation or Isolation: The Australian Cul de Sac? The Case of Contract Law' (Paper presented at the 20th Anniversary Symposium, The Internationalisation of Law: Legislating, Decision-Making, Practice and Education, Bond University, Gold Coast, 26–27 June 2009)

HM Treasury, *PFI: Strengthening long-term partnerships* (2006) <https://www2.unece.org/wiki/download/attachments/23758291/Treasury%20-%20PFI%20Strenghtening%20long%20term%20partnerships.pdf?api=v2>

Horrigan, Bryan, 'Good Faith from a Drafting and Pleadings Point of View' (Paper presented at the Commercial Court CPD Seminar, Melbourne, 4 June 2014)

Horrigan, Bryan, 'New Frontlines in Regulating Unconscionable, Unfair, and Bad Faith Business Conduct', *The Monash Law E-Briefing* (Melbourne), 2nd ed, 18 June 2014 <http://themonashlaw-e-briefing.blogspot.com.au/2014/06/expert-legal-commentary-new-frontlines.html>

House of Representatives Standing Committee on Industry, Parliament of Australia, *Science and Technology, Parliament of Australia, Finding a Balance: Towards Fair Trading in Australia* (1997)

Infrastructure Australia, *National Public Private Partnership Guidelines: Commercial Principles for Social Infrastructure*, vol 3 (2008) <http://www.infrastructureaustralia.gov.au/public_private/files/National_PPP_Guidelines_Vol_3_Commercial_Principles_Social_Infrastructure_Dec_08.pdf>

Infrastructure Australia, *National Public Private Partnership Guidelines: Commercial Principles for Economic Infrastructure*, vol 7 (2011) <http://www.infrastructureaustralia.gov.au/public_private/files/Vol_7_Commercial_Principles_Economic_Infrastructure_Feb_2011.pdf>

Infrastructure Australia, *The National Public Private Partnership Policy and Guidelines*, Overview (2008) <http://infrastructureaustralia.gov.au/policy-publications/public-private-partnerships/national-ppp-policy-guidelines.aspx>

Lee, Stephen, 'The State as Model Litigant' (Paper presented at Lunchtime Seminar Series, Victorian Government Solicitor's Office, 28 September 2006) <www.vgso.vic.gov.au/.../The%20State%20as%20Model%20Litigant.pdf>

Macedo Jr, Ronaldo Porto, 'Relational Consumer Contracts: New Challenges for Brazilian Consumer Law' (Paper presented at the 8th International Consumer Law Conference, Auckland, New Zealand, 9–11 April 2001)

Mackaay, Ejan and Violette Leblanc, 'The Law and Economics of Good Faith in the Civil Law of Contract' (Paper presented at the 2003 Conference of the European Association of Law and Economics, France, 18–20 September 2003) <http://www.crdp.umontreal.ca/fr/productions/textes/T12.pdf>

Mason, Anthony, 'Contract and its Relationship with Equitable Standards and the Doctrine of Good Faith' (Paper presented at Cambridge Lectures, Cambridge 8 July 2003)

Moise, Bojinca, 'Solidarism as Theoretical Foundation of Good Faith' (Paper presented at the Fourth Year of the International Conference: Days of Law (COFOLA 2010), Czech Republic, 2010) <http://dvp.sehnalek.cz/files/prispevky/05_obcan/Bojinca_Moise_(4721).pdf>

New South Wales Government, *Working with government: Guidelines for privately financed projects*, (2006) <http://www.treasury.nsw.gov.au/__data/assets/pdf_file/0009/3141/wwggui_1.pdf>

O'Brien, Leighton, '"Good Faith: Practical Applications in Contract Law" in Contracts 2010: Optimising Contract Performance and Mitigating Risk' (Paper presented at the 10th Annual Conference Series, Sydney, 9–11 February 2010)

Official Commentary, *UNIDROIT Principles of International Commercial Contracts* (1994)

Partnership Victoria, *Annexure 1A—Commercial Principles for Social Infrastructure* (2009) <http://www.dtf.vic.gov.au/files/b6329ae3-835d-4e13-bb60-a1dc00d32493/Victorian-Jurisdicational-Requirement-Annexure-1A.doc.>

Ross, Jim, 'Introduction to Project Alliancing' (Paper presented at Alliance Contracting Conference, Sydney, October 2003)

Schlechtriem, Peter, 'Good Faith in German Law and in International Uniform Laws' (Paper presented at Centro di studi e ricerche di diritto comparator e straniero, Saggi, Conferenze e Seminari 24, Rome, February 1997) <http://servizi.iit.cnr.it/~crdcs/crdcs/frames24.htm>

Scottish Law Commission, *Report on Formation of Contract: Scottish Law and the United Nations Convention on Contracts for the International Sale of Goods* (1993)

Trade Practices Committee of the Business Law Section of the Law Council of Australia to the Senate Economic References Committee, *Inquiry into Whether the Trade Practices Act 1974* (Cth) *Adequately Protects Small Business from Anti-Competitive or Unfair Conduct* (2004)

《关于审理买卖合同纠纷案件适用法律问题的解释》[Interpretation of the Supreme People's Court on Issues Concerning the Application of Law for the Trial of Cases of Disputes over Sales Contracts] (People's Republic of China) Supreme People's Court, Interpretation No 8, 10 May 2012

《最高人民法院关于适用〈中华人民共和国合同法〉若干问题的解释(一)》[Interpretation I of the Supreme People's Court of Several Issues Concerning the Application of the Contract Law of the People's Republic of China] (People's Republic of China) Supreme People's Court, Judicial Interpretation No 19, 19 December 1999

《最高人民法院关于适用〈中华人民共和国合同法〉若干问题的解释(二)》[Interpretation II of the Supreme People's Court of Several Issues Concerning the Application of the Contract Law of the People's Republic of China] (People's Republic of China) Supreme People's Court, Judicial Interpretation No 5, 24 April 2009

《最高人民法院关于适用〈中华人民共和国民法典〉合同编通则若干问题的解释》[Interpretation by the Supreme People's Court of Several Issues Concerning the Application of Title One General Provisions of Book Three Contracts of the Civil Code of the People's Republic of China] (People's Republic of China) Supreme People's Court, Judicial Intrepretation No 13, 4 December 2023

《最高人民法院印发〈关于案例指导工作的规定〉的通知》[Notice of the Supreme People's Court on Issuing the Provisions on Case Guidance] (People's Republic of China) Supreme People's Court, Notice No 51, 26 November 2010

The manufacturer's authorised representative in the EU is Springer Nature Customer Service Centre GmbH, Europaplatz 3, 69115 Heidelberg, Germany. If you have any concerns regarding our products, please contact ProductSafety@springernature.com

Printed and bound by CPI Group (UK) Ltd, Croydon, CR0 4YY
01/10/2026
02225963-0004